EARLY HISTORY OF MASSACHUSETTS.

LECTURES

DELIVERED IN A COURSE BEFORE THE LOWELL INSTITUTE, IN BOSTON,

BY MEMBERS OF THE

Massachusetts Historical Society,

ON SUBJECTS RELATING TO THE

EARLY HISTORY OF MASSACHUSETTS.

BOSTON:
PUBLISHED BY THE SOCIETY.
1869.

CAMBRIDGE:
PRESS OF JOHN WILSON AND SON.

PREFATORY NOTE.

THE Committee charged with the publication of this volume of Lectures, must not allow it to go before the public without a grateful acknowledgment of the indebtedness of the Society to their associate, the Hon. JOHN AMORY LOWELL, for his liberal and obliging cooperation in the arrangements for their delivery and for their publication.

It should be distinctly understood, in view of any conflicting opinions which may perhaps be found in these Lectures, that the author of each Lecture is individually and exclusively responsible for whatever he has advanced.

CONTENTS.

I.

PAGE

Massachusetts and its Early History: Introductory Lecture. By Hon. Robert C. Winthrop. Jan. 5, 1869 1

II.

The Aims and Purposes of the Founders of the Massachusetts Colony. By George E. Ellis, D.D. Jan. 8, 1869 29

III.

Treatment of Intruders and Dissentients by the Founders of Massachusetts. By George E. Ellis, D.D. Jan. 12, 1869 . . 75

IV.

History of Grants under the Great Council for New England. By Samuel F. Haven, A.M. Jan. 15, 1869 127

V.

The Colony of New Plymouth and its Relations to Massachusetts. By William Brigham, A.M. Jan. 19, 1869. . . . 163

VI.

Slavery as it once prevailed in Massachusetts. By Emory Washburn, LL.D. Jan. 22, 1869 191

VII.

Records of Massachusetts under its First Charter. By Hon. Charles W. Upham. Jan. 26, 1869 227

VIII.

The Medical Profession in Massachusetts. By Oliver Wendell Holmes, M.D. Jan. 29, 1869 257

IX.

PAGE

EARLY RELATIONS WITH THE INDIANS. By SAMUEL ELIOT, LL.D. Feb. 2, 1869 303

X.

THE REGICIDES SHELTERED IN NEW ENGLAND. By CHANDLER ROBBINS, D.D. Feb. 5, 1869 319

XI.

THE FIRST CHARTER AND THE EARLY RELIGIOUS LEGISLATION OF MASSACHUSETTS. By JOEL PARKER, LL.D. Feb. 9, 1869 . . . 355

XII.

PURITAN POLITICS OF ENGLAND AND NEW ENGLAND. By EDWARD E. HALE, A.M. Feb. 12, 1869 441

XIII.

EDUCATION IN MASSACHUSETTS: EARLY LEGISLATION AND HISTORY. By GEORGE B. EMERSON, LL.D. Feb. 16, 1869 463

MASSACHUSETTS AND ITS EARLY HISTORY.

Introductory Lecture

BY

HON. ROBERT C. WINTHROP.

MASSACHUSETTS AND ITS EARLY HISTORY.

INTRODUCTORY.

AN Introductory Lecture, my friends, like an overture to an oratorio or an opera, has, proverbially, a wide scope; and I shall avail myself, with your indulgence, of the largest privileges of my position. It is no affectation in me, however, to say to you at the outset, that I have little hope of satisfying even the reasonable requisitions of the service which has been assigned me. I am conscious, indeed, of coming here this evening to offer an apology, rather than to deliver an historical lecture. Most gladly would I have prepared myself to do something worthy of such an occasion, and of such an audience as I see before me. Most gladly would I have prepared myself, had it been in my power, to deliver something suitable to the position which I am called to occupy here, as the President of the old Historical Society of Massachusetts, the oldest historical society in our country; which, for more than three-quarters of a century, has devoted itself to the illustration of the Colonial history of New England, publishing more than forty volumes of invaluable historical materials, which ought to be in the library of every town and village of New England, but which, I am sorry to say, have had fewer patrons, or certainly fewer purchasers, than they deserved and needed.

Most gladly, too, would I have prepared myself, had it proved to be possible, to say something appropriate and proportionate to the great theme of that series of lectures which I am privileged to introduce, — the historical merits and virtues of the founders and builders-up of this old Puritan Commonwealth, — not second, certainly, to any Commonwealth beneath the sun, for the influence it has exerted upon the welfare of the world, and the examples it has afforded for the admiration and imitation of mankind. Such a theme, I am sensible, deserves and demands the best treatment of which any of us are capable. The praises of the New-England Fathers should not be feebly uttered. To preface a course of lectures on such a subject, and by such lecturers as are to succeed me, by any vapid commonplaces, or any mere vaporing and boastful panegyrics, were like putting up a lath-and-plaster portico to some stately Doric temple, or a façade of stucco upon some solid mausoleum of marble or porphyry. Better let the structure be, without any façade at all, — as the grand Cathedral of Florence, with that majestic dome which so roused the emulation of Michel Angelo, has stood for so many centuries, — than impair its grandeur, and offend its majesty, by any cheap or incongruous frontispiece. There was nothing of *sham* in the character or the conduct of those with whom our lectures are to deal; and nothing of *sham* should be associated with their commemoration.

Why, then, am I here at all, — seeing that I must needs be so reckless of my own rede, and do only what I feel to be so far short of my own conception, at least, of what is due to the occasion? The answer to this question, my friends, will supply me with a subject, and will furnish the substance of the apology which I am here to offer you.

Allow me, at the outset, to recall the circumstances under which I first heard of these lectures. It was about the end of last January, just as I was leaving the pleasant city of Nice, recently included in the Empire of France, that I received a kind letter from my valued friend, Dr. George E. Ellis, — the original proposer of these lectures, and without whom they would not and could not have been undertaken, and who is himself to address you next Friday evening on the "Aims and Purposes of the Founders of the Massachusetts Colony," — a letter announcing that such a course was in process of arrangement between Mr. Lowell and himself, and suggesting the hope that I might return home in season for its opening or its close. I had just taken leave of our grand Admiral Farragut, who, throughout that eventful circumnavigation from which he has recently returned, made friends for his country, as well as for himself, wherever he went; and the carriage was already at the door, which was to bear me along that magnificent Corniche road, — on the very brink of the Mediterranean, — of which any one who has ever been over it will require no description, while to those who are still strangers to its marvellous attractions and its magic beauty, no words of others, certainly not of mine, could convey any adequate conceptions of them. I drove along this incomparable road during three days of delicious weather, and on the fourth day entered that superb city which a grander Admiral even than Farragut might well have been proud to claim as his birthplace, — Christopher Columbus, a native of Genoa. A noble monument to Columbus, recently finished, surmounted by a striking statue of him, and adorned by a series of bas-reliefs illustrating the strange, eventful story of his life, — from which, I need hardly say, the Discovery of America was not wholly omitted, — greeted us at the gates, with the simple inscription in Italian, "To Christopher Columbus from his Country;" and, as I gazed upon it with admiration, I could not help feeling that it was not there alone that a monument and a statue were due to his memory, but that upon the shores of our own hemisphere, too, there ought to be some worthy memorial of the discoverer of the New World. I could not help feeling, indeed, how fit it would be, if we could have at New York,[1] or in Boston, or at Washington, or at Worcester, — under the auspices of our excellent American Antiquarian Society, which has taken the supposed date of Columbus's discovery as the date of its own anniversary, — an exact reproduction of this admirable monument at Genoa, so that hemisphere should seem to respond to hemisphere in a common tribute to the heroic and matchless old navigator. It would be some sort of atonement, I thought, on the part of America, — tardy and inadequate, indeed, but better than nothing, — for having allowed the name of another, however meritorious, to usurp the place to which his name was so pre-eminently entitled in the geographical nomenclature of the globe.

No one, however, who observes the course of things in our own land, if not in other lands, in regard to monuments and statues, can be surprised that the claims of Columbus should have been postponed. Shakspeare has portrayed the whole

[1] See p. 27.

philosophy of the matter, in that most impressive passage which he has put into the mouth of the not altogether reticent Ulysses of ancient Greece. You all remember it: —

> "Time hath, my lord, a wallet at his back,
> Wherein he puts alms for oblivion,
> A great-sized monster of ingratitudes:
> Those scraps are good deeds past; which are devour'd
> As fast as they are made, forgot as soon
> As done: . . . . .
> One touch of nature makes the whole world kin, —
> That all, with one consent, praise new-born gawds,
> Though they are made and moulded of things past;
> And give to dust, that is a little gilt,
> More laud than gilt o'er-dusted.
> The present eye praises the present object."

How true is it, my friends, here and elsewhere, now as in Shakspeare's time, that the man who discovered a continent, or founded a great commonwealth, is postponed to some living hero, or to him who died but yesterday! For a time the heroes of our Revolution crowded out all commemoration of the Pilgrim or Puritan Fathers. Then came the heroes of a later war with England to crowd out the Revolutionary patriots. Next followed the heroes of the conquest of Mexico. More recently, the heroes and martyrs of our late civil war have absorbed all our sympathies and all our means. It is not unnatural; nor is it a subject for reproach or complaint, or for any thing but satisfaction. We grudge no tribute, certainly, however costly, to those heroic young lives which were offered up so nobly for the recent rescue of the National Union. Yet it may be hoped that a day will still come, when America may have time to look back, even as far as Columbus; and, coming down through the various stages of her early colonial settlement, and her later constitutional government, may provide some fit memorials of the men to whom she has owed her rise and progress. It may be hoped that a day will come, when Massachusetts may have leisure to examine that "wallet of oblivion at the back of Time," and to rescue from it some names and deeds of her own earlier and later history, which she would not willingly let die. It may be hoped that a day will come, when our own city may have time to review her roll of honor, and may realize that no

Campo Santo, or Santa Croce, or Père la Chaise, or Westminster Abbey of the Old World, contains dust more precious, or more worthy of commemoration, than that which lies almost unmarked in some of her own ancient graveyards. I will mention but a single name; that of the great minister of our first Puritan church, in honor of whose intended coming our city is said to have been called:— We sent, indeed, over the Atlantic, not many years since, a considerable sum of money to repair the little chapel of his noble church in Boston, Lincolnshire, Old England; but there is nothing to tell the passer-by, unless he stoops over the mouldering stone with the microscope of an Old Mortality, where, in the Boston of New England, have reposed for two centuries the ashes of JOHN COTTON.

But the statue of Columbus was not the only thing I saw in Genoa, which awakened reflections and associations connected with my own land. I did not fail to grope my way through the old Historic Hall, with its double row of original portrait statues of the old Genoese nobles, formerly known as the Bank of St. George, but now desecrated to the use of the dingiest department of what, I should hope and believe, is the dingiest custom-house in the world. Heaven forbid, thought I, that any historic hall of my own land should ever suffer such a profanation. Yet when I remembered how inadequately cared for our own Faneuil Hall, and still more our own old State House, had often been; and how much of their sanctity and of their safety had been sacrificed in years past, if they were not still, to any and every purpose which might increase the rents, and add a few more hundreds of dollars to a treasury from which so much goes out from year to year for more than doubtful expenditures,— I was less emboldened to indulge in any wholesale strictures upon other cities. But better, a thousand-fold better, let me say in passing, that all such structures, whether in Genoa or in Boston, should be razed to the ground at once, and live only as they are photographed on the hearts of those who have held them sacred, than that they should be left cumbering the ground and blocking the highway, only to signalize the more conspicuously that indifference and irreverence towards the noblest scenes and associations of a glorious past, which have been engendered by the rush and crush of modern improvement and modern traffic.

But pardon me, my friends, for such a digression, and bear with me kindly as I roll rapidly again along the Riviera, resting at mid-day on the lofty hill at Rota, which commands so wonderful a view, and reaching Sestri di Ponente just in season to enjoy one of those indescribable Italian sunsets. The necessity of an early start, the next day, not only secured us an opportunity of witnessing what Jeremy Taylor had so vividly in mind when he quaintly recommended to the readers of his "Holy Living," that they should sometimes "be curious to see the preparations which the sun makes, when he is about to quit his chamber in the East;" but enabled us also to reach the summit of the last mountain on our route, in season to look down upon the lovely harbor of Spezia, just as the daystar was once more sinking beneath the blue waters of the Mediterranean, and casting those ineffable roseate hues upon the snow-capped Apennines in the distance, while at the same instant a full-orbed moon was rising majestically from behind them. A more delightful and inspiring view it has hardly entered into the imagination of poet or painter to conceive. Shall I be forgiven, however, for saying that there was an added beauty to that view, — to American eyes, certainly, — when we descried in the harbor below us, safely riding at anchor, and surrounded by its companions of the squadron, and surmounted by the stars and stripes, the same noble propeller, bearing the name of the "Great Bostonian," — Franklin, — which we had left at Nice, and which had come round there that very day? I do not envy the apathy of any American, young or old, who can suddenly find himself face to face, in a foreign land, with the flag of his country, flying from the mast-head of one of its noblest frigates, and symbolizing more especially the personal presence and authority of an admiral who went into action lashed to a mast-head himself, — I do not envy, I say, the composure of one who can confront that flag, under such circumstances, without emotion; or, who would not consider any prospect, which sun and moon and azure waves and snow-capt hills combined can make up, as beautified and glorified by such an additional feature.

The next morning, I found myself in the train with Farragut and his party, and went on with them to Pisa, where we all ascended "the tower which leans and leans and leans, but never falls." On the following day, I was where I could read the inscription on the ancient residence of Americus Vespucius; and where I was led to wish again, as I had more than once wished before, that Boston would follow the example of Florence, and so inscribe its local history on the names of its streets, and the walls of its houses, that it might be read by every boy and girl on their way to school.

But what, you may well ask, my friends, what has all this to do with the course of historical lectures which I am here officially to introduce? What has it all to do even with the apology which I proposed to offer you? Not so much, perhaps, with either as might be wished, yet by no means so little as some of my hearers may at first be disposed to think. For as I drove along that magnificent road, during those five or six days of superb weather, when sun and moon and each particular star would seem to have shed their selectest influence upon our pathway (and be it always borne in mind, that one may as well look for the beauties of a landscape while passing through a tunnel, as attempt to form any idea of the grandeur of the Corniche by traversing it in a fog or a storm), — as I drove along that marvellous road which, too soon, I fear, is to be abandoned for the greater despatch and economy of an already half-finished railroad, the letter of my friend Dr. Ellis, announcing these lectures, and which had been opened as I entered the carriage, was fresh in my mind and frequently in my hand. I read it certainly more than once, or twice, or thrice; and the subject to which it referred kept strangely blending itself with all I was observing and enjoying, entering unbidden alike into my thoughts by day and my dreams by night. As I gazed, at one moment, on the glorious sea at my side, and marked the matchless blueness of its waters; and at another, on the gorgeous hues of sunrise, or of sunset, around and above me, fulfilling, as hardly anywhere else is so completely fulfilled, the exquisite idea of the Psalmist, — "Thou makest the outgoings of the morning and the evening to rejoice;" — as I contemplated the varied luxuriance of the climate and the soil, where, on those last days of January and first days of February, the vine and the olive were still wearing their leafy honors side by side; and oranges and lemons still ripening on the branches; and the rose and the sweet pea still blooming on the walls and in the gardens; — as I inhaled that balmy air which made it a luxury to breathe; — as I turned to the thousand forms of beauty and of grandeur which greeted me from the distant hills and mountains, the Maritime Alps or Ligurian Apennines, with their robes of ice and diadems of snow: — all the while, old Massachusetts and its history and its Historical Society, and this very course of Lowell lectures, were still uppermost, or undermost, or somewhere in the midst of my thoughts, — sometimes in the way of comparison and sometimes of contrast, sometimes of yearning and sometimes, I do confess, of dread.

I could not help feeling, of course, that whatever else my native State might have to boast of, she had nothing in the way of sea, or sky, or soil, of climate or of scenery, to be compared for an instant with what I was beholding. I could not help contrasting the genial temperature and glowing atmosphere which I was enjoying, with the bleak winds and deep snows and drenching storms and freezing cold, which my fellow-citizens at home must have been at that moment enduring. And while I was thus meditating and musing, the fire kindled, and I found myself seriously asking myself, whether I would permanently exchange, were it in my power to do so, such sea and sky and soil, as we have here in New England to-day, for those of southern France or central Italy; and suddenly I found myself resolving, that if I should reach my home safely and in season, and should be called on to take either an opening or a closing part in this course of lectures, — ignorant, as I was, what other subjects might be left open to me, — I would give my reasons for saying no, — emphatically *no*, — to this question; and would devote my little hour to some thoughts on the influences upon the character and career of our earlier and our later people, and on the supreme results to our history as a Commonwealth, of that very soil and climate about which we are so often disposed to complain, and of which my letters from home were at that moment saying, "that it was feared the Gulf Stream had changed its current, and that we might soon look out for polar bears and other arctic curiosities!" And soon the subject and its treatment began to expand and shape itself in my mind. I bethought me that Massachusetts, too, had a sea of her own,

— an historical sea, if I may so speak; that, indeed, she had risen out of the sea, that she could not have been Massachusetts had she not been founded on the coast. And I followed that coast around, on the map of my memory, from the farthest point of Cape Cod, to which Captain John Smith, — one of the pioneers of New-England exploration, of whom my friend Hillard has given us so good a Life; and who himself deserves a statue or a monument somewhere along shore, — attempted to affix the name of King James; round to the extremest verge of Cape Ann, to which the same bold, though erratic — I had almost said vagabond — navigator essayed to give the portentous and not altogether musical title of Cape Tragabigzanda. I found myself pausing in this survey, as you will not doubt, to mark the spot in Provincetown Harbor, where, in the cabin of the "Mayflower," the first written Constitution known to the history of the world, was drawn up, agreed upon, and signed. I found myself pausing again, as you will not doubt, to mark the spot in Plymouth Harbor, where the Pilgrim Fathers left the "Mayflower" at that terrible wintry season, and landed on that consecrated rock. I found myself pausing once more, you may be sure, to mark the spot in the gentler waters which wash that charming Beverly shore in the harbor of Salem, where the "Arbella," with the charter of Massachusetts, and its governor and company, came to anchor ten years later. Nor did I altogether forget the little islands on which Bartholomew Gosnold had landed and built a house, before Puritan or Pilgrim, or even John Smith, had ventured within our bay. And then there came over me a more vivid impression than ever before, of all that that bay, with the great ocean of which it is an inlet, had done for the character and enterprise and industry of our people, from those early days to this. I bethought me of those whale-fisheries, of which it had been the cradle and the nursery, and which elicited that well-remembered and magnificent tribute of Edmund Burke, in his speech on conciliation with America, — a tribute, which, at the end of nearly a hundred years, cannot be read without stirring our blood like a trumpet, and which is worthy of being read and re-read, as a piece of glorious prose which neither Macaulay nor Milton often, if ever, surpassed: —

"Look at the manner in which the people of New England," said Burke, "have of late carried on the whale-fishery. Whilst we follow them among the tumbling mountains of ice, and behold them penetrating into the deepest frozen recesses of Hudson's Bay and Davis's Straits, whilst we are looking for them beneath the arctic circle, we hear that they have pierced into the opposite region of polar cold, that they are at the antipodes, and engaged under the frozen serpent of the South. Falkland Island, which seemed too remote and romantic an object for the grasp of rational ambition, is but a stage and resting-place in the progress of their victorious industry. Nor is the equinoctial heat more discouraging to them, than the accumulated winter of both the poles. We know that whilst some of them draw the line and strike the harpoon on the coast of Africa, others run the longitude, and pursue their gigantic game along the coast of Brazil. No sea but what is vexed by their fisheries. No climate that is not witness to their toils. Neither the perseverance of Holland, nor the activity of France, nor the dexterous and firm sagacity of English enterprise, ever carried this most perilous mode of hardy industry to the extent to which it has been pushed by this recent people; a people who are still, as it were, but in the gristle, and not yet hardened into the bone of manhood."

I bethought me, too, of the cod fisheries which our bay had nourished and cherished, until they became at one time so far the very staple of our Commonwealth, that their emblem,—as I have the best reason for remembering,—was suspended, where it still hangs, over the chair of the presiding officer of the representatives of the people in our legislative halls. I bethought me, again, of the mercantile marine it had built up, until Salem became one of the great seats of the East-India trade; and Captain Robert Gray, of Boston, discovered the Columbia River; and Boston itself rose to be the third,—as it not long ago was, I know not where it stands now,—while New Bedford was hardly less than the fifth, in the commercial tonnage of the Union. Nor, certainly, did I fail to remember what our bay and our sea had done for the national navy, and the thousands of gallant tars it had supplied for fighting their country's battles on the ocean,—whether under Bainbridge and Lawrence and Chauncey and Hull and Decatur, in those days when George Canning declared, in the House of Commons, that "the spell of British invincibility on the ocean was at last broken;" or in these latter days of not inferior glory, under Porter and Rodgers and Winslow and Foote and Farragut. Was this a sea, I asked myself, to be disowned, or abandoned, or exchanged for any other sea beneath the sun? It was no Mediterranean, indeed. It did not run between vine-clad hills and romantic villages; and one could hardly sail an hour upon it, in a straight course, without leaving capes and headlands and snug harbors behind him, and going out to buffet with the big rollers and swelling billows of the vast Atlantic, with nothing but the sea and the sky, and the God above the sky, to witness the encounter. But, for this very reason, it was a sea to impart the bravery it demanded; to stimulate the adventure it invited; and to breed and educate, as it has bred and educated, a race of hardy and intrepid mariners, taking to the water, — as Dr. Palfrey once so happily said, — as naturally as so many ducks to a pond; whose enterprise and exploits have supplied, and are still destined to supply, the theme of solid history, as well as of brilliant romance, to the end of time; mariners of New England, who are as worthy of being famous in song and story, as those mariners of Old England, whose memories are embalmed in the immortal song of Campbell.

And then I bethought me of the climate of Massachusetts, which had so marvellously co-operated with the sea, in giving vigor and energy and hardihood to our people. True, we had no Januarys or Februarys like those I was experiencing. True, our winters were almost always long and dreary and dreadful, and our summers too often brief and scorching. A glorious autumn we might generally boast of, kindling our forests into a thousand glories, as the inexorable Frost King blazes his pathway through the valleys and along the hill-sides, in colors such as never adorned the train of any other earthly monarch: but we have had recent experience that even this cannot be counted on; while as to spring, — why, if our poet Bryant had seen fit to vie with Thomson, — as I think he might have done, — and to depict the Seasons of New England, he could have done nothing but include spring in a parenthesis.

Yet, would I alter all this? Would I, if the wand of Prospero, to lay or lift a tempest, were in my hand, exchange even our Boston east wind, eager and nipping as it is, for some sweet but treacherous south, breathing, indeed, over a bank of violets, but bringing in its track the lassitude, the self-indulgence, the aversion to labor, the inaptitude for liberty, the incapacity for self-government, or for sustained and manly effort of any sort, which characterize so many of the inhabitants of those sunny climes through which I was then passing? Admit that our east wind may have imparted not a little of its harsh and acrid quality to the tempers of those who first weathered it, which has not been wholly eradicated, which perhaps never can be eradicated, from the tempers of their descendants; for I am disposed to think, that the acrid quality of the climate was, in part at least, primarily responsible for creating that "acrid spirit of the times," which Longfellow tells us, at the close of one of his graceful New-England tragedies, "corroded the true steel" of one of the earliest and bravest of the old Puritan leaders. But what other climate could have given them the muscle, the grit, the gristle (as Burke called it), the strong right arms, and the stern and dauntless souls, which enabled them to endure the deprivations of a wilderness, and to subdue a soil which would have repelled and defied all feebler hands or hearts?

And, next, I bethought me of that soil: What a soil it was, here in New England, what a soil it is still, compared with that then beneath my feet! And I remembered but too vividly the dreary and desolate look of a Massachusetts landscape for six or seven months of the year, not only without fruit or flowers, like those which were on all sides around me, but without a spire of grass or a leaf on the trees. But I remembered, too, a little dialogue which I had once heard from the lips of Edward Everett. Would that those lips had language still, and could repeat it, in their own inimitable way, once more! He was accompanying Henry Clay, during the month of April, I think it was in the year 1833, through the county of Middlesex, which Mr. Everett then represented in Congress, on a visit to Lowell. "Everett," exclaimed Mr. Clay, "in Heaven's name, what do your constituents live on? I see nothing hereabouts capable of supporting human life, or animal life of any sort." "Why, Mr. Clay," replied Everett, "don't you see that tree in the middle of yonder field there?" "Yes, I do," said Mr. Clay; "and a very small and miserable specimen of a tree it is; there is not a leaf or a bud on it; it looks dead already, and hardly fit for firewood." "Ah!" said Mr. Everett (in playful resentment of an old impertinence to a neighboring New-England State), "it makes capital wooden nutmegs!" Yes, my friends, the barrenness of our ground has made our brains fertile; and even the invention which built up Lowell, has owed not a little of its stimulus to the sterility of the surrounding acres. The willing and luxuriant harvests of other latitudes, are, indeed, unknown to us; but who shall complain of a soil which has so enforced industry; which has so quickened and sharpened the wits; which has so nourished independence and freedom; which has presented no temptation to make woman a yoke-fellow with the brutes, exhibiting her, like those I saw around me, subjected to the hardest labors of the field; and which, above all, — far, far above all, — has so repelled and repudiated from its culture every form of human servitude! Boast as we will, and as we well may, of the influence of free schools and free governments in moulding and training the characters and careers of New-England men, — and my friend, Mr. Emerson, will tell you all about that, when his turn to lecture comes, — we must not forget that there are influences underlying and overlying all these, — the influences of the earth beneath us and of the sky above us. One of the most popular of Old England's poets, even in the very piece in which he proposed to illustrate the influence of education and government upon mankind, — a piece which, though fragmentary and unfinished, is not unworthy to stand beside his own exquisite elegy in a country churchyard, — has given expression to this idea in some noble lines: —

> "Not but the human fabric from the birth
> Imbibes the flavor of its parent earth;
> As various tracts enforce a various toil,
> The manners speak the idiom of their soil.
> An iron race the mountain-cliffs maintain,
> Foes to the gentler genius of the plain."

One might almost imagine, indeed, that Gray had New England, and New-England men, distinctly in his mind, when he adds: —

> "For where unwearied sinews must be found
> With side-long plough to quell the flinty ground,
> To turn the torrent's swift-descending flood,
> To brave the savage rushing from the wood, —
> What wonder if, to patient valor train'd,
> They guard with spirit what by strength they gain'd?"

And you all remember that good, dear, pious Mrs. Barbauld has condensed the whole thought into one of the grandest couplets in all poetry: —

> "Man is the nobler growth our realms supply,
> And souls are ripened in our northern sky."

Yes, my friends, we of New England, after all, may well thank Heaven that our Pilgrim Fathers landed upon nothing softer than a rock,[1] and that the Puritan founders of Massachusetts were not persuaded, — as Oliver Cromwell endeavored to persuade them, and would fain have forced them, had he dared to try it, — to abandon their flinty glebe for the rich mould of the tropics. It is not enough for us to be grateful, that the region to which they so firmly adhered, was not a region exposed to such inundations as have recently devastated so many of the fields and villages of Switzerland, and made such a claim upon the sympathy and succor of all who have witnessed the glories of the Alps, and the simple virtues of those who inhabit them. It is not enough for us to be grateful, that the clime to which they clung so tenaciously, is not a clime subject to such convulsions as have recently swallowed up whole cities on our own hemisphere; and the mere liability to which is itself sufficient to unnerve and demoralize even those who may escape all actual damage to person or property. It is not enough for us to be grateful, that the bay around which they nestled and clustered, had no smouldering volcano on its right hand or on its left, threatening at every outbreak, like Vesuvius or Ætna at this moment, to overwhelm all within its reach with a torrent of burning lava. It is not enough for us to be grateful, that the land and the sea which they refused so obstinately to abandon or exchange, were free alike from the corrupting and distracting influences of mines of silver or of gold, and of fisheries of coral or of pearl; though I may not forget that, in these latter years, some of our not very distant hills have occasionally been suspected of gold, and that a few exquisite pearls have actually been found, in the streams near Sandwich, not far from where the Pilgrims landed. But, beyond and above all this, may we not well thank God, as we review our history, even for that springless climate, of short summers and long winters, of late and early frosts,

1 See p. 27.

of sharp and sudden vicissitudes, which has demanded, from first to last, the steady and sturdy struggle of intelligent freemen for existence and for bread? May we not well thank God for a soil, from which no North-western Ordinance or Missouri Compromise, no Wilmot Proviso or Constitutional Amendment, was ever needed to shut out slavery; and for a temperature which has braced up our children to a manly, vigorous, independent, self-sustaining, and self-relying exercise of their own thews and sinews and brains in every field of useful labor or worthy enterprise?

Who is not willing to unite with me in exclaiming, in this sense at least, — Let Massachusetts be "left out in the cold" for ever, with nothing but ice and granite for her natural exports, rather than have all the manhood melted and thawed out of her children, as it was out of so many of those whom I saw by the way-side, too limp for any thing but to bask in the sun and beg? Who can say that upon a different soil, and under other skies, even New-England principles, as we call them, would have been proof against the temptation of establishing, or at least permanently tolerating, domestic institutions which have been so fatal elsewhere, and which it has cost at last such a deluge of blood and treasure to abolish? Who can say that if the pilot of the Pilgrims, to whom, justly or unjustly, treachery has sometimes been imputed, had conducted the Mayflower nearer to the Southern Cross, instead of steering her ever by that blessed North Star; and if the Massachusetts colony had followed in their wake, — we, their descendants, might not at this moment be suffering, as so many of our brethren elsewhere are suffering, from the destitution and desolation, directly or indirectly brought upon ourselves, by a vain struggle, in the interests and under the influence of slavery, to overthrow that National Government, and rend asunder that Constitutional Union, which it is now our pride and glory to have defended and preserved for our children?

Such, my friends, were some of the thoughts, on the influence of soil and climate upon the character and history of New England, which came swarming through my mind as I whirled along that magnificent Corniche road last winter, with the letter of my friend Dr. Ellis in my hand. Such were the leading ideas of the lecture I then conceived, and proposed to prepare deliberately, if I should be called on to prepare any thing, for this occasion; and which I thought might be worked up into a not altogether inappropriate Introductory to such a course. But a thousand unforeseen circumstances of foreign travel, and of domestic and personal experience, soon occurred to obliterate the whole subject from my mind; and I returned home, not long ago, without ever thinking of it again, and without a note on which I could rely for reviving and reconstructing the train of ideas. And all that I have been able to do, since my return, has been to recall thus hastily the associations of time and place, to gather up the tangled threads wherever I could lay hold of them in my memory, and to present to you thus crudely, what I would so gladly have elaborated, illustrated, and perfected. If, however, by throwing myself into the gap, — as I have done, at the last moment, and at the imperative call of others, — I shall have prepared the way for the instructive and well-considered and eloquent discourses which I know are to follow, my hour will not have been spent in vain; and you, I am sure, will all pardon me for so desultory and discursive an utterance.

I must not let you go, however, without reverting, in a few closing remarks, to the original purpose of these lectures, and to the general objects of the Society under whose auspices they have been undertaken. There is something remarkable, and more than remarkable, — there is something quite wonderful, I think, — about the way in which the history of this old Commonwealth of ours, and the history of New England, of which it was the capital colony, have been preserved, cared for, and "treasured up as for a life beyond life," from the very outset of their career. Not only are we spared the pains of seeking the story of our origin in myths and fables, in traditions and legends, like the people of so many other lands, but we may find it written out for us at the moment, by those who could tell us all that they saw, and a most important part of which they were.

Hardly had the Pilgrims landed at Plymouth in 1620, before William Bradford, who was so soon to succeed the lamented Carver as their governor, began to collect the original letters and papers, which, ten years afterwards, he commenced "piecing up at times of leisure" (to use his own phrase), until he had completed a connected and careful account of the first twenty-seven years of that pioneer plantation. This invaluable work, — after remaining in manuscript for more than two hundred years, known only by a few citations which had been made from it by later writers, who had enjoyed the privilege of consulting it, — after having disappeared from all view, and eluded all search, for more than half a century; and after having been lamented over like one of the lost books of Livy — to us, if not to the world at large, a thousand times more precious than the whole of Livy, — was at last discovered in 1855, on the other side of the Atlantic Ocean, in the library of the Bishop of London at Fulham, and was printed for the first time, by this Society, in 1856, from an exact copy made for the purpose, under the faithful editorship of our present accomplished Recording Secretary, Mr. Charles Deane.

On the other hand, the Massachusetts Company proper, with their charter, had not left their final anchorage at the Cowes, near the Isle of Wight, in 1630, before the governor of that colony (John Winthrop) had made the first entry in a journal or history, which he continued from day to day, and from year to year, until his death in 1648–9. That work, too, remained in perishable manuscript for a century and a half. The original was in three volumes; the two first of which were printed, for the first time, at Hartford, in 1790, from an inaccurate copy, which had been commenced by Governor Trumbull, with a preface and dedication by the great lexicographer, Noah Webster, who subsequently confessed that he had never even read the original manuscript. It remained for one whom we now recognize, since the death of our veteran Quincy, as the venerable senior member of our Society, and its former President (James Savage), to decipher and annotate and edit the whole; for lo! in 1816, the third volume, of which nothing had been seen or heard for more than sixty years, turned up in the tower of the Old South Meeting-house! The Rev. Thomas Prince, the pastor of that church, who kept his library in that tower, and is known to have had all three of the volumes in 1755, died without returning this third volume to the family of the author, from whom I have the best reason to think they were all borrowed. And so in 1825–6, one hundred and ninety-five years after that first entry, on that Easter Monday, while the "Arbella" was "riding at the Cowes," these annals of the first nineteen years of the Massachusetts colony were published in a correct and complete form. But as if to illustrate the risks to which they had been so long exposed, and to signalize the perils they had so providentially escaped, one of the original volumes was destroyed by a memorable fire in Court Street, before Mr. Savage had finished the laborious corrections and annotations to which he had devoted himself.

Here, then, we find the striking fact of the two governors of the two originally independent colonies of Plymouth and Massachusetts Bay, which afterwards, in 1691, were combined in a single Commonwealth, — the two men who were the leading witnesses of all that occurred, and the leading actors in all that was done, — preparing careful histories of the rise and progress of each, and leaving them in manuscript at their death: Those manuscripts we find remaining unprinted, uncopied, and seemingly uncared for, during a period of a century and a half and two centuries respectively; exposed to all and more than all the common accidents which wait upon ancient papers, — the moth, the bookworm, the damp, the flames, — owing to the unsettled and troubled condition of the colonies, from time to time, and almost all the time: For instance, when the British cavalry occupied the Old South Church, as a riding-school and a stable, in 1775, and took Governor Winthrop's old house (which stood next) for firewood, both of these precious manuscripts were in the tower, where Prince had left them; and both were doomed, to all human eyes, to be used as kindling; but they were really destined for another sort of kindling: Both of them we find reappearing in the end, — substantially every leaf of them; — one of them, and a large part of the other, turning up at last where they would least have been looked for, or have been imagined to be; and both of them waiting, — waiting, as it were, for the fulness of time, — to be published, as they have been, by those most capable of appreciating them and doing them justice.

What is there in the curiosities of secular literature more striking! Surely, we may say, so far as Massachusetts history is concerned, "There's a divinity that shapes our ends, rough-hew them how we will." But this is but the beginning of the story. While these original and more authentic accounts of the infant Commonwealth were still scarcely known to exist beyond the family circle of their authors, — as early as 1654, — Edward Johnson, one of the intensest of Puritans, publishes in London, his "Wonder-working Providence of Sion's Saviour in New England," which, though written in a most inflated and bombastic style, and full of blunders and doggerel, contains many most important and valuable facts, and is worthy of being remembered as the first printed book of New-England history. A beautiful edition of it, with a valuable Introduction, has recently been published by Mr. W. F. Poole, the late faithful Librarian of the Boston Athenæum. Then came Nathaniel Morton, a nephew of Governor Bradford, with his "Memorial of Plymouth Colony," abounding, also, in important references to the Massachusetts Colony proper, published originally at our Cambridge in 1669, and republished in 1826, under the admirable editorship of another former President of this Society, — the late excellent Judge Davis.

And now "draws hitherward, — I know him by his stride," — the giant of New-England early literature, — the marvellous and marvel-loving Cotton Mather, with a voracity for every thing relating to our colonial condition and history as insatiate as his own vanity; seeking and searching for something new and strange, like those men of ancient Athens whom Paul depicted; of a credulity which swallowed every thing which was told him, and a diligence which digested almost every thing which he swallowed; and publishing, in London, in 1702, after a prodigious amount of strugglings and wrestlings, of prayers and fastings, of visions by day and dreams by night, a huge folio volume, entitled "Magnalia Christi Americana," or, as the titlepage has it, "The First book of the New-English History, reporting the Design where*on*, the Manner where*in*, and the People where*by*, the several Colonies of New England were planted, by the endeavour of Cotton Mather;" — containing a monstrous mass of information and speculation, of error and gossip, of biography and history, of italics and capitals, of classical quotations, Latin and Greek, and of original epitaphs, Latin and English, in prose and in verse, which, as old Polonius said of Hamlet's actors, "either for tragedy, comedy, history, pastoral, pastoral-comical, historical-pastoral, tragical-comical, scene individable or poem unlimited," has hardly a parallel in the world. Let me not seem to disparage or undervalue Cotton Mather,—a perfect Dr. Pangloss, as he was in many particulars,—for with all his foibles and all his faults, all his credulity and all his vanity, it cannot be denied that he did a really great work for New-England history. The lives of our Worthies could not have been written without him; while his "Essay to do Good" is known to have given the earliest incentive to the wonderful career of New England's most wonderful son,—Benjamin Franklin.

Passing rapidly now over Church's "King Philip's War," first printed in 1716, of which a beautiful edition has recently been added to "the New-England Library" by the Rev. Henry Martyn Dexter; and John Dunton's "Letters from New England," in 1686, just printed for the Prince Society, from the original manuscript in the Bodleian Library, under the careful editorship of Mr. W. H. Whitmore,—we come next, in order of date, to the "Chronological History of New England" by the accurate and indefatigable Thomas Prince himself, whose first volume was published in 1736; and, who in 1755, began a second volume, of which only three serial numbers were printed before his death, in 1758. Then we have the valuable historical "Summary" of Dr. William Douglas, published in Boston, in numbers, the first of them in 1746–7; and the whole two volumes of which were completed in 1751.

And now appears upon the scene, as an historian of Massachusetts, another of her colonial governors, whose name was so identified, justly or unjustly, with the Stamp Act, and others of those acts of British oppression which drove us to rebellion, and through rebellion to independence, that it long was held in too much of passionate abhorrence to allow of any justice being done to any thing he did or said or wrote; but who, take him for all in all, did as much for the history of this his native State, and did it as well, as any man who has lived before or since. Let us not fail to do justice to his memory in this respect. Governor Hutchinson's first volume was published in 1764. The second volume, almost ready for the press, was in his house in Garden-Court Street, on the 26th of August, 1765, when it was so shamefully sacked and pillaged by a mob. Hutchinson, as the mob approached, was engaged in bearing to a place of safety a beloved daughter who had refused to quit his side, and was thus compelled to abandon his precious papers to their fate. Every thing was destroyed, or thrown out of the windows; and the scattered pages of this second volume of his history were left lying in the street for several hours in a soaking rain. But thanks to the care and pains of the Rev. Andrew Eliot, one of the servants, then and always, of the good God to whom we owe the marvellous preservation of those other and earlier manuscripts of those other and earlier governors, all but eight or ten sheets were collected and saved; and so much of them was still legible that, in spite of the muddy footprints of the Vandals who had trampled on them, the author was able to supply the rest, transcribe the whole, and publish it in 1767. Still a third volume, hardly less valuable than either, and written with an almost judicial fairness and a wonderful freedom from prejudice, considering the treatment he had received, remained in manuscript for half a century after his death in 1780, and was only rescued from perdition, and published in 1828, through the persevering efforts of Mr. Savage, and other members of our Society.

I must not forget that still another governor of Massachusetts, James Sullivan, the first President of our Society, early devoted his leisure from professional and public labors to the preparation of a history of his native Province of Maine,—then a part of Massachusetts,—and published it in 1795. I must not forget the excellent account of that great epoch in Massachusetts history, commonly called "Shays's Rebellion," published in 1788 by George Richards Minot (the father of our venerable William); and followed, in 1798 and 1803, by two substantial volumes of the history of the province, from 1748 to 1765. I must not forget either the really great work of one who was so long our Corresponding Secretary, and whose accomplished son,—who so well illustrates the idea of ancient mythology, "one power of physic, melody, and song"—is announced among the lecturers of our course; I mean the "American Annals" of the late Dr. Abiel Holmes, published in 1805, and abounding in dates and facts of Massachusetts and New England, as well as of National interest. Still less must I forget the elaborate History of New England, by the Rev. William Hubbard, an early minister of

Ipswich, completed in manuscript as long ago as 1682, but which it remained for this Society, with the patronage of the Legislature of Massachusetts, to publish for the first time as lately as 1815.

Time would fail me, or certainly your patience would be exhausted, my friends, were I to attempt to speak, as I ought to speak, of all the more recent contributions and contributors to the historical illustration of our Commonwealth, and of New England; of the Rev. John Eliot, and of Alden Bradford; of Dr. Felt's Ecclesiastical History, and Governor Washburn's Judicial History; of Drake's comprehensive and elaborate History of Boston; of Quincy's Harvard University; of Young's Chronicles of Plymouth and of Massachusetts, and of the Records of those old Colonies, edited by our worthy Mayor, Dr. Shurtleff; of Mr. Savage's Genealogical History of New England; of Tudor's James Otis; of Richard Frothingham's Siege of Boston, and Life of Warren; of Sabine's Fisheries and Loyalists; of Dr. Holland's Western Massachusetts, and General Schouler's Massachusetts in the late Civil War, with its admirable portrait of the lamented Andrew, and its vivid presentment of many of the stirring scenes through which we have so lately passed; of the Life and Letters of John Adams by his distinguished grandson; of Barry's Massachusetts; of Bancroft's Colonial Period; of Upham's recent and most interesting History of Witchcraft; and of Palfrey's consummate and crowning work on New England, which may fitly complete the calendar, and which is worthy, I need not say, of far more than any mere passing commendation of mine.

I have omitted, I doubt not, in this running catalogue, many names which deserve to be mentioned; and I have said nothing of what has been done so well, in their Collections and Registers, by our sister societies of other States, and by kindred associations in our own State; or of the numerous town histories, and church histories, which have been so faithfully written. But I have said enough to recall to your remembrance the fact, that while New England has furnished not a few able and brilliant historians and biographers for some of the great political and literary epochs of other lands, ancient and modern, and for some of the great statesmen of other parts of our own land, — in our lamented Prescott and Sparks and Felton, and in our living Ticknor and

Motley and Parkman and Kirk, — her own history has by no means been neglected; but that there has been a most striking succession of men, — many of them governors, judges, ministers, counsellors, men of renown, famous in their generation, — who have been moved, as by a common impulse, to keep the record of New England, and of Massachusetts in particular, and to illustrate the history of their rise and progress; some of whose works, like those of William Bradford and John Winthrop and Thomas Hutchinson, have come down to us under circumstances of almost romantic interest; and all of which together can hardly fail to leave the impression on a thoughtful mind, — I will not admit that it need be a superstitious mind, — that for good or for evil, for encouragement or for warning, for our glory or for our shame, that history was not destined to be lost to mankind.

But I could not be forgiven, — I could not forgive myself, — were I to close without an allusion to one other name, which I have purposely reserved to the last, — the name of the Rev. Dr. Jeremy Belknap, the recognized founder of our Society, whose History of New Hampshire, in three volumes, published in 1784, 1791, and 1792, and his two volumes of early American biography, published in 1794 and 1798, are full of importance to the work of which I have been speaking. Under his lead, our Society was organized in 1791, — to gather up the fragments, that nothing be lost, — composed of ten members, at the outset, increased to thirty, and afterwards to sixty in all, and now limited to a hundred members throughout the Commonwealth. Beginning their career upon the most economical scale; ordering their Treasurer, Judge Tudor, to buy "twelve Windsor green elbow-chairs, a plain pine table, painted, with a drawer and lock and key, and an inkstand;" and with no resources but an assessment of two dollars a year upon each member, — they proceeded to collect papers and pamphlets and books, and to publish, scrap by scrap, as an appendix or a preamble to a magazine called "The American Apollo," whatever original manuscripts, relating to New England, they were able to pick up; the very first of these scraps having been published on the 6th of January, 1792, just seventy-six years ago to-morrow. In these latter years, the liberal and noble benefactions of Samuel Appleton and Thomas Dowse and George Peabody have added greatly to their library and to their funds, and have enabled them to go on with their work more conspicuously and more confidently. But the enormous cost of printing, and the inadequate sale of their volumes, are serious impediments to their progress; and this very course of lectures has been arranged, as a labor of love on the part of the members, not without at least a secondary view to eking out the insufficiencies of our treasury.

Forty-five volumes of Collections and Proceedings have already been printed, — many of them containing papers of unspeakable importance and interest; and some of them throwing a light upon the formation of our institutions, the establishment of our towns and schools, and the inner life of the earlier and later settlers of New England, which can be found nowhere else. Other papers of equal interest and value are awaiting the press. Without any very large addition to our resources, if it were only secured before some of our members, now in my eye, but whose names I forbear to mention, shall have lost the taste and the faculty for this sort of labor, our valuable manuscripts might be printed, and placed beyond the reach of accident, as fast as is desirable. And it is easy to suggest a legitimate and effectual mode of relief, — in the wider circulation and sale of our Collections, — if we could only accomplish its adoption. We cannot hope, indeed, that our volumes will find any great number of purchasers or readers, in competition with the illustrated poems or sensation novels, of which the tenth or the twentieth thousand are advertised in successive months. But there are more than three hundred towns in Massachusetts. In the public or social libraries of every one of them, there ought to be a complete set, or as complete a set as is still possible, of these Historical Collections. Everywhere we observe liberal men, residents or natives of these towns, founding, or endowing, or aiding these public libraries. If we could find enough of such liberal men, who, severally or jointly, would be responsible for placing sets of these Collections in only one-half of the town libraries, — and I know not what more appropriate New-Year's present could be made by any one to the place of his nativity, or of his winter or summer residence, — I should feel the greatest confidence, that we and our successors could go on, without let or hindrance, to continue the story of this noble Commonwealth in all its earlier, and in all its later, relations to

New England and to the nation at large,—"nothing extenuating, nor setting down aught in malice," but giving the truth, the whole truth, and nothing but the truth, after the manner and example of those who have preceded us.

It is a work, my friends, which, you will all agree with me ought not to be left incomplete. We owe it to the memory of our fathers, that no authentic account of their lives and labors should be lost. We owe it to our children, that the great examples of piety and purity, of endurance and enterprise, of wisdom and patriotism and heroism, with which our earlier and our later annals abound, should be handed down to them in all the exactness of contemporaneous records. We owe it to ourselves not to be behindhand, at this day of our prosperity and abundance, in doing our share towards completing a history, which so many good and great men, under so many disadvantages and discouragements, have labored at so lovingly and so successfully, and which would almost seem to have been watched over from the beginning by a higher than human Power.

NOTES.

Page 5, Line 24.

I am glad to say that, only six weeks after the delivery of this lecture, a colossal statue of Columbus, by an accomplished American artist (Miss Emma Stebbins), which is described as "grand in its conception and beautiful in its execution," was presented to the Commissioners of the Central Park at New York, by the Hon. Marshall O. Roberts, an eminent and munificent merchant of that city, and is immediately to be added to the decorations of that noble park.

Page 16, Line 8.

An accomplished and classical friend has reminded me that Herodotus (the old father of History), at the end of his last book (Calliope), makes Cyrus say: "*Φιλέειν γὰρ ἐκ τῶν μαλακῶν χώρων μαλακοὺς ἄνδρας γίνεσθαι.*"

THE AIMS AND PURPOSES

OF THE

FOUNDERS OF THE MASSACHUSETTS COLONY.

"Tantum Religio Potuit."

By REV. GEORGE E. ELLIS, D.D.

THE AIMS AND PURPOSES

OF THE

FOUNDERS OF THE MASSACHUSETTS COLONY.[1]

"TANTUM RELIGIO POTUIT."

I AM to speak of the Aims and Purposes of the Founders of the Colony, now the State, of Massachusetts. What were the ends and objects of their enterprise? what its motive and its design? It ought to be easy for us to meet these questions with a full and sufficient answer. We have many and very distinct avowals from most of the leaders in that enterprise. From these, digested and harmonized, we might well expect to learn their real intent. And if it be suggested — as it often has been — that these avowals of theirs were not frank disclosures of their real motives, but were misleading or deceptive, designed to cover their secret purposes, which it would not have been safe or for their own ultimate success to reveal, then we have another means of reaching the truth. On the principle that actions speak louder than words, we have a sure interpretation of their motives in their deeds, in the course which they pursued, in the measures which they originated, in the records of their legislation and administration, and in their practical management of their affairs.

If the views which are now to be presented have the warrant of truth, it will appear that there is no occasion for charging them with insincerity, or with secrecy; and that their avowed motives were put into their actions.

[1] Less than half of the matter of the following Lecture, with the authorities quoted in it, was read on its delivery. The extracts from documents on which its statements and arguments are based, are here printed at length.

It may as well be stated distinctly, at the start, that I intend to controvert, or at least to qualify and correct, the current opinion, the so-called popular and generally accepted idea, of the motive of their enterprise. An error, of the sort defined as the suppression of the truth, has worked into our history. By some strange process, the key has been lost to modern use which alone can make it intelligible as a whole, and reveal the consistency of its parts. Inadvertence and misconstruction, rather than any intentional unfairness, have confused and mystified this subject.

Dr. Palfrey, the latest, and incomparably the best, of our historians, — so thorough and able and trustworthy indeed, that there is no reason why he should not always be the last of them, — after rehearsing preliminaries, and bringing the founders of Massachusetts to these shores, gives us this sentence : —

"As a corporation, the company had obtained the ownership of a large American territory, on which it designed to place a colony which should be a refuge for civil and religious freedom." [1]

But on the very preceding page the historian has quoted the words of Winthrop, the governor and master-spirit of the colony, as found in a beautiful little treatise, called "A Model of Christian Charity," written by him on his ocean passage hither. These are the words : —

"It is by a mutual consent, through a special overruling Providence, and a more than ordinary approbation of the churches of Christ the work we have in hand, to seek out a place of cohabitation and consortship, under a due form of government, both civil and ecclesiastical." [2]

1 Hist. of New Eng., vol. i. p. 314.

2 The spirit of earnest and gentle devoutness which runs through this little essay gives us an engaging revelation of the character of the writer. Though it is anticipating a point to be more emphatically insisted upon by and by, another quotation from the essay may be introduced here. It will prepare us for a further dealing with more matter that is like it.

"Thus stands the cause between God and us. We are entered into Covenant with Him for this worke. We have taken out a Commission. The Lord hath given us leave to drawe our own articles. We have professed to enterprise these and those accounts, upon these and those ends. We have hereupon besought Him of favour and blessing. Now if the Lord shall please to heare us, and bring us in peace to the place we desire, then hath hee ratified this covenant and sealed our Commission, and will expect a strict performance of the articles contained in it ; but if wee shall neglect the observation of these articles, which are the ends wee have propounded, and, dissembling with our God, shall fall to embrace this present world

There is a wide discrepancy between the statement made by the historian and that made by the Governor. The variance is great even, as measured by words. — by words, which change their meanings with time and use, and are charged with more or less of meaning according to the intelligence of readers or hearers. But far greater than the difference between the verbal statements is the variance in the substance and the matter of the two assertions. What Governor Winthrop so distinctly affirms about the intentions of his company, taken for what it signified at the time when it was written, conveys something amazingly different, wide apart, from the idea which those who read the sentence of Dr. Palfrey would draw from it. Now, the difference in the substance and purport of what goes respectively with those two statements, to my mind, corresponds exactly to the erroneous writing and reading of our early history, which has dropped out of recognition the real aims and purposes of the founders of Massachusetts, and substituted for them other motives and ends, avowed or secret.

The difference between the Governor's "place of cohabitation and consortship, under a due form of government, both civil and ecclesiastical," and the historian's "place of refuge for civil and religious freedom," is, one may say, immeasurable by comparison or contrast. The purpose which the Governor recognizes, positively and completely excluded every thing that is conveyed to us in the phrase used by Dr. Palfrey and by ourselves. We have civil and religious freedom in this State now. But what we have as such was not in the minds of the Fathers. They never designed it or planned for it. On the contrary, in view of their real intent and aim, the purpose which mastered and put them willingly and heroically to its service, what is civil and religious freedom to us, would have been to them a dread and woe.

I might quote a long and suggestive series of statements from the pens of the ablest writers in Massachusetts, who have found occasion to give their own views as to the purpose and aim of

and prosecute our carnal intentions, seeking greate things for ourselves and our posterity, the Lord will surely breake out in wrathe against us, be revenged of such a [sinful] people, and make us knowe the price of the breache of such a covenant." — *Mass. Hist. Collections*, xxvii. p. 46.

the original colonists. My space restricts me here within narrow limits.

Governor Hutchinson says, —

"It was one great design of the first planters of the Massachusetts colony to obtain for themselves and their posterity the liberty of worshipping God in such manner as appeared to them to be most agreeable to the sacred Scriptures. — Upon their removal, they supposed their relation both to the civil and ecclesiastical government of England, except so far as a special reserve was made by their charter, was at an end, and that they had right to form such new model of both as best pleased them."[1]

Judge Story says, —

"The fundamental error of our ancestors, an error which began with the very settlement of the colony, was a doctrine which has since been happily exploded; I mean the necessity of a union between church and state. To this they clung as to the ark of their safety."[2]

This *error* is what we see. The colonists found in it their obligation and motive.

Mr. Quincy says the colonists did not come here "to acquire liberty for all sorts of consciences, but to vindicate and maintain the liberty of their own consciences. They did not cross the Atlantic on a crusade in behalf of the rights of mankind in general, but in support of their own rights and liberties."[3] But all depends upon the view which the colonists had of the extent, nature, and use of "their own rights and liberties."

There are those who charge themselves with the responsibility of defending and vindicating the Fathers of Massachusetts, alike against censures and assertions which are perfectly true, as well as against aspersions and slanders which are false and malignant. Their defence in either case is made difficult, and always will be unsatisfactory and insufficient, unless we start fairly with an understanding of their real motive and design. This may prove, on the search, to have been one of such a nature, such an inspiration, that they shall need no vindication or apology for having been guided by it. It may prove that, in the light and under the sway of a supposed obligation which furnished

1 History, vol. i. pp. 368–9.

2 Commemoration of the Settlement of Salem.

3 Address: Second Century of Boston.

them their enterprise, they will as little need to be relieved of any censure for what they did to others, or to each other, in attempting to accomplish it, as to be condoled with, pitied, or wept over for the stern sufferings to which they subjected themselves in pursuit of their great aim.

The attempts which are made to vindicate the Fathers of Massachusetts — to extenuate their errors, to reduce or apologize for their harsh spirit and their severe and, to us, cruel dealings — do not reach to the bottom of the matter; they are not successful; they are not consistent with truth. By some strange oversight, many of their descendants have failed to inform themselves how they may wisely deal with criticisms and censures visited upon an ancestry whom they feel bound to defend. On no subject dealt with among us, in lectures, orations, sermons, poems, historical addresses, and even in our choice school literature, has there been such an amount of crude, sentimental, and wasteful rhetoric, or so much weak and vain pleading, as on this. Those old forefathers who are thus patronized, flattered, and stood for, if they could listen to or read what is thus offered in their behalf, would themselves repudiate the larger part of it. They would feel aggrieved equally, perhaps, by their champions as by their defamers. The root of the whole error, common alike to those who censure and those who defend those ancient Fathers, is in the assumption that they came here mainly to seek, establish, and enjoy liberty of conscience; that this was their inspiration, their motive, their aim. Their assailants and their defenders both agree, in the main, in asserting or allowing this; and they are both wrong.

Starting from this assumption, their assailants proceed to say, that these Fathers very soon showed that it was only liberty of conscience, and that a very peculiar conscience, of *their own*, which they sought for, — liberty to indulge their own notions and intolerant spirit; that they at once became the relentless persecutors of every opinion and belief varying from their own, and stopped at no severity or cruelty in repressing and punishing every form of dissent; imprisoning, banishing, whipping, fining, mutilating, and hanging all who questioned their ways. They did all these harsh and cruel things. They were deadly enemies of every form of what they called heresy; and some free-thinking, if they could have reached it, they would have regarded as punishable as some free-speaking. They restricted the right of citizenship, in the franchise, — the right of choosing and of being chosen to office, — to those who had accepted their religious covenant and become church-members. They not only punished strangers and interlopers coming into their jurisdiction whose ways and opinions offended them; but they also proceeded, almost to the last penalties of their rigid code, against a succession of men and women in their own religious fellowship, who raised strife or dissent. They even fettered themselves by disabling covenants and compacts, and bound themselves in severe subjection to tests and obligations of the sternest sort; willingly renouncing a large measure of that liberty which we so naturally exercise.

These, certainly, were strange doings for men and women professing liberty of conscience, self-exiled for the purpose of providing a safe harborage for it. If they did all these things by a rule of their own opinionativeness, measured by a standard of their own devising, with no appeal, outside of themselves, to an authority held by them as equally supreme for their own guidance and that of all others, — their course would indeed present the most marvellous phenomenon in history. If they had intended to afford such an asylum, and had in writing or in spoken word avowed it, one would have thought that the first instance in which they violated or impaired it, would have opened their eyes to the marked and glaring inconsistency of their course. At any rate, how easy would it have been for the first victim of their intolerance to have quoted their own professions against them! — an opportunity never availed of from first to last by any one of their victims, for the very excellent reason, as we shall soon see, that the founders of Massachusetts had made no such professions, but were consecrated to an enterprise so pledged and constrained in itself that it would not have admitted of any laxness.

The simple truth is, that the founders of Massachusetts never professed or promised any thing that is implied to us in the phrase "liberty of conscience." After having read every thing that I know of as extant in print, or manuscript, from the pens of those exiles, I feel justified in stating positively that they did not come here to seek, nor even to indulge themselves in, "liberty of conscience," — in any thing like the meaning which that phrase has to us. We mislead ourselves when we assert or allow that they recognized any thing of the sort. Not a single sentence can be quoted from any one of them committing them to it. You may find the words, the phrase, in their writings, often repeated and very emphatic; but when it is used to express any thing of what we mean by it, that thing is sternly repudiated; and when the phrase is a part of their own vernacular, it covers something which is only a part of a much larger whole, and which defined rather a limitation, a subjection, than an enfranchisement, of natural liberty. We must not put our meaning into their phrase, but their meaning.

It can hardly be necessary to avert here the suggestion of a quibble or a cavil, to the effect that these self-exiled colonists were still exercising that same free will and private judgment, alike in what they renounced and in what they accepted and pledged themselves to believe and do, — which practically defines liberty of conscience. The subject of a Jesuit novitiate may exercise that "liberty" in putting himself under a rule which henceforth binds him to forego it. If, as I shall attempt to show, the Fathers of Massachusetts felt, avowed, and put themselves under the sway of, an obligation to an external rule, which overbore henceforward the exercise of any natural freedom for changing or qualifying their allegiance and subjection to it, then it would seem that we should bring them before us rather as the awed and pledged subjects of a yoke to which they had submitted themselves, than as free rovers not as yet persuaded to what they should commit themselves, if to any thing or to anybody. They certainly were not "fancy-free."

Every conception which those men had of liberty, civil or religious, was of something subjected to the sway and restraint of law, — a qualified, dependent, conditioned, and reduced freedom. Liberty under law was their motto, and it depended upon the nature and the quality of the law to decide the nature and the quality of the liberty. In any province or exercise of liberty, they recognized, frowning or presiding over it, some symbol or dispensation of authority.

In a great controversy rising here in the Court from a small occasion, in 1645, and leading to what is called "the impeachment" of Winthrop, then Deputy Governor, he made an admirable speech, in which we find him giving his idea of liberty as follows: —

"For the other point concerning liberty, I observe a great mistake in the country about that. There is a twofold liberty, — natural (I mean as our nature is now corrupt) and civil or federal. The first is common to man with beasts and other creatures. By this, man, as he stands in relation to man simply, hath liberty to do what he lists; it is a liberty to evil as well as to good. This liberty is incompatible and inconsistent with authority. The exercise and maintaining of this liberty makes men grow more evil, and in time to be worse than brute beasts: *omnes sumus licentiâ deteriores.* This is that great enemy of truth and peace, that wild beast, which all the ordinances of God are bent against to restrain and subdue it. The other kind of liberty I call civil or federal; it may also be termed moral, in reference to the covenant between God and man, in the moral law, and the politic covenants and constitutions amongst men themselves. This liberty is the proper end and object of authority, and cannot subsist without it; and it is a liberty to that only which is good, just, and honest. This liberty you are to stand for, with the hazard not only of your goods, but of your lives, if need be. Whatsoever crosseth this is not authority, but a distemper thereof. This liberty is maintained and exercised in a way of subjection to authority; it is of the same kind wherewith Christ hath made us free." [1]

De Tocqueville, in his "Democracy in America," [2] quotes the above, and describes it as a "fine definition of liberty."

Of liberty of conscience, either as an abstraction or as an absolute right, they with whom we are dealing had no conception, as of a good thing. Certainly, they had no respect for it, no confidence in it. They would have dreaded it beyond our power in these days to imagine. They had begun to see around them, in their native England, the threatenings of some of the effects and results of just what we mean by liberty of conscience, and they shuddered at them. Their dread of those consequences was one of the satisfactions which they afterwards found in their exile. It would be much nearer to the truth, — indeed, it is the truth itself, — and it would be truer to all the facts of the case, to the integrity of history, and to the right use of terms

1 Life and Letters, vol. ii. pp. 340, 341.

2 Bowen's ed., vol. i. p. 52.

which get changed in their import and burden, to say, frankly and boldly, that our Fathers came here to get away from, to get rid of, such liberty of conscience, as to them a hateful, pernicious, and ruinous thing, sure to result in impiety and anarchy. They did not claim it for themselves, except under a restriction and limitation, soon to be defined, which would render the claim almost nugatory in our view of it. They would have shuddered at indulging themselves in what is now known as such liberty. To have expected them to approve of it in others, and to provide for it, would be an absurdity. It was the one horrid, dreaded bugbear of their fancies, — the one proscribed iniquity of their religion. A conscience free, in our loose sense of the word, would have been to them far worse than no conscience at all.

Attracted as I was, years ago, to the study of their enterprise, as one of the most striking episodes in the world's annals, considering what great and marvellously prospered issues have come from it, I soon learned, that the fulsome panegyrics and the sentimental rhetoric spent upon those stern old Fathers, were worse than wasted; that the superficial way in which their history has been read and referred to, was introducing misrepresentation and misunderstanding; and that they had become the subjects of false praise and of unjust censure, the joint product of which had come to be visited upon them in the form of a facile and flippant ridicule. No one among the living generation here, native or alien, is called upon to undertake their championship in terms which will vindicate their superstitions or their severities, or which will cover an approbation of the fundamental principles assumed or adopted by them. They are, however, justly entitled to be set forth in the light of their own age, under the guidance of their own sincere convictions, and with an intelligent, truthful recognition of their master-motive, which was as lofty a one as has ever engaged sages, philanthropists, or saints in any earthly enterprise. It is painful to any one who, inheriting their blood and sharing the blessings of their sufferings and labors, is also versed in their history, to hear them either falsely praised or unfairly criticised, ridiculed, and maligned. In the mixtures of populations in our northern cities, and in the spirit of religious partisanship which is rife among us, those who are very glad to avail themselves of the freedom and thrift of our Puritan heritage, often allow themselves to speak contemptuously and derisively of the original colonists. What has come of their enterprise and institutions, is found to be desirable by all who share in it; but not only gratitude, truth itself, is often forgotten in the enjoyment of the inheritance. The story of the intolerance of the colonists is curtly told in epigrams and stinging jests. Their grim and morose manners, their superstitions, austerities, and cruel enactments are enlarged upon. Some of their lineal progeny give them over to travesties and railleries of light and bitter tongues.

Any thing that could be viewed as a defence or vindication of them; any thing, even, which, falling short of that, would claim for them an average measure of intelligence and common sense, — must be given over, if it takes in the fancy that these old Fathers had main regard for what we mean by liberty of conscience, or by civil freedom.

Read their history searchingly, penetrate to the motives and convictions of the men and women themselves, and the truth will reveal itself to you, that never was there in this world a company of persons who, individually and in their joint fellowship, held their consciences as subject to a more constraining obligation than they did theirs. I never find any one of their pleas or avowals alleging a claim to, or an exercise of, liberty of conscience, which fails to qualify it by a recognition of their subjection to a Scripture rule, in indulging themselves in that liberty. Thus, in the Humble Petition and Address of the General Court to Charles II., in 1660–1, Endicott being governor, they say: "Our liberty to walk in the faith of the Gospel, with all good conscience, according to the order of the Gospel, was the cause of our transporting ourselves," &c.

A rule, or mastery, which they accepted over their consciences, became to them, in fact, a substitute for conscience. You must look behind, deeply below, this pretence of freedom of conscience, in the ordinary use of the phrase, for the influence, the sway, the conviction, the purpose, aye, the inspiration, which moved them. They were the last men in the world to trust to a natural conscience. They were a covenanted people. The Puritan Bible was the Lord of their consciences; and they put themselves under the most implicit and unlimited subjection to what they owned as its just authority over them. True, it may be said they followed their individual consciences, and allowed them exercise in approving and putting themselves under a rule, which, for them, represented a supreme authority. But, in so doing, they understood that they parted with what others, "uncovenanted," might regard as their liberty. Their Bible training had preoccupied and restricted their freedom. Their opinions, their motives, their actions, their laws, their institutions, were all restrained — we should say, hampered — by their religious belief, reducing their natural freedom within rigid limitations. We may in these days of ours question the reasonableness of that belief of theirs; and we may deny that the Bible has the kind and degree of authority over the natural conscience which they assigned to it. But these are our opinions, not theirs; and in order to see and know them, we must get into their atmosphere. The fact is, that a conscience in subjection to a severe rule, and not a free conscience, guided them. So little did they think of what they might do, if they indulged their own notions and speculations, that their whole earnestness of purpose was concentrated in putting themselves under a disabling restriction of their own wills and wishes. The free exercise of their individual consciences would have divided them in opinion, and prevented any harmony of action. Only as they consented to forego individualism in speculation and belief, through a common conscientiousness subjecting them to the rule of the Bible, could they walk and act together.

I will endeavor to state, in a plain way, the simple and authentic truth, which will furnish the key to the motives and intent of the colonists.

Certain proprietary rights and privileges on land and water, in a region defined as Massachusetts Bay, had been secured by royal charter to a trading company of adventurers in England. Twenty patentees were named as constituting that company; viz., a governor, a deputy governor, and eighteen assistants, — seven beside the governor and deputy governor being a quorum for business. The company, by its charter, could make as many more persons free of it, freemen, so called, — that is, members or partners, voters, proprietors, — as they pleased, and on such terms, conditions, and qualifications as they pleased. The company had absolute jurisdiction over its territory; and the charter gave it full powers of legislation and administration, subject only to accordance with the laws of England. The charter provisions for this power and these rights are explicit, full, and emphatic. To the company was given "full and absolute power and authority, to correct, punish, pardon, and rule" all English subjects that should at any time adventure to, or inhabit within, the precincts of its jurisdiction; and, "for their special defence and safety, to encounter, expulse, repel, and resist by force of arms, as well by sea as by land, and by all fitting ways and means whatsoever, all such person and persons, as shall at any time hereafter attempt or enterprise the destruction, invasion, detriment, or annoyance to the said plantation or inhabitants."

Here, certainly, was a large franchise, with broad privileges and well-fortified rights. Yet nothing short of all this would have secured the enlistment of able and well-disposed men in an enterprise that stood out alone hopefully among many similar enterprises in those days which had disastrously failed. The company needed all that the charter pledged to it by the royal seal: the right of self-administration; of deciding and imposing the terms on which it would admit free associates, who might advance or ruin its schemes; legal rights over its jurisdiction; and power to punish, expel, and thwart the designs of all who might threaten or practise harm or annoyance to it.

Certainly the question may be raised, and a very vigorous and equal-handed discussion may be maintained upon it, whether the three provisions in their charter, on which they insisted so strenuously, and with their own self-favoring interpretation of them, — the absolute jurisdiction of the soil, the authority to define their own terms for admitting freemen, and the right to drive out those whose presence troubled them, — allowed of the strained use and application to which the proprietors applied them. It is to my purpose, however, only to accept the fact, that the authorities did so interpret those provisions, and did, in the open face of day, act upon such interpretations. This they did, not only in their secret confidences with each other, but equally in public avowals. They could not expect to make a secret of their pretensions, not even of their bold denial of a right of appeal from them to English courts; for there was almost a worn track and highway on land and sea, between the Massachusetts court and those courts, made by complainants. Indeed, even to the last death-struggle of the authorities to retain their charter against commissioners and against Charles II., they stood stoutly to their first construction of it.

It was probably intended and expected, though not a word was covenanted or intimated to that effect, that the company and its charter should remain and be administered in England; vessels and servants being sent hither to fish and trade. As to the legality of its transfer by charter and local government to this spot, it is not within the scope of my lecture to argue or pronounce. Nor is any discussion of that matter needful here and now. For, as we have seen what powers of local jurisdiction the charter assured to the company, it would seem that its officers might have done, through their resident agents here, substantially what, and all that, they did when they were established in their jurisdiction. They could make laws for all who were living here; they could admit or reject at their pleasure, and on their own terms, any who sought to vote in their affairs; and they could warn off and drive out intruders. Had the charter and administration never been transferred, the company would still have had rule here.

A merely mercenary spirit, bent on pecuniary gains, had, in the main, guided the company in its origin, as it had similar patentees corporated by prior grants and charters. But there were in its membership men strongly swayed and leavened by Puritanism; and the extraordinary excitement, the religious fervor, and the civil and political agitations of the crisis in England, — fast working towards civil war and revolution, — increased and strengthened that influence. While Endicott at Salem, with a body of associates and servants, was acting as local governor and agent of the company, and receiving his instructions from the charter administration in England, we find the following entry on the original records, — of matter of business, as the company was assembled in its General Court, at the house of its deputy governor, Thomas Goff, in London, July 28, 1629: —

"Mr. Governor (Cradock) read certain propositions conceived by himself; viz., that for the advancement of the plantation, the inducing and encouraging persons of worth and quality to transport themselves and families thither, and for other weighty reasons therein contained, to transfer the government of the plantation to those that shall inhabit there, and not to continue the same in subordination to the company here, as now it is. This business occasioned some debate: but by reason of the many great and considerable consequences thereupon depending, it was not now resolved upon; but those present are desired privately and seriously to consider hereof, and to set down their particular reasons in writing *pro* and *contra*, and to produce the same at the next General Court; where, they being reduced to heads, and maturely considered of, the company may then proceed to a final resolution thereon; and in the mean time they are desired to carry this business secretly, that the same be not divulged."

For any thing we know to the contrary, this significant proposition, as well as the purpose which it proposed, may have originated in the mind of Governor Cradock. That it does not appear to have surprised or at all displeased some of those, at least, who heard it as "conceived by himself," would indicate that preparation had been made for its bold utterance, and for its entry upon the records, by previous suggestion and consultation. At any rate, the purpose of transferring the charter and government was not of a sort to have been born full-shaped for the occasion of its public utterance, on the spur of a moment. The matter was made the especial business of the Court at a meeting a month afterwards; the point under consideration being, "to give answer to divers gentlemen intending to go into New England, whether or no the chief government of the plantation, together with the patent, should be settled in New England or here." Committees were appointed representing both alternatives, with liberty to get advice and opinions from others not belonging to the company; and they were to prepare their respective arguments, from which a report might be digested for the General Court the next day. The deliberateness of the method, and yet the short time allowed for the decision, is another indication of much previous conference. The decision was made on the next day, August 29, when, after a hearing of reasons on both sides, and a long debate, the question was called for, whether the patent and the government be transferred, "so as it may be done legally." By erection of hands, it appeared by the general consent of the company, that the transfer should be made; "and accordingly an order to be drawn up." At the Court held on September 29, following, the orders above agreed upon having been read, further decisive action was deferred, on account of the absence of some of the leading assistants, who had been at the previous meetings. But in the mean while some preliminary measures were provided for, especially "to take advice of learned council, whether the same may be legally done or no."

At the meeting of the General Court, October 15,—at which, significantly, Mr. John Winthrop, and some others of like spirit, appear for the first time,—the transfer, and arrangements incidental to it, were fully decided. On the 20th of the same month, a General Court was held, for the purpose of choosing new officers of the company, with reference to the enterprise agreed upon, as neither the governor nor the deputy intended to go over at that time. Mr. John Winthrop, "both for his integrity and sufficiency," was chosen governor, and Mr. John Humphrey deputy; but as the latter, when the time for embarkation came, was to stay behind, Thomas Dudley was put in his place. One other entry on the records must be copied here. At the Court on November 25,—

> "Upon the motion of Mr. White, to the end that this business might be proceeded in with the first intention, which was chiefly the glory of God; and to that purpose, that their meetings might be sanctified by the prayers of some faithful ministers, resident here in London, whose advice would be likewise requisite upon many occasions,—the court thought fit to admit into the freedom of this company Mr. Jo: Archer and Mr. Philip Nye, ministers here in London, who being here present kindly accepted thereof. Also Mr. White did recommend unto them Mr. Nathaniel Ward, of Standon." [1]

This last extract must convey to us all that it reports, all that it suggests, and a great deal more also. It gives us explicitly a fragment from a history which we have the means of setting into a more full narration. A change had evidently passed upon the Massachusetts Company,—a change in purpose, aim, and membership. So far as its business proceedings had now come to embrace a prayer meeting, the token is a reminder of much beside. Some of the preparatory agencies which wrought to the result may be indicated. When Deputy Governor Dudley had

[1] Court Records, vol. i. pp. 49–63.

got a rude cottage for himself here, less than a year after his arrival, he addressed a letter, of singular interest and pathos, to the Countess of Lincoln, the mother of the wife of Isaac Johnson, his associate. In this letter he says, —

"Touching the plantation which we have here begun, it fell out thus. About the year 1627, some friends, being together in Lincolnshire, fell into discourse about New England, and the planting of the Gospel there; and, after some deliberation, we imparted our reasons, by letters and messages to some in London and the west country; where it was likewise deliberately thought upon, and at length, with often negotiation, so ripened," &c.,

as to result in the procuring of the royal charter, and in the plantation. These "Boston men," so called, reinforced the funds of the company. It was the coming in of the religious spirit into the business plans, by the new membership of the company, which alone induced the transfer of the charter and the government. In the little treatise of Winthrop, written on the Atlantic Ocean, already quoted, he says, "We are a company professing ourselves fellow-members of Christ." Some links out of the chain which connected the trading company with the religious colony, were wanting, until the recent discovery of a large mass of the papers of Governor Winthrop revealed to us certain night rides, secret consultations, and deliberate negotiations, weighing of arguments and devotional exercises, which brought him into membership of the company, committed him to its bold and consecrated enterprise, and led to his choice, as its all sufficient leader.

Nearly at the same time on which the valuable mass of "Winthrop Papers" came to light in New London, Conn., containing, among others, the governor's autograph copy of that significant document called "General Considerations for the Plantation in New England," &c., John Forster, Esq., published in London a biography of that noble patriot Sir John Eliot. The Hon. R. C. Winthrop having published the above named document in the "Life and Letters" of his ancestor, with the reasons for assigning the authorship to him, had shortly afterwards noticed an allusion by Mr. Forster, to a paper found among Eliot's, alluding to New-England colonization. The Earl of St. Germans, a descendant of Eliot, on being applied to by Mr. Winthrop, kindly sent to our Society a transcript of the paper, which proved to be a copy, with some variations, of the "Considerations." It was made by Eliot himself, in the Tower, to be sent to his illustrious compeer, John Hampden. We have now four copies of that important document which did such service of a religious sort in our enterprise.[1]

The enterprise was eminently one which was originated, controlled, and guided by a leadership. It had favorers, coadjutors, subordinates, sympathizers, and servants; but its aim, its quickening motive, and its inspiration, came from a very small number, perhaps from only half a score of persons, — its master-spirits. These devised and purposed; they bore the sacrifices and renewed the pledges of self-consecration under dark and discouraging aspects. They furnished in council the practical wisdom adapted to the development of the scheme, and its only security in emergencies. They were men who could confide in each other.

I feel justified in adopting Winthrop as my chief authority and guide in interpreting the motives of his associates for whom he speaks, as well as for his own. The crisis in the affairs of the company in England was marked by his coming into it, and his coming in brought in a religious intensity in its purposes. He was himself at the time under deep religious impressions. The colony for the twenty remaining years of his life was more influenced by him than by any other person, alike in its civil and religious administration, — not excepting even Cotton. We have more full and frank disclosures and avowals from his pen, than from all others of his associates. These are cogent reasons for implicit trust in him.

It was the working of the religious leaven in the company which ensured the end of colonizing by the transfer of the government. Such members of the company as had no heart or zeal for the work, dropped out of it; and new members were, for its new consecration, drawn into it. Friends and well-wishers in the kingdom, not belonging to it, nor intending to join it, made generous and valuable gifts to it, because of its new designs.

The counsellor of the company, Mr. White, who had procured

[1] Historical Society Proceedings, 1864–5, pp. 413, &c.

the drafting of its charter, and by whose calculation or foresight it may perhaps have been contrived, that neither London nor any other place was specified for its local administration, had certified to the legality of its transfer. Had the intent been known by the English authorities, — we are not certain that it was not known, — the transfer would perhaps have been prevented. Had those authorities been privileged with a prevision of what was to come from establishing the charter here, they certainly would have retained it in England; in fact would never have allowed it to have passed the seals.

Coincidently with the departure of the colonists, the Rev. Mr. White, of Dorchester, the chief prompter of the enterprise, published his "Planters' Plea," in explanation and justification of it. In this, he says, —

"I should be very unwilling to hide any thing I think might be fit, to discover the uttermost of the intentions of our planters in their voyage to New England; and therefore shall make bold to manifest, not only what I know, but what I guess, concerning their purpose. As it were absurd to conceive they have all one mind, so were it more ridiculous to imagine they have all one scope. Necessity may press some; novelty, draw on others; hopes of gain in time to come may prevail with a third sort: but that the most, and most sincere and godly part, have the advancement of the Gospel for their main scope, I am confident. That of them some may entertain hope and confidence of enjoying greater liberty there than here in the use of some orders and ceremonies of our church, it seems very probable."

The chosen leader of the enterprise was a providential man; and from that hour till his death, twenty years after, he was its hero and its saint. The members of that transported trading company, represented by its officers, its freemen, and their servants, present themselves on this side of the great dreary ocean, as a band of religious exiles. They appear in, they assume, that character, at once. As such they prayed together under a huge forest tree, and recognized the consecration of their enterprise.

And what was it? Now, in place of that silly fancy that they were seeking to provide a refuge for freedom of conscience, let us substitute their real inspiration and aim. Liberty of conscience, in our full sense of the phrase, was preparing to assert and exercise itself in England, at the time of their exile; and it was this fact, with "the prophaneness" and "disorder" there fermenting, which frightened our Fathers away from their dear old home. We have a multitude of queer books and pamphlets, the relics of those days,—quaint, odd, wild, eccentric, in their contents, gleaming here and there with grand and startling truths, and proving fully this affirmation, that there is not a cobweb nor a fancy, a notion nor a theory, a conceit nor an opinion in any living brain to-day, in Boston, which was not soon after the emigration held and avowed then and there. And this positive statement, if it does not exhaust, at any rate puts to trial, the utmost power of language. These dreams and heresies of visionaries, mystics, and bold thinkers, were, as we shall note by and by, especially and painfully odious to those from whom we inherit this Commonwealth. They wanted to get away from all such hateful license, and to find protection from its risk in a pledged and covenanted purpose. The Fathers of Massachusetts, parting with their lands and houses at home, finally, with no intent of return, once for all, agreed by a most solemn compact at their own charges, and by an investment of all their worldly goods, to avail themselves of their charter rights over the territory covered by their patent, to try here an experiment, which seemed to them alike noble, practical, and religious.

And here I must avail myself of the privilege indulged to one who, in a historical review, infers from results and developments the nature of the primary causes and motives which originated and guided them. From the frank and earnest and reiterated avowals of the leaders and the master-spirits of the enterprise, and from their steadfast purpose and aim manifested in all their subsequent measures, plans, legislation, and administration, I infer the design which they had in view. I should have a right to draw such an inference, if I had to do it solely as an interpreter of actions, without any avowals of a direct sort to aid me. But these avowals in words are not wanting, and they are in full harmony with the deeds done. It is not necessary, to assure the position which I take, that I should be held to show that, if the question of purpose and motive had been put to each and every party to this enterprise, including all its subordinates and servants, he would have answered as I answer for its leaders. Even the leaders may not all have seen the full shape of their vision. But I have no misgiving as to what it was. The enterprise was no hap-hazard experiment in drifting, no waiting on the luck of events. The serious earnestness with which it was undertaken, corresponds to the resolute purpose with which it was pursued by them.

Their lofty and soul-enthralling aim — the condition and reward of all their severe sufferings and arduous efforts — was the establishment and administration here of a religious and civil commonwealth, which should bear the same relation to the spirit and the letter of the whole Bible that the Jewish commonwealth bore to the Law of Moses. This was the significance and purport of the remarkable words written by Governor Winthrop, on his passage hither, "to seek out a place of cohabitation and consortship, under a due form of government, both civil and ecclesiastical." The difference between the aim so defined and the providing "a refuge for civil and religious freedom," will appear as we go along. An experiment was to be put on trial here which, even we must say, had a right to be tested, and which was worthy of being tested; but which was regarded by our Fathers as holding them under a consecrated obligation to commit themselves to it. They organized here a body politic, all whose laws, functions, and institutions had rigid reference to their one supreme aim. Their own consciences were held under thrall by it, and were free only in one direction of obligation to it, — that of whole-souled and life-lasting loyalty to it. Two misgivings or fears, and only two, were known to them: first, that they themselves, by fault or infirmity, might fail of fidelity to it; or, second, that it should be brought under peril from the wickedness or waywardness of any who might creep in or start up among them. Against the first danger, they sought security under a solemnly pledged agreement and covenant, binding themselves to each other and to God. Against the second risk, they believed they could protect themselves under their charter, by choosing only such associates as they desired, and on their own terms, and by exercising their royally sealed authority to resist, thwart, punish, and drive out every one who might oppose or annoy them.

Mark the qualification in the statement just made, — that the projected religious commonwealth was to be founded and administered by the Bible, the whole Bible, not by the New Testament alone. If, as Christians, they had adopted what is generally held in these days as to the substantial substitution of the New Scripture for the Old, their whole creed and rule and legislation would have been different. But they revered and used and treated the Holy Book as one whole. A single sentence from any part of it was an oracle to them: it was as a slice or a crumb from any part of a loaf of bread, all of the same consistency. God, as King, had been the Lawgiver of Israel: he should be their Lawgiver too. They had found so little satisfaction under the legislation of men that they longed to put themselves under the legislation of the Deity. Israel, as a commonwealth, had been administered by his statutes: those same statutes should bind their consciences, ratify their laws, and rule their lives. They would make the support of religion compulsory, as did the Jewish legislator. The Sabbath-breaker and the blasphemer should stand as high criminals. The Church should fashion the State, and be identical with it. Only experienced and covenanted Christian believers, pledged by their profession to accordance of opinion and purpose with the original proprietors and exiles, should be admitted as freemen, or full citizens of the commonwealth. They would restrain and limit their own liberty of conscience, as well as their own freedom of action, within Bible rules. In fact, — in spirit even more than in the letter, — they did adopt all of the Jewish code which was in any way practicable for them. The leading minister of the colony was formally appointed by the General Court to adapt the Jewish law to their case; and it was enacted, that, till that work was really done, "Moses, his Judicials," should be in full force. Mr. Cotton in due time presented the results of his labor in a code of laws illustrated by Scripture texts. This code was not formally adopted by the Court; but the spirit of it, soon rewrought into another body, had full sway.

It was known that Winthrop had written what he calls "a small treatise," in 1644, at a period of some internal variance in the colony, in which treatise he undertook to vindicate the government from the "aspersion" of being arbitrary in its conduct. This treatise came to light only a few years ago, among some family papers, in the Governor's original autograph. In it are found the following very decisive statements: —

"By these it appears that the officers of this Bodye politick have a Rule to walke by, in all their administrations, which Rule is the Worde of God, and such conclusions and deductions as are or shalbe regularly drawn from thence. . . .

"The ffundamentalls which God gave to the Commonwealth of Israell were a sufficient Rule to them, to guide all their Affaires; we havinge the same, with all the Additions, explanations and deductions, which have followed; it is not possible we should want a Rule in any case: if God give wisdome to discerne it."[1]

In the life of Mr. Cotton by his friend Mr. Davenport, we find the following most explicit statement, which shows how far these Fathers were from recognizing the plea for liberty of conscience: —

"Considering that these Plantations had liberty to mould their civil order into that form which they should find to be best for themselves, and that here the churches and Commonwealth are complanted together in holy covenant and fellowship with God in Christ Jesus, Mr. Cotton did, at the request of the General Court in the Bay, draw an abstract of the laws of judgement delivered from God by Moses to the Commonwealth of Israel, so far forth as they are of moral, that is, of perpetual and universal, equity among all nations; especially such as these Plantations are; wherein he advised that Theocrasie, *i.e.* God's government, might be established as the best form of government, wherein the people that choose rulers, are God's people in covenant with him, that is, members of churches, and the men chosen by them to be rulers, such also, and the laws of God, and the ministers of God, are consulted with by the Governor, magistrates and people, in all hard cases and in matters of the Lord, that is, of religion," &c.[2]

In July, 1634, the hearts of the colonists were gladdened by the receipt of "Certain Proposals made by Lord Say, Lord Brooke, and other persons of quality, as conditions of their removing to England." Hutchinson has preserved these for us, by printing them "with the answers thereto."

Besides proposing an aristocratic class for recognition in the colony, these noblemen desired that the franchise should depend

[1] Life and Letters, vol. ii. p. 445. [2] Hutchinson's Coll. of Papers, p. 161.

upon property. The answer vindicates, wholly from Scripture texts and examples, the law of the colony which restricted the franchise to church-members.

Hutchinson also gives us a letter, on the same occasion, from Mr. Cotton to Lord Say and Sele, which is in itself conclusive as to the intent of the authorities. He writes in vindication of their rule: —

"God hath so framed the state of church government and ordinances, that they may be compatible to any commonwealth, though never so much disordered in its frame. But yet, when a commonwealth hath liberty to mould its own frame (*scripturæ plenitudinem adoro*), I conceive the scripture hath given full direction for the right ordering of the same. It is better that the Commonwealth be fashioned to the setting forth of God's house, which is his church, than to accommodate the church frame to the civil state. Democracy, I do not conceive, that ever God did ordain as a fit government either for church or commonwealth. If the people be governors, who shall be governed? As for Monarchy and Aristocracy, they are both of them clearly approved and directed in Scripture, yet so as referreth the sovereignty to himself, and setteth up Theocracy in both, as the best form of Government in the Commonwealth, as well as in the church."[1]

Captain Edward Johnson, that serviceable man in so many capacities, civil and military, came over with Winthrop's company. He understood well, and heartily sympathized with, the purposes of the colonists, whose toils he shared, and whose fortunes he sought to record, though anonymously, in poetry and verse, — distressing as some of the latter is. His quaint and grotesque but still instructive book — "Wonder-working Providence of Sion's Saviour in New England" — is strewn all over with the tokens characteristic of the Biblical model of the Commonwealth.

As a deputy of the Court, and himself one of the most laborious and efficient members of the committee engaged in the protracted work of digesting a body of laws, he may be regarded as competent, as he certainly was frank, a witness of the intent which underlaid all our early legislation. The following words of his are certainly candid enough: —

"This year, 1646, the General Court appointed a Committee of divers

[1] Hutchinson History, vol. i., Appendix.

persons to draw up a Body of laws for the well ordering of this little Commonwealth: and to the end that they might be most agreeable with the rule of Scripture, in every county there was appointed two Magistrates, two Ministers, and two able persons from among the people, who having provided such a competent number as was meet, together with the former that were enacted newly amended, they presented them to the General Court, where they were again perused and amended; and then another committee chosen to bring them into form, and present them to the Court again, who the year following passed an Act of confirmation upon them, and so committed them to the Press; and in the year 1648, they were printed, and now are to be seen of all men, to the end that none may plead ignorance; and that all who intend to transport themselves hither, may know this is no place of licentious liberty, nor will this people suffer any to trample down this vineyard of the Lord, but with diligent execution will cut off from the City of the Lord, the wicked doers; and if any man can shew wherein any of them derogate from the Word of God, very willingly will they accept thereof, and amend their imperfections (the Lord assisting); but let not any ill-affected persons find fault with them, because they suit not with their own humour, or because they meddle with matters of Religion, for it is no wrong to any man, that a people who have spent their estates, many of them, and ventured their lives for to keep faith and a pure conscience, to use all means that the Word of God allows for maintenance and continuance of the same, especially they have taken up a desolate Wilderness to be their habitation, and not deluded any by keeping their profession in huggermug, but point and proclaim to all the way and course they intend, God willing, to walk in; if any will yet, notwithstanding, seek to justle them out of their own right, let them not wonder if they meet with all the opposition a people put to their greatest straits can make," &c.[1]

These extracts, and a score of others of a similar purport might be culled from the writings of the leading exiles, tell the whole story. The actual code of laws adopted by the colony — called "The Bodie of Liberties," prepared mainly by the Rev. Nathaniel Ward of Ipswich — differs essentially from Mr. Cotton's abstract, especially in dispensing for the most part with scriptural citations; but in no single particular did the legislation indicated by it, look away from or loosen its hold upon the supreme purpose of the authorities, to establish and administer here a strictly Biblical Commonwealth. Ward, who had had an

[1] Book iii. chap. v., Poole's ed., p. 206.

early legal training in England, stood for that aim and experiment as firmly as did Cotton.

And then we are to remind ourselves that their Bible faith was not merely a simply vague and general reverence for it, like the sentiment which lingers now with their descendants. They had no theory about the Bible: they never criticised it; and they rarely suggested amendments, even of the English translation of it. They loved, honored, and revered it, and gave to it the homage of their awed spirits. What testimony is borne to this fact in their letters and diaries, in the implicit faith with which they took down the texts and expositions of their ministers, and quoted illustrations and parallelisms from the Bible, as decisions for all cases! How earnestly did they strive to incorporate into their private and family life, not only the preceptive, but as much as they could of even the ceremonial, matter of the Scriptures!

That frankly avowed and practically applied purpose of the Fathers, of establishing here a Bible Commonwealth, "under a due form of government, both civil and ecclesiastical," furnishes the key to, the explanation of, all the dark things and all the bright things in their early history. The young people educated among us ought to read our history by that simple, plain interpretation. The consciences of our Fathers were not free in our sense of that word. They were held under rigid subjection to what they regarded as God's Holy Word, through and through in every sentence of it, just as the consciences of their Fathers were held, under the sway of the Pope and the Roman Church. The Bible was to them supreme. Their church was based on it, modelled by it, governed by it; and they intended their State should be also. Two very striking and emphatic sentences from the pen of Governor Winthrop convey the substance of volumes; and who had better right than he to tell us his own aim and that of his associates?

"Whereas the way of God hath always been to gather his churches out of the world; now, the world, or civil state, — must be raised out of the churches." — "The Magistrates are limited, both by their church Covenant, and by their oath, and by the duty of their places to square all their proceedings by the rule of God's Word [why did he not say by the law of England?] for the advancement of the Gospel and the weale publick," &c.[1]

This was their master aim, — this was the vision of the soul which led those exiles hither, — and by the inspiration of which alone, would they have come, or remained, or prospered. Constrained, compulsory, and rigidly enforced subjection to the consecrated purpose and rule of their enterprise required of those who imposed or recognized it, a personal suffering under it, a painful loyalty to it, fully as severe, as tasking to the energies of human nature, as were the disabilities and penalties which they stood ready to inflict upon all opponents and mischief-makers. It is worth our while to remember that the heads of that Commonwealth, its legislators and magistrates, found their own yoke a very hard one in the bearing. Winthrop, Dudley, Saltonstall, and others, the highest among them, were called to question, put under discipline, and bound to penalties. While their scruples forbade the kissing of the Bible, in the administration of an oath, their conduct and "carriage" were tried by the statutory authority of that Book.

We must consider this also: these Fathers were proprietors by purchase, members of a private joint-stock company, holding this territory under mercantile conditions. They had the rights of corporators. After parting with their property in England to commit themselves to their enterprise, they subjected it to risks in the transfer and occupancy here, which, as local residents on their own territory, it was wise in them to foresee, and prudent to provide against. They did not put the right of franchise among them at a money value. It was not to be purchased at any price. They would confer it on conditions of their own, but never sold it to any one. No one, resident or stranger, could lay claim to it. The mass of those who came over with

1 These very significant statements are from Winthrop's "Reply," &c., to Vane's "'Briefe Answer,'" &c., to "A Defence of an Order of Court made in the year 1637," concerning the giving the magistrates power to deny to any, by their own rule, the right of residence here. It must be owned that Mr. Vane presses the honored governor with very able and cogent objections to the assumption of the magistrates. Winthrop, certainly, has recourse to special pleading. But the specialty is based, like all the early legislation of the colony, upon the foregone conclusion of a Bible Commonwealth. (Hutchinson's Coll. Papers, pp. 88–98.)

the company, were simply hired servants of the company; and those whom they found here were interlopers and squatters.

The proprietors had a right to say on what terms other persons should come here to abide, to vote, to take any part in the administration of affairs, — perilling either their property or their enterprise, — which was a consecrated experiment. Mark these words of Governor Winthrop, when he found occasion, in the controversy with Vane, to stand for these proprietary rights: —

"Let the Patent be perused, and there it will be found, that the incorporation is made to certain persons by name, and unto such as they shall associate to themselves, and all this tract of land is granted to them and their associates.

"None other can claim privilege with them but by free consent."

It is true the original proprietors and exiles were most glad to welcome new-comers of spirit and purpose like their own; but they were very keen and rigid in their scrutiny. Yankee inquisitiveness, which was but old English shrewdness, sharpened on our granite whetstones, began then its famed skill in interrogations put to all strangers. They wished to know every newcomer thoroughly, outside and inside; whence he came; what he wanted; what he believed; if possible, what he thought; what he intended to do; what was his substance; what was his spirit. And these conditions were perfectly well understood in the Old World, by those likely to come hitherwards. No man, who is meditating an assault upon a hornet's or a wasp's nest, better understands the nature of his enterprise, and the sort of reception he will have, than did the Familist, Antinomian, Anabaptist, or Quaker, know beforehand how Massachusetts would entertain him. Courtesy, honesty, all fair principles, required that the rights and purposes of the legal proprietors should be respected by all others.

The conclusion is obvious. These exiled colonists, having embarked all their worldly goods in this enterprise, would be dismayed and ruined by its failure. Having solemnly covenanted with separate churches as Englishmen at home, they had entered into another solemn agreement with each other, outside of their court-meeting, before they embarked.

This "Agreement" was made at Cambridge, England, on Aug. 26, 1629, and was subscribed by those who pledged themselves to embark on the following March. In it they say they have engaged themselves to their enterprise, after having "weighed the greatness of the work, in regard of the consequence, God's glory, and the churches' good." They face "the difficulties and the discouragements" before them. They considered this "withal, that this whole adventure grows upon the joint confidence we have in each other's fidelity and resolution herein, so as no man of us would have adventured it without assurance of the rest." The agreement was conditional, on this proviso, "that before the last of September next, the whole government, together with the patent for the said plantation, be first, by an order of court, legally transferred and established to remain with us, and others which shall inhabit upon the said plantation."[1]

One other paper, very important in its bearings on this point, is to be carefully noted, because as it was prepared and circulated on the other side of the water, as preliminary to, and designed to induce, the emigration, it exposes to us the intent of the leaders in the enterprise. It is entitled, "General Considerations for the Plantation in New England, with an Answer to Several Objections," to which reference has already been made. We have now four copies of the substance of this paper, with variations and comments from the different hands under which it passed. It was a document which served a high agency in promoting the enterprise, being passed from friend to friend, and used in those cross-country rides and night consultations which drew its master-spirits into it. One copy of it, as has been related, came from the hands of that noble patriot, Sir John Eliot, in the Tower; and was sent by him to his friend and compeer, John Hampden. There is a religious spirit and tone in the whole paper. The seventh of the considerations reads thus:—

> "What can be a better work, and more noble and worthy a Christian, than to help to raise and support a particular church while it is in its infancy, and to join our forces with such a company of faithful people," &c.[2]

There is a remarkable recognition in this document of a deeply ominous foreboding, often finding utterance from the pens and hearts of the leading colonists, that a catastrophe of utter anarchy

[1] Hutch. Coll. Papers, p. 25. [2] Hutch. Coll. Papers, p. 27.

and ruin was impending threateningly, at the time, over the realm and the religion of England. From that awful wreck they would save the gospel, by transplanting it, and rearing for it a church which should guide the Commonwealth. The following solemn sentences meant more to devout hearts in those days than they mean to us: —

> "Secondly, all other churches of Europe are brought to desolation; and it may be justly feared that the like judgement is coming upon us: and who knows but that God hath provided this place [New England] to be a refuge for many whom he means to save out of the general destruction."

This was indeed a reason for regarding it "a service to the church of great consequence, to carry the Gospell into those parts of the world."

These Fathers of Massachusetts having thus solemnly covenanted with each other, in the terms of their august experiment, were bound to stand for it, and to try it with heart and soul and life. Any thing or any body that perilled it, any stranger or interloper coming among them, or a troublesome spirit rising up of themselves, must be dealt with in a summary way. He brought under risk every thing which they had, or hoped for, or revered. They were themselves under the same bond and pledge which they exacted of others. They were all in the wilderness. They were straitened of their own natural and lawful liberty in many ways and things. They were held to personal and mutual covenants of the most stringent sort. They could not say what they pleased, still less do as they pleased. They had made themselves amenable to what they called "the Gospel rule;" and, if they swerved or broke terms, the penalty was sure and stern. They were no triflers, no summer-day dreamers, no fancy theorists, such as we have in our day. They knew well what an opinion like theirs cost; what a conviction and a belief meant; what the enterprise which they had in hand involved to those who were determined to embark in it. They had looked before them very deliberately: they had fronted the conditions of their work, and come to meet them. They encountered no opposition or discomfiture which they had not provided for.

At the first General Court of the company held on this soil, May 18, 1631, one hundred and eighteen persons applied to be admitted as freemen, voters, new and full partners. Here was a startling and critical predicament for the company, represented by less than a dozen of the actual proprietors and administrators under the charter. What was to be done? Some of the applicants for the franchise were "old planters," or squatters; some had been sent here, and others had been just brought here, as hired servants of the company; and others still were suspected or disaffected persons, of a sort which a Quarter court had already judged "unmeet to inhabit here." Should this miscellaneous multitude be at once lifted to a place and power which put the whole enterprise effectually at their mercy? The court was alarmed, as well it might be. It was alarmed, but it confronted the juncture. These applicants were admitted to the franchise, having first taken the freeman's oath. The oaths formally entered upon the Records, for every officer and member of the company, furnish in themselves very significant matter bearing upon the intent of the colonists as already set forth, to establish here a Biblical Commonwealth. Before the transfer of the charter, the form of oath for the governor, deputy, and assistants, bound them "to admit none to be free of this fellowship but such as may claim the same by virtue of our privileges." But after the charter had been transferred, and the government had been set up here, these official oaths had been significantly changed into this form: the governor and magistrates bound themselves to administer the government "according to the laws of God, and for the advancement of his Gospel, the laws of this land, and the good of the people of this plantation." This change in the form of the oath meant all that it implies.

And whoever took the first freeman's oath here, swore as follows: —

> "I do freely and sincerely acknowledge that I am justly and lawfully subject to the government of the Company: and do accordingly submit my person and estate to be protected, ordered, and governed by the laws and constitutions thereof."

Yet before letting in this crowd of citizens, "the generalitie," as they were called, the Court agreed and ordered, that henceforward the freemen should vote for the body of assistants, who, after being chosen, should elect a governor and deputy out of their own number, and should be the legislators, and also should appoint all officers of the law. This restriction was, however, removed the next year, and the freemen resumed their right of voting directly for governor and deputy. Of the newly admitted freemen, more than half were already church-members, and others soon became so. A few of them proved intractable or mischievous persons, and had afterwards to be dealt with by summary or deliberate process. The shock of apprehension, almost of dismay, to which the Court had been subjected, led to the adoption of that rule and order, for prospective operation, which has been made the reproach and jeer of the early legislation of Massachusetts. It stands on our Records in these words: —

> "To the end the body of the commons may be preserved of honest and good men, it was likewise ordered and agreed, that for time to come no man shall be admitted to the freedom of this body politic, but such as are members of some of the churches within the limits of the same."[1]

Looked at in the light of our days, or even by the contemporary working of the rule as experimental trial tested it, we, of course, may denounce it, or ridicule it. But we must be fair to those who lived by their own light, and tried a serious enterprise. In establishing that rule, the company exercised a charter-right, by their own interpretation clearly conferred upon them; and sought, without doing wrong to any, to protect and defend themselves, their own franchise, their own property, their own great design. What else, what less, than this could they have done for their own security? Even if only as the responsible administrators of a

[1] Court Records, vol. i. p. 87.

Mr. Cotton, in a letter to Lord Say, Lord Brook, &c., in 1636, says (Hutch. Hist., vol. i. Appen. 435), that no church-members "are excluded from the liberty of freemen." But the being a church-member did not, of itself, constitute a freeman. The application for the privilege must be made to the Court, and there be submitted to the vote of the other citizens; and then, if the candidate passed, he had to take the freeman's oath. It would seem, however, that there was soon a considerable number of church-members who did not seek the privilege of citizenship; perhaps shrinking from its annoyances and responsibilities. For, in 1643, the Court "Ordered, concerning members that refuse to take their freedom, the churches should be writ unto, to deale with them." (Records, ii. p. 38.)

Lechford, just before this time, wrote that "Three parts of the people of the country remain out of the church."

local government, they had had an ordinary concern to avert disorder and anarchy, and to maintain morality and religion, they could hardly, in those days, have stopped short of that rule, at least in its substance, or in an equivalent alternative. In every Christian State, religion was then established; and uniformity of subjection to it was imposed by laws and penalties.[1]

The inference, then, seemed to be that the more scriptural, authoritative, pure, and practicable a method or type of religion was, the better was it entitled to the legislative warrant.

But if the Fathers of Massachusetts were under the sway and in the service of the aim which has been defined as theirs, they had especial reason, as they had legal right, in requiring of all who sought to vote about their property and their experiment, that they should be in accord with them. They chose to put foremost this condition, and to insist upon it: 'Commit yourselves to our opinion, conviction, and purpose, then we will let you in: join our religious fellowship, and you shall share our civil rights, without money or price.' They thought confidently — for them, reasonably — that they should thus make sure for a stock of citizens, if not of saints, yet of those who were outwardly, visibly, and constrainedly free from the more scandalous and mischievous human failings. At any rate, they did thus make sure of men who, before God and their fellows, had voluntarily pledged and covenanted themselves, by a well-defined standard of obligation, the bond of a rigid intercommunion. No

[1] In maintaining their form of administration of religion by a public tax, and making an attendance upon its services compulsory, the colonists did but follow the example of their native country. In the colony of Virginia, in 1610, attendance at church twice every Sunday was enjoined "upon pain, for the first fault, to lose their provision and allowance for the whole week following; for the second, to lose said allowance, and also to be whipped; and for the third to suffer death." (Force's Tracts iii. (ii.) 11.) Subsequent modifications of the law in Virginia were as follows: "The Governor published several edicts, — That every person should go to church Sundays and holidays: or lie Neck and Heels that night, and be a slave to the colony the following week; for the second offence he should be a slave for a month; for the third, a year and a day." (Stith, p. 147. 1618.)

In Virginia Assembly, Aug. 4, 1619. "All persons whatsoever upon the Sabbath days, shall frequent divine service and sermons, both forenoon and afternoon, and every one that shall transgress this law, shall forfeit three shillings a time, to the use of the church: all lawful and necessary impediments excepted. But if a servant in this case shall wilfully neglect his master's commands, he shall suffer bodily punishment."

man could get into a church except through profession, confession, and the taking of a vow, and the putting himself under the discipline of a brotherhood. Those who had passed that ordeal, and were still held to its continuous control, were to be regarded as Christians; and Christians might be trusted as citizens. So far were the Fathers of Massachusetts from feeling that they wronged any one by establishing this rule, that they were assured that they were adopting an eminently wise way in conferring a privilege which they might have withheld. It was fully competent for them to have declined making any more freemen on any terms. They made more because they wished for more, provided they could have them of their own sort, which was not our sort.

Those who were not freemen or voters had rights and privileges secured to them which still made them members of "ye body politique." The twelfth of the "Bodie of Liberties" made this provision:—

"Every man, whether inhabitant or foreigner, free or not free, shall have libertie to come to any publique Court, Councel, or Towne meeting, and either by speech or writing, to move any lawfull, seasonable, and materiall question, or to present any necessary motion, complaint, petition, Bill or information, whereof that meeting hath proper cognizance, so it be done in convenient time, due order, and respective manners."

To construct a commonwealth out of a church, as the honored and noble Winthrop so frankly avowed it, and to administer all civil affairs by church-members,—that was the intent of the founders of this colony. They meant that the rulers and those who chose the rulers should be upright, God-fearing men, as, in a most emphatic sense, they were themselves. Enough of such men, they believed, could be found,—men renewed, baptized in the Spirit, gifted with wisdom, in faithful covenant with Christ, their Master. Yet they were not to depend upon, nor to trust to, their own wisdom, nor to follow their natural consciences. They had God's Word,—divine statutes, an inspired oracle. Some of our ancestors used the Bible in earlier English versions; but our version had won its way to the hearts of many of them. The free and authorized circulation of the royal version wrought an effect in England which we can scarcely make real to ourselves. It took the place of pope, church, and minister for thousands, whom it brought under the direct teaching of God. Those who read it with that moderated control of their own eccentric tendencies which would insure a common influence from it, brought themselves under subjection to it. Individual fanatics and "private interpreters" put it to strange uses. By that Book, even without the aid of the new covenant Scriptures, the chosen people of old — between whose circumstances and their own our Fathers found many parallels — had been trained in a wilderness, and fashioned into a commonwealth. They intended to repeat the process under fairer auspices. With a stern and heroic spirit, in awful sincerity, earnest men and gentle women, made calmly resolute for their own share in it, set themselves to the work, after counting its cost so wisely that they met with nothing which they had not anticipated. Many died of the earliest hardships, in full faith of a blessed success to be realized by their posterity. And these were accounted happy by their survivors, who looked on their fresh wilderness graves as the seed-bed of a glorious harvest.

It is not strange, though it is in many respects sad, that so many of those high-souled exiles should have had to meet the vexations of all the stages of a gradual, but finally a complete, disappointment in the thwarting and failure of their experiment. They could not create a State out of a church; for a State grew up which would not come into their church, and which they would not have allowed to come into it. They could not administer a civil government by Biblical statutes; for those statutes have God, not man, for their administrator. That liberty of conscience which they themselves, and for themselves, had put under restraining subjection to their own covenants and religious limitations, was irresistibly exercised by some among them, and by a continual succession of new-comers. They were made dreadfully uncomfortable by dissentients and intruders and interlopers, — honest and pure persons, men and women, but eccentric, fanciful, and strong-headed, with strange conceits, theories, and notions of their own. For a time, the magistrates and ministers tried to stand by their first purpose and aim, at all cost. Their legislation was pursued into the most minute details. It was inquisitorial, severe, fearless, and without respect of persons. They maintained their proprietary rights, and clung to their Theocratical experiment against all intruders and heretics. Their Court (Sept. 4, 1639), in passing a law against "the common custom of drinking one to another," as an occasion of much waste and sin, held it to be a duty to prevent such wickedness, — "especially in plantations of churches and common weales, wherein the least known evils are not to be tolerated by such as are bound by solemn covenant to walk by the rule of God's word in all their conversation."[1]

Whatever the expectations of the leading colonists may have been, before they crossed the seas, of the relations of dependence and oversight which would continue to exist between their remote home and England, and however vague or definite may have been their intentions of setting up for themselves, as a matter of fact they did find themselves charged with the whole responsibility of administering a government. Their necessities and emergencies settled that point for them. England gave them no help whatever; and all her attempted commissions about their affairs were regarded and rejected, or resisted, as mischievous interference. The home government could not have wisely disposed the affairs of this colony at any time during its charter administration. For a large part of that term England itself was in a distracted condition, through its own civil war; and its intermeddlings here would but have caused confusion and increased dissension. Charged, then, with the full responsibility of legislative, judicial, and executive offices, the authorities developed their own scheme, and worked toward the realizing of their Theocracy. Their experiment proved impracticable. Its weak points answered exactly to the kind of assaults and the sort of weapons which were tried against it by their own more restless spirits and by their ingenious tormenters. In one aspect of the case, and in some moods of our minds, in these days we cannot but smile as if we found fun in reading some of their experiences; for there certainly is an element and aspect of the ludicrous in some of them. It seems as if all the ingenuities and whimsies, all the crotchets and extravagancies, of crude and conscientious enthusiasm and fanaticism, were conjured up at the time, and for the occasion of teasing and worrying the poor sheep who had sought this fold. The tor-

[1] Court Records, vol. i. p. 271.

menting troublers of the new Israel were of every style and pattern, of every variety of sting and venom. One who in our dog-day season is trying to do diligent work with eye, hand, and mind engaged, and who finds himself made the sport and prey of flies, gnats, mosquitoes, and all summer bugs, may realize what was often the vexed and harried experience of our Fathers, as, from over the seas, or out of the woods, or in one of their own cottages or congregations, some "extraordinary," "exorbitant," or "unsavory spirit," in man or woman, presented itself, — to indicate a swarm in persistency and variety.

Beside the buffetings and distractions caused by strangers or troublers among themselves, the authorities had soon to meet with many serious perplexities arising from the practical working of their own theory. Thus, as the Court had made church-membership the condition of eligibility to the franchise, they found it essential for them to have a word to say about the rightful constitution of churches whose prerogative it was to decide the terms of admission for members. To prevent variance and undue privilege or license in this matter, the independence of the churches was brought under risk. In 1634–5, we find the following on the Records:[1] —

"This Court doth intreate of the elders and brethren of every church within this jurisdiction, that they will consult and advise of one uniform order of discipline in the churches agreeable to the Scriptures, and then to consider how far the magistrates are bound to interpose for the preservation of that uniformity and peace of the churches."

In the next year, the Court subjected the mode of gathering churches to the order and approbation of the magistrates, and refused the franchise to members of churches otherwise gathered.[2]

The "New-English Canaan" was the jesting title which the roguish Thomas Morton gave to the site of the Puritan State; showing how well he divined the nature of the enterprise which he tried to vex and thwart. The experiment of the Fathers of Massachusetts to form and administer a Commonwealth, in which all civil affairs should be disposed by members of one order of churches, is classed by us now among the visionary fancies

[1] Records, vol. i. p. 168. [2] Vol. i. pp. 142–3.

which have beguiled good but weak men, and which, on the trial, have exposed their folly and error. So we judge; and then, too often, condemn. Those covenanted legislators are not to be held accountable for the logical or the practical consequences which followed from their scheme when put on trial. They were not bound to foresee these consequences, nor to be ready to abandon, or even to re-adjust, their theory, as its experimental working brought perplexities and unlooked-for resistance. They were right, after having recognized what their faith and piety held to be a constraining duty which would consecrate and bless them in the doing of it, to throw their souls into its discharge, and defy and resist all opposition.

The quotations which have been so abundantly made in the preceding pages, from the authentic writings of the leading founders of Massachusetts, and from their legislative records, are alike confidential and public testimonies of the design which prompted them. It was not that they intended, however conscientiously they might have done so, to construct a theory or form of government of their own devising, for ends of civil and religious freedom. All motive to do this, if they had felt its influence, was overruled by a profound conviction, the result of their religious training and belief, that the Bible offered them an already perfected model and guide for a Commonwealth; and that they were at liberty only, or could only safely use their liberty, in following that model. Many pages more, from diaries, letters, and more public documents, might be covered with confirmatory and illustrative matter, similar to what has already been given.

But there is a record of such marked and emphatic significance in its bearing upon the same point, that it must not be passed over unnoticed.

Massachusetts alone, of all its sister colonies of New England, with positive avowal, and with consistent efforts and measures to realize it, aimed to establish a Bible Commonwealth. The colonies of Plymouth, Connecticut, and New Haven, approximated to that aim, but fell short of it in actual legislation for it.

What, then, was more natural than that Massachusetts should have attempted to induce her sister colonies to follow her own example, in making the church estate the condition of citizenship? This attempt she did make in all sincerity, though with but partial success. As early as 1638, at a meeting held at Cambridge, Connecticut had proposed a confederation with the other three colonies. The proposition, failing of effect at the time, was held in mind, till it resulted in a union of the four in 1643, by formal articles, providing for regular annual meetings of two commissioners for each of them, appointed by their several General Courts. The preamble of the Confederacy begins thus: —

"Whereas, we all came into these parts of America with one and the same end and aim, namely, to advance the Kingdome of our Lord Jesus Christ, and to enjoy the liberties of the Gospell in puritie, with peace," &c.

The object of the Union was chiefly for purposes of mutual aid in defence against the Indians. They entered into "a firme and perpetuall league of friendship and amytie, for offence and defence, mutuall advice and succour, upon all just occasions, both for preserving and propagating the truth and liberties of the Gospell, and for their own mutuall safety and welfare."

After the organization had become familiar, and the commissioners, instructed by the General Courts which they severally represented, and to whom they were to report the advisory measures recommended in their Congress, had experience of what business might properly come before them, we find the following proposition on their Records, at a meeting held in due order of place and time, at New Haven, in September, 1646. It bears on its face that it came from Massachusetts: —

"Upon serious consideration of the spreading nature of Error, the dangerous growth and effects thereof in other places, and particularly now the purity and power both of religion and of civill order is already much corrupted, if not wholy lost in a parte of New England, by a licentious liberty graunted and setled; whereby many casting off the rule of the word, professe and practise what is good in their owne eyes: And upon information of what petitions have beene lately putt in some of the Colonies against the good and straite wayes of Christ, both in the Churches, and in the Comon Wealth, the Commissioners remembering that those Colonies for themselves and their posteritie did enter into this firme and perpetuall league, — as for other respects so for mutuall advise that the truth and liberties of the Gospell might be preserved and propagated, thought it their duty seriously to comend it to the care and consideration of each Generall Corte within these United Colonies, that as they have laid theire foundations and measured the temple of God, the worship and worshippers by that straight Reed God hath putt into their hands, soe they would walke on and build up (all discouragements and difficulties notwithstandinge) with an undaunted heart and unwearied hand, according to the same rules and patternes. That a due watch be kept and continued at the doores of God's house, that none be admitted as members of the body of Christ, but such as hold foorth effectuall callinge and thereby union with Christ the head, and that those whome Christ hath received, and enter by an expresse covenant to attend and observe the lawes and dutyes of that spirituall Corporation, that Babtisme, the seale of the Covenant, be administred onely to such members and their ymediate seed, that Anabaptisme, familisme, Antinomianisme, and generally all errors of like nature, which oppose, undermine and slight either the scriptures, the Sabboth, or other ordinance of God, and bring in and cry up unwarrantable Revelations, inventions of men, or any carnall liberty, under a deceitfull colloure of liberty of conscience, may be seasonably and duely supprest, though they wish as much forbearance and respect may be had of tender consciences seeking light as may stand with the purity of religion and peace of the Churches."

The record adds:—

"The Commissioners of Plymouth desire further consideration concerninge this advise given to the generall Corts." [1]

Massachusetts had been consistent with herself in pressing her Bible theory of State upon her sister colonies, but she could not legislate for them.

Now look at, examine, that aim or scheme or experiment of the first colonists, as it stands in the line of history, and holds a place, certainly not a mean one, among the enterprises of men. It was one of a hundred schemes, visions, lures, or devices of men, which have floated before their busy and quickened fancies, and engaged their whole souls, their worldly means, their lives and heroism in attempts to realize them. The possible nobleness of humanity has often gone into some of the dreamiest and most impracticable of these schemes. The Fathers of Massachusetts had doubtless read the "Republic" of Plato, and the "Utopia" of Sir Thomas More. But they had also read

[1] From the Plymouth Copy of the Records of Commissioners.

their Bible as they had read no other book. And if they had seen the Book float down from the sky, and had received it by a clutch of the hand from out of a mountain cloud, they could not have given to it a more revering love, trust, and divine authority than they did yield to it. It suggested to them the conception and experiment of a Christian state, a commonwealth in which human legislation should be patterned from the divine.

The conditions of time, opinion, opportunity, and persons, for the practical trial of a Biblical Commonwealth, were as follows:

1. A religiously earnest period, characterized by an implicit faith in the divine authority, and in the literal, inspired infallibility of the whole Bible; and a mode of valuing it, and a sense of subjection to its teachings conformed to that view of it.

2. A class of men and women to whom that belief should be a bond of sympathy and fellowship.

3. Unfavorable or antagonistic circumstances forbidding the practical trial of an ecclesiastical commonwealth where they were then living.

4. The opening of a new field remote and sheltered in the distance, with vested rights secured for its occupancy and jurisdiction.

I have used by preference the term a "Biblical Commonwealth:" I might have confined myself to the use of the term "Theocracy," which has been quoted more than once, as used by the Fathers as applicable to their form of government. And it is applicable, if by it we mean the direct recognition of a Divine Headship to a state. Our Fathers used it in that legitimate sense of the term which subordinates all views of expediency, custom, and human prerogative to a profound sense of subjection to a Divine Ruler, and an obligation to accept and to follow what is believed to be an intelligible revelation of His will, as the basis and guide of legislation.

That conception was sure, in its turn and season, to come to practical trial in this world. It stood entered on the docket of time, awaiting human agents, fit field and opportunity, with the prime condition of faith and self-renunciation in man and woman. Then it would be entitled to a trial.

Glance with a single backward thought, over the long and varied, generally interesting, but often melancholy, series of the visionary fancies, the social and political theories, by which men and women with only good aims have sought to organize and govern themselves. We have had the schemes of St. Simon, of Fourier, and of Owen. You may have read Mr. Hepworth Dixon's sketch of some of the experiments on trial among us, in Shakerism and Communism. And it hardly becomes an age and an indulgence, which, like our own, tolerate the filthy experiment of Mormonism, to be very critical in judging about any of the past theories which have failed. There have been many experiments of a purely religious sort, tried by men and women devoutly sincere and high-minded, which had far less of grandeur, nobleness, and practical feasibility to offer as motives, than had that of our Fathers. Among the fashionings of the millennium, and the plannings for it, theirs, certainly, was not one which will unfavorably compare with others. They took care to guard against the extravagancies and the follies of the Fifth Monarchy men; and they had a sober, and never a fanatic, spirit. Their experiment, as I have said, was sure of, and was entitled to have, its time and trial. We may criticise and even ridicule it, if we choose, on its weak side. But there was an august grandeur, an attractive and spell-like power in it, a beckoning promise of some unspeakable blessing with it, which would be certain to give it an enthralling influence over devout and high-souled men and women. Its time for trial came at the most earnestly religious age which has as yet been chronicled in the history of the church.

It is from the failure and from the success of great visions and schemes, that men have learned all their practical and political wisdom. We will not undertake to cast the proportions of success or failure in the original enterprise, which is represented now by the Commonwealth of Massachusetts.

Puritanism, in the strictly Bible theory and embodiment of it, as accepted by our Fathers, had a thoroughly sincere discipleship, and a hearty earnestness of purpose engaged for it, only for a little more than half a century and for two generations. During that period, and for those full believers of it, it was transiently consistent, because it was parallel with, and at the level of, the degree of intelligence which had been reached in some portions of Christendom, — especially in England, — for it never had the same sway on the continent of Europe. Under those temporary conditions, Puritanism secured the devout confidence of noble and eminent men, statesmen, jurists, and scholars; and of such votaries as in those times there were, of science and philosophy, as well as the profoundest reverence of meek women, sturdy yeomen, and craftsmen in ordinary life. But Puritanism could not outlast its own age, nor hold its unquestioned control beyond the limitations of time and generations, except by living on its traditions among people in secluded places not reached by increasing light and extended knowledge.

It started with an estimate of, and a way of using, the whole Bible, which have been discredited by more intelligence, independence of thinking, critical, scholarly, and scientific culture, and the exercise of a higher grade of what we call common sense in common people. But the theory and faith on which our Fathers proceeded, though steadily impaired, modified, and diminished, have only gradually yielded, only a little for each generation, — retaining enough of inherited or traditional influence to avert the catastrophe of a complete revolutionary repudiation at any one time. The spirit and shadow, the tone and savor of Puritanism, still remain and have influence in our State. Doubtless, there are members of our present Legislature, certainly there are constituents of some of them, who in heart and mind are persuaded, that it would be well if we could restore Puritan legislation in our franchise, in our churches, in household management and discipline, in Sabbath laws, in many social customs and indulgences, against dissipation and gambling. But the dream is of the past.

No reader can engage his mind, candidly and seriously, upon the original papers left to us by the Fathers of our colony, without being impressed with the thought, that they subjected themselves to all the sacrifices involved in their enterprise, bore willingly all the sharp inflictions of suffering incident to it, and cheered themselves with great religious hopes of its issues, under the quickening impulse of a belief that they were putting under practical trial the loftiest aim which had ever inspired high-minded and devout men.

True, it is unspeakably to our advantage and enjoyment in the freedom and cheerfulness of life, that we have been released from the severe sway of what we call, conventionally, the rigidness and superstition of Puritan institutions and ideas. We may, however, question the fairness of describing as the outgrowth of Puritanism, what a more just view of facts recognizes as a general and comprehensive progress and enlightenment, by many agencies of advance on the past.

Yet are we sure that the change, as all relaxing and liberalizing, is pure gain to us, and no loss? A large and liberal-minded man might easily defend the position, that there were elements and usages of Puritanism, which we are none the wiser, none the better, none the freer, none the happier, for having left them. Our domestic, civil, and religious life; our amusements, vices, and wicked haunts, — all testify that our Fathers had some virtues and safeguards which we have not.

Meanwhile, not with alarming and dangerous reaction of revolution or anarchy, but slowly and safely relaxing its sway in our Commonwealth, eight generations born and nurtured here, and many bands of new exiles, have realized that Puritanism has prepared for them a most pleasant heritage. So that this noble and honored State has a repute of which all living in it, who are not justly proud, will not increase its credit by staying here, but had better avail themselves of their liberty by moving out of it without process.

The Commonwealth in this our present age of it has these four conspicuous honors: —

1. Its money bonds are set at a higher premium than are any American paper obligations in the marts of the world.

2. Its educational system, and the high and general culture produced by it, give us the pre-eminent advantages and safeguards of intelligence.

3. Its charitable, benevolent, and reformatory institutions are most numerous, munificent, and humane. The State is treated by the whole Union, as a bank for gathering, and a deep free pocket for dispensing, all manner of pecuniary gifts; and those who are for leaving us out in the cold, strangely enough, have to come here to get warm.

4. There are in this Commonwealth more peaceful and happy homes, palatial in our towns and cities, and simple and frugal in our sheltered valleys and on our hill-sides, filled with those who

are favored beyond any people on the earth in an opportunity to make the best thing possible out of life.

I have said nothing to rebut, or even as recognizing, the charge against our Fathers of having a worldly outlook for trade and profit. It is enough to say that they were in the body and found it necessary to keep themselves alive, — to be fed, housed, and clothed, as human beings always do, wherever they may be, and whatever experiment they have on trial. Some of them did keep alive. After stern and varied hardships, a few of them gathered a comfortable substance. But as to the profit of their undertaking, nearly the whole of that has come to the generations between them and our own, — most largely to our own. It would not have been agreeable or desirable, for such persons as we are, to have lived with our Fathers; but it is an inestimable privilege to us to live after them, in their own places.

TREATMENT

OF

INTRUDERS AND DISSENTIENTS

BY THE

FOUNDERS OF MASSACHUSETTS.

BY REV. GEORGE E. ELLIS, D.D.

TREATMENT

OF

INTRUDERS AND DISSENTIENTS

BY THE

FOUNDERS OF MASSACHUSETTS.

A CORRECT view of the aims and purposes of the Founders of Massachusetts carries with it a certain consistent course of treatment, which might be expected to be visited upon all who should interfere with them, or cause them trouble. Their project was in itself of such a nature, that it would very easily afford a test for distinguishing between a friend and an enemy, — between measures, intentions, and even opinions, which would tend to advance it, and those which would thwart and wreck it. Once committed to their enterprise, and holding in their hands a royal instrument, which they regarded as securing to them the territorial rights and jurisdiction necessary for a practical trial of it, they felt that it would be their own fault or folly if it failed in that trial. To keep possession of their charter was their first security. For this they trusted to law, to policy, to shrewd management; and to a final reinforcement from obstinacy, and something that looks like cunning, — the last, however, brought into use only in opposition to cunning. There were in their view, or construction, three privileges secured to them by that charter, which were their main reliance: —

First, An absolute jurisdiction over the soil included in their patent;

Second, The right to define and impose terms on which alone new members should be admitted into their company;

Third, The right, "for their special defence and safety, to incounter, expulse, repel, and resist, all such person and persons, as shall at any time attempt the destruction, invasion, or annoyance to the plantation or its inhabitants."

No doubt they had some intelligent apprehensions of the nature and sources of the hostility from parties and individuals which they would have to deal with. They had reason to believe that their hold upon their charter would always be under peril, from their enemies residing in England, and from those smarting under their discipline carrying ill reports from hence. These they would need to circumvent in one way. Their internal troubles they would meet in another way.

Only the actual reading of the early volumes of the original Records of the colony, page by page, carefully and intelligently too, can put their case before us, as they might claim that we should look at it. And we should need to begin with them at their own beginning. Their enterprise in colonizing had been preceded by a series of like undertakings, which had proved costly and disastrous failures. Unfit men, and insufficient or unblessed purposes or aims, had brought those enterprises into painful discomfiture, and stained them with reproach. If a new one was to be undertaken, it was with cautions and warnings learned from those which had been blasted. The excellent and revered John White, of the English Dorchester, the most effective promoter of the Massachusetts colony, in his "Planters' Plea," 1630, had well defined the sort of persons who alone might hope to prosper in such an enterprise. He wrote: —

> "The persons chosen out for this employment, ought to be willing, constant, industrious, obedient, frugal, lovers of the common good, or, at least, such as may be easily wrought to this temper; considering that works of this nature try the undertakers with many difficulties, and easily discourage minds of base and weak temper."

With equal force and frankness, he describes the sort of persons not wished for, as not suitable: —

> "Men nourished up in idleness, unconstant, and affecting novelties, unwilling, stubborn, inclined to faction, covetous, luxurious, prodigal, and generally men habituated to any gross evil, are no fit members of a colony."

We have one letter by Governor Cradock, and two from the company in England, addressed to Endicott, as their representative here before the charter was brought over. The explicit directions which they contain indicate the measures which the authorities themselves would pursue when established here. Endicott is told, "that the propagating of the Gospel is the thing we do profess, above all, to be our aim in settling this plantation." He is instructed to press a rigid restriction upon the sort of persons allowed to reside here; and "that none be partakers but such as be peaceable men; and of honest life and conversation, — and desirous to live amongst us and conform themselves to good order and government." The company had yielded to the desire of the Rev. Ralph Smith to come over, "before we understood his difference of judgment in some things from our ministers." The order to Endicott is, "that, unless he will be conformable to our government, you suffer him not to remain within the limits of our grant." Explicit directions also are given him for settling all single persons and servants in families, that they may have part in morning and evening devotions.[1]

Such hints as these prepare us for what we find when the government was established here. An agreement had been made with their ministers in England. The first business of the first Court, held on this soil, is entered thus: "Imprimis, it was propounded how the ministers should be maintained. It was ordered that houses should be built for them, with convenient speed, at the public charge;" and salaries paid in money and in produce. Following on with the Records from that page, we find the development of their purpose to establish here a Bible Commonwealth formed out of a church, — the legislators of which, should be bound by solemn covenant, as professed Christians pledged to one sacred design. We find in those records, too, a series of legislative acts, and of cases of enforcement of them, which are now pronounced absurd, arbitrary, intolerant, and even of merciless cruelty. These are candidly entered, never apologized for, but always justified by those responsible for them. From these and other original records, we

[1] Col. Rec., i. 386–397.

have a fair and full presentment of the materials for dealing with this subject, — The Treatment visited by the authorities of the colony of Massachusetts upon the Intruders who came into their jurisdiction, and upon the Dissentients who, from time to time, individually, or in company, started forth among themselves. Readers generally, among us, know that that treatment was severe. The occasions and reasons they do not generally know. And even though it may be unnecessary for me to say so, yet let me distinctly and emphatically avow, that I am not to argue for the abstract justice or fairness of the course pursued by the authorities of Massachusetts; nor to attempt to vindicate it as necessary; nor to palliate its severity; nor even to assert its wisdom or expediency under the circumstances. If a faithful exposition of the facts shall avail in either of these directions, those who now stand charged with folly, harshness, and cruelty, will, so far, have the benefit in judgment. I am not undertaking a vindication of those Fathers, in the sense of an approval or justification either of their religio-political theory, or of their measures for a practical trial of it. I hold myself simply to the obligation to make a fair statement of the facts of the case; to set what is to us an historic past, in the light, — or under the darkness, if such it were, — of the times when it was living, present experience; to expound the views, the actions, and, if possible, also the motives of those who, in the exercise of what they held to be rightful authority, as under covenant and oath, did what they believed to be their duty to themselves in doing as they did towards others.

We must first put ourselves into the light or — if, as suggested, it was — under the darkness of those times. The basis of fellowship, of accord, and of legislation in Massachusetts, was different from that of either of her sister colonies of New England. That stern and strong form of faith, founded on a reverential regard for the letter of the Bible, which was held here, was also substantially held by the leading spirits of the other colonies. But it was more especially wrought in with the spirit, the purposes, and the measures, which had sway in Massachusetts; and the peculiar working and shaping of that belief here account for all the peculiarities of our early history. As we read that history, we are at times surprised at the kind and degree of unanimity, of accordance in opinion and purpose, of so many persons of strong and really independent spirits. Why did they not fall out oftener and more threateningly among themselves? What was it that kept enough of them of one mind and of one will for the ends of legislation and administration? It was simply and solely their common aim, founded upon their common faith; their idolizing, so to speak, of the Bible; their way of thinking about it, interpreting it, and using it. This common religious sentiment and purpose — restraining an indulgence of what we mean by liberty of conscience — held them firmly in sympathy and mutual confidence. To a certain extent, and that a large extent, it repressed and checked the tendency to diversity of judgment. That diversity of judgment, individualism, opinionativeness, was the most marked characteristic of the age that was then opening, and even of the class of persons with whom they had many strong affinities. Their common faith discouraged, averted, much of what would have been utterly fatal to their enterprise. Had they allowed individualism, or tolerated any of the crotchets of eccentric and independent speculation, their scheme would have come to an end before it had had a beginning. There were many occasions and emergencies — such were furnished indeed in every case of their dealing with opposers and dissentients — in which variance of judgment among themselves would have fatally discomfited them. The strength of their one bond of harmony enabled them to deal as with one mind with all who differed with them.

This suggestion brings us directly to the point from which we have to start. The especial dread of the Fathers of Massachusetts was of all individuality and eccentricity of opinion. They had an intense — by us an unappreciable — horror and distrust of those who professed to be favored with private interpretations, revelations, and inspirations. And, strangely enough, it so proved, that nearly every one of their troublers — Antinomians, Gortonists, and Quakers — laid claim to those oracular qualities and gifts. The epithets of description and reproach attached to the names of such intruders and dissentients, carry with them a key to the history. They were "exorbitant" persons, "heady," "fantastic," "blasphemous," "malignant," "unsavory spirits," &c. The decisive blow which fell on the head of Mrs. Hutchinson, on her trial before the court, came from the testimony of a reverend fellow-passenger with her on her way over the sea, that, in the ship, "she had vented her revelations" about some calamity that was coming on the country. Gorton's mystic creed was to the authorities the very hyperbole and quintessence of crazy enthusiasm. The Quaker's "inward light" and "testimony-bearing by the Spirit" was utter blasphemy to the pious ears that heard it. It is a very curious fact, that not a single one of those men or women, who were treated with the severest or most cruel penalties by the authorities of Massachusetts, was of immoral character or of impure life; not one of them. On the contrary, they were especially such as we should regard as blameless, even excellent and exemplary, in their moral character and conduct, — honest, truth-speaking, kind, and tender-hearted. But erratic individuality of opinion or interpretation, or a claim to a "revelation" of their own, would bring the best and purest of them under judgment. In one point of view, this whole series of the troublers of the New England Israel gives us a most interesting and even fascinating study of characters. They were such as make especial favorites for the mystic, the pietist, and the transcendentalist. They would have made an admirable stock for "Brook Farm." They did make a most miscellaneous and heterogeneous stock for the early Rhode-Island and Providence plantations. With the single exception of that sad scapegrace Captain Underhill,[1] even the Antinomians were all free of moral reproach. But they were not wanted, and they could not be tolerated in Massachusetts. "Transcendentalism" was wasted on our Fathers. It was a thing of which they would very soon have had too much, if they had admitted any of it. We must get ourselves as far away as possible from the atmosphere and liberalism of this modern Boston, with its free invitation and its large hos-

[1] Underhill, though very serviceable in his military capacity, was a man of a shaky morality and a cloudy theology. He was "convented" on grave suspicions of impurity, but explained his conviction that he was one of the elect, by saying, that, "having lain under a spirit of bondage and a legal way five years, he could get no assurance till the Spirit set home an absolute promise of free grace, as he was taking the moderate use of the creature called tobacco." — *Winthrop's Journal*, vol. i. p. 270.

pitality for all novelties and individualisms, — its churches, synagogues, cathedrals, halls and theatres for preaching, — its conventions, fraternities, and woman's club, — if we would have before us the Boston that once was. Did it enter into the imagination of its first occupants to conceive what a posterity they should be responsible for?

Their dread of all persons professedly illuminated by special revelations was by no means the result of a merely imaginary apprehension of a possible evil that might befall them. I have affirmed that it might with truth be alleged, and with full evidence, that the Fathers of Massachusetts, instead of coming hither to provide for liberty of conscience, left their old home to keep themselves clear of the workings and effects of the license, lawlessness, and mischief, which had already begun to threaten a wild indulgence in England. Any one who is well read in the history of England, either in its capital or in its by-places, during the period just following the planting of this colony, needs not to be told that that period, of all the Christian ages, was most rife in religious fancies, speculations, eccentricities, and frenzies. Some persons, without this knowledge, take for granted that sectarianism, individualism, and free thinking, with all their developments, moderate or extravagant, healthful or harmful, are the especial products of our modern age. They are strangely and egregiously mistaken. It is just as difficult to devise a new heresy or a new fancy or a new oddity in religious belief or practice, as it is to discover a new truth. There is no opinion, conceit, or notion in such matters, recognized among us, which had not its living belief and avowal at the period of which I am speaking.

Before me lie three quaint and time-worn old books, very communicative witnesses as to what I am now saying. They were written and published after the time when our General Court began to legislate on this soil, but their contents cover materials that were familiar and notorious. I will copy and read their titles, which, I think, will serve the purpose, without asking you to read their contents.

1. "Gangræna: or A Catalogue and Discovery of many of the Errors, Heresies, Blasphemies, and pernicious practices of the Sectaries of this

time, vented and acted in England in these four last years, &c. By Thomas Edwards, Minister of the Gospel."

2. "Heresiography, or a Description of the Heretics and Sectaries sprung up in these latter times, &c. By Ephraim Pagitt, late Minister of St. Edmonds."

3. "The Dippers Dipt. Or the Anabaptists Duck'd and Plunged over Head and Eares, at a Disputation in Southwark, &c. By Daniel Featley, D.D."

This was Milton's "year of sects and schisms."

A precious medley do these books, and others like them, "adorned with cuts," present us, of the workings of individualism and sectarism in England then. And there were on the stage of life earnest and fantastic characters, answering to each belief and opinion, each notion, scruple, and extravagance, by garb, behavior, habit, and speech. There were then in England men who wore long hair and women who wore short hair; the bearded and the shaven; the dandy and the drab-coated; those who said *Thee* and *Thou*, and those who kept on their hats, where others took them off, before Fox became the apostle of such.

To assume, as some carelessly do, that when Roger Williams and others asserted the right and safety of liberty of conscience, they announced a novelty that was alarming, *because* it was a novelty, to the authorities of Massachusetts, is a great error. Our Fathers were fully informed as to what it was, what it meant; and they were familiar with such results as it wrought in their day. They knew it well, and what must come of it; and they did not like it; rather, they feared and hated it. They did not mean to live where it was indulged; and, in the full exercise of their intelligence and prudence, they resolved not to tolerate it among them. They identified freedom of conscience only with the objectionable and mischievous results which came of it. They might have met all around them in England, in city and country, all sorts of wild, crude, extravagant, and fanatical spirits. They had reason to fear that many whimsical and factious persons would come over hither, expecting to find an unsettled state of things, in which they would have the freest range for their eccentricities. They were prepared to stand on the defensive.

Now we turn back again to the Colony Records, without an actual perusal of which, page by page, as I have said, will the history, as it is apt to be written, not stand before us as truth. On those pages we are impressed at once by the high-handed, resolute, straightforward, and systematic way, — never faltering, halting, doubting, or justifying themselves, — in which the authorities proceeded to put the soil and its inhabitants under their mastery. They proceeded on the calm, full assurance, that it was for them to begin with a clear, or a cleared, field. Exactly as one who, having purchased a large freehold, on which he contemplates improvements, runs his eye over it to see what nuisances he must remove; the stumps to be grubbed up, the holes in the fences, and so forth. The colonial proprietors by charter found here some chance and irregular residents; "old planters," and others, who, with a mysterious history behind them in England, — rogues, adventurers, or romantic spirits loving solitude and the wilderness, — had occupied many of the headlands and promontories of our Bay. These had to be packed off, sent home to England, or brought under the authority and discipline of the colonists. Some of these, getting before the Privy Council with the tale of their grievances, and with ill reports of what was going on here, originated that suspicion and jealousy towards the colony which brought its charter and authorities under threats and peril. The only effect which such complaints had here was, to make legislation and oversight more rigid and watchful, and the dealing with mischief-breeders more sharp and stern. Never in a single instance were the authorities intimidated or thwarted. All interlopers here, all roving characters, seeking the delights of a proximate return to the state of nature, were at once looked after. The roisterous and reckless Morton, of Merry Mount, has the honor of coming first under their discipline. At the very first Court held in the Bay, it was "Ordered, that Morton, of Mount Woolison, should presently be sent for by process." They had him in hand in less than a fortnight, set him in the "bilbowes," and then sent him to England, confiscating his goods to make satisfaction to Indians whom he had wronged, and then burning his shanty as a scene of wicked revelry. In a few months after, six persons have a passage home provided for them against their will; the all-sufficient reason being given that they are "persons unmeete to inhabit here." At the same time, as one of two prisoners to be sent to England, is that dark and mysterious character, Sir Christopher Gardiner, "an undoubted Papist," professedly a Knight of the Sepulchre, sorely charged as having temporary and contemporary wives, two in England, and a certain Italian woman here. On the same date, the first quack was treated in a way which reminds us how different the law was then from what it is now.

"Nich. Knopp is fined five pounds for taking upon him to cure the scurvey by a water of noe worth nor value, which he sold at a very deare rate, to be imprisoned till he pay his fine, or give security for it, or els to be whipped, and shall be liable to any man's action of whome he hath received money for the said water." [1]

Again, —

"Thomas Gray is enjoined under the penalty of ten pounds to attend on the Court in person this day three weeks, to answer to divers things objected against him, and to remove himself out of the limits of this patent," before six months. (p. 77.)

Another unaccounted-for old planter, who seems to have had dangerous relations with the Indians, was Thomas Walford, of Charlestown.

He was, May, 1631, "fined forty shillings, and is enjoined, hee and his wife, to depart out of the limits of this pattent, before the 20th day of October nexte, under pain of confiscation of his goods, for his contempt of authority, and confronting officers," &c.

"Capt. John Stone for his outrage comitted in confronting authority, abuseing Mr. Ludlowe, both in words and behavour, assalting him and calling him a just ass &c. is fined 100 pds, and prohibited coming within this pattent without leave from the Government under the penalty of death." (p. 108.)

Again, —

"Mr. Thomas Makepeace, because of his novile disposition, was informed we were weary of him unlesse hee reforme." (p. 252.)

Mr. Blaxton, an old planter on the peninsula of Boston, a mysterious man, shrewdly foreseeing what sort of a sway was

[1] Records, vol. i. p. 83.

about to be established here, quietly took himself off, selling out to the settlers his own squatter rights and improvements.

While the soil was thus cleared of intruders, and the proprietors asserted their rights of jurisdiction over strangers, they were none the less resolute in putting their own magistrates and servants under rigid discipline. Sir Richard Saltonstall, and others of the highest among them, were fined for absence or tardiness at the Court-meetings, or for irregularities of conduct. It is hard to read the Records without feeling the motions for many a smile, or even for more marked demonstrations. So rigid was the inquisition, so petty were many of the offences punished, and so severe were the penalties, that we find our smiles repressed. But those stern and grim legislators understood themselves. They knew what were their aims, and the caution, severity, and resoluteness requisite to realize them, or, at least, to guard the trial of them. Before we hear of their making stocks or whipping-posts, such conveniences seem to have been all handy for use as subjects were sentenced to them.

It would seem from the following order of the Court, that the use of the Boston stocks was very fittingly inaugurated: —

"Edward Palmer, for his extortion, takeing 1l. 13s. 7d. for the plank and wood-work of Boston stocks, is fined five pounds, and censured to bee set an hour in the stocks. This fine was remitted to 10s."[1]

"Robert Shorthose, for swearing by the blude of God, was sentenced to have his tongue put into a cleft stick, and to stand so by the space of halfe an houre."

"Elizabeth, the wife of Thomas Apelgate, was censured to stand with her tongue in a cleft stick, for swearing, raileing, and revileing."

"Edward Woodley, for attempting a rape, swearing, and breaking into a house, was censured to be severely whipt 30 stripes, a yeares imprisonment, and kept to hard labour with course dyot, and to weare a coller of yron."[2]

"Capt. Lovell was admonished to take heede of light carriage."[3]

A specimen of the severity of their discipline on a grievous offender, a servant on Governor Cradock's farm, is as follows: At the Court, June 14, 1631.

"It is ordered that Philip Ratliffe shall be whipped, have his eares cut off, fined 40 pounds, and banished out of the limitts of this jurisdiction,

[1] Records, vol. i. p. 260. [2] Id. p. 177. [3] Id. p. 193.

for uttering malicious and scandalous speeches against the government," &c.

Again, at the Court, in March, 1638, —

"Mr. Ambros Marten, for calling the Church covenant a stinking carrion and a human invention, and saying he wondered at God's patience, feared it would end in the sharpe, and said the ministers did dethrone Christ, and set up themselves; he was fined 10 pds. and counselled to go to Mr. Mather to be instructed by him."

These last two extracts are very significant to us of a fact, evidence of which is strewn all over the Records, that the authorities were especially stern, unflinching, and unrelenting, in dealing with those whose offence was a contumacious trifling with the dignity of the government, or an irreverent reproaching of their church covenant. Security and harmony, respect and submission, as to both those vitally fundamental matters, held at stake the prosperity or the absolute ruin of the enterprise.

Yet it would be doing harsh injustice to the early legislators of Massachusetts, to recognize in their records only a stern spirit. Gentleness and mercy show many pleasing and impressive manifestations even there. The reader is constantly reminded of the same characteristic in the Jewish code, in which severity is set in contrast with mildness. The tender regard for the widowed and the fatherless; the privileges secured to the gleaners, as illustrated in the beautiful pastoral in the Book of Ruth; consideration for the impoverished and the honest debtor; the distinction between disciplinary punishment and inhuman vengeance, — are admirably paralleled between the Old-Testament code and that of Massachusetts. Our legislators stood for absolute equity between man and man. They protected the unfortunate and the wronged. They provided for the fair settlement of estates, and the adjustment of private controversies. Their legislation was rigidly impersonal and sternly impartial. They remitted fines on confession and submission. As has been already said, the ever-upright Winthrop and the other associates in the chief magistracies, stood in turn at the same bar where offenders and culprits were held to judgment. Here, certainly, is an act of even-handed justice, done by the Court, in September, 1631: —

"It is ordered that Josias Plastowe shall (for stealeing four basketts of corne from the Indians) returne them eight basketts againe, be fined five pounds, and hereafter, to be called by the name of Josias, and not Mr., as formerly hee used to be." [1]

Some distinction of difference is certainly to be recognized by us, for it was recognized by the authorities, in their mode of treating, respectively, intruders or strangers who caused them annoyance, and the dissentients from their opinions, measures, or policy, members of their own company and churches. The harshness which in either case is rightly charged upon the authorities, and the injustice and cruelty which, with less ground of reason, are also ascribed to them, can be fairly judged of by us only when we keep in mind the distinction between the two classes of troublers. As regards those who were not proprietors, members of the company, or freemen, but chance residents, strangers, interlopers, adventurers, or visitors, the authorities felt that their rights of self-protection and privacy, with security from molestation, were as plain and sufficient as are those of any householder among us on his own premises, or those of any joint-stock company in managing its corporate affairs. They did not feel themselves bound in any case, beyond their own inclinations, to give a reason for keeping out, warning off, or expelling, such as came under the description just named. It was enough if any such person was thought "unmeete to inhabit here." If he was not wanted, he must stay away, or he might be sent away. If he did any thing wrong while here, he might be fined, whipped, or otherwise punished first, and then be ordered and helped to take himself off. So the authorities insisted their charter gave them a right to judge and act in every case for themselves; and so they knew it was wise and necessary for them to proceed, if they meant that their profoundly sincere and exacting religious enterprise should have a fair trial. The issue stood thus between the two parties, — the housekeepers and the visitants, the proprietors and the outsiders. Here were the owners of certain property, and proprietary rights of local government and jurisdiction. They understood each other, and were solemnly covenanted with each other, in a pur-

1 Records, vol. i. p. 92.

pose which had brought them hither, at their own charges, furnished with the means of self-protection. They must stay here, identifying themselves and their fortunes with their experiment. They had parted with their homes and possessions in the old world; and, if they could not make and keep such here, they would be vagabonds on the earth.[1]

The other party to the issue were those who came unasked, for curiosity, adventure, or caprice. They did not intend to stay except for private ends of their own. They had no property here. They did not love the air of the place, nor its society. Very many of them were possessed of the whimsies and crotchets which the colonists intended to be clear of, as one reason for coming hither. Others of those intruders had the "prophetical spirit," which classed them as nuisances of the most offensive character. It certainly was easier and more reasonable for the visitors to leave, than for the householders to break up their establishment, or to live in a constant ferment and dissension. And it is to be frankly and distinctly admitted, that not a single such intruder, however summarily he was dealt with here, would have escaped legal process and punishment under like circumstances in England. Any one who will search curiously into the vagrant laws of the mother country, and mark what a careful watch was kept, and what discipline was visited upon the unthrifty and those who had no visible means of a livelihood, will find abundant evidence that our Fathers followed precedents; though, it must be owned, they did not care for such support.

The case was somewhat different when dissent and variance sprang up within their own fellowship in state or church. The grievance was a deep and a sore one, in each instance of it, when those who had the rights of freemen, and the sanctity of

1 In a "Declaration" issued by the Court, in 1659, in the course of the proceedings against the Quakers, this ground is assumed: "There is no man that is possessed of house or land, wherein he hath just title and property as his own, but he would count it unreasonably injurious that another who had no authority thereto should intrude and enter into his house, without the owner's consent." The argument proceeds, that, if the intruder in such a case should be killed by the householder, the latter will be guiltless; and if an individual may thus defend his private rights, how much more the authorities of a government. — Miscellaneous MSS. in the State House.

the covenant of church-membership raised diversities of judgment or variances of purpose, and so caused distraction. It was evident in all such cases, that the umpireship, the appeal, would be found in referring to the common pledge of aim and enterprise which had bound the proprietors together, and to the seal which they had set upon their pledge in their church vows and in their civil oath. It was perfectly fair, as they were held themselves, that they should hold each other to the most stringent terms of their joint and common obligations. It was to be taken for granted, that each and every one of them was concerned to avert the failure of their enterprise; and if that was risked by any variance of opinion in civil or religious matters, such variance was to be held in check before it resulted in sedition or dangerous heresy.

Roger Williams was the first conspicuous subject of what is called the intolerance, the severity, aye, the cruelty, of the authorities of Massachusetts. Fact and fiction, or great misapprehension and misrepresentation, are about equally mingled in the popular reading of his story. An enterprise to which he fortuitously committed himself, helped alike by the sort of discomfitures and compulsory straits which it encountered, as well as by any deliberate and intentional purpose of his own thrown into it, was crowned with the same success as was reached by Massachusetts through another process. His purity of character, his integrity, perseverance, and magnanimity, and his lengthened life, give a personal and historic interest to his career. But none the less was he the occasion of much trouble here. The quarrel which he had on this soil was of his own originating. If he had had his way a grievous wrong would have been visited on the colonists. He found occasion, indeed, to reconsider, with maturer wisdom, the course he had pursued here, when the adoption or imitation of it by some of his own associates in Rhode Island led him to ask sympathy and aid from Massachusetts.

Sir William Martin, a warm friend of the colony and of Governor Winthrop, in a letter to the latter from England (in March, 1636), after Williams had come under censure, wrote as follows:—

"I am sorry to hear of Mr. Williams' separation from you. His former good affections to you and the plantations were well known to me, and make me wonder now at his proceedings. I have wrote to him effectually to submit to better judgements, and especially to those whom formerly he reverenced and admired; at least, to keep the bond of peace inviolable. This hath been always my advice; and nothing conduceth more to the good of plantations. I pray show him what lawful favor you can, which may stand with the common good. He is passionate and precipitate, which may transport him into error; but I hope his integrity and good intentions will bring him at last into the way of truth, and confirm him therein. In the mean time, I pray God to give him a right use of this affliction."[1]

This kindly and impartial estimate of Williams was made by one who evidently knew him well. It corresponds at every point with the view which a fair-minded reader would take of his case as history.

Williams came here in 1631 as a young, ardent, and strongly self-willed man, at his own prompting. He was not a proprietor in the company, and never became a freeman of it. He was a rigid separatist from the English Church, in which he had been a minister; while the authorities of Massachusetts were not so rigid, certainly not in avowal, as Williams wished them to be. He was invited, on his arrival, as he long after affirmed, though there is no other testimony to the fact, to become the teacher of the Boston Church; which he says he refused to do, because its members would not humble themselves for their former communion with the English Church, and renounce it. He served a short time in the ministry at Salem, though the Court remonstrated at his being put into that office, both because of that severe judgment of his already mentioned, as also because of an opinion for which he stood stoutly, that the power of the magistrates and of government should be limited to civil affairs, taking no cognizance of an infraction of the first four commandments. This opinion and avowal of Williams, of course struck a fatal blow at the very life of the "Theocrasie," which the Fathers of Massachusetts were establishing. He made warm friends in Salem, notwithstanding the restlessness of his spirit. Yet, for reasons not known to us, he left there within a year, and shared a more congenial ministry with the separatist pastor, Mr. Smith, at Plymouth. The excellent and

[1] Hutch. Coll. Papers, p. 106.

gentle Elder Brewster, and the judicious and even-tempered Governor Bradford, both had occasion to mark his hastiness of spirit and his "unsettled judgment," though they loved him. They were glad to have him go away; and on his return to Salem, in 1633, they addressed a word of caution on his account to his old friends. While he was at Plymouth, he had shown to the authorities there a written paper, in which he struck another blow against the very fundamentals of any local government to be administered on this soil, by denying the validity of any rights conferred by the patents held by the colonists. This treatise coming to the knowledge of the authorities of Massachusetts on his return to Salem, he was summoned to answer for it. In the only single instance known to us in his life, of his yielding in judgment or pertinacity, — and even this instance, as it proved, was not to be permanently an exception, — he penitently confessed that he was in error, submitted to the judgment of the Court, and consented that his treatise should be burned. The magistrates in vain tried to prevent the Salem Church from putting him into office in 1634, and withheld a grant of land from that town on account of this contumacy. He was again summoned before the Court in 1635, for having broken his promise by renewing his assault upon the patent, for calling the English churches, reproachfully, anti-Christian, and for denying the right to put an unregenerate person under oath in a civil court. Altercation and acrimony mingled in this dispute. The result which might reasonably — and shall we not say, fairly? — be expected, came in the form of this judgment, by the Court, Sept. 3, 1635: —

"Whereas, Mr. Roger Williams, one of the elders of the Church of Salem, hath broached and divulged divers new and dangerous opinions against the authority of magistrates, as also writ letters of defamation both of the magistrates and churches here, and that before any conviction, and yet maintaineth the same without retraction, it is therefore ordered,"

that he depart from the jurisdiction within six weeks, failing of which he was to be sent away, never to return without leave. On account of the season, his time was extended to the next spring. As he was planning for a settlement on Narragansett Bay, and continued to keep Salem in a ferment, the magistrates concluded to ship him for England. This coming to his knowledge, he anticipated the measure by starting off, as his last biographer, Mr. R. A. Guild, thinks, in a shallop, and "coasting probably from place to place during the 'fourteen weeks' that he 'was sorely tossed,' and holding intercourse with the native tribes, whose language he had acquired."[1]

Less than a dozen close friends accompanied Williams; and the supporters which he left behind him were reduced to about the same number, when the nature and tendency of his self-willed course were fully realized. Much romantic and sympathizing interest has been connected with his supposed wilderness experience. But all the settlers were in a wilderness then, and it would have been a wilder one than it was, on the edge of our Bay, if the disorganizing notions of Williams had had sway. There was no intentional inhumanity in the treatment of him. He might have gone to friends in Plymouth. He had no right of residence here, and his course was not such as to give him a claim on courtesy or hospitality. We must not transfer our sense of security, our tolerance, and our familiarity with what are to us harmless extravagances, to our Fathers, and then wonder why they allowed this well-meaning but troublesome man to visit upon them such fears. It was a matter of life or death with them.

Cotton Mather's oft-quoted saying about Williams, "that he had a windmill in his head," is not exactly true. A windmill admits of being adjusted to breezes and currents, however fickle; and its use depends upon its turning these breezes to account in ministering to the homely necessities of the body's life. Williams had in him neither mechanical nor moral appliances or impulses for seeking any selfish ends. He was sound to the core in integrity, frank, disingenuous, and large-hearted.

John Quincy Adams best characterized him on the less agreeable side of his nature, when young, by calling him "a conscientious contentious man."

In the old age of a long life, Williams, mellowed by time, and taught patience by having to deal in his own colony with such opponents and troublers as he himself had been to Massachusetts, became, even more benignantly and lovingly, what he had

[1] Publications of the Narragansett Club, vol. i. p. 32.

always been in the real temper of his heart. His noble magnanimity disposed him to be of the highest service to Massachusetts, in averting from her peril, and establishing for her friendly relations with the Indians in threatening times. He appreciated, too, the personal kindness which he had received from individuals, who, in the exercise of their authority, had had to deal with him as a dangerous and mischievous offender. There is great tenderness in the tones and words in which, in his old age, he speaks of "that ever-honored Governor, Mr. Winthrop," who, he says, "advised him, for many high and heavenly and public ends," to steer his course to the Narragansett Bay; and also of the bounty of "that great and pious soul, Mr. Winslow;" and of others.

Mr. Williams may be classed either among the intruders or the dissentients against whom, as individuals or as classes, Massachusetts exercised its charter authority or its ecclesiastical discipline. As one who came hither unbidden, not as a member of the company, and never made a freeman under it, he might be said to have been here only on sufferance, liable to be warned off at the pleasure of the proprietors whenever his presence should prove undesirable. But as having exercised a ministry in one of the regular church assemblies of the jurisdiction, it might be claimed that he had been adopted as a full citizen. Yet that his having come into full standing in the colony would have made little, if any, difference in the course pursued towards him, may fairly be inferred from the facts now to be recognized in the dealing with a large company of dissentients springing up here, alike in full civil and church relations. These are known to us as Antinomians, and as the followers and sympathizers with Mrs. Hutchinson.

The agitation and strife connected with the Antinomian controversy, opened by Mrs. Ann Hutchinson, came dangerously near to bringing the fortunes of the young Massachusetts colony to a most disastrous ruin. Discord and division, of the most imbittered sort, among brethren, proposing a recourse to open violence with blows and arms, reached an advanced stage of sedition, and threatened complete anarchy. The peril overhung at a time when the proprietary colonists had the most reasonable and fearful forebodings of the loss of their charter by the interference of a Privy Council Commission, and also were waging war against the Pequot Indians. Those were dark and wretched days here, for the colonists, whose all was at stake. Ominously enough, too, Mrs. Hutchinson arrived here, Sept. 18, 1634, in the vessel which brought the copy of that commission. Winthrop describes her as a woman of a "ready wit and bold spirit." Strongly gifted herself, she had a gentle and weak husband, who was guided by her. She had at home enjoyed no ministrations so much as those of Cotton, and her brother-in-law, Mr. Wheelwright. She came here to put herself again under the preaching of the former. On her passage, she had raised the fears of Symmes, the minister of Charlestown, by "venting some private revelations," and by uttering some strange opinions. By his interference and warning, the admission which she sought to membership of the Boston Church was delayed, though afterwards granted. She had been here for two years, known as a ready, kindly, and most serviceable woman, especially to her own sex in their straits and sicknesses. But she anticipated the introduction of "the woman question" among the colonists in a more troublesome form than it has yet assumed for us. Joined by her brother-in-law, who was also admitted to the church, after those two quiet years she soon made her influence felt for trouble, as he did likewise. There were no newspapers in those days, no clubs, no daily mails, no gatherings for friendly intercourse, no food for the mind other than religious discoursing to vary the strain upon one class of thoughts, or to occupy the listless or social hours.

Besides the regular substantial repast of listening to many sermons, the dessert consisted of talking them over. As a general rule, men are apt to leave out something, and women are apt to put in something, in their respective reports and criticisms of sermons. The male members of the Boston Church had a weekly meeting, in which they discussed the ministrations of Cotton and Wilson. Mrs. Hutchinson organized and presided over one, held soon twice in a week, for her own sex, attended by nearly a hundred of the principal women on the peninsula and in the neighborhood. It was easy to foresee what would come of it, through one so able and earnest as herself, even if she had no novel or disjointed or disproportioned doctrine to inculcate; which, however, it proved that she had. Antinomian means a denying, or, at least, a weakening, of the obligation to observe the moral law, and to comply with the external duties; to do the works associated with the idea of internal, spiritual righteousness. It was a false or disproportioned construction of St. Paul's great doctrine of justification by faith, without the works of the law, — a doctrine which is safe only exactly as St. Paul defines and limits it, — easily misrepresented and exposed to dangerous application. Its truth is restricted to its Divine relations, and fails as it is applied between man and man. God takes the right and sincerely earnest heart-purpose for the deed, and pities and forgives shortcomings. Man sometimes will do the same, but not always: nor can man always be expected to do it, for he cannot be sure of a heart-purpose, even if it would satisfy him. A debtor burdened with obligations, with a sincere desire to pay, asks that that desire be accepted as payment. This is satisfactory to all except to the creditors. Mrs. Hutchinson was understood to teach, that one who was graciously justified by a spiritual assurance, need not be greatly concerned for outward sanctification by works. She judged and approved, or censured and discredited, the preachers whom she heard, according as they favored or repudiated that view. Her admirers accepted her opinions. Winthrop [1] ascribes to her "two dangerous errors, from which grew many branches:" "first, that the person of the Holy Ghost dwells in a justified person; second, that no sanctification can help to evidence to us our justification." Word soon went forth that Mrs. Hutchinson had pronounced in her meetings, that Mr. Cotton and her brother-in-law Wheelwright, alone of all the ministers in the colony, were under "a covenant of grace," the rest being "legalists," or under "a covenant of works." These reports, which soon became more than opinions, were blazing brands that it would be impossible to keep from reaching inflammable material. The matter of dissension was just of the sort to cause contention of the most alarming character, because concerned with matters already exaggerated in their interest, and entertained in the community with a morbidness of zeal. As the contention extended it involved all

[1] Journal, vol. i. p. 200.

the principal persons of the colony. Cotton and all but five members of the Boston Church — though one of these five was Winthrop, and another was Wilson — proved to be sympathizers with Mrs. Hutchinson; while the ministers and leading people outside in the other hamlets were strongly opposed to her. She had a partisan, moreover, of transcending influence in the young Governor Sir Henry Vane. The son of a Privy Councillor, and one of the Secretaries of State, he had (not with the sympathy of his father) given himself to zeal for the Puritan form of religion; and, by suggestion of the King, had a three years' leave of residence in New England. He had come here the year before the Antinomian controversy opened; and was but twenty-three years old. Though pure and devout, and ardent in his zeal, he had not then the practical wisdom for which Milton afterwards praised him in his noble sonnet: —

"Vane, young in years, but in sage counsels old."

So gushing was the admiration quickened in the colony toward their noble visitor, that the people at once chose him for their governor, electing Winthrop as deputy. Vane, sincere and right intentioned as he was, erred in judgment; and the results of his administration of a single year were so unsatisfactory to himself, as well as prejudicial to the colony, that he soon returned to England, disappointed and under a cloud.[1] With his strong support, and that of two other prominent magistrates and of so overwhelming a majority of the Boston Church, Mrs. Hutchinson naturally felt emboldened. The other ministers of the Bay coming to Boston to the Court, took up, and in conference, heightened the strife. The Boston Church was for introducing Wheelwright to office over them; and this design was with difficulty frustrated. He then was invited to a church gathered at Mount Wollaston. The cloud grew very dark over the colony, as the terrible war with the Pequots was coincident with

[1] Richard Baxter gives us an account of the trouble which he had, when chaplain to the garrison in Coventry, with "one or two persons who came among us from New England, of Sir Henry Vanes party, and one Anabaptist tailor." (Life, Part I.) Baxter unfairly attributes to the Anabaptist party, as largely composed "of abundance of young, transported zealots, and a medley of opinionists," the responsibility of bringing forth "the horrid sects of Ranters, Seekers, and Quakers, in the land." (Life, Part II.)

the threatenings of sedition. Meetings of ministers and of magistrates, separately and jointly, were held; at one of which the plain-spoken Hugh Peter opened his mind, without compliment of matter or manner, to the young governor.

Mrs. Hutchinson and some of her followers rose and went out of meeting when Wilson officiated. Bitterness and rancor came between former friends. A General Fast Day was appointed for pacification. But Wheelwright preached a sermon of an exciting character, quoting passages from the Old Testament intimating a recourse to arms and violence. He was at once proceeded with for sedition. Members of the Boston Church presented a petition in his behalf, for which they were disarmed and otherwise censured. He himself made an appeal to the King, which only aggravated his offence; and as Winthrop writes, "refusing to leave either the place or his public exercisings, he was disfranchised and banished." Seven years afterwards, having lived away, he reviewed his course with regret and manfully apologized for it in a letter, to the Governor for the Court, in which he said that, after long and mature consideration, he had found that the main point of difference in the controversy about justification and the evidence of it —

"is not of that nature and consequence as was then presented to me in the false glass of Satan's temptations and mine own distempered passions, which makes me unfeignedly sorry that I had such a hand in those sharp and vehement contentions raised thereabouts, to the great disturbance of the churches of Christ."

He also regrets the censoriousness of his sermon, and the countenance which he gave in it to persons of corrupt judgment; —

"and that, in the Synod, I used such unsafe and obscure expressions, falling from me as a man dazzled with the buffetings of Satan, and that I did appeal [to the King] from misapprehension of things."

He "confessed that herein he had done very sinfully, and he humbly craved pardon." This letter was dated at Wells, Sept. 10, 1643, probably after he had learned of the tragic death of his sister. His sentence of banishment was revoked.[1]

[1] Winthrop's Journal, vol. i. p. 162.

This penitence was an after work. He stood stoutly for his sister through her convention before the Court.

The civil sentence passed against her, Nov. 2, 1637, was as follows: —

"Mrs. Hutchinson (the wife of Mr. Wm Hutchinson) being convented for traducing the ministers and their ministry in this country, she declared volentarily her revelations for her ground, and that shee should be delivred, and the Court ruined, with their posterity; and thereupon was banished, and the meane while comited to Mr. Joseph Weld untill the Court shall dispose of her."[1]

After she had been sentenced to civil banishment, she was dealt with by the Church, and excommunicated. She lost her temper, and seemed once to part with veracity, on her trial. Her "revelations" were especially offensive. At one time "she made a retraction of near all" the errors attributed to her, and "declared that it was just with God to leave her to herself, as he had done, for her slighting his ordinances, both magistracy and ministry." A question involving her veracity arose, when she affirmed that she had never advanced some of the opinions charged upon her; and for this, Winthrop says, "the church with one consent cast her out," for "having impudently persisted in untruth." Many of her sympathizers at once fell away. As the summing up of the strife, seventy-six persons were disarmed;[2] two were disfranchised and fined; two more were fined; eight more were disfranchised; three were banished; and eleven who had asked permission to remove, had leave, in the form of a limitation of time within which they must do it. The more estimable and considerable of them apologized, and were received back. Those who did not, proved troublesome persons where they went. After various removes with her husband, and a vexed and troubled life, Mrs. Hutchinson, a widow, with many children and grandchildren, living on the shore opposite

[1] Records, vol. i. p. 207.

[2] There was thought to be need of especial caution in this measure of disarming. The military power of the colony had recently been organized into three regiments, carefully officered, and for the time admirably well equipped. The sound of war was in the land; and Wheelwright, in his sermon, had carried the rhetoric of battle and violence, from the Old Testament, as far as it was safe to use it for Bible champions. The authorities reasonably apprehended a direct recourse to arms.

Long Island, was murdered in the summer of 1643, on an inroad of the Indians. A daughter of eight years of age, the only survivor, was carried into captivity. Four years afterwards, she was recovered by the General Court, and brought back to Massachusetts. Edward Hutchinson, a son of this excellent though perhaps ill-balanced woman, had been among those who were disfranchised and fined. His fine of forty pounds was remitted, though I do not find any record of his restoration to full citizenship, which probably he obtained. He remained in Boston, on the removal of the family, and was a brave captain, doing good service in Philip's war, and receiving a mortal wound in Quaboag [Brookfield] fight. He was the great-grandfather of Thomas Hutchinson, our provincial governor and historian, who, in his latter capacity, seeking to subordinate filial sentiment to impartiality, has hardly done justice to his ancestress in his narration of her troubles.

Thomas Savage, another of the disarmed, had married a daughter of Mrs. Hutchinson, and afterwards he became son-in-law of her strongest enemy, Rev. Zachariah Symmes. The Hon. James Savage, his descendant, as editor and commentator of Winthrop, gives us another example of impartiality in his faithful annotations concerning the Antinomian controversy.

A period of twenty years elapsed between the struggle against Antinomianism and the special legislation against the Quakers. But the interval was divided by another contentious issue, which threatened to put the ecclesiastical basis of the government to a severer strain than it could safely bear, though still it triumphed. Again the issue was one which engaged both intruders and dissentients against the Government, though the disaffection was mainly that of transient residents and non-freemen. Mr. William Vassall, one of the original assistants, had come over with Winthrop; but, from some disaffection, had very soon returned to England. After residing there five years, he came hither again, but, by preference, to Plymouth colony. He was intensely opposed both to the civil and ecclesiastical rule set up by his old associates. Being, as Winthrop says,[1] "a man of a busy and factious spirit," and "never at rest but when in the fire of contention, he had practised with such as were not

[1] Jour., vol. i. pp. 26 and 321.

members of our churches" to initiate a new strife. Robert Child and six others, accordingly, in May, 1646, addressed a Remonstrance and Petition to the General Court, complaining that the residents here were not governed by the laws of England; that they were kept out of civil privileges as not being church-members, while church-membership was to be secured only by a covenant which was not fairly framed; that their children were denied Christian baptism, and they themselves compelled by fine to support and attend religious ministrations: for all which grievances they asked redress. The Court, having made arrangements for a synod of churches, issued, on Nov. 4, 1646, a stiff "Declaration" in answer. They insist that "y[e] Government is framed according to our charter and y[e] fundamental and common laws of England, and carried on according to the same;" adding, however, these important clauses, which we know now how to fill in with all the meaning they then implied, — "taking the words of eternal truth and righteousness along with them, as that rule by which all kingdoms and jurisdictions must render account of every act and admistration in the last day." What was so "taken along" with the laws of England, was the Bible, not by any means as of secondary authority. The "Declaration" is followed by a series of parallelisms between Magna Charta and the Colony Laws, a liberal allowance being made for statutes "alterable for occasions."[1]

The petitioners carried their appeal to Parliament, but without avail, there being then a good understanding between that Court and ours. The complaints which were zealously urged in England against the rigid and persecuting course of the authorities of Massachusetts, drew from their old associate, the noble Sir Richard Saltonstall, a letter of sharp rebuke, addressed to Cotton and Wilson, somewhere between 1645 and 1653. A leading and highly honored assistant, he had arrived here with Winthrop, June 12, 1630; but, after some trifling alienating experiences, he went back to England at the close of the following March, leaving here some of his family, but never returning himself. He continued, however, to exert his powerful influence to befriend the colony, and to circumvent its enemies at the English courts. The difficulty of his task in that capacity, rather than any doubt

[1] Hutchinson's Coll., pp. 188–218.

that he had not shared, or had lost his interest in, the religious designs of his former associates, may have prompted some of the stinging rebukes of that letter. He writes, —

"Reverend and deare friends whom I unfaynedly love and respect: It doth not a little grieve my spirit to hear what sadd things are reported dayly of your tyranny and persecutions in New England, as that you fyne, whip and imprison men for their consciences. First, you compel such to come into your assemblies, as you know will not join with you in your worship, and when they show their dislike thereof or witniss against it, then you styrre up your magistrates to punish them for such (as you conceyve) their public affronts. Truly, friends, this your practice of compelling any in matters of worship to doe that whereof they are not fully persuaded, is to make them sin, for so the Apostle (Rom. 14 and 23) tells us, and many are made hypocrites thereby, conforming in their outward man for fear of punishment."

He prays for them and hopes they will —

"not practice those courses in a wilderness which you went so farre to prevent. These rigid wayes have layed you very lowe in the hearts of the saynts. I doe assure you I have heard them pray in the publique assemblies, that the Lord would give you meeke and humble spirits, not to stryve so much for uniformity, as to keep the unity of the spirit, in the bond of peace. — I hope you do not assume to yourselves infallibilitie of judgement, when the most learned of the Apostles confesseth he knew but in part, and saw but darkely as thro a glass. Oh that all those who are brethren, tho yet they cannot thinke and speake the same things, might be of one accord in the Lord."[1]

Cotton, for himself and for his brother Wilson, replied to this letter of frank and friendly rebuke, in a spirit of loving respect for the writer, but disclaiming all blame, and standing stoutly for their Bible model in their proceedings. Saltonstall had been at least fourteen years withdrawn from any present share of administering "the church in the wilderness." Away from the tentative processes and the actual difficulties of the scheme on trial here, he had the equally tasking responsibility of meeting the perplexities which it involved on the other side of the water.

The saddest and darkest stain upon the early annals of Massachusetts attaches to the treatment of the people called Quakers. And yet the fair and full rehearsal of the facts which

[1] Hutchinson Papers, pp. 401–407.

compose a faithful narrative of what, beginning in comedy ended in tragedy, will certainly avail to relieve the burden of wanton and ruthless cruelty cast upon our legislators. Two leading positions must be taken at the start.

First, it is to be frankly admitted, that those legislators, though beyond measure provoked and goaded to the course which they pursued, and though they acted with slow deliberation, and were always ready to interpose mercy for judgment, did nevertheless, as seen in the light of our day, act very unwisely; allowed their timid fears to master their reason, and committed themselves to a dilemma, either horn of which humiliated and tortured them.

Second, it is to be as frankly and positively affirmed, that their Quaker tormentors were the aggressive party; that they wantonly initiated the strife, and with a dogged pertinacity persisted in outrages which drove the authorities almost to frenzy; while with a stiff temper of audacity, as the authorities saw it, but of fidelity to holy duty as they felt, they courted the extreme penalties which they might at any moment have escaped, except through constraint of their "inspirations."

This episode in our history, mingled of the ludicrous and the dismal, dates from more than a quarter of a century after the planting of the colony. Many of the wiser and gentler spirits which at first had sway here, and whose judgment would doubtless have stopped short of the tragic inflictions visited on four so-called Quakers, had gone to their rest. Winthrop, Cotton, Wilson, and others like them, as they passed away, left the administration of affairs in State and Church to men more stern and less wise than themselves. In the mean while, foreign and domestic troubles and perplexities had contributed to endanger the colony, to threaten its liberties, and to make the management of its affairs even more difficult. The emergencies of the time made it of the most critical necessity to keep out all disturbers, to secure internal harmony, and to cling to the well-proved safeguards of the first enterprise.

The root of the prevalent superficial opinion, founded upon an unintelligent, cursory, and hap-hazard way of writing and reading our history, and which heaps an unrelieved burden of censure upon our colonial court for its proceedings against the Quakers, presents itself at once to an impartial inquirer. Misapprehension and error, leading to positive injustice to our legislators, come in the popular mind, from identifying modern Quakers with the sort of persons whom our Fathers knew and dealt with under that name. When one or a group of those excellent people known as Friends is seen quietly passing our streets, if any descendant of our colonists, or any foreign-born citizen, trusting to ignorance in the lack of knowledge, should say to himself, "Those are the sort of people who, two hundred years ago, were imprisoned, whipped, and mutilated here, and four of whom were hung on Boston Common," he would need to be sent back to the record.

The intrusive, pestering, indecent, and railing disturbers of early Massachusetts, lawless and ignorant as most of them were, have scarcely a single point of affinity with the dignified and highly esteemed Friends of our day. These last are, and for several generations have been, especially noted for quietude of spirit, for a grave solemnity of demeanor, and a modest unobtrusiveness. Indeed, it would be hard to define stronger points of contrast in speech, conduct, and even in some important matters of opinion and religious belief, than those which really distinguished between the first and the modern Quakers. Those whom our Fathers knew were of the type of Fox and Burroughs and Naylor.[1]

[1] In vol. i. pp. 10 to 158, of Burton's Parliamentary Diary, may be read the curious and wearisome debate upon the case of Naylor, extending over eleven days. That the wise and gravè men of the English Parliament of 1656 should have found material in that case for so long a discussion, when so much important business had to be postponed by it, is in itself a suggestive fact. The perusal of that tedious story will nevertheless reward a reader, if he will take it as a chapter of the struggle and development of opinion concerning full liberty of conscience. Naylor, however, was indicted and condemned for blasphemy. He had rode into Bristol in a guise, and with observances, imitating the entry of Jesus Christ into Jerusalem. The indictment against him was: "That he assumed the gesture, words, names, and attributes of our Saviour, Christ." Narrowly escaping capital punishment, he was sentenced to be pilloried and whipped in two places in London, to have his tongue bored with a hot iron, to be branded on the forehead with the letter B, to be sent to Bristol, there to ride "on a horse bare-ridged, with his face back," to be whipped again, and then brought back to prison in London, debarred the use of pen, ink, and paper, and of all food but what he should labor for. Cruelly treated as he had been, the victim for a time of an insane enthusiasm, and of the fanatical folly of some admirers, he was for a time disowned by the Quakers. Coming to his senses after two years' imprisonment, he grieved over his delusions, and became an approved and effective preacher. His utterances just before his death have a deep tenderness, sweetness, and beauty.

In "An addition to the book entitled, 'The Spirit of the Martyrs revived,'" published just one hundred years after the first coming of the Quakers to Massachusetts, Joseph Bolles, one of the earnest Friends, draws a censorious contrast, "concerning the difference between the former Quakers, that suffered Persecutions and these in this day," as follows: —

"If we may know them by their Fruits, they were two manner of People; the first often going to Meeting Houses, and bearing a godly testimony, after the speaker had done [not always waiting for that, however], also Teaching and Exhorting at other public places, for which they suffered much Persecution, which they took joyfully, being upheld by the Power of God. And these, only holding Meetings of their own in a formal way, as other Professors do, having a form of Godliness, and not the Power and Life thereof, as the suffering Quakers had; minding earthly things, being adulterated and living in the friendship of the World, which is enmity with God. So these, not having the spirit as the first Quakers had, are no more to be compared with them, than a dead Tree may be compared to a living Tree."

The writer was certainly unjust in thus making the difference wrought by a century to consist only in this, that the first Quakers kept themselves alive by disturbing other people, while his contemporaries stagnated among themselves. The Friends did not settle into quietude, till they had secured a general recognition of the vitalities of their system of truth. They have ever since met the unpopularity of standing for advanced and unwelcome truths, and for reforms.

Those whom we know are of the type of Penn, Barclay, and Whittier. The conduct, at least, of those who first bore the name, would find its severest rebukers in such as now bear it. As to religious opinions, or theology, distinctly characteristic of the intruders here, it is curious to note how little those had to do with the strife. Penn and Barclay wrought out for the Friends, a religious system for belief and practice which would do honor to any fellowship of Christians at the present time. But that was the product of a later age of Quakerism, calmly, intelligently, and even philosophically elaborated by nobly endowed men. The crude and indigested notions which the early Quakers uttered "in a prophetical way," sounded like the wildest rant, to be relieved of the reproach of blasphemy only by being referred to a besotted stupidity or a shade of distraction. Our Fathers cared little, if at all, for the Quaker theology. They did not get so far as that in dealing with them. Not being inclined to accept the account which the Quakers gave of themselves as being under the peculiar guidance of the Holy Spirit, our Fathers dealt with them on the score of their manners, their lawlessness, and their offensive speech and behavior. Yet it is also true that the peculiar set of Quakers who came and testified, and defiantly insisted upon returning and staying here, would not have been in all respects exactly what they were, nor have done all that they did, and as they did, if they had not had just such persons to deal with them as they confronted here.

We, indeed, in the calm retrospect by which we study past developments of new opinions, and in the intelligent analysis which we make of the working elements that go to the production of a fresh truth, can apprehend the high and pure motive which not only led, but really inspired, those unwelcome missionaries to our Bay. They were the advanced pleaders for a liberty which is now our life, for a form of faith and piety which alone has power for a free soul. The most illiterate and incoherent of them had the Divine gift. They put their sincerity beyond all question, by their often meek, but always unflinching, endurance of contumely and violence. And, without doubt, much of their terrible abusiveness of language was wholly free from malice and any ill-intention, but was prompted wholly from an honest and severely righteous sense of the errors and superstitions which they assailed. But all this, we must again remind ourselves, is from our own point of view, not from that of our Fathers. The colonists had themselves suffered for opinion's sake. They, too, had their visions, not "of private interpretation," and they thought they had a skill in "trying spirits," and must look for the devil always under a disguise.

George Fox, the reputed founder of the system of belief and practice known as Quakerism, has come to stand in many sketchy and æsthetic essays, as a profoundly original genius, a man of nature's own large endowing, a seer and an organizer. He was nothing of the sort. A cursory perusal of those old books describing the heresies and sectaries then abounding in England, to which I have referred, will convince a reader that, before Fox came upon the stage, all the fancies, scruples, and oddities of opinion and behavior by which he and his companions first won their notoriety, were all ready for their adoption. Fox was an eclectic. He picked up in the various places where he wandered, and from the mixed and multiform company with which he associated, every one of his peculiar ideas and crotchets.

Though he had a native vigor of understanding, and a soul of sincerity and purity, he was an illiterate and ill-balanced man. Shoemaker and shepherd as he was by turns, he was given to hypochondriac meditations; and when, with his seeking and inquisitive mind, he commenced his rovings, he found stimulant and food for his morbidly eccentric nature in any shred of truth which he gathered on the way. The fellowship which he drew around him was of those like himself, waiting — as the phrase went — for some one who would "speak to their condition," and then ready by public or private harangues, "testimonies," or "prophetical burdens," to make that condition of theirs a standard for trying other peoples' spirits. Some of the sect did get hold of, and urge with earnest, simple eloquence, living truths which lay latent in the Christian Scriptures, unrecognized and unapplied, according to their due value and authority, by the Church of their day. But the Quakers threw these fresh truths out of their proportions and relations in dealing with them.

If Fox, as he once purposed, had gone into physic, instead of into divinity, he would not have led so harmless a life. But, as a preacher, he was known as a disturber of the peace, a reviler of other ministers of religion, and of magistrates. His tongue was a sharp one, though he referred its sharpness to the Spirit. He railed and testified in all public places and assemblies, and of course was buffeted, mobbed, and put into jail. He was one of those harmless enthusiasts, who are best reduced to soberness by being to a degree listened to, and then let alone. But neither he nor his fellows would have been satisfied with being slighted: nor were those whom they abused and reviled, inclined to give them the benefit of indifference. Some of his associates far exceeded him in their offensiveness of speech and behavior. The English jails soon became filled with Quakers, who, curiously enough, were by many regarded as disguised Popish emissaries of the Franciscan order in the service of Rome. Baxter rashly asserts that many such friars had been found speaking in the Quaker assemblies.

The home-field of England, Ireland, and Scotland, inviting and rewarding as it was, soon proved too limited for the missionary zeal of the new enthusiasts. Men and women of the sect soon found "the burden and call of their spirit" to carry their testimony over the earth. The continent of Europe, with its princes and peasants, offered them promising opportunities, and the Pope and the Grand Turk received visits from them.

Our Fathers were on the watch for an inroad of these despised but dreaded intruders some considerable time before they found their way hither. Through letters from friends at home, and the abounding pamphlets of religious controversy of those days, the people of Massachusetts were well informed as to the spirit and actings of the Quakers. Dangerous books had already been found circulating in the colony, and had been proscribed by law in 1654; especially some of those of John Reeves and Ludovick Muggleton, "the two last Witnesses," which contained similar notions to those advanced by Fox. The authorities were on the alert. Indeed, but a few weeks before the first two Quakers arrived here, a solemn Fast-day had been kept in the colony, the first object of which was stated to be, "to seek the face of God in behalf of our native country, in reference to the abounding of errors, especially those of Ranters and Quakers."[1]

It was not till July, 1656, ten years after the first preaching of Fox, that the unwelcome news was circulated in Boston, that a ship in the harbor, from Barbadoes, had on board two women Quakers. One of these, Mary Fisher, had visited the Grand Turk, at Adrianople. By order of the magistrates, they were searched and committed to jail, and their books were burned; the master of the vessel being put under bonds to take them away again. Hardly were they got rid of, than a vessel arrived from England, having on board four Quaker men, and as many women, together with a ninth passenger, a man, who, having come on board at Long Island, had been converted by his companions. They were committed to jail, examined, and found by their abusive

[1] Rec., iv. (1) 276.

speech to belong to a class of persons for whom there was no room or welcome here. Gorton, from Rhode Island, found means to communicate with them in jail, proposing to get them out of the vessel somewhere along the coast, as the master of it, in conformity with his heavy bonds, was carrying them out of this jurisdiction. But the magistrates thwarted Gorton's purpose.

Then began a series of deliberative and legislative measures on the part of our authorities, founded, as they believed, on their full right to secure themselves from the seditious and rancorous visitors; either by warning them off from coming, or by at once banishing them on their arrival, with some form of punishing for a return those who, having come more than once, were to be shipped off again. There was a gradation and an adaptation of the penalties enacted, designed to be fitly and righteously adjusted to the measure of provocation, insolence, and defiance exhibited by the intruders themselves. In every previous instance in which any offender had been banished from the jurisdiction, the sentence had been effective. No one who had suffered it had ever defied it by returning hither again. The magistrates had reason to suppose that that measure would be sufficient for their protection in the case of the Quakers. When it is considered, too, that any shipmaster who should bring such as passengers, was liable to a heavy fine, and to other enforced charges; and also, that any resident who should harbor or encourage a Quaker, would be severely dealt with for the offence, — it might appear as if good manners, and generosity and magnanimity of spirit, would have kept the Quakers away. Certainly, by every rule of right and reason, they ought to have kept away. They had no rights or business here, and a simple prohibition ought to have been sufficient even to release their consciences from all obligation to meddle with other people's consciences. Most clearly, they courted persecution, suffering, and death; and, as the magistrates affirmed, "they rushed upon the sword." Those magistrates never intended them harm, nor would have done them harm, except as they believed that all their successive measures and sharper penalties were positively necessary to secure their jurisdiction from the wildest lawlessness and an absolute anarchy.

But they erred in their calculation, reasonable as it was. They little knew how stiff and indomitable was the will of a Quaker, what a new energy and persistency of purpose came of a conscience reinforced and guided by a supposed inspiration from above. An hour's meditation, in some favorable mood of mind or feeling, would lead a Quaker to the persuasion, that a certain utterance from his lips, or a certain course of conduct, was as clearly indicated to him by God, as if a commission had floated down to him from the visible heavens.

These "revelations" came in a very simple form, as promptings or directions, which the subjects of them seem to have been persuaded that they could distinguish, by some test of quality or intensity, from the mere impulses or inclinations which it would be unwise to yield to. Thus, two of the victims on whom fell the last penalty of Massachusetts law, as we shall soon have to read, gave this account of their reasons for provoking that penalty. William Robinson, being in Rhode Island, felt that "the Lord had commanded him to go to Boston, and to lay down his life there." Marmaduke Stevenson, at Barbadoes,

> "heard that New England had made a law to put the servants of the living God to death, if they returned after they were sentenced away. Immediately came the Word of the Lord unto me, saying, 'Thou knowest not but that thou mayest go thither.' — So after that, a vessel was made ready for Rhode Island, which I passed in; and the Word of the Lord came unto me, saying, 'Go to Boston with thy brother William Robinson,'" &c.[1]

It was in vain that ministers and magistrates pressed any Quaker who returned here, after being banished the second, third, and fourth time, and complained of persecution, with the argument, that the Master, in whose name he professed to preach, had expressly instructed his disciples, that, "when persecuted in one place, they should flee to another." The Quaker had a revelation which nullified that command.

With the purpose and aim of impartiality held in the mind of one who is historically dealing with this episode, it seems as if the only way to secure it, is to divide between the parties either censure or palliation. The facts cannot be written with-

[1] Miscellaneous Papers in the State House.

out the use of the stronger and the harsher adjectives on both sides. There was no down, or rosewater, or language of compliment, in use among them. Stern, sinewy, Saxon speech, and a calling of things by their right names, and a setting before us of pitched combatants in the attitude of striking and striking back, alone befit the facts. We like to feel that the fight was fair on both sides. One party represented a renovated Israel on the ocean border of a wilderness, seeking, with wrong or malice for none outside of them, to obey the call of God in planting a religious Commonwealth. They required peace and harmony. The other party had new light; and they felt upon them the obligation of making the darkness comprehend it The Quakers had hold in common of an advanced truth, quick with the energy of the Spirit. There was accord enough among them to assure them that their oracles were not private delusions. Their oracles were, indeed, better than the utterance of them.

There was much that was irritating and aggravating in the sharpest degree, — and intended to be such — in the language and conduct of the Quakers. Their persistency, their seeming wilfulness, and aimless spirit of annoyance, indicated a set purpose of defying all remonstrance, and of inviting a violent handling.

I do not know that an essay has ever been written upon the satisfactions of being *persecuted*, as the word is, especially when that persecution is incurred by persecuting other people.[1] But there is matter for such an essay, and for its copious and rich illustration. The men and women who regarded themselves as led by the Spirit to give "testimony," which, as things then were, would subvert all civil and religious order in this colony, and overwhelm it with confusion and anarchy, — while travelling through the wilderness, or coursing inland waters, or pinched in the stocks, or screaming out through barred windows,—doubtless took an appreciable comfort in their own "sufferings." They felt that they entered thereby into the fellowship of prophets and martyrs. An hour of brooding and elated thought lifted them

[1] Worcester defines *persecute* thus: "To pursue with malignity or enmity; to harass with penalties; to afflict; to distress; to oppress; — generally on account of opinions." Webster's definition is, "To pursue in a manner to injure, vex, or afflict; to cause to suffer pain from hatred or malignity; to harass; to beset in an annoying way." The reader may make his own selection and application.

to heights of intense enthusiasm. A spell wrought upon their spirits; and they yielded themselves, as they thought, to a guidance from above. Their full sincerity was proved by their shrinking from no burden, mortification, sacrifice, or pain, which lay in their way of obligation. Modest and pure women, under this spell, would rush into the public highways, or into a crowded place of worship, and, independent of all the art or materials of dressmakers, would make a distressing spectacle of themselves. One such, coming into a meeting-house in this condition, had smeared herself with black paint, — as a sign, she said, of the black-pox, which she prophesied God would send on this cruel jurisdiction.

I have before me a copy, which I made from a miscellaneous mass of manuscripts in our archives in the State House, of official papers connected with the legislation and the proceedings against the Quakers. Among these are many original letters, on scraps of paper, written, in the jail, by imprisoned Quakers to their friends or to the magistrates. Most of these, even those whose grammar, diction, and chirography indicate the least of culture, express, often with great sweetness and gentleness of spirit, a heroism of heart and a self-centred calm of conviction fully befitting witnesses for the truth of God. In general, these papers fail of bearing out the charge of our own authorities, that the Quakers were beyond measure abusive in their speech. And it is probable that the sternness of face which was set against them, the rough handling which they received, and the offensive epithets applied to them, occasionally irritated them into coarseness and violence of language not habitual with them.

Some livelier specimens of their rhetoric than any which I have found in our own records, passed under my eyes among the rich stores of the British Museum.

Among these is a tract[1] bearing this title: —

"N. England's Ensigne, It being the Account of Cruelty, the Professors' Pride, and the Articles of their Faith; signified in characters written in blood, wickedly begun, barbarously continued and inhumanly finished (so far as they have gone) by the present power of darkness possest in the Priests and Rulers in N. England, with the Dutch also

[1] Numbered in Catalogue, 493. h/6

inhabiting the same land. In a bloody and cruel birth which the Husband to the Whore of Babylon hath brought forth by ravishing and torturing the seed of the Virgin of Israel," &c. "Written at sea, by us whom the wicked in scorn call Quakers."

Of this, Humphrey Norton was the writer. The Massachusetts people are described as "Cruel English Jewes." New England is "the most vainest and beastliest place of all Bruits [brutes], the most publicly prophane, and the most covertly corrupt." One of his company, he says, went to the meeting-house in Martha's Vineyard; "and after the Priest Thomas Maho [Mayhew] had done his speech, unspake a few words." Being thrust out for this, he repeated his visit in the afternoon. Here is a graphic piece of etching: —

"A man that hath a covetous and deceitful rotten heart; lying lips which abound among them, and a smooth, fawning, flattering tongue, and short hair, and a deadly enmity against those that are called Quakers and others that oppose their wayes, such a hypocrite is a fit man to be a member of any N. England church.

"J. Rous and H. Norton were moved to go to the great meeting house at Boston upon one of their Lector days, where we found John Norton their teacher set up, who like a babling Pharisee run over a vain repetition near an hour long (like an impudent smooth fac'd harlot, who was telling her Paramoors a long fair story of her husband's kindness, while nothing but wantonness and wickedness is in her heart.) When his glass was out he begun his sermon, wherein, amongst many lifeless expressions, he spake much of the danger of these who are called Quakers. Some of his hearers gaped on him as if they expected honey should have dropped from his lips. And amongst other of his vain conceits he uttered this, (whereby he plainly discovered the blindness and rottenness of his heart,) that the Justice of God is the Armor of the Devil: the which, if true, then is the Devil sometimes covered with Justice: which is more than ever I heard any of his servants say on his behalf before," &c.

"13th of 2d Month, 1658 Sarah Gibbins and Dorothy Waugh spoke at Lector. Death fed Death through the painted sepulchre John Norton." And, "as a sign of his emptiness," the women broke two empty bottles over him.

The same lively journal contains an impudent letter to Governor "Indicot." If there was an epithet beyond all others offensive to a New-England minister, it was that of "Priest" which the Quakers so freely used. "Baal's priests," "the seed of the Serpent," "the brood of Ishmael," were other titles. We can hardly conceive of the indignation caused by these wanton disturbances of the exercises of the "Thursday Lecture."

It is possible, that, when a Puritan congregation was startled and shocked by such an apparition among them as that of an unclothed woman, or by a less indecent method of Quaker testifying, the minister may at the moment have been reading from the Bible, how one of the old prophets had, without his garments, delivered himself in a similar prophetical way of his burden. Our Fathers listened to the holy record of such doings with the profoundest reverence; but the living imitation infuriated them. They could not, or they would not, on the bare word of the Quakers themselves, believe that they were inspired directly from the Holy God. They had another way of accounting for the phenomena. Yet who can doubt but that some high-wrought fervors, or some sweet inward satisfactions, compensated the reproachings, buffetings, and whippings which the victims drew upon themselves. Indeed, they often contrived to make rather a good thing of it. They rallied and comforted and reinforced each other. They would not work in the prisons, nor pay jail fees. They excited the sympathy of some of the tender and less rigid members of the colony, who would introduce food into the windows of the prison, and who very soon began to protest against the cruelty used towards them, and to listen favorably to their utterances. This sympathy for the Quakers, so likely to be, and so soon actually, followed by discipleship among our own people, was what the magistrates greatly dreaded. Many of their harsher measures they regarded as simply cautions and safeguards against the spread of Quaker notions with the weaker and more sympathetic among themselves. If a Quaker in prison could get pen, paper, and ink-horn, — or, failing the last, blood from a pricked finger would serve, — he would address a missive to magistrates and ministers, not always conciliatory. There are many of these preserved in our State House. As the parties to this terrible struggle came better to understand each other, the terms of either party were as follows: —

The magistrates, regarding the opinions and conduct of the Quakers as seditious and blasphemous, resolved, in the exercise of their charter-rights, to keep them out, or to drive them out, of their jurisdiction; steadily increasing the penalties against such as, having been again and again banished, returned.

The Quakers, on their part, — assured that persecution among Christians was wicked, that the Puritan church-way was oppressive and wrong, and that its intolerance could be worn down and worn out only by the most resolute defiance and endurance of penalties, — professed their purpose, in the name and under the power of God, to persecute the persecutors till they ceased to persecute. It was a struggle between two indomitable wills; the one fortified by a parchment charter and a church covenant, the other borne up by an intense conviction of direct spiritual guidance. Our sympathies must go — for go they will — with those who thus held to a still inspiring and revealing God, beyond the contents of a Book taken by its letter.

There is something more yet to be said, in order that we may set the constituted authorities of Massachusetts in the light in which they themselves stood and acted. Their horror of fanaticism in religion had been learned and intensified from the terrible extravagancies and the bloody tragedies connected with the wild doings of the Anabaptists of Munster under King John, the tailor of Leyden, in the century preceding. Visions of a repetition of these frenzies came up before the horrified minds of our magistrates and ministers; and they felt the responsibility of averting what they so often in their records call up in reference to these mad Anabaptists. Again, mutilation of the body had been made familiar to them in England, as a penalty for malignity, sedition, and heresy. They may have seen Leighton, Burton, Prynne, and Bastwick,[1] as thus mutilated by the

[1] Dr. Leighton, for his book against Prelacy, had been sentenced "to suffer the loss of both ears, to have his nostrils slit, his forehead branded, to be publicly whipped, fined ten thousand pounds, and perpetually imprisoned." The sentence was executed to the letter, save that he was set at liberty by the Long Parliament, after twelve years' confinement, when he could neither see, hear, nor walk.

Henry Burton, Dr. Bastwick, and William Prynne were mutilated in a similar manner. The last of these having been sentenced a second time to a part of the punishment, the stumps of his ears were sawed out. These acts were done under Episcopal and Royal sanction. It is melancholy to think that they should have to

highest English law. And, once more, our Fathers regarded Quakers as representing for them, of danger and evil, exactly what plotting Jesuits represented to the realm of England. The penalty of death, on Quakers coming here a fourth time after banishment, was copied by them from the English statute against Jesuits. The mutilation law was never but partially enforced here.

The miscellaneous manuscripts of scraps of paper, to which I have referred as now among the old files in the State House, enable us to trace the course of proceedings in this harassing experience, and contain much curious matter. By an order of Court, June 10, 1658, the Rev. John Norton was appointed to write and publish a treatise against the Quakers. This he did, under the title of "The Heart of New England rent by the Blasphemies of the present Generation," &c.; and he received a grant of land for his remuneration. The Court had been moved to ask this service of him; and to other measures, by the zeal of the sterner portion of their constituents. In October, 1658, a petition was addressed to the Court from leading citizens of Boston, in which they asked for severer laws against the Quakers. The dangers and ruin threatening from their behavior and testimonies, and the darkly drawn apprehensions of the same horrors as followed from Anabaptism at Munster, are alleged as justifying a law inflicting death upon such as should return from banishment. Singularly enough, the names of several of the signers of this petition indicate them as some of those who had been censured and disarmed, for having signed the petition in behalf of Mr. Wheelwright. Some persons here had evidently changed sides, from that of sufferers to that of advocates of the sternest discipline.[1]

As I have said, there was a steadily progressive legislation of enactments and penalties undertaken by Massachusetts, designed to meet and punish the successive acts of boldness and con-

a degree been imitated by the Puritan against the Quaker. It is remarkable, however, that, even after his second barbarous punishment, Mr. Prynne should have written a book to prove "that Christian Kings and magistrates have authority, under the Gospel, to punish idolatry, apostasy, heresy, blasphemy, and obstinate schism, with pecuniary, corporal, and, in some cases, with capital punishments." (Wood's Athen Ox., ii. pp. 811-827.)

[1] Vol. of Miscel. Papers in the State House, p. 246, &c.

tumacy, on the part of the Quakers, — prison, fines, whippings, mutilation of ears and tongue, branding, and the gallows. Sad, sad indeed, was the climax to which our Fathers were led on, from an error at the start. They sought, with only partial success, to induce the other New-England colonies to keep pace with them in legislation against the Quakers. Rhode Island, as furnishing a harborage for all sorts of consciences, made our Fathers uncomfortable, because from it the Quakers had such a ready access to our jurisdiction. Would that Massachusetts, in her own course with them, had anticipated the method suggested in the sly wisdom of the reply which she received from Benedict Arnold, the President of Rhode Island, in answer to a request that that colony would imitate the legislation of the Bay colony against the Quakers. Arnold, speaking for his associates, says : —

"We find that in those places where this people aforesaid, in this Colony, are most of all suffered to declare themselves freely, and are only opposed by arguments in discourse, there they least of all desire to come. And we are informed that they begin to loathe this place, for that they are not opposed by the civil authority; but with all patience and meekness are suffered to say over their pretended revelations and admonitions. Nor are they like or able to gain many here to their way. Surely, we find that they like to be persecuted by civil powers; and, when they are so, they are like to gain more adherents by the conceit of their patient sufferings, than by consent to their pernicious sayings." (R. I. Records, i. 377.) [1]

But even the all-including tolerance of Roger Williams suf-

[1] Our historian, Hutchinson, tries to divide equally his censure upon our magistrates and the Quakers, when he speaks (Hist. i. 380) of "the strange delusion the Quakers were under, in courting persecution; and the imprudence of the authorities in gratifying this humour, as far as their utmost wishes could carry them."

The famous Richard Baxter, of Kidderminster, who had been greatly exercised and annoyed by the personal abuse visited on him by Quakers, came at last to learn the same wise way of humoring them. He writes in his Life : —

"The Quakers would fain have got entertainment, and set up a meeting in the town, and frequently railed at me in the congregation; but when I had once given them leave to meet in the church for a dispute, and, before the people, had opened their deceits and shame, none would entertain them more, nor did they get one proselyte among us."

One of his most pertinent questions to them concerning their doctrine of the "inner light," which they said all men had, was this: "If all have it, why may not I have it?"

fered a strain too much from the Quakers. Rowing in a skiff over the Narragansett Bay, quickened by his ever-ardent love of disputation, to match himself against some of them, the keen-spirited old man had a sore trial of his patience. He afterwards wrote of Quakers, —

> "They are insufferably proud and contemptuous. I have, therefore, publicly declared myself, that a due and moderate restraint and punishment of these incivilities, though pretending conscience, is so far from persecution properly so called, that it is a duty and command of God unto all mankinde, first in Families, and thence into all mankinde Societies." [1]

The summing up of the severities in our own colony is as follows: twenty-two Quakers were banished on pain of death; four were hung, one a woman; three lost the right ear; one was branded in the hand with the letter H; between thirty and forty were whipped.

The death penalty was legalized by only a majority of two in the General Court; and was so strongly resisted, as soon to be left in abeyance.

The Court, from time to time, urged to the most stringent measures by some of the more austere spirits, and discouraged

[1] "George Fox digged out of his Burrowes," &c., p. 200. This curious book, of which, though it was published in Boston, in 1676, there are only four copies known to be extant, — one being in the Boston Athenæum, — is promised in a reprint by the Narragansett Club. It is to be hoped, that a few of those who had known of Roger Williams's youthful experiences in Massachusetts survived to enjoy its perusal. The old fire of disputation had not gone out in its writer. Its severity of bitterness and invective, its unsparing contemptuousness, streaked with real good-nature and the old "conscientious contentiousness," — make it one of the curiosities of literature. Williams had evidently been beyond measure provoked and horrified by the Quakers. He had tried his skill upon them in a meeting at Newport, in 1671; but he says, that, while he was speaking, one cut him off by "falling to prayer," and then another by singing. George Fox being then in the country, Williams challenged him and his followers to a public discussion on fourteen propositions, the thirteenth of which is that, "Their many Books and writings are extreamly poor, lame, naked, and swelled up with high titles and words of boasting vapour." Williams, says Fox, was afraid to meet him. "This old Fox thought it best to run for it; and leave the work to his journeymen and chaplains." The disputation was held at Newport, and rare sport it must have afforded to uncircumcised listeners. "God graciously assisted me in rowing all day with my old bones, so that I got to Newport towards the midnight of the day before the meeting" (p. 24.) It was in August, 1672.

There is a double joke in the title of the book, as it includes a sly hit at Burroughs, one of Fox's chosen companions.

by a steadily increasing number of opponents, moved either by pity or by a sense of the utter futility of the legislation, were evidently, as shown by scraps of paper still extant, most sorely perplexed. Under a sense of their responsibility, and moved by their convictions, that Quakers were to the colony they were guarding from ruin and anarchy, precisely what Jesuits were to the realm of England, they felt justified in enacting and inflicting the death penalty against the most obstinate and insidious offenders. They issued several formal vindications and arguments in support of their successive measures. The pleas which they set up were all minutely and elaborately illustrated by Scripture texts and examples, like that of Solomon's putting to death of Shimei.[1]

The stern issue was to be fully tried. Four Quakers were banished, Sept. 12, 1659, on pain of death if they returned. Two of these, Mary Dyer being one, "found freedom to depart." But she returned again in a month, with the other two, who were attended by a woman from Salem, bringing with her some linen, which she showed to the Governor, as intended for the winding-sheets of the victims.

The rest is best narrated by the Court Record: —

"SECOND SESSION, GENERAL COURT, OCTOBER 18, 1659.

"It is ordered that William Robbinson, Marmaduke Stephenson, and Mary Dyer, Quakers, now in prison for theire rebellion, sedition, and presumptious obtruding themselves upon us, notwithstanding their being sentenced to banishment on paine of death, as underminers of this government, &c., shall be brought before this Court for theire trialls, to suffer the poenalty of the lawe (the just reward of their transgression) on the morrow morning, being the nineteenth of this instant."

Being "brought to the barre, they acknowledged themselves to be the persons banished. After a full hearing of what the prisoners could say for themselves, it was put to the question, whether the prisoners, who have been convicted for Quakers, and banished this jurisdiction on paine of death, should be putt to death according as the lawe provides in that case. The Court resolved this question on the affirmative; and the Governor, (Endecott) in open Court, declared the sentence to W. Robbinson, that was brought to the barr: W. R. yow shall goe from hence to the place from whence yow came, and from thence to the place of exe-

[1] 1 Kings, chap. ii.

cution, and there hang till yow be dead. The like sentence the Govr., in open Court, pronounced against Marmaduke Steephenson and Mary Dyer, being brought to the barre one after another, in the same words:

"Whereas" — the above named — "are sentenced by this Court to death for theire rebellion, &c., it is ordered that the Secretary issue out his warrant to Edward Michelson, marshall generall, for repairing to the prison on the 27th of this instant October, and take the said persons into his custody, and then forthwith, by the aid of Capt. James Oliver, with one hundred souldiers, taken out by his order proportionably out of each company in Boston, compleatly armed with pike and musketteers, with powder and bullett, to lead them to the place of execution, and there see them hang till they be dead, and in theire going, being there, and retourne, to see all things be carried peaceably and orderly. Warrants issued.

"It is ordered that the Reverend Mr. Zackery Simes and Mr. John Norton, repaire to the prison, and tender theire endeavors to make the prisoners sencible of theire approaching dainger by the sentence of this Court, and prepare them for theire approaching ends.

"Whereas Mary Dyer is condemned by the Generall Court to be executed for hir offences, on the petition of William Dier, hir sonne, it is ordered that the said Mary Dyer shall have liberty for forty eight howers after this day to depart out of this jurisdiction, after which time, being found therein, she is forthwith to be executed, and in the meane time that she be kept close prisoner till hir sonne or some other be ready to carry hir away within the aforesaid time; and it is further ordered, that she shall be carried to the place of execution, and there to stand upon the gallowes, with a rope about her necke, till the rest be executed.

"Itt is ordered, that thirty-six of the souldiers be ordered by Capt. Oliver to remain in and about the towne as centinells, to preserve the peace of the place, whiles the rest goe to the execution.

"It is ordered that the selectmen of Boston shall, and heereby are required and impowred to presse tenn or twelve able and faithfull persons every night during the sitting of this Court to watch with great care the toune, especially the prison," &c.[1]

This last order is an evidence, among others which the Records show, that the magistrates, charged as they felt with the gravest responsibility in vindicating the authority of the law against all trifling and defiance, were still well aware that a protesting and indignant spirit, widely working among the citizens, was ready to manifest itself in a threatening way.

On the 27th of October, 1659, a gallows stood on Boston

[1] Vol. iv. pt. 1, pp. 383–4.

Common, for the execution of three condemned Quakers, who, after repeated banishments, refused to accept their lives on the condition that they would go away and keep away, — W. Robinson, Marmaduke Stevenson, and Mary Dyer. The train-band accompanied them, and drums were beat to drown their testimony. The town, also, was put under guard, by thirty-six soldiers, against apprehended tumult. The two men were hung, and buried beneath the gallows. Mary Dyer, who for more than twenty years had been a trouble to Massachusetts, after having the noose put round her neck, was pardoned, and sent back to Rhode Island, though with difficulty prevailed on by her son to go. She must have been past middle age, if not in the decline of life. In the Antinomian troubles, she had been prominent as a fast friend of Mrs. Hutchinson, and had suffered from the poor superstition of the times, because of an unhappy incident in her maternity. She walked to the gallows between her two condemned companions, holding each of them by a hand. The marshal asked her, "If she was not ashamed to walk, hand in hand, between two young men?" She replied, "It is an hour of the greatest joy I can enjoy in this world. No eye can see, no ear can hear, no tongue can speak, no heart can understand, the sweet incomes and refreshings of the Spirit of the Lord which now I enjoy."

When she understood, on being returned to the prison, upon what account she was reprieved, she wrote to the authorities repudiating the ground of it, and tendered the sacrifice of her life against the law. It was only by compulsion that she was got out of the jurisdiction on horseback. She came back again the next spring. On the gallows the second time, June 1, 1660, she was offered her life, if she would promise to keep out of Massachusetts. Her reply was: "In obedience to the will of the Lord I came; and in his will I abide faithful to the death." She did so.

I have before me, as I write, the autograph, on sadly stained paper, of a poor and sorrowful letter, dated at Portsmouth, R.I., May 3, 1660, and addressed to Governor Endicott, by his "most humble suppliant, W. Dyer." The letter draws tears now, if it did not from the eyes that first read it. The husband pleads to save his wife from death on the gallows: —

"Honored Sir, — It is no little grief of mind and sadness of hart, that I am necessitated to be so bould as to supplicate your honored self, with the Honbl Assembly of your Generall Court, to extend your mercy and favor once agen to me and my children. Little did I dream that I should ever have had occasion to petition you in a matter of this nature, but so it is that throw the divine providence and your benignity, my sonn obtained so much pity and mercy att your hands, as to enjoy the life of his mother.

"Now my supplication to your Honors is to begg affectionately the life of my deare wife. Tis true I have not seene her above this halfe yeare, and therefore cannot tell how in the frame of her spirit she was moved thus again to run so great a hazard to herself and perplexity to me and mine, and all her friends and well-wishers: so it is, from Shelter Island about by Pequid, Narragansett and to the town of Providence, she secretly and speedily journied, and as secretly from thence came to your jurisdiction. Unhappy journey may I say, and woe to that generation saye I that gives occasion thus of grief and trouble to those that desires to be quiet, by helping one another (as I may say) to hazard their lives for I know not what end, or to what purpose. If her zeale be so greate as thus to adventure, oh, let your favour and pitye surmounte itt, and save her life. Let not your forewonted compassion be conquered by her inconsiderate madness, and how greately will your renowne be spread, if by so conquering you become victorious. What shall I say more? I know you are all sensible of my condition, and let the reflect be, and you will see what the petition is and what will give me and mine peace. Oh let mercies wings once more soar above justice ballance, and then whilst I live shall I exalt your goodness. But otherwise twill be a languishing sorrowe, yea, soe great that I should gladly suffer the blow att once muche rather. I shall forbear to trouble your Honors with words, neither am I in a capacitye to expatiate myselfe at present. I only say this, yourselves have been and are, or may be, husbands to wife or wives, and so am I, yea, to one most dearlye beloved. Oh, do not you deprive me of her, but I pray give her me out again, and I shall bee soe much obliged forever, that I shall endeavor continually to utter my thanks, and render your Love and Honor most renowned. Pitye me. I beg it with tears."

Those tears are in the paper still. If he could have answered for his wife, she would have lived. She answered for herself.

The next year, one more banished Quaker, William Leddra, who had been a weary nuisance in many places, refused to accept his life, and was executed on the Common, March, 1661.

Another condemned and sentenced man was in the prison, but he wrote to the magistrates, —

"I, the condemned man, do give forth under my hand, that if I may have my liberty, I have freedom to depart this jurisdiction, and I know not that ever I shall come into it any more. W. CHRISTOPHERSON."[1]

The Quaker will had overcome the Puritan will. The magistrates relaxed. The people withstood the death penalty. It has been often affirmed, and has been generally supposed, that the authorities were arrested in their course by a mandate procured by a Quaker, who had been whipped in Salem, from Charles II., which forbade any further capital proceedings against Quakers, and required that the condemned be sent to England. Such a royal letter was written by the King, Sept. 9, 1661, and received by our Court in November. But before it was even procured from the monarch, the Court had evidently been convinced of the utter folly of its measures. It had wavered in suspense, vacillated, and failed to enforce its capital law against victims in its power, while it shrunk from using its appliances to secure others whom it might easily have reached.

It may be that the king's command was a welcome salvo to the chagrin or mortification of the authorities. Certain it is, that the Quakers revelled over the discomfiture of the magistrates, and played some of their most offensive antics of railing and defiance. But they were by no means left to their liberty. The whip and the cart-tail, the prison and the pillory, were still kept in service against them, even by allowance of the King, and the course pursued in England. The General, the Quarterly, and the Magistrates' and Local Courts found subjects in them for penalties, more or less severe, till perfect tolerance was found to be the lesson of wisdom, and the condition of peace.

The Puritan Commonwealth, after a resolute struggle against the successive shocks, personal and practical, which its essential elements invited, as well as were sure to encounter, yielded even then only gradually, though I can hardly add gracefully, to a steady modification of its original theory. Yet there was more of success than of failure in the experiment. All of profound sincerity, and of God-fearing self-consecration, and of stern resolve, which put that august experiment on trial, planted for it foundations, giving to it its early security, and constituting the

[1] Miscel. Papers.

stability and glory of the Commonwealth which succeeded to it.

Sometimes, as I walk in our city streets, or ride through our clustering towns and villages, I imagine myself as having by my side one of the old first comers to this wilderness; some grave man, in church or magistracy, who, after his coming, may have lived and wrought here more than half a century, in laying the hard and deep foundations of things. I raise him up — in a shadow — for my companionship. He goes along with me, looks round him, puts questions, and turns to me to relieve his surprise, to refix landmarks, to relate and account for the changes and developments of things on our way. He is stern and sharp: but I am not afraid of him; for I know that what I have of him is only dust, and that something more substantial represents him elsewhere. Shadow as he is, we can hardly keep our footing in the crowded streets. He is inclined, at a glance, favorably to regard our humanity in providing bird-roosts in the wires which run over our roofs in the air, unless he surmise them to be snares for catching birds. But these rows of shops and stores, with all their gilded gew-gaws and displays of trifles and luxuries, are about to prompt his utterance, just as he is choked by a whiff from some "tobacco-taker" passing by. The theatres, and palaces of vice for gambling or intemperance, make him sad and sour. But the great school-houses offer a temporary relief. He wishes to rest awhile in the burial-grounds, and study their stones, — asking where is his own. The hardest part of the explanatory work which falls to me, is as we pass many churches, — Jewish Synagogues, the Roman College and Cathedral, at the sight and name of which those shadowy lips seem to utter something that sounds like a very bad word. The lists of voters, with the un-English names upon them, and the prevalence of Hibernian patronymics, are evidently too much for him. The explanation of the national flag plainly engages his sympathies. He remembers that he and his old contemporaries were rather tame in their loyalty, and that he died thinking, — perhaps hoping, — that things would one day come about so, that we should have a flag of our own. On the whole, though the facts which he would have to hear and face, and to take for just what they are and mean, would fearfully exercise him, and lead him to ask how all this freedom and license had worked in among us, and whether Church and State had not been wrecked over and over again in the process; on the whole, I think, he would rather remain alive with us, and take his chance, and take things as they are, than go back into the ground again. One thing, I know, would reconcile him to taking things as they are; viz., the clear conviction, that if he and all his generation could come again into their old places, they could not introduce a force which would turn back the current. They would have to take things as they are, and submit to the dispensation of human freedom, as safer than Puritan sway.

Freedom, — sad and fearful and wicked things are done in that name, by that plea, for that good; but we must accept it, with all its risks, which sometimes frighten or dismay us. Any thing but the most perfect and unfettered freedom of thinking, speaking, and acting among us, would peril the experiment we are trying here, grander than that of our Fathers, — of making one nation out of fragments of all the populations of the globe. There is no form of force, no method of restraint, no devices of imperial, ecclesiastical, military, or even constitutional sway, which could possibly control the processes of risk involved in the contact and citizenship of all the races, colors, temperaments, and classes, which we hold in solution here. No: the wit of man, piety, wisdom, statesmanship, would in vain attempt, by any repressive or coercive measures, any interference, however gentle or however stern, to introduce any agency of external authority in the mighty process which is working here. Nothing but perfect freedom, absolute soul-liberty for the individual, can make the process safe on the trial. We can dam rivers. We can imprison thousands of pounds of steam. We can use a flash of lightning for a common carrier. But we cannot overmaster the workings of human nature.

HISTORY OF GRANTS

UNDER

THE GREAT COUNCIL FOR NEW ENGLAND.

BY SAMUEL F. HAVEN.

HISTORY OF GRANTS

UNDER

THE GREAT COUNCIL FOR NEW ENGLAND.

THE subject assigned to me for a lecture to-night is, "History of Grants under the Great Council for New England."

However important this may be in a historical point of view, so far as pleasurable interest is concerned it certainly has a rather dry and unpromising aspect.

Moreover, it was said of this Great Council for New England, by the learned Dr. Belknap, after he had tried in vain to harmonize their proceedings, that —

"Either from the jarring interests of the members, or their indistinct knowledge of the country, or their inattention to business, or some other cause which does not fully appear, their affairs were transacted in a confused manner from the beginning; and the grants which they made were so inaccurately described, and interfered so much with each other, as to occasion difficulties and controversies, some of which are not yet ended."

So, too, Governor Sullivan in his work on "Land Titles in Massachusetts" declares that the legislative acts of the Council for New England and their judicial determinations "were but a chain of blunders;" and "their grants, from the want of an accurate knowledge of the geography of the territory, were but a course of confusion."

Possibly, it was with the hope of obtaining additional light upon these obscurities and perplexities, to the extent of reconciling apparent discrepancies, that the subject was selected for treatment in this series of historical lectures. But intricacies which learned historians and acute lawyers have failed to elucidate, it may be presumed are not susceptible of a distinct and definite solution, such as Courts require for the establishment of a title to property; and we may be compelled to find in a narrative of the circumstances under which they had their origin their only reasonable explanation.

You will therefore be spared a technical dissertation upon charters, patents, grants, and other methods of conveying territorial rights, and be asked to listen to a relation of the rise, the character, the operations, and the end of the great corporation in England created by James I. on the 3d of November, 1620, consisting of forty noblemen, knights, and gentlemen, and called "The Council established at Plymouth, in the County of Devon, for the Planting, Ruling, and Governing of New England in America."

It will be necessary to go back a little; not indeed to the days of Adam and Eve, as did our distinguished New England chronologer, Dr. Prince, who devoted so much time and space to the preliminary annals of the *world*, that he died before completing those of this limited portion of the globe, which were the real object of his work, — but to the beginning of England's conventional title to American possessions. It was a *conventional* title, inasmuch as it rested upon an understanding among the so-called *Christian* powers, that the rights of nations and peoples, who were not at least nominally Christian, should be entirely disregarded. The sovereigns of Europe carried out in practice the principle which the Puritans of Cromwell's parliament were said to have asserted in theory, and apparently regarded the scripture promise that the saints shall inherit the earth as a mere statement of their own just prerogative. Among Catholics, the Pope, as an inspired administrator, distributed newly discovered regions according to his inclination and infallible discretion. His assignments of continents and seas by the boundaries of latitude and longitude were valid in Spain and Portugal and France; but in England the King, when he had become also the head of a church, claimed authority to empower his subjects to discover "remote, heathen, and barbarous lands, not actually possessed of any Christian prince or people, and the same to hold, occupy, and enjoy, with all commodities, jurisdictions, and royalties, both by sea and land;" of course, in subordination to his own paramount authority, but with no reference to the supremacy of the Roman pontiff.

John and Sebastian Cabot were commissioned, in like phraseology, by Henry VII., "to seek out countries or provinces of the heathen and infidels, wherever situated, hitherto unknown to all Christians, and to subdue and possess them as his subjects." If their discoveries had been followed at once by possession, the papal sanction might have been deemed essential to a sound title; but England had long been a Protestant country before steps were taken to maintain her claims to a portion of the New World. Remote events, like distant objects, are apt to seem crowded together, for want of a perspective to make the intervals which separate them evident to our perceptions. Thus we often fail to realize the duration of uneventful periods of history which come between the strifes and commotions, or other great occurrences which chiefly occupy the attention of both the historian and his reader. From A.D. 1495, the date of the commission to the Cabots, to A.D. 1578, the date of the letters patent to Sir Humphrey Gilbert, under which possession was first taken for the English crown, the lapse of time exceeds that of two generations of men, as these are usually estimated.

Meanwhile, circumstances were silently and indirectly, as well as slowly, preparing for the settlement of this portion of the American continent. Unrecorded voyages were annually made to our coasts for fish by the Spaniards, Portuguese, and French; the fasts of the church causing a large demand for that article of food in Catholic countries. The people bordering on the Bay of Biscay were hereditary fishermen. Their ancestors had captured whales in their own tempestuous sea; and Biscayans, or *Basques*, as they were more frequently termed, were in great request as experts for the fisheries at Newfoundland, and along the shores of New England. They professed to believe that their countrymen visited the same fishing-grounds before Columbus crossed the ocean. The business was so lucrative that the reports first brought home by the Cabots of the great abundance of codfish in those regions produced an excitement among the people engaged in that trade, not unlike that which rumors of gold in California and Australia have created in more recent times.

No account has been preserved of the *commencement* of fishing voyages to the American seas; but they can be traced back to within half a dozen years of the return of the Cabots; and twelve or fifteen years later as many as fifty vessels of different nations were employed on the Grand Banks.

Of such voyages no journal was kept and no history was written; because it was the policy of the adventurers to keep these prolific sources of wealth, as much as possible, from attracting the attention of competitors.

The presence of European vessels on our shores, in considerable numbers, a century before the arrival of the Pilgrims, may account for traditions among the natives, and the occasional discovery of articles of European manufacture in their graves, that have been supposed to point to the visits of the Northmen at far more distant periods.[1]

A process of preparation not less marked and effective was at the same time going on in England itself. Until the reign of Henry VII., that kingdom had been behind all other European States in mercantile enterprise. Italy, Spain, Portugal, Holland, and even Germany, were before her in commerce or manufactures. The fluctuations of trade, in the removal of its seats from one place or country to another, are among the marvels and curiosities of history. The chief wonders of the world — the costly and gigantic remains of decayed cities, where now all is silence and desolation — are the fruits of accumulated capital in what were once the forwarding and distributing stations of trade. Thebes, Babylon, Nineveh, Palmyra, Tyre, and Carthage were great and magnificent, because, as the prophet Nahum saith of Nineveh, "They multiplied their merchants above the stars of heaven."

Wherever traffic has found a seat and centre, art, architecture, enterprise, and political power have been its inevitable fruits. The growth and decay of these local influences, and their distribution in turn among the kingdoms of the earth, though springing from natural causes, belong no less to the mysterious operations of Providence. It was the commercial decline of Italy (the industrial Italy of the Middle Ages), whose prodigal remains of æsthetic splendor are the memorials of her merchant princes, that

[1] When Captain John Smith visited the Susquehanna Indians, in 1608, they had utensils of iron and brass, which, by their own account, originally came from the French of Canada.

carried Venetian navigators to England, among them the family of Cabots, seeking employment for the exercise of their native arts.[1] At the same time, the incessant wars upon the continent were driving tradesmen and manufacturers from the free cities of central Europe, which they had built up and enriched; many of whom took refuge in the British Isles, which thus easily acquired the advantages of skill and experience in the production and sale of important fabrics. England's opportunity had come. Though not lying in the course of the world's great thoroughfares, yet, by insular position, favorably formed for maritime pursuits, her chances of wealth and power from the magic agencies of commerce had at length arrived. Through the reigns of Henry VII., Henry VIII., Edward VI., and the bloody Mary, to their full fruition in the Augustan era of Queen Elizabeth, these causes were not only increasing the riches, but developing wonderfully the mental and physical character and capacities of the British people. More independent, politically and socially, than their neighbors in Holland, they shared with them the accumulation of the precious metals which flowed from American mines, through Spain and Portugal, to the chief marts of trade, and experienced the stimulating effects of capital in all departments of life and action. Enterprise, extravagance, ambition, emulation, greed, were the healthy and unhealthy consequences of a prosperous and excited community.

The tendency to a sort of theatrical exaggeration in sentiment and manners that followed upon this development of physical resources and mental energies was perhaps a natural result. Man has often been declared to be the product of the peculiarities of the period in which he was born. Well might Shakespeare say of his own time, "All the world is a stage, and all the men and women are mere players;" for the whole reign of Elizabeth was a theatrical pageant, where Leicester and Essex, Sidney, Southampton, and Raleigh, and not excepting Bacon, the representative of philosophy, personated the various characters of an heroic drama; while the many-sided Shake-

[1] The superior naval advancement of Italy at that period is illustrated by the fact, that the leaders of discovery in the western hemisphere — Columbus in the service of Spain, Cabot in the service of England, Vespucius in the service of Portugal, and Verazzano in the service of France — were Italians.

speare was himself a dramatic embodiment of the entire intellectual expansion of his age.

There lived then a certain remarkable woman, — remarkable for having two sons of different fathers, whose heroic temperament and versatile talents must have been derived from their common mother. The half-brothers, Humphrey Gilbert and Walter Raleigh, were more alike in tastes and genius than is often seen in a nearer relationship. It was the blood of the *Champernons*, — a name that has a place of its own in our colonial history, — and not that of the *Gilberts* or *Raleighs*, which made them what they were.

To these two men, of honorable birth and social standing, each of whom combined the habits and qualities of a soldier with those of a studious scholar, and could handle with equal skill the pen and the sword, we owe it that this New England where we live, and this entire Union of vigorous States, are not dependencies of France or Spain, or such as are those feeble provinces which sprang from French or Spanish colonization.

Whatever constructive right or title England had acquired by the discoveries of the Cabots, a little more delay, and their assertion would have been no longer practicable, except at the point of the sword. It was Gilbert and Raleigh who, in the nick of time, gave this direction to British energies; and apparently nothing but the grand ideas and exhaustless resolution of these great minds, and their inspiring influence amid disappointment and disaster, saved an indefinite and uncertain claim by means of a positive and substantial possession.

The rival claims of the leading European powers, at this juncture, to the soil of our continent north of the Gulf of Mexico, were not better defined, or more easy of satisfactory adjustment upon legal and equitable principles, than are those of the grantees of the Great Council for New England, which are now the particular subject of consideration. The rules and precedents of national and international law furnish a convenient phraseology for the discussion of questions relating to territorial ownership and boundaries, as phrenology provides a convenient nomenclature for describing the faculties of the mind although it may not be admitted to determine their actual position and limits. In larger divisions of land, even where private citizens alone are concerned, the most tenacious grasp is apt ultimately to acquire the legal title. Time heals defects, and the pertinacious possessor finds his right to hold and convey secured by circumstances, and protected by judicial tribunals.

The English jurists of the reign of Elizabeth maintained, that discovery and possession united could alone give a valid title to a new country. But how far asunder in point of time might these acts be, and yet retain their virtue when brought together? And what if another discovery and a possession came between them? Will a possession fairly taken, but not continued by uninterrupted occupancy, avail for a completion of title?

The answers to these questions are not so distinctly given as to enable us to found upon them, clearly, the right of the British crown to issue patents and charters, empowering its subjects to hold and distribute the regions which, under the names of Virginia and New England, embraced a large portion of the North American continent.

John and Sebastian Cabot discovered, and to some extent explored, the American coast (A. D. 1497–8) from Labrador to the Carolinas, more than a year before the continent had been seen by Columbus or by Americus Vespucius; but the subjects of other powers had visited these shores familiarly, and some of them had taken formal possession in the name of their sovereign, long before Sir Humphrey Gilbert came to Newfoundland in 1583.

On behalf of the King of Portugal, Cortereal ranged the northern coast only two years later than the Cabots, and gave the name Labrador to the country still so called.

A map of the Gulf of St. Lawrence and the neighboring country was made by the French, from their own observations, as early as 1507.

It is said, that in 1522 there were fifty houses at Newfoundland occupied by people of different nations. There were probably some English among them, although the English fisheries were then chiefly in the direction of Iceland.

In 1524, an expedition for discovery was sent by Francis I. of France, under John De Verazzano, a Florentine, who explored our coast from the Carolinas to Newfoundland, as the Cabots had done, but with more particularity, and called the country

NEW FRANCE; and in the same year Stephen Gomez, in the service of Spain, sailed from Florida to Cape Race; his object being, as was then the case with almost all the navigators that preceded him here, to find a passage through to the Pacific Ocean, then called the South Sea.

After this, while the Spaniards were seeking a foothold in Florida, the French, in a series of expeditions from 1534 to 1542, with Cartier as chief leader, were, on behalf of France, erecting monuments in token of possession, and planting colonies, in the region of the gulf of St. Lawrence. Having endured several seasons of trial and suffering, these colonies came to an end, as settlements; leaving, it is claimed, some of their members still in the country. With the exception of a disastrous expedition in 1549, when Roberval and a numerous train of adventurers were supposed to have perished at sea, no farther measures were taken by the French to re-establish themselves in the North till near the close of that century.

Thus, while England had neglected to maintain her rights as a discoverer, Spain, Portugal, and France had explored the same parts of North America; and France had planted her subjects on the soil, without formal remonstrance, so far as is known, from any other power. The English fishery at Newfoundland had become important in 1548; but no record has been preserved of any attempt at colonization.

This negligence, or indifference, was first broken by Sir Humphrey Gilbert. He had written a discourse to show the probability of a passage by the north-west to India, which may have promoted the voyage of Frobisher to the Arctic Sea in 1576; and, in 1578, he received from Queen Elizabeth authority to discover and take possession of remote and barbarous lands unoccupied by any Christian prince or people, as the Cabots had been empowered to do by Henry VII. It is noticeable, that the patent to Gilbert contains no allusion to the Cabots, or to any rights of the crown derived from former discoveries. For aught that appears in the instrument itself, this was an independent and original enterprise for discovery and conquest, with a right on the part of Gilbert to possess and govern the discovered and conquered lands in subordination to the Queen. But such was not the view of the grantee himself. He did not survive to be his own historian; but we learn from the narrative of Edward Haies, "a principall actour in the same voyage," —

1st, That the enterprise of Gilbert was based upon the consideration, that "John Cabot, the father, and Sebastian, his son, an Englishman born, were the first finders out of all that great tract of land stretching from the Cape of Florida unto those Islands which we now call the Newfoundland; all of which they brought and annexed unto the crown of England."

2d, That if a man's motives "be derived from a virtuous and heroical mind, preferring chiefly the honor of God, compassion of poor infidels captived by the devil, tyrannizing in most wonderful and dreadful manner over their bodies and souls," and other honorable purposes specified, "God will assist such an actor beyond the expectation of man." Especially as, "in this last age of the world, the time is complete for receiving also these Gentiles into his mercy; . . . it seeming probable by the event of precedent attempts made by the Spaniards and French sundry times, that the country lying North of Florida God hath reserved to be reduced unto Christian civilization by the English nation."

"Then seeing the English nation only hath right unto these countries of America, from the Cape of Florida northward, by the privilege of first discovery, . . . which right also seemeth strongly defended on our behalf by the powerful hand of almighty God, withstanding the enterprises of other nations; it may greatly encourage us upon so just ground, as is our right, and upon so sacred an intent as to plant religion, to prosecute effectually the full possession of these so ample and pleasant countries appertaining unto the crown of England; the same (as is to be conjectured by infallible arguments of the world's end approaching) being now arrived unto the time by God prescribed of their vocation, if ever their calling unto the knowledge of God may be expected."

This conviction, that the end of the world was near, was the source of much of the heroic adventure, and the excuse for much of the merciless barbarity towards the natives, which attended the occupation of this continent by Europeans. The WORD was first to be preached among all nations; and soldiers and priests alike believed themselves agents of heaven in the fulfilment of prophecy, when, acting under papal or royal authority, they compelled the submission of heathen nations to the

Christian faith by violence and bloodshed. Columbus thought he had ascertained by calculation, that there remained but one hundred and fifty years from his time before the final catastrophe. "My enterprise," said he, "has accomplished simply that which the prophet Isaiah had predicted, — that, before the end of the world, the gospel should be preached upon all the earth, and the Holy City be restored to the church." Nearly ninety years of that remnant of time had expired, when, influenced by similar sentiments, Sir Humphrey Gilbert set forth on a similar errand.

It was his intention to take possession at Newfoundland for the northern portion of the country, and at some point nearer Florida for the southern portion of the English claim; going first to Newfoundland to gain the advantage of a favorable season of the year, and the period when fishing vessels were most numerous at that station. The ships of different nations then engaged in that employment, were one hundred from Spain, fifty from Portugal, and one hundred and fifty from France, to fifty from England. But England had become full-blooded and dangerous, and already aspired to rule the seas. She had the best ships, which, as Haies expresses it, were "admirals" over the rest, and controlled the harbors.

Gilbert landed, and calling together the merchants and ship-masters of the several nations, took possession with all the prescribed formalities. He promulgated laws, to which the people, by general voice, promised obedience; and made grants of land, the recipients covenanting to pay an annual rent, and yearly to maintain possession of the same by themselves or their assigns as his representatives.

We know that Gilbert was lost at sea, without having been able to make a like demonstration elsewhere. But his proceedings at Newfoundland have been regarded by all English writers as substantiating the English title to the whole country. No distinct colony was left behind him; but the British domination continued to be recognized by the mixed population on the shore, and was, when necessary, enforced by summary process among the ships.

On learning the death of his heroic half-brother, Sir Walter Raleigh, his partner in the enterprise, immediately obtained a similar commission and patent in his own name, and sought to complete their purpose by planting a colony at the South. It was his fortune, too, to fail in that part of his design which contemplated the establishment of settlements under his own rule and tributary to himself; but he was the first to possess and occupy the soil of Virginia; and, although interrupted for a time, the occupancy of British subjects in that region became permanent, without the interference of rival attempts at colonization.

It was under such circumstances, and in such manner, that the title of England, be it good or bad, to a portion of our continent, was originally acquired and maintained.

It seemed to be desirable to refer to the nature of that title, to the civil condition of England, to the operations of trade and fishery, and to the colonial projects which preceded the incorporation of that semi-commercial, semi-political body known as the Great Council for New England. For it was the wealth of the mercantile classes, resulting in some degree from the discovery of new sources and new courses of trade in distant regions, that made the nobility and gentry eager to partake of their gains. The "Fellowship of English Merchants for the Discovery of New Trades," sometimes called also the Muscovy or Russian Company, which had a charter as early as 1554–5, had been remarkably successful. Immense fortunes, like those of Sir Thomas Smith and Sir John Wolstenholm, and others who took part in the Virginia enterprises, had been realized by merchants who became knights and baronets. The wealth of the House of Commons far exceeded that of the House of Lords. The great increase of extravagance in private expenditure had become a serious drain upon the resources of the nobility; and it was the hope of profit from the fur trade and fisheries, combined with the advantage and dignity of territorial proprietorship, that caused the formation and governed the conduct of the New-England Company, while ignorance of business and embarrassments arising from conflicting claims, domestic and foreign, brought it to an end.

There is another preliminary fact, which is of great interest to New England, and especially to Massachusetts. At the beginning of a new century, A. D. 1602, Raleigh's colonies had disappeared, and all traces of them were lost. Dr. Holmes, in his Annals, remarks, that then "in North America north of Mexico not a single European family could be found." If we understand by *family* a household of men, women, and children, this statement may be nearly correct; and yet it is estimated that there were at that time, at Newfoundland, as many as ten thousand men and boys employed on board and on shore in the business of taking and curing fish. Colonization, however, had been virtually abandoned in despair. At that critical period, it was revived by two men whose service to this country in that respect has never been properly or sufficiently acknowledged. These were the Earl of Southampton and Bartholomew Gosnold: the first, the friend and patron of Shakespeare, and the subject of many of his sonnets, who had impaired his fortune by his liberality to men of letters; the other, an intrepid mariner from the west of England, who became the leading spirit, and one of the first victims, of the attempt to renew the settlements of Virginia.

You are all familiar with the story of Gosnold's visit to Massachusetts Bay, in 1602; and it hardly needs to be stated, that the expedition was undertaken with the consent of Raleigh, as coming within his jurisdiction; that the cost was chiefly defrayed by the Earl of Southampton; that the design of the voyage was to find a direct and shorter way across the ocean and a proper seat for a plantation; that the company consisted of thirty-two men, twenty of whom were to remain in the country; that, in fact, they were the first to take a straight course across the Atlantic, instead of the usual passage to Virginia by the West Indies; that they reached land near Salem Harbor; that from them came the familiar names of Cape Cod, Martha's Vineyard, the Elizabeth Islands, &c.; and that they built a fort at Cuttyhunk in Buzzard's Bay. They were delighted with the country, but were compelled to return home for larger supplies. Before they could come back better provided for a permanent settlement, Queen Elizabeth died, Raleigh was thrown into prison by her successor, and all schemes for American colonization were of necessity to be abandoned, or organized upon a new basis under a new sovereign himself destitute of energy and enterprise. Fortunately, Gosnold and his companions were not merely men of action, but could write and speak as well; and to their glowing narratives and zealous exertions, aided by the famous Hakluyt, and men of influence at Court, historians ascribe the procurement of the charter of 1606, from which the ultimate settlement of the United States and the resulting heritage of territorial rights are to be dated.

The fact of Gosnold's selection of our own coast for an intended colony is sufficiently well known; but I am sure, that the characters and services of the leaders of that little company are not sufficiently understood and appreciated, or, instead of the farce which was enacted over the later and inconsequential landing and brief continuance of a body of outlaws on the coast of Maine, all New England would have united in measures to honor the memory of the real founders of permanent habitation and indisputable title within our national bounds.

For some reason, the charter of 1606 did not embrace the whole of the British claim. It extended no farther south than the present limits of North Carolina, and no farther north than the present limits of the State of Vermont; that is, from the thirty-fourth to the forty-fifth degree of latitude. Within these bounds there were to be two colonies under separate administrations, subject to a paramount administration in the mother country. The southern colony could plant anywhere between the thirty-fourth and forty-first degrees, and the northern colony, anywhere between the thirty-eighth and forty-fifth degrees; leaving three degrees, or the space from the southern point of Maryland to the southern point of Connecticut, as common ground.

The northern company had need of hot haste in choosing a location; as, in the race for possession, the French had once more taken the lead, and renewed their plans of founding an American empire. Having before sent over a ship-load of felons from the jails, who were left to take care of themselves at the Isle of Sables, a more formidable expedition was organized in 1603, the year succeeding Gosnold's memorable voyage. Henry the Great being then King of France, a gentleman of his household, named De Monts, received from him a patent of the American territory from the fortieth to the forty-sixth degree of north latitude, with power, as lieutenant-general, to colonize and rule it. It will be noticed that this grant almost exactly covers the territory assigned to the northern colony of Virginia by the English charter of 1606. De Monts lost no time in entering upon his dominion; and he and his followers settled themselves in Nova Scotia, at *Monts désert* (now called Mount Desert), and along the coast of Maine as far as the Penobscot. They looked into Boston Harbor in search of a more genial climate, but were repelled by the hostile attitude of the natives.

The company of outlaws which, in imitation of the French, Chief-Justice Popham sent to the mouth of the Sagadehoc or Kennebec River, in 1607, was undoubtedly intended and expected to check the advances of that nation. It not only failed, but its failure paralyzed the energies of the northern company of Virginia for many succeeding years.

That portion of the duplex contrivance of James I. accomplished nothing important of itself until, after much opposition, a separate organization and charter were obtained in 1620. In the mean time, its twin-brother, at Jamestown, flourished, after a fashion; it is doubtful whether most aided or hindered by the frequent interference of the English monarch, that "Dominie Sampson" spoilt into a king, who believed himself to be the fountain of wisdom, not less than the fountain of honor. It was able, in 1613, to fit out an armed vessel, commanded by Captain Argall, which broke up the French settlements at Port Royal, Mount Desert, &c., and compelled their inhabitants to retire towards Canada; protesting all the while, that whatever abstract rights Great Britain might possess, if any there were, the Virginia charter expressly excepted in its grants regions already occupied by any Christian prince or people; they (the French) being a Christian people, in occupation of the places from which they were driven two years before the Virginia charter was made; which was very true.

Upon the island of Manhattan at the mouth of Hudson's river, on the common ground of the two so-called Virginia companies, the Dutch had located themselves, claiming title from its discovery by Hudson, in their service. While returning from his expedition against the French, Captain Argall called on them also, and required submission. They were too feeble to resist; but the next year a new governor came from Amsterdam, with reinforcements, asserting the right of Holland to the country, and refusing the tribute which his predecessor had consented to pay to the English.

It was to this inheritance, of not undisputed possessions, to which the new corporation, styled "The Council established at Plymouth, in the County of Devon, for the Planting, Ruling, and Governing of New England in America," succeeded on the 3d of November, 1620.

The charter, after referring to the previous charter of 1606, and the changes that had since been made for the benefit of the southern company, states that Sir Ferdinando Gorges, and other principal adventurers of the northern company, with divers persons of quality who now intend to be their associates, resolving to prosecute their designs more effectually, and intending to establish fishery, trade, and plantation, within the precincts of the said northern company; for that purpose, and to avoid all confusion and difference between themselves and the other company, have desired to be made a distinct body.

It proceeds to grant to the persons named, the territory from the fortieth to the forty-eighth degree of north latitude and through the main land from sea to sea, to be called NEW ENGLAND; that is, from the latitude of Philadephia to the middle of Newfoundland, and through all that width from the Atlantic to the Pacific; varying a few degrees of latitude from the bounds prescribed in the original patent.

They were to be one body politic and corporate, to consist of forty persons, and no more, with perpetual succession. Vacancies were to be filled by the members. They were empowered to establish laws not contrary to the laws of England; and to their "governors, officers, and ministers," according to the natural limits of their offices, was given authority to correct, punish, pardon, and rule all English subjects that should become colonists, according to the laws and instructions of the Council; and in defect thereof, in cases of necessity, according to their good discretions, in cases criminal and capital as well as civil, and both marine and others. Such proceedings to be, as near as conveniently may be, agreeable to the laws, statutes, government, and policy, of the realm of England. The continent, from the fortieth to the forty-eighth degree, from sea to sea, was absolutely given, granted, and confirmed to the said Council and their successors, to be holden, as of the manor of East Greenwich, in free and common socage,[1] as distinguished from the feudal tenure of personal service; and all subjects were forbidden to trade or fish within their limits without a license from the Council under seal.

The rank and personal standing of the grantees corresponded to the extent of territory and the magnitude of the powers bestowed upon them. They consisted of many of the highest nobility of the kingdom, and knights and gentlemen of prominence and influence. Their aims and purposes were not less lofty and aristocratic. Upon the general ground, that kings did first lay the foundations of their monarchies, by reserving to themselves the sovereign power (as fit it was), and dividing their kingdoms into counties, baronies, hundreds, and the like, they say, —

> "This foundation being so certain, there is no reason for us to vary from it; and therefore we resolve to build our edifices upon it. So as we purpose to commit the management of our whole affairs there in general unto a governor, to be assisted by the advice and counsel of so many of the patentees as shall be there resident, together with the officers of State."

Among the "officers of State" were to be a treasurer, a marshal, an admiral, and a master of ordnance. Two parts of the whole territory were to be divided among the patentees, and the other third reserved for public uses; but the entire territory was to be formed into counties, baronies, hundreds, and the like. From every county and barony deputies were to be chosen to consult upon the laws to be framed, and to reform any notable abuses. Yet these are not to be assembled but by order of the President and Council in England, "who are to give life to the laws so to be made, as those to whom of right it best belongs." The counties and baronies were to be governed by the chief, and the officers under him, with a power of high and low justice, subject to an appeal, in some cases, to the supreme courts. The lords of counties might also divide their counties into manors and lordships, with courts for determining petty matters. When great cities had grown up, they

[1] "An estate of the highest nature that a subject under any government can possibly receive and hold." — *Sullivan, Land Titles in Massachusetts,* p. 36.

were to be made bodies politic to govern their own private affairs, with a right of representation by deputies or burgesses.[1]

There was a provision in the charter for its renewal and amendment, if changes should be found expedient; and measures were taken for a new patent, omitting the requirement that their government should be as near the laws of England as may be, and inserting authority to create titles of honor, and establish feudal tenures.

The chief managers of the affairs of the Council were Sir Ferdinando Gorges, a friend and fellow-soldier of Raleigh, who, ever since the failure of the Popham enterprise in Maine, had been striving to settle a plantation for trade and fishing there on his own account; Captain John Mason, who had been governor of Newfoundland; and the Earl of Warwick, the President. The patents issued to colonists, whether companies or single adventurers, were intended to conform to the political system they had adopted.

The influence of Gorges is seen in the project, which was early started, of laying out a county, on the general behalf, forty miles square, on the Kennebec River, and building a great city at the junction of the rivers Kennebec and Androscoggin. Two kinds of patents were provided for by the Council: one for private undertakers of petty plantations, who were to have a certain quantity of land allotted them at an annual rent, with conditions that they should not alienate without leave, and should settle a stated number of persons with cattle, &c., within a definite period; the other for such parties as proposed to build towns, with large numbers of people, having a government and magistrates, who were to have power to frame such laws and constitutions as the majority should think fit, subordinate to the State which was to be established, "until other order should be taken."

The grand schemes of the Council were not destined to experience even the promise of success. They began to fail from the very beginning of their operations. They had to contend not only against the active hostility of the Southern corporation, the remonstrances of the French, and the pertinacity

[1] Brief Relation of the President and Council. In Mass. Hist. Soc. Col., vol. xix.

of the Hollanders, who said little, while they encroached upon the fisheries, and inclined to take possession of Connecticut River; but the fishermen and fur-traders of England itself, whose rights, become prescriptive by long enjoyment, were so summarily interfered with. The matter was taken up by Parliament, and Sir Ferdinando Gorges was summoned to their bar. His argument, that the enlargement of the King's dominions and the advancement of religion were of more consequence than a disorderly course of fishing, which, except for their plantation, would soon be given over, (as so goodly a coast could not long be left unpeopled by the French, Spanish, or Dutch), if it did not satisfy the Commons, had weight with the King, who continued his favor and protection.

Gorges was to be the Governor of the new State; and, in 1623, the attempt was made to transfer an operative government to the American soil. The King had issued a proclamation enforcing their authority; and now Robert Gorges, son of Sir Ferdinando, was sent over as Lieutenant-General and Governor of New England, with a suite of officers, to establish his court at Massachusetts Bay; where a tract extending ten miles on the north-east side of the bay had been granted to him personally by patent.

This proved an unfortunate procedure. It increased the hostile feeling in England, so that, in a list of public grievances brought forward by Parliament, the first was the patent for New England. This public declaration of the House's dislike, Gorges tells us, "shook off all adventurers from the plantation, and made many of the patentees quit their interest." The Lieutenant-Governor and his military and ecclesiastical officers were advised to return home; and thus the plan of a State ruled by a Company, such as we have seen to succeed in India, failed in New England.

The other purpose of the Council, viz., to derive a profit from the fisheries and the fur-trade, with a view also to the ultimate advantages of territorial proprietorship, was continued in a feeble and desultory way. The great object was to get the country occupied at all events, and grants of land were made with a singular disregard of boundaries and of previous conveyance. Gorges and Mason were the only persons at all acquainted with localities here, and Gorges had become despondent and almost desperate. Many members of the corporation gave up their partnership rather than pay their shares of the expenses; and it was difficult to find others to take their places. They tried the policy of dividing the whole territory among their members, in severalty, which came to nothing. Dissensions arose, and the Earl of Warwick withdrew from their meetings, but still kept the great seal, and evaded the calls that were made upon him to deliver it to the treasurer. They did not know what patents had been issued, and the President was "entreated to direct a course for finding out." It was proposed to send over a surveyor to settle limits, and commissioners to hear and determine grievances. The company became reduced from forty to twenty-one, notwithstanding recruits had been diligently sought among the merchants. Their records from November, 1632, to January, 1634, are wanting. When they begin again, the only remaining objects aimed at seem to have been a renewal of the policy of assigning to members distinct portions of the region embraced in their charter, and a surrender of the charter to the King, who is besought to graciously ratify the division, and confirm it by his own decree. This he does not appear ever to have formally done; and the Great Council for planting, ruling, and governing New England, came to an end in 1635, leaving no other incumbrances upon the soil than such as arose from a few larger patents, which depended for their force and validity very much upon the royal sanction they ultimately received, and some grants whose proprietors were in the country engaged in actual occupancy or management.

Dr. Palfrey, in his history, gives a list of twenty-four grants made, or supposed to have been made, by the Council for New England before the final partition attempted among themselves. From these we must take the doubtful, or at any rate futile, division among the partners alleged to have been effected in 1622; also the Charter of Nova Scotia to Sir William Alexander, which came directly from the King with the assent of the Council, how signified does not appear; also the supposed grants to Thompson, Weston, and Wollaston, which, if ever formally executed, were soon forfeited or abandoned, like some others that might be added from the Records; also the patent of Connecticut,

March 19, 1631, which proceeded from the Earl of Warwick personally, and was apparently founded on an actual or expected title passed, or to be passed, from the Council to himself. It is possible that, like the deed of Cape Ann to the Pilgrims, by Lord Sheffield in 1623, it was based on a contemplated division among the Council that was never perfected.[1] Grants were sometimes spoken of as made that were not drawn up; and sometimes the execution, long delayed, was not formally completed, so that the Council felt at liberty to confirm or reject them. To some patents there were conditions attached; such as rent, and the introduction of settlers within a certain time, to remain a certain time, which, if not complied with, might occasion a forfeiture.

Four in Dr. Palfrey's list are for the benefit of the Pilgrims at Plymouth; but the last and amplest absorbed or cancelled the others.

The first act of this nature for the benefit of the Pilgrims, was dated June 1, 1621. The other grants to them of 1622, 1627, and 1630, enlarged their property and powers at Plymouth, and gave them a large tract of land on the Kennebec, for trade with the Indians; by the special favor, it is said, of the Earl of Warwick, who seems to have been devoted to the interests of the Puritans.

There remain to be mentioned fourteen grants professedly emanating from the Council: —

1st, To Captain John Mason, March 9, 1622, of the coast and islands between Salem River and the Merrimack, called by him "*Mariana*." It is said to have been imperfectly executed; and was disregarded in subsequent conveyances.

2d, To Gorges and Mason jointly, Aug. 10, 1622, of the country between the Merrimack and Kennebec Rivers, and sixty miles inland from their mouths, "which they intend to name the PROVINCE OF MAINE."

3d, To Robert Gorges, of ten miles from Boston towards Salem, just

[1] Historians have stated, without giving any authority, that the Connecticut territory was granted by the Council to Warwick, in 1630, and even that it was confirmed to him by the King. But the Council Records show that "a rough draft" of a patent for the Earl of Warwick, relating to the same territory, was under consideration three months after his conveyance to Lord Say and Sele, &c.

before he came over as Lieutenant-Governor. The *tenure* was by the sword, or *per gladium comitatus*.

4th, To a grandson of Sir F. Gorges and his associates, of twenty-four thousand acres, on both sides of York River in Maine, with the islands within three leagues of the coast. This patent, though referred by Gorges to 1623, was not executed till Dec. 2, 1631, and was reissued the following March, with a partial change of associates. The consideration was their engaging to build a town.

5th, To the Massachusetts Company, which, as confirmed by the royal charter, March 4, 1629, covered Mason's Mariana, the tract of Robert Gorges, and a part of the territory of Gorges and Mason; as it was to embrace the country from three miles north of every part of the Merrimack River to three miles south of Charles River.

6th, To Captain John Mason, Nov. 7, 1629, from the middle of the Merrimack River to the middle of the Piscataqua, and sixty miles inland from their mouths, and all islands within five leagues of the coast; "which he intends to name NEW HAMPSHIRE."

A series of grants succeeded, that are well known as prolific of suits and legal questions to the inhabitants of Maine. These are —

1st, The joint patents of what are now the towns of Saco and Biddeford.

2d, The Muscongus, or Lincoln grant, between the Muscongus and the Penobscot Rivers, which became the famous *Waldo* patent.

3d, The Lygonia, or Plough patent, of forty miles square, between Cape Porpoise and Cape Elizabeth, including the now City of Portland. The date and the grantees are both uncertain.[1]

4th, The Swamscot patent, covering the towns of Dover, Durham, and Stratham.

5th, The Black Point grant of fifteen hundred acres in Scarborough.

6th, To Gorges and Mason, and certain associates, of lands on the Piscataqua, where some of their people had settled.

7th, To Richard Bradshaw, fifteen hundred acres above the head of "Pashippscot," where he had been living.[2]

8th, To Trelawney and Goodyear, a tract between the Black Point patent and the Casco River.

9th, The well-known Pemaquid patent of twelve thousand acres, Feb. 29, 1632, to be land "not *lately* granted, settled, and inhabited by any English."

[1] Willis, in Hist. of Portland.

[2] This is added from the Council Records.

All writers, until recently, have called the grant of Aug. 10, 1622, the *Laconia* grant. It was not till a copy of the grant of August, 1622, was obtained from England, by the Maine Historical Society, for publication in 1863, that the error became apparent. The real Laconia grant was dated Nov. 17, 1629, and conveyed to Gorges and Mason "all those lands and countries bordering upon the great lake, or lakes and rivers known by the name of the River and Lake, or Rivers and Lakes of the Iroquois," meaning thereby Lake Champlain. The final and effective grant of the Province of Maine was to Gorges, directly from the King, April 3, 1639, when the Council for New England had ceased to exist.

The heirs of Gorges and Mason, after vain efforts to sustain their title to Maine and New Hampshire, ultimately surrendered their claims for a moderate consideration; while the minor tracts, in process of time, came to be defined and adjusted by legislative and judicial interference.

It may be said, with probable truth, that, but for the success of Massachusetts, all other grants or patents from the Council would have come to nought; and that, on one side the French, and on the other the Dutch, or else the original natives, would have become possessed of all New England. It was so asserted when Massachusetts was summoned to show cause why its charter should not be revoked.

Yet the charter of the Massachusetts Company gave the death blow to the Council for New England. In connection with the litigious attacks of the Virginia Company, who desired to break up the monopoly of the fisheries, and the protest of the French ambassador, it is assigned, by themselves, as the principal cause of the surrender of their charter. They complained that their own grant to this company had been unfairly obtained and unreasonably enlarged, absorbing the tract of Robert Gorges, and riding over the heads of all those lords who had portions assigned them in the King's presence; that its members wholly excluded themselves from the government of the Council, and made themselves a free people, "whereby they did rend in pieces the first foundation of the building." On account of these troubles, and upon these considerations, they resolved to surrender their own patent to the King.

The political purpose of the founders of Massachusetts, and its friends in England, when clearly understood, will be seen to shed a new light upon many obscure points of our own and also of English history.

It is curious to observe, among the men who intended to come to New England, Pym, Hampden, Sir Arthur Hazlerig, and Oliver Cromwell. It is instructive to notice, that it was the Earl of Warwick who managed to obtain the patent for the Massachusetts Company, as Gorges relates; that it was the same earl who, on his own responsibility, conveyed Connecticut to Lord Say and Sele, Lord Rich, Charles Fiennes, John Pym, John Hampden, Herbert Pelham, and others; and then to remark that, in the revolution which soon took place in England, the Earl of Warwick, Lord Say and Sele, and Lord Mandeville, the son-in-law of Warwick, are designated by Clarendon as chief managers among the Peers; while in the House of Commons, Pym, Hampden, Sir Harry Vane, and Nathaniel Fiennes, brother of Charles, were principal leaders. From these, and many other coincidences, it looks as if the revolution at home was only a carrying out and extending of the political experiment which it had first been their intention to try in New England. And the impression is strengthened, when we learn that members of the original Massachusetts Company took a prominent part in all the public movements of the revolutionary party, — in Parliament, in the Army, in the Assembly of Divines at Westminster, and among the Judges appointed for the trial of the King. It is not strange that the lesser purpose, and the more limited intention, should have been forgotten or obscured, amid the exciting events of the grander and more comprehensive undertaking.[1]

A more particular account of the grants made or proposed by the Council, which would have been tedious in a lecture before a general audience, is given in a supplement.

[1] Dr. Palfrey (Hist. of N. E., vol. i. p. 308) refers to the probable purpose of a renovated England in America entertained by the Puritan leaders, in view of the clouds that were gathering over the political prospects at home; and quotes a remark of Burke, to whom the same reflection had occurred. See also Hist. of N. E., vol. i. p. 390, n.

SUPPLEMENT.

Every one at all familiar with the grants from the Council for New England must be aware that their history would properly fill the pages of a large volume. All that a single lecture can accomplish, even with the aid of a supplement, is to take the place of an introductory chapter, giving some account of the subject-matter, and an abstract of the most important facts and conclusions. It is believed that the list of grants here presented is more full and more correct than any before attempted; but in a case where our most careful historians have been led into remarkable errors, it would be unreasonable to demand absolute accuracy or completeness. The patience required for the selection and verification of the particulars now brought together, the reader will hardly be able to appreciate.

Summary of Grants from the Great Council for New England.

No. 1.—The first grant from the Council, of which there is any record, was taken out in the name of John Peirce, citizen and clothworker of London, and his associates, June 1, 1621, for the benefit of the Pilgrims at Plymouth. It allowed one hundred acres to each planter within seven years, free liberty to fish on the coast of New England, and fifteen hundred acres for public uses. After seven years, a rent of two shillings for every one hundred acres to be paid annually. The lands having been properly surveyed and set out by metes and bounds at the charge of the grantees, upon reasonable request within seven years they are to be confirmed by deed, and letters of incorporation granted, with liberty to make laws and constitutions of government. In the mean time, the undertakers and planters are authorized to establish such laws and ordinances, and appoint such officers, as they shall by most voices agree upon. This patent was first printed from the original manuscript, with an introduction and notes, by Charles Deane, Esq., in 1854. The land was to be taken anywhere not within ten miles of land already inhabited, or located by authority of the Council, unless it be on the opposite side of some river.

No. 2.—1622, March 9. Captain John Mason's "*Mariana.*" The headland "known by the name of Tragabigsenda, or Cape Anne, with the north, south, and east shores thereof," from Naumkeag River, to a river north-westward from the Cape (the Merrimack), then up that river to its head, thence across to the head of the other river; with all the islands within three miles of the shore. Hubbard, Hist. of N. E., pp. 614–16.

No. 3.—1622, April 20. To John Peirce. This was an attempt of Peirce to surrender the indenture of June 1, 1621, and take a deed of the lands to himself, his heirs, associates, and assigns. When it was ascertained that his associates were not privy to this movement, he was compelled to agree to submit the matter to the authority and pleasure of the Council. See Council Records, in Proceedings of American Antiquarian Society of April, 1867.

No. 4.—1622, May 31. In the Records of the Council of this date, it is stated, that "order is given for patents to be drawn for the Earl of Warwick, and his associates, the Lord Gorges, Sir Robert Mansell, Sir Ferdinando Gorges." Dr. Palfrey regards this order as referring to a division of the country, from the Bay of Fundy to Narraganset Bay, among twenty associates, in which the region about Cape Ann fell to Lord Sheffield, who sold a patent for it to the New-Plymouth people. Captain John Smith, in his "Generall Historie," published in 1624, says that New England was "engrossed by twenty patentees who divided my map into twenty parts, and cast lots for their shares." Mr. Thornton, in his interesting work on Cape Ann, has a map from Purchas representing this division, and a fac-simile of the patent from Lord Sheffield above mentioned. There may have been such a division suggested when Captain Smith wrote, and Purchas, writing at the same date, may have prepared the map to correspond with that expectation. The above order from the Records of the Council seems, however, to be limited in its application to the Earl of Warwick, and *three* associates; and there is no account of such a division as the map exhibits in the Records, as we have them, or in the "Relation of the President and Council," or in the "Briefe Narration" of Gorges, or in the act of the Resignation of the Charter, where it would naturally appear. The division referred to by Gorges in his "Briefe Narration," and which is described in the proceedings for the surrender of the charter, is a very different one, and quite inconsistent with that exhibited by the map. It is not improbable that the distribution mentioned by Smith, may be alluded to in the agreement for the division, Feb. 3, 1634–5, thus: "Forasmuch as . . . in the 8th (? 18th) year of the reign of King James, of blessed memory, in whose presence lots were drawn for settling of divers and sundry divisions of land, on the sea-coast of the said country, upon most of us, *which hitherto have never been confirmed in the said lands so allotted*, and to the intent that every one of us according to equity, and in some reasonable manner answerable to his adventures or other interest, may enjoy a proportion of the said country to be immediately holden of his Majesty, we therefore," &c. The deed from Lord Sheffield, dated Jan. 1, 1623–4, is in direct conflict with the grant from the Council to Mason, March 9, 1622. (See above, No. 2.) Lord Sheffield's conveyance of Cape Ann, like that of Connecticut by the Earl of Warwick, was probably based upon a proposed division that was never legally completed. See note at the end of this Supplement.

No. 5.—1622, Aug. 10. By indenture to Sir Ferdinando Gorges and Captain John Mason, "All that part of the mainland in New England lying upon the sea-coast, betwixt the rivers of Merrimack and Sagadahoc, and to the furthest heads of the said rivers, and so forwards up into the land westward, until threescore miles be finished from the first entrance of the aforesaid rivers, and half way over; that is to say, to the midst of the said two rivers," "together with all the islands and islets within five leagues' distance of the premises," which, it is stated, the grantees with the consent of the President and Council intend to name "*The Province of Maine.*"

The error of Dr. Belknap in supposing this to be the *Laconia* grant, has been repeated by historians to the present time. Mr. Deane, who saw the true Laconia deed in the Record Office in London, two years ago, gives the correct statement in the Report of the Council of the American Antiquarian Society, Oct. 21, 1868. The grant of Aug. 10, 1622, is given in full in the Provincial Papers of New Hampshire, edited by Dr. Bouton (Concord, 1867), who also makes the correction. Hutchinson, Hist., vol. i. p. 282, ed. of 1795, says this grant "did not appear to have been signed, sealed, or witnessed by any order of the Council." See Provincial Papers of New Hampshire, p. 28, *note*. For an interesting opinion of Sir William Jones, the King's Attorney-General, in 1679, on the validity of the several grants to Mason, on the absence of any right in the Council for New England to confer powers of government, and on the requirement of their charter that their grants should appear to be the acts of a majority of the Council present at a lawful meeting, see Hubbard's Hist. of N. E., pp. 616–621.

No. 6. — 1622, Nov. 16. The Council Records speak of Mr. Thompson's patent as "this day signed." In the Appendix to the memorial volume of the Maine Historical Society, is a copy of an ancient, but imperfect list of New-England patents, from the Record Office, London, in which the first named is "a patent to David Thompson, M. Jobe, M. Sherwood, of Plimouth, for a pt. of Piscattowa River." Whatever Thompson's grant may have been, it came to nothing. He was a Scotchman, apparently in the service of the Gorges' family, and lived at one time on the Piscataqua River; and at another, on "*Thompson's Island*," in Boston Harbor.

No. 7. — 1622. Thomas Weston was supposed to have a patent of land at Wessagusset (Weymouth, Mass.). Bradford, p. 122. "Weston's patent is not extant, and little is known respecting it." Deane, in Bradford, p. 124, *note*.

No. 8. — 1622, Dec. 30. To Robert Gorges, son of Sir Ferdinando, "All that part of the mainland commonly called Messachusiac, on the north-east side of the Bay known by the name of Massachuset, together with all the shores along the sea for ten English miles in a strait line towards the north-east, and thirty miles into the mainland through all the breadth aforesaid," including the islands, within three miles of any part of said land, not before granted. The grant is given at length in the "Briefe Narration," chap. xxiii. Its tenure is by "the sword," *per Gladium Comitatus*. When Robert Gorges came over, he located himself at Wessagusset, which was not within his grant. Among the manuscript records of Massachusetts is a memorandum to the effect, that, Robert Gorges having died without issue, the land descended to his eldest brother, John, who conveyed it to Sir William Brereton, Jan. 10, 1628. Brereton died, leaving a son and a daughter. The son died, and the daughter married Edmund Lenthall; and their only daughter and heir married Mr. Levett, of the Inner Temple, who claimed the land in right of his wife. See note to the "Briefe Narration" of Gorges, in Coll. of Me. Hist. Soc., vol. ii. p. 46.

No. 9. — 1623. To Ferdinando Gorges, grandson of Sir Ferdinando, and his associates, among whom were "Walter Norton, Lieutenant-Colonel Thomas Coppyn, Esq., Samuel Maverick, Esq., Thomas Graves, Gent. (an engineer), Raphe Glover, merchant, William Jeffryes, Gent., John Busley,

Gent., Joel Woolsey, Gent., all of New England." The date of 1623 is derived from the "Briefe Narration," chap. xxv., where Gorges says his grandson, and some of his associates, hastened to take possession at the time, carrying with them their families; but according to the Council Records, the date of sealing the patent was Dec. 2, 1631. It was renewed March 2, 1632, with some change in the associates, and the former patent cancelled. The grant was first, of one hundred acres to each person transported within seven years, if he remained three years; second, of twelve thousand more, to the associates, on the east side of the river Agamenticus, on the coast three miles, and into the land so far as to contain twelve thousand acres, and one hundred acres more for each person; third, to F. Gorges himself, besides the above, twelve thousand acres on the opposite or western side of the river along the coast westerly to the land appropriated to the plantation at Pascataquack (Portsmouth), and so along the river Agamenticus, and the bounds of Pascataquack, into the mainland so far as to contain twelve thousand acres; with all the islands within three leagues into the ocean. In consideration that they have undertaken to build a town. Two shillings to be paid yearly for every one hundred acres of arable land after seven years. This description is from the Records of the Council, in Proceedings of the American Society of April, 1867. See also respecting this grant, Coll. of Me. Hist. Soc., vol. ii. pp. 49, 50, *note*. At a meeting of the Council, March 22, 1637 (after the surrender of their charter), it is stated that this grant was renewed to Edward Godfrey and others, and "this day the seal of the company was set thereunto."

No. 10. — 1628. To the Plymouth people, of lands on the Kennebec. Renewed and enlarged the next year. Bradford, p. 232.

No. 11. — The Massachusetts patent of March 19, 1628, made into a Royal charter, March 4, 1629. Dr. Palfrey expresses an opinion, that the patentees among whom the coast of New England had been partitioned six years before surrendered their claims, founded on the following record of the Massachusetts Company: "Sept. 29, 1629. — It is thought fit, and ordered, that the secretary shall write out a copy of the former grant to the Earl of Warwick and others, which was by them resigned to this company, to be presented to his lordship."

The patent of the Massachusetts Company from the New-England Council is not extant; and there is some mystery attending the manner of its procurement, as well as about its original extent. Sir F. Gorges says, that, on the request of the Earl of Warwick, he consented to a grant that should not be prejudicial to the interests of his son Robert. In the act of resignation of their charter by the Council, they say, that the Massachusetts Company, "presenting the names of honest and religious men, easily obtained their first desires; but those being once gotten, they used other means to advance themselves a step beyond their first proportions to a second grant, surreptitiously gotten, of other lands also, justly passed unto Captain Robert Gorges long before." Robert Mason, petitioning the King, in 1676, for possession of the lands granted to his grandfather, declares that the Massachusetts Company "did surreptitiously, and *unknown to the said Council*, get the seal of the said Council affixed to a grant of certain lands;" and did, by their subtile practices, get a confirmation under the great seal of England. In their answer to this petition, the Massachusetts authorities deny the charge, no doubt with sincerity; but all circumstances leave an impression on the mind that, by the influence, perhaps by the *management*, of the Earl of Warwick, advantages were gained, which many, if not most, of the Council would have objected to. By the favor of Warwick, the Plymouth people obtained their lands on the Kennebec; and the patent of Connecticut was made in his own name, by what authority does not sufficiently appear. These facts may explain the dissatisfaction which arose between the Council and Warwick, their president, and the efforts of the Council to get the seal out of his possession. He seems not to have cared for personal proprietorship, but to have desired to give his Puritan friends the advantage of his official position and influence.

No. 12.—1629, Nov. 7. By indenture, to Captain John Mason, part of the same territory which was conveyed by a similar deed to Gorges and Mason, jointly, Aug. 10, 1622. The difference being, that instead of extending from the middle of the Merrimack River to the middle of the *Sagadahoc*, on the coast, and back into the interior sixty miles between those limits, this grant extends no farther than the middle of the Piscataqua River, but the same distance into the interior, between the Merrimack and the Piscataqua, including also islands within five leagues of the shore; "which the said Captain John Mason, with the consent of the President and Council, intends to name *New Hampshire*." In the deed to Gorges and Mason, it was proposed to call the whole territory the *Province of Maine*. The form and general phraseology of the two deeds are alike. If the first instrument was valid, this one, of necessity, could be of no effect. See above, No. 5; Provincial Papers of New Hampshire, pp. 21 and 28, *note*; Hazard, vol. i. p. 289.

No. 13.—1629, Nov. 17. This is the true *Laconia* grant, which, by a mistake, originating doubtless in a misprint, has sometimes had the date Nov. 27, instead of Nov. 17, assigned to it. There is a copy of it in the office of the Secretary of State of Massachusetts. It embraces, in substance, the lands bordering upon the great lake (Champlain), or lakes and rivers commonly known by the name of the river and lake, or rivers and lakes, of the Iroquois; together with those lakes and rivers, and the land within ten miles of any part of them on the south or east, and from the west end or sides so far to the west as shall extend half-way into the next great lake to the westward; thence northward into the north side of the main river running from the great western lakes into the river of Canada, including all islands within the precincts.

The nullity of this grant is shown by the fact, that so many careful historians have confounded it with that of Aug. 10, 1622, another imperfect and ineffectual instrument. See N. H. Provincial Papers, vol. i. pp. 28 and 38. Hubbard, Hist. of N. E., chap. xxxi., says, that after three years of fruitless endeavors for the more full discovery of "an imaginary Province called Laconia," the agents of Gorges returned to England with a "non est inventa Provincia."

No. 14.—1629, o.s., Jan. 13. The last Plymouth patent, to William Bradford and his associates, in consideration that they have lived nine years in New England, and planted a town at their own cost, and are able to relieve new planters: All that part of New England between the middle of Cohasset River and the middle of Narraganset River, and up from the mouths of those rivers in a strait line into the mainland as far as the utmost limits of the country called "Pokenacutt, alias Sowamsett;" and bounded on the east by the ocean, without including islands on the coast. And as the grantees have no convenient place for trading or fishing within their own precincts, there is also conveyed to them all that tract of land, between, or extending from, the utmost limits of Cobbisconte, which adjoins the river Kennebec, towards the western ocean, and a place called the Falls at Nequamkike; and the space of fifteen miles on each side of the river Kennebec, and all the said river Kennebec that lies within the said limits and bounds, eastward, westward, northward, or southward, last above mentioned. The patent gave a right of passage to and from the ocean, and the right of fishing on the neighboring shores, not inhabited or otherwise disposed of, and also privileges of administration. It appears to have no other signature than that of the Earl of Warwick.

The Plymouth people tried in vain to procure a charter from the Crown, with powers of government. They strengthened their rights in Maine by deeds from the Indians, and endeavored to establish settlements; but tired of the vexation which that property gave them, they sold their entire interest, in 1661, to four persons, for four hundred pounds. In 1753, the then owners became a corporation, by the name of "the Proprietors of the Kennebec Purchase;" and, after much controversy and litigation, the obscure boundaries were ultimately adjusted. See Gardiner's "Hist. of the Kennebec Purchase," in Coll. of Maine Hist. Society, vol. ii. The patent is in Hazard, vol. i. pp. 298–303.

No. 15. — 1630, Feb. 12. At this date, two deeds were issued of the land between Cape Elizabeth and Cape Porpoise in Maine, each of four miles along the coast, and eight miles into the mainland; one on the north side of the Saco River to Thomas Lewis and Richard Bonython, the other on the south side of the Saco River to John Oldham and Richard Vines. From these grants have sprung the two towns of Saco and Biddeford, retaining nearly the same limits. Hist. of Saco and Biddeford, by George Folsom.

No. 16. — 1630, March 13. The Muscongus grant, afterwards known as the Waldo patent. The abstract of this grant, in Hazard, Coll. vol. i. pp. 304, 305, taken from the Maine Records, is unintelligible. Williamson, Hist. of Me. vol. i. p. 240, describes it as extending from the seaboard, between the rivers Penobscot and Muscongus, to an unsurveyed line running east and west so far north as would, without interfering with any other patent, embrace a territory equal to thirty miles square; and adds, in a note, that the north line, as since settled, is in the south line of Hampden, Newbury, and Dixmont. The grant was to John Beauchamp and Thomas Leverett, of England. Leverett is said to have succeeded to the property on the death of Beauchamp. John Leverett, President of Harvard College, as sole heir of his grandfather, became the owner in 1715. By the admission of partners, a company was formed, consisting of thirty proprietors, who first employed Brigadier-General Samuel Waldo as agent, and ultimately assigned to him the largest interest in the patent. Coll. of Me. Hist. Society, vol. vi. art. xv.

No. 17. — 1630. The Lygonia, or Plough patent, considered to extend from Kennebunk River to Harpswell in Casco Bay, or, as usually stated, from Cape

Porpoise to Cape Elizabeth, and forty miles inland. Hubbard, Ind. Wars, part ii. p. 9, says the patent was granted in the year 1630, and signed by the Earl of Warwick and Sir Ferdinando Gorges. Willis, Hist. of Portland, p. 29, says he has never "been able to discover this patent, nor ascertain its date, nor who are the patentees." Different names are given in different accounts. An unsuccessful attempt at settlement was made in 1631. In 1643 the patent was transferred to Alexander Rigby, a rich English lawyer, who appointed George Cleaves as his deputy. The contest of conflicting jurisdictions between the representative of Rigby and the representatives of Gorges was only ended when Massachusetts took possession of the whole territory in 1672. Sullivan, Hist. of Me., pp. 309–319; ib., "Land Titles," p. 44; Williamson, Hist. of Me. vol. i. p. 238; Folsom, Hist. of Saco and Biddeford, pp. 26–28.

No. 18. — 1631, March 12. To Edward Hilton, "all that part of the river Piscataqua called Hilton's Point, with the S. side of the said river up to the falls of Squamscot (or Swamscot), and three miles into the mainland for breadth." Following Dr. Belknap and Dr. Palfrey, I stated in the lecture that this grant covered the towns of Dover, Durham, and Stratham. But in the recently published Provincial Papers of New Hampshire, p. 29, Dr. Bouton, the editor, says, "No document relating to New Hampshire has been so grossly misrepresented as this. . . . It covered only Hilton's Point; . . . and the whole did not exceed a township five miles square." Its extent and its ownership, in 1656, as shown in a record of partition, by authority of Massachusetts, may be seen in ibid., pp. 221–223.

No. 19. — 1631, Nov. 4, by the Council Records (Willis, and others, say Nov. 1). To Thomas Cammock, fifteen hundred acres, lying upon the mainland along the sea-coast, on the east side of Black Point River. This is now a part of Scarborough, and included Stratton's islands. Possession given in 1633; patent confirmed by Gorges in 1640. The tract is now held under this title. Willis, Hist. of Portland, p. 31.

No. 20. — 1631, Nov. 4. To Richard Bradshaw, "fifteen hundred acres, to be allotted above the head of Pashippscot (Pejepscot), on the north side thereof, *not formerly granted to any other*." Council Records. This, and the grant to Cammock, were in consideration that the grantees had been living on the premises for some years.

The Council Records of Dec. 2, 1631, say, that Lord Gorges and Sir Ferdinando Gorges gave order for two patents, one for Walter Bagnall for a small island, called Richmond Island, and fifteen hundred acres on the mainland, to be selected by Walter Neale and Richard Vines; another for John Stratton, of two thousand acres, on the south side of Cape Porpoise, and "on the other side northwards into the south side of the harbor's mouth of Cape Porpoise." Sainsbury's Calendar, p. 137, has it "John Stratton of Shotley, co. Suffolk, and his associates."

Bagnall was at Richmond Island in 1628, where he was killed by the Indians, Oct. 3, 1631 (previous to the date above stated). Willis, Hist. of Portland, p. 25.

No. 21. — 1631, Nov. 4. To Sir Ferdinando Gorges and Captain John Mason, and their associates, a portion of land on the Piscataqua River, "along the seashore westward five miles, and by an imaginary line into the mainland, north to the bounds of a plantation belonging to Edward Hilton; and the islands within the same river eastward, together with three miles along the shore to the eastward of said river, and opposite to the habitation and plantation where Captain Neale lives, and up into the mainland northerly, by all the breadth aforesaid, thirty miles; with the lakes at the head of said river." In consideration of service formerly done, and the settlement there by Captain Neale, the erection of salt-pans, &c.

They were to pay to the Council forty shillings sterling, payable at the Assurance House, Royal Exchange, London, if demanded. First payment at the Feast of St. Michael, 1632, "and so for all service from year to year." Abstract in the Council Records. Hubbard, Hist. of N. E., chap. xxxi., says, that in his time, a copy of this indenture was extant at Portsmouth. He makes the date Nov. 3, 1631, and the instrument to be without signature or seal; but he says, "it seems to be of as much force as other instruments of like nature produced on such like accounts at the present time." The Council Records state that the patent was *sealed* Nov. 4. Hubbard calls the sum to be paid forty-eight pounds per annum, instead of the forty shillings mentioned in the Records. The names of the associates are in Hubbard.

No. 22. — 1631, Dec. 1. To Robert Trelawny and Moses Goodyear, the tract lying between Cammock's patent "and the bay and river of Casco, and extending northwards into the mainland, so far as the limits and bounds of the lands granted to the said Thomas Cammock, do and ought to extend towards the north." It was claimed that this grant included Cape Elizabeth, and nearly all the ancient town of Falmouth, and part of Gorham and Richmond island. A contest was maintained, in reference to boundaries, for many years, extending beyond the lives of the first settlers. Willis, Hist. of Portland, pp. 32, 33; Council Records.

No. 23. — 1632, Feb. 29. To Robert Aldworth and Giles Elbridge: first, one hundred acres for every person transported by them within seven years, adjacent to twelve thousand acres, afterwards mentioned, and not lately granted, or settled and inhabited, by any English. Second, twelve thousand acres more to be laid out near the river Pemaquid, along the sea-coast as the coast lieth, and up the river as far as may contain the said twelve thousand acres and the hundred acres for each person transported, together with all the islands opposite their coast within three leagues into the ocean. In consideration that they have undertaken to build a town, &c. Powers of government, or administration, are also expressed in the deed, which was signed by the Earl of Warwick and Sir Ferdinando Gorges. Pemaquid, like other territories in Maine, has been a subject of much controversy, and has experienced many vicissitudes. It is said that one of its sons is preparing a history of its fortunes. "*Ancient* Pemaquid" has already been the subject of an Historical Review, by Mr. Thornton. A notarial copy on parchment of the original deed, and two volumes of the records of its proprietors, from 1743 to 1774, are in the library of the American Antiquarian Society.

No. 24. — 1632, June 16. Under this date, in Mr. Sainsbury's Calendar of Colonial Papers in the State Paper Office, London, is the following entry: "Grant of the Council for New England to George Way and Thomas Purchas, of certain lands in New England, called the River Bishopscotte, and all that bounds and limits the mainland adjoining the river to the extent of two miles." By Bishopscotte is meant *Pejepscot*, now Brunswick. Purchas, it is said, took possession in 1628, and lived there many years. In 1639, he conveyed the title and jurisdiction to Massachusetts, reserving the interest and possession of such lands as he should use and improve within seven years. Hazard, vol. i. p. 457. The country was depopulated during the Indian war of 1675; after which, Richard Wharton obtained the claims of both Purchas and Way, expecting a confirmation from the King, but died before his plans were completed. See Willis, Hist. of Portland, p. 24; Coll. of Me. Hist. Society, vol. iii. articles v. and vi.

The original deed to Way and Purchas has long since been lost, and no record of it remains. This grant was the subject of a long and bitter controversy between the Pejepscot proprietors and other claimants, not finally settled till about 1814. Willis, Hist. of Portland, p. 64, *note*.

The efforts of the Council to divide New England into provinces, or lordships, and distribute these among themselves, remain to be noticed. There are indications that such a design was entertained at an early period; but the charter was found to be defective, and arrangements were soon made for a new one, from which all the patentees who had not paid their dues were to be excluded. To entitle a partner to the benefit of the lands and the privileges of a patentee, a payment of £110 was required. It was voted that delinquents should forfeit all interest under the charter, and their rights and privileges be transferred to persons willing to take their places and make the payments. Not more than half of the original patentees accepted the conditions of membership, and fewer still seem to have redeemed their pledges.

At various dates in the Records, — May 31, 1622, July 24, 1622, June 21, and 26, 1632, — agreements and orders are introduced having in view the assignment of territory, more or less particularly designated, to certain members. But all these orders and agreements, whatever may have been the intentions of the Council at the time, were treated as of no validity when they came to surrender the charter to the King. In preparation for that event, they met on the 3d of February, 1634–5, and divided the coast of New England into eight parts; viz.: —

1st, From the southern limits in the fortieth degree of latitude to Hudson's River.

2d, From Hudson's River to a river or creek ("near a place called Redunes or Reddownes") about sixty miles eastward.

3d, From that river eastward about forty-five miles, to a river or creek called Fresh River.

4th, From the Connecticut River to the Narraganset River, accounted about sixty miles.

5th, From Narraganset River around Cape Cod to Naumkeag (Salem).

6th, From Naumkeag to Piscataqua Harbor and River.

7th, From Piscataqua Harbor to the Kennebec River.

8th, From the Kennebec River to the St. Croix.

By comparing the Council Records, the "Briefe Narration" of Gorges, and Hubbard's History of New England, we find that the *First* portion was assigned to the Earl of Arundel (Gorges says Lord Mulgrave, who was originally Lord Sheffield); the *Second* to the Duke of Richmond (in place of the Duke of Lenox); the *Third* to the Earl of Carlisle; the *Fourth* to Lord Gorges; the *Fifth* to the Marquis of Hamilton; the *Sixth* to Captain John Mason; the *Seventh* to Sir Ferdinando Gorges; the *Eighth* to Lord Alexander.

Each of these divisions was to extend back into the interior sixty miles, except the last, which reached to the "river of Canada."

Each division, except the last two, was to have, in addition, ten thousand acres on the "east part of Sagadahoc." The seventh division was to have with it the north half of the Isles of Shoals and the Isles of Capawock, Nautican, &c., near Cape Cod; and the eighth division the Island called Mattawack, or the Long Island, west of Cape Cod. The south half of the Isles of Shoals was to go with the division of Captain Mason.

There is apparently a space omitted between "Fresh River," wherever that was, and the Connecticut.

These divisions are described with particularity in the Records of the Council. It is stated that the grants were signed and delivered on the fourteenth day of April; that, on the eighteenth, leases, for three thousand years, of the several divisions, were made to the persons interested; and that on the twenty-second, deeds of feofment were made to them.

To every one that had previously a lawful grant of lands was reserved the freehold with its rights, he "laying down his *jura regalia* (if he have any) and paying some small acknowledgment, for that he is now to hold his land anew of the proprietor of the division."

It is to be inferred that this remnant of the Council included all who were then desirous, or qualified, to receive assignments of territory.

The account of this division by Hubbard, Hist. of N. E., chap. xxxi., differs from that in the Records in many important particulars, and is less likely to be correct.

On the 26th of April, 1635, the Council prepared a petition to the King that he would cause patents to be made for the several divisions, to be held immediately from himself; and on the 5th of May resolved that the deeds should be acknowledged before a Master in Chancery, and enrolled before the surrender of the charter, and the King be requested to confirm them under the Great Seal; *also to prosecute a suit at law for the repeal of the Massachusetts patent.* They also prepared the form of an acceptance for the King to adopt on their surrender of the charter, and a declaration of the reasons on account of which the surrender was made. The formal resignation was dated June 7, 1635.

The acceptance of the surrender may have been held in abeyance for a time, as meetings of the Council are recorded, Nov. 26, 1635, March 22, 1637, and Nov. 1, 1638, at which business was transacted. The Earl of Lindsay desired to have a proportion of land allotted to him; which was assented to, to be "on ye river where the Flemings are seated," above the Duke of Richmond. Lord Maltravers wished for "a degree more in longitude and latitude joining his limits (had he taken the place of some one of the eight grantees?), which the

Council were willing to assent to, if he would declare in what direction he wanted it. The Earl of Sterling's (Lord Alexander's) proportion was carried more distinctly to the Kennebec River; and Lord Gorges, and Sir Ferdinando Gorges, were each allowed sixty miles further up into the mainland.

Our supplement can afford no space for comments or inferences; but it is apparent that no such division as is referred to by Captain John Smith in 1624, and laid down on the map published by Purchas, was recognized by the Council as valid, and that no territorial rights were admitted as having belonged to the Earl of Warwick. The charter of Massachusetts was to be annulled, the entire coast of New England divided among the eight Proprietary's above named, and all remaining rights and powers belonging to the Grand Patent surrendered to the King, Sir Ferdinando Gorges to be made his Lieutenant or Governor over the whole country as a province of the Crown. Political events at home prevented the accomplishment of this design. Captain John Mason and Sir Ferdinando Gorges alone contrived to secure permanent advantages to themselves. No other executed deed of any of the proposed divisions has come down to us but that to Mason, April 22, 1635, without, however, a confirmation from the King. Gorges received his division, with the additional sixty miles into the interior, in the form of a charter from the Crown, dated April 3, 1639. Obscurity of description, the overlapping of boundaries in different deeds, the introduction of powers which the Council could not legally confer (such as those of government and administration), and imperfect execution, seem to have rendered most of their early grants unsound in their own estimation; and perhaps all of them would have proved to be void or voidable if subjected to a strict legal test. It will simplify the subject, if we strike from the list of those which preceded the final division the first eight and the thirteenth as of no subsequent consequence, and rest the claims of Mason and Gorges upon the deeds to Mason of Nov. 7, 1629 and April 22, 1635, and the charter to Gorges of April 3, 1639, as some of their representatives appear to have done (see Prov. Papers of N.H. p. 28, *note*). Massachusetts ultimately took the place of these great proprietors, and extended her jurisdiction over most of the territory covering the minor patents, whose adjustment among the parties interested was the work of much time, and a great deal of law.

NOTE.

In Hubbard's History of N. E., pp. 231–2, is what purports to be an attested copy of so much of the agreement for a division among themselves, by the Council, as relates to the portion assigned to Captain John Mason. It is signed by the other seven Council members. It contains also the paragraphs which, in the Records of the Council, precede and follow the list and descriptions of the several divisions; and an error in copying the first paragraph has increased the confusion heretofore attending this subject. The *agreement*, as the Records show, was dated Feb. 3, 1634; and the copyist of Hubbard's document introduced that date into the first paragraph, which alludes to an attempt in the lifetime of King James, and in his presence, to effect a similar division, making it appear as if the attempt occurred on that date. In the second edition of Hubbard, the editor, Mr. Harris, observing that there must be a mistake, altered the figures from 1634 to 1624; a worse error, as it has led to the belief that a division was actually made on the 3d of February, 1624. The *Records* mention no such date.

It is proper to state, that the original Records of the Council for New England are not extant. The copy printed by the American Antiquarian Society, in 1867, was obtained by me in London, at the State Paper Office, where the parts so recovered exist in the form of a transcript, apparently made for a judicial purpose. Our historians were already familiar with them there.

THE COLONY OF NEW PLYMOUTH

AND

ITS RELATIONS TO MASSACHUSETTS.

By WILLIAM BRIGHAM.

THE COLONY OF NEW PLYMOUTH

AND

ITS RELATIONS TO MASSACHUSETTS.

THE colony of New Plymouth comprised all the present territory of the counties of Plymouth, Barnstable, and Bristol, with the exception of Hingham, which was a part of the colony of Massachusetts Bay. It had also an additional strip on its southern border, now included in the State of Rhode Island. Its history as a civil community begins on the signing of the compact, on the eleventh of November, 1620, in the cabin of the "Mayflower," while she lay at anchor in the harbor of Cape Cod; and ends on its union with Massachusetts, under the province charter, in 1691, — a period of seventy-one years. It began with a population of about one hundred persons; and terminated with a population of about nine thousand. It began in doubt and uncertainty, in what they called a "remote corner of the earth;" but the threescore and eleven years of its existence enabled its people to accomplish the great purposes for which they endured and suffered so much, and to establish institutions and principles of civil government, which are now, and will ever be, the pride and admiration of every true friend of freedom.

This colony was the first permanent European settlement in New England. Other and earlier attempts had been made, but had failed. An English colony had been established at Jamestown, in Virginia, a few years before; and the French had made a feeble settlement in Canada. These two colonies were their only European neighbors; and either of them was as incapable of affording aid to the Pilgrims at Plymouth, if they had been so disposed, as if they had been on the other side of the Atlantic. Previous to this settlement, Smith and Gosnold had sailed along the shores of New England, explored various places on its coast; and had published accounts of their voyages at home, giving a most favorable impression of its climate and soil, and the thousand sources of wealth which must follow its occupation.

Early in the seventeenth century, the people of England were looking with intense interest towards the new world, not only as a place for the acquisition of wealth, but as a refuge from the oppressions and burdens which they began so severely to feel. It was this state of feeling which induced James I., in 1606, to grant a charter to two companies to settle Virginia, which was then the name given to the whole country. This charter granted a strip of land on the coast, about one hundred miles wide, and extending from the thirty-fourth to the forty-fifth degree of north latitude. The first, or southern colony, had permission to settle anywhere between the thirty-fourth and forty-first degrees; and the northern colony, anywhere between the thirty-eighth and forty-fifth degrees; but neither colony was permitted to settle within one hundred miles of the one which should make the first settlement.

I refer to this charter now, and shall refer to other charters, merely to enable us fully to understand some of the difficulties, under which the Plymouth colony labored, during their whole history. The Pilgrims before leaving home had obtained a charter from the southern colony, undoubtedly expecting to settle within its limits; but when they arrived at Cape Cod, they found themselves beyond the limits of the southern Virginia company, and, of course, their charter was of no use to them in that position.

It was under these circumstances, and for these reasons, that they established, under their own hands, a Constitution of government in the famous compact of Nov. 11, 1620, in which they acknowledged themselves the subjects of King James, and say, —

"That having undertaken for the glory of God, and advancement of Christian faith, and the honor of our king and country, a voyage to plant the first colony in the northern parts of Virginia, do by these presents, solemnly and mutually, in the presence of God and one another, covenant and combine ourselves in a civil body politic, for our better ordering and preservation, and furtherance of the ends aforesaid. And by virtue hereof, do enact, constitute, and form such just and equal laws, ordinances, acts, constitutions, and offices, from time to time, as shall be thought most meet and convenient for the good of the colony, unto which we promise all due submission and obedience.

"In witness whereof, we have hereunder subscribed our names at Cape Cod, the eleventh of November, in the year of the reign of our sovereign lord, King James of England, France, and Ireland, the eighteenth; and of Scotland, the fifty-fourth. Anno Domini, 1620."

This was their whole constitution of government then, and for ten years afterwards, and was in fact their real constitution, during the whole history of the colony. Subsequent events gave them other claims of authority; but how valid these claims were, we shall see in what thereafter took place.

This agreement bearing the names of nearly all the adult male members of the company, and executed on the very day of their arrival at Cape Cod, and before any one had left the ship, for the purpose of establishing a civil government, under which they could enact laws, and protect and control their little community, is certainly one of the most remarkable acts of these remarkable men. The history of the world had afforded them no precedent of this character. This is the first of written constitutions the world ever knew, and is the sole invention of the Pilgrims. It established principles which were then new and untried. All were made equal before the law, and had an equal voice in the government. All were compelled to submit to the majority, and to give obedience to such laws as the majority should enact. There was no division of powers, no creation of offices, no restraints or checks upon the government. The majority rule of all the people was their only guide. These principles have since become familiar to the American mind, and have in fact become the basis of all our governments; and two and a half centuries have proved the truth of the remark of Governor Bradford, that "such an act, under their circumstances, might be as firm as any patent, and in some respects more sure."[1]

At about the time of the signing of this compact, and without

[1] Bradford's Hist., p. 89; Morton's Memorial, p. 37.

the knowledge of the Pilgrims, the great patent of New England was granted to forty persons, called the "Council established at Plymouth, in the County of Devon, for the Planting and Governing of New England in America." It superseded the first grant to the northern Virginia colony; and granted all the territory from forty to forty-eight degrees north latitude, and from sea to sea. It was this extensive grant, and those that followed it, that afterwards created conflicting claims among the American colonies, which were not fully settled till after the Revolution, and the Independence of the country.

This charter gave the company most extensive powers, and included within its limits the territory which the Pilgrims had settled. As this was a charter from the King, it gave to that company rights superior to those of the Pilgrims, which rested on no higher claim than "squatter sovereignty."

As soon, therefore, as the Pilgrims had learned what this grant was, they applied to the Council at Plymouth, for a grant of the soil which they had taken possession of. A charter was obtained in the name of John Pierce, in 1621; but it was so imperfect, and so little suited to their wants and condition, that the colonists never used it. It gave them no distinct and separate territory; but a grant of a certain number of acres to each settler. It really accomplished nothing towards the establishment of a civil government, which the Pilgrims had so much at heart.

In 1629, another charter was granted to William Bradford and his associates, which, if it had been ratified and approved by the King, would have fully answered the purposes in view. It defined the boundaries of the territory, and gave them, nominally at least, power to make such laws and regulations as should be necessary.

But this charter came from the Council at Plymouth. That Council could grant the soil, but could not confer on the colony powers of government. A grant of these powers could come only from the King. And it was for this reason, that, during their whole history, they exhibited constant anxiety about it, and were from time to time seeking the King's ratification. They sought it from Charles I., and also at the restoration of Charles II.; but they met with no success from either. It was from this want of authority that they lost the territory on their southern border, — the charter to the Rhode Island colony from the King extending over and beyond the boundary of the Plymouth colony, and being regarded as of higher authority than the charter of the latter, which the King had never sanctioned.

The colonists of Massachusetts Bay were more fortunate. They had a grant of their charter both from the King and the Council at Plymouth. It was made before they left home, and was brought with them as their constitution of government.

It will thus be seen that the compact of 1620 was the basis of the Plymouth Constitution. Under it they enacted laws and accomplished the great ends of civil government, and it was always referred to as affording the highest evidence of their authority. In 1636, the General Court, in declaring the sources of the authority of this government, and the title to its lands, cited this compact, the treaty with Massasoit, the grant from the Indians, and the charters to Pierce, and to Bradford and his associates. But the enumeration of so many grounds of authority betrays a consciousness of the weakness of their several claims, and this may have been a prominent cause of a less determined resistance to the demands of the commissioners of Charles II. than was made by their neighbors of the Massachusetts Bay.

During the first ten years the Plymouth colony was very feeble. At the end of the first winter there were but fifty-one persons, three-fourths of whom were women and children. In 1627, their number had increased to one hundred and sixty-six. There was some increase afterwards, but at the time of the settlement of Boston in 1630, they probably did not exceed two hundred and fifty. In the charter to Bradford, it is stated that the population of the colony was near three hundred persons. This was undoubtedly an exaggeration, for the whole evidence shows that it did not exceed the number before-mentioned. But feeble though it was, it was nevertheless a real success. Ten years had made it a well-established community. They had built their dwellings and had established their farms, cultivating the soil, and obtaining therefrom ample means for their support. They had suffered from famine and endured almost every privation, yet they did not complain; nor were they discouraged, but trusted in God, believing that better things were in store for them. Their faith in the future was never shaken. They never doubted that this was their home, and that they should be the founders of a free,

God-fearing people. When the "Mayflower" left them in April, 1621, on her return voyage, not one of the surviving Pilgrims went back with her; but all stayed in their new home, already consecrated by the graves of one-half of their number. They planted their seed, and when the harvest was gathered, appointed a day of thanksgiving for their mutual rejoicing, and thus unconsciously established an institution which has already become national, and has given joy to at least eight generations of their descendants.

Fortunately, we have a record of most of the public acts of this colony; and from that record, as it appears in their laws, judicial proceedings, conveyances of land, wills, and inventories of property, we have the means of learning their character and condition almost as accurately as if they had been our contemporaries. It was the custom of the day to record in the inventory of every deceased person's property, a detailed statement of every article, so that we can now ascertain how many shoes, what clothing, and what articles of furniture each man had. If he had any books, all the titles were given, and it would not be difficult to give a list of every volume found in the colony.

For the first ten years most of the people resided in Plymouth. This was necessary for their protection. They had no officers but a governor, with at first one assistant, — afterwards increased to seven, — and a constable. All the freemen met in General Court, enacted such laws and made such orders as they needed, and tried and punished offenders. The legislation during this period was very meagre. The first law recorded established trial by jury in all cases, both civil and criminal. This was in 1623, showing their strong attachment to an institution of their native country, which has ever been regarded as the protector and birthright of the English race. In 1626, they enacted that no boards or timber should be exported from the colony without the consent of the Governor and Council; and this was done too, as the act expressed it, from fear that they should not have timber enough for their own use, though the whole country was filled with it, — a fear that the experience of two hundred years has proved to be wholly groundless.

The right of the franchise during the early history of the colony was confined to the freemen: afterwards in the election of deputies, and in the management of town affairs, other persons were allowed to vote; and so general was the franchise, that in some towns a majority of voters were not freemen. In 1669, none were allowed to vote in town affairs but freemen, or freeholders of twenty pounds' ratable estate. The General Court alone admitted freemen; but the same was often done on the recommendation of the towns, and for many years no special qualifications were required; but in 1671 it was provided —

> "That none shall be admitted a freeman of this corporation, but such as are one-and-twenty years of age, at the least, and have the testimony of their neighbors that they are of sober and peaceable conversation, orthodox in the fundamentals of religion, and such as have also twenty pounds of ratable estate in the government."[1]

In this respect they differed from their neighbors in Massachusetts, where a voter must have been a member of a church. The right of taking away the franchise in case of crime or loss of character was always claimed and frequently exercised by the General Court. The right of suffrage created a duty on the part of the freeman, and if he failed to attend the Court, he subjected himself to a penalty of ten shillings. The right of suffrage was regarded by them, as it always will be by all men who value free institutions, as a right which should never be neglected, and one in which the whole public, as well as the individual, have an interest.

The right of inquiring into the fitness of the deputies was always exercised, and in 1658 it was provided, that —

> "The General Court should, on being assembled, first take notice of their members, and if any were found unfit for such a trust, that they and the reasons therefore be returned to the town from which they were sent, that they might make choice of more able and fit persons to send in their stead;"

a right which, if exercised properly and fairly in some modern assemblies, would leave them without a quorum.

The success of this colony, though comparatively small, undoubtedly did much to promote other settlements in New England. The reports of Winslow and Bradford were read eagerly at home, and may have been an influential cause in promoting the settlement of Massachusetts Bay. But whether so or not, the settlement of Massachusetts was a most auspicious event to

[1] Plymouth Laws, p. 258.

the colony of New Plymouth. It established at once as their neighbors a community of intelligent people, having the same great objects in view, and ready at all times to exercise towards them their friendly offices, and afford them such aid and protection as their situation required. The Massachusetts colonists were soon numbered by thousands, and were guided by men of great intelligence and purity. Compared with the people of Plymouth, they were rich, and able to supply themselves with such things as were necessary to the successful planting of a colony. They imported at once large numbers of neat cattle, horses, sheep, goats, and swine, so that in four or five years they had an ample supply for all their wants, and by the introduction of such agricultural implements as were known and used at that day, they were enabled at once to cultivate and improve their lands, and to obtain abundant crops.

The prosperity of Massachusetts soon reacted on Plymouth; and of the great tide of emigration which soon set in, Plymouth received her proportional part, so that in 1643 its population had increased to three thousand, and had extended beyond Plymouth, establishing several other towns in the colony.

This increase and extension of population required a more extensive system of legislation, and in 1636 there was a revision of the laws, and something like a code adopted. Before they adopted their code, however, they made a declaration as a fundamental law —

"That no imposition, law, or ordinance be made by ourselves or others at present or to come, but such as shall be made or imposed by consent, according to the free liberties of the state and kingdom of England, and no otherwise."

The very doctrine maintained by their descendants in the Revolution, and the violation of which led to American Independence. The early enunciation of this doctrine would indicate, that even then they expected and intended to make their own laws, and not to be governed by those of any other country.

At this period, there was a secretary who kept their records, and it was not unusual to record the repeal of a law by a simple erasure, giving the date of such repeal. This appears in the forms of the oaths of office, which as first drawn required the officer to swear to be truly loyal to our Sovereign Lord, his heirs and successors. After the Rebellion in England, these words were erased, and the words, "the State and Government of England as it now stands," were interlined. At the Restoration, these were in turn erased, and the original restored.

During this period a law was enacted, making it penal in the sum of twenty pounds sterling for any one elected to the office of governor to decline the service; a fact showing that the race of gubernatorial candidates, so abundant in our times, had not then begun to exist.

Till 1639, all the freemen assembled together for the enactment of laws. As the settlements extended, this became inconvenient, and their families were left exposed. At first, proxies were allowed, then delegates were chosen who could enact laws; but they were subject to repeal by the whole body of freemen at the general election. In fact, during the whole history of the colony, though most of the laws were enacted in a meeting of delegates from the towns, yet the right of all the freemen to come together and take the legislation into their own hands was never entirely abandoned.

In 1658, there was a new revision of the laws, and the secretary was directed to send a manuscript copy of this revision to every town in the colony, and the towns were required to furnish the secretary with the necessary paper to make a copy, and to have them read publicly once a year. One of these copies, at least, is still in existence. The third revision was in 1671, when the laws for the first time were printed. Massachusetts printed her first code in 1648, anticipating Plymouth in this respect twenty-three years.

These laws show more fully than any thing else, what were the wants, opinions, and policy of the people. The charter to Bradford declared that the tenure of their lands should be, as of the manor of East Greenwich, in the county of Kent, — an old Saxon tenure, by which the lands descended to the sons equally, to the exclusion of the daughters. This tenure was adopted in their code of 1636; and there is no provision of law making any change till 1685, when it was provided that all the lands should descend to the sons equally, except that the oldest son should have a double portion; and if there was but one son, he should have the whole, even if there were a dozen daughters excluded. There was, however, a provision by which the daughters could be protected. They could apply to the County Court for an allowance, and thereupon the Court would order the son or sons to pay a fixed sum of money to them, if they thought it expedient.

Massachusetts early adopted a more equitable rule, dividing the lands among all the children, the sons and daughters alike, except that the oldest son had a double portion, — a system that continued through the whole history of the province, and was not abolished till 1789, nine years after the adoption of our State Constitution.

This rule of descent in Plymouth, though different from that of Massachusetts, was often rendered inoperative by the making of wills. These often provided lands for the daughters, and in some cases gave the oldest son a double portion. Captain Standish gave a double portion to his oldest son. This system of a double portion to the oldest son was borrowed from the Jewish law, and seemed to our ancestors more equitable than the English law of primogeniture.

The authority to make disposition of property by will was fully recognized; and many of the colonists availed themselves of it. It is from these wills that we learn more fully than from any other source the true views of the colonists. They often refer to the object of their coming to this country, express their religious belief, and a desire to distribute their property for the glory of God, and the good of the colony, not forgetting to provide for the education of their children, and for works of charity. Their estates were very small, varying from £50 to £600; and, of course, their charitable contributions were necessarily small. As they had no money, they were compelled to make contributions from their domestic animals and other personal property. The church to which they belonged was seldom forgotten. Dr. Samuel Fuller, whose will was proved in 1633, after providing for his family and friends, says, —

"I give, out of my stock of cattle, the first cow-calf that my brown cow shall have, to the church of God, at Plymouth, to be employed by the Deacon or Deacons of the said church, for the good of the said church, at the oversight of the ruling elders."

Others of equal generosity, but of less means, gave smaller

things, frequently a ewe-lamb, which was not only a common gift to the church, but to all grandchildren throughout the colony. These gifts appear small, but it must be recollected that they were poor; and even fifteen years later, when the Commissioners of the United Colonies proposed a contribution through the colonies, for the benefit of poor students at Harvard College, they asked only for a peck of corn from each family. And at a later date there was an actual contribution through the colony, for the benefit of Harvard College; and the people of the colony showed their interest in that institution, by contributing from their scanty means corn and other grains, in quantities which appear at this day very small. Yet even these were most acceptable gifts; and, by this universal good will, that institution, created "to prevent learning from being buried in the graves of the fathers," was sustained, and its usefulness extended.

The inventories which were presented by executors and administrators, show some very curious facts. I have stated that they present every article in detail, so that we can see and know, after two hundred years, exactly what furniture and clothing they had, even to the number of chairs and shoes. They were all provided with some kind of gun or arms. Some of them had armor. Their cattle, at the end of twenty years, had become numerous, and constituted a considerable part of their personal property. The titles of all their books are given in detail, with some few exceptions. Dr. Fuller's medical works are described in his inventory, as "Physic Books," and were valued at £1; and his chest of surgical instruments was appraised at £5, making the whole stock of books and instruments of the physician of the colony, of the value of £6. All of them had one or more Bibles; and generally a psalm-book, together with various religious books, generally an exposition of Revelations, or some of the books of the Old Testament. They had spinning-wheels almost without exception, together with a small quantity of hemp and flax, from which they manufactured their own clothing.

In the inventory of Miles Standish, the military man of the colony, I find about the usual kinds of property. He had a library of some twenty volumes, among which were three Bibles, Cæsar's Commentaries, and a law-book. It is not stated what the law-book was, but it is one of the few found in the colony for thirty years; and whether it contributed any thing to a knowledge of the common law of England, does not appear. Of his instruments of war, he had one fowling-piece, three muskets, four carbines, two small guns, one old barrel, one sword, one cutlass, and three belts.

Of his furniture, he had a warming-pan, a frying-pan, and a cullender. He also had two saddles, a pillion, and a bridle; sixteen pieces of pewter, a still, a malt-mill, and some spinning-wheels. It also appears that he was a successful farmer, as well as warrior; for he had a large herd of cattle, including four oxen; and the product of his farm was twenty-five bushels of corn, eleven bushels of wheat, fourteen bushels of rye, and thirty bushels of pease. His whole property amounted to £358.

Governor Bradford had a much larger estate; and from the inventory of his property, it appears that he had three match-lock muskets; a snaphance musket; a birding-piece; a pistol, and cutlass; and one pair of old bandelaires. Of his furniture, he had four leather chairs; one great leather chair; two great wooden chairs, and two stools; also two spinning-wheels. Of his clothing, he had a stuffe suit, with silver buttons; a cloth cloak, faced with taffety; a pair of black breeches, and a red waistcoat; one black hat, and one colored one; one pair of boots, and twenty-one pairs of shoes. He had some hundred volumes of books, among which are two Bibles; also Mr. Cotton's answer to Mr. Williams, which, at that time, excited much interest in the Plymouth colony, where Mr. Roger Williams resided for a time, and was treated with great kindness and consideration by many of the leading men.

I give this as a specimen of the property which some of the principal men of the colony had. Most of them had only the furniture necessary to furnish a log hut, or a dwelling equally humble; and I have no doubt that there is more furniture, in value, in any one of fifty houses in Boston, at the present day, than there was in the whole Plymouth colony in 1650. A full statement of all their property, as it appears in their inventories, would give almost as accurate an idea of their condition as we could obtain from a daguerreotype.

In the judicial proceedings there was great simplicity. They intended to follow, as far as they could, the common law of England. But they had few law-books and no lawyers; and it was not always easy to ascertain what the common law was. They discarded all the cumbersome forms in use at that time in England; and adopted such forms as their own good sense dictated. The General Court was the only Court for some years; and the Governor and assistants tried most of the cases during the whole history of the colony. For some years their deeds of land were neither signed nor sealed; but an acknowledgment of the sale was made before a magistrate, who made a memorandum of it. They had a grand jury to find an indictment; but when one was found, it was often contained in two or three lines, and meant what it said; and a common man could understand far better what the charge was, than he could in the excessive verbiage of some more modern indictments.

The punishments were often left to the discretion of the Courts; but they were chiefly fines, whipping, placing in the stocks, or town cage, — for every town was compelled by law to have a cage.

Their criminal law was remarkably mild for that day, and was mildly administered. At the revision of 1636, there were but eight capital offences. At that time there were twenty in Massachusetts, and thirty-one in England, where they afterwards increased to upwards of two hundred. Baylies informs us, that no execution ever took place in the colony for any crime but murder. In this he is not strictly correct; though executions for other crimes were very rare, and perhaps there was but a single exception to the statement which the historian of the colony has made. At any rate, more trials for a capital offence have taken place in Massachusetts, during the year 1868, than all the trials of that character which took place in this colony during its whole existence. Crimes of the highest character were very rare. Most of the offences actually punished would have been passed over at the present day without notice. Taking tobacco, smoking, laughing in public religious meetings, inveigling the affections of young girls without the consent of their parents, were all offences which they could not tolerate; and they, and others of like character, make up the great part of the crimes which entitled the guilty one to a moderate whipping, or a temporary confinement in the stocks, or town cage.

There is nothing more erroneous than to suppose that the Pilgrims, or the people of Plymouth, were harsh or severe in their laws, or in their mode of executing them. The reverse is the actual truth. There is not an instance of a civilized community, certainly not of that day, whose criminal code was so mild, or whose citizens were more obedient to the laws under which they lived. Where their own laws were defective, they had recourse to the law of God. There was a law against witchcraft, or compaction with the devil; but no person was ever tried for that offence. There was a law against Quaker Rantors; but no Quaker had a hair of his head hurt. Gorton presented to the Court a railing accusation, which, in modern times, would have sent him to the lunatic asylum; yet they took no further notice of it, than to order it to be recorded in their public records, thus perpetuating the evidence of their own forbearance and discretion, and the folly and malice of their accuser.

They intended, undoubtedly, in their judicial proceedings, t follow the common law of England. This they claimed as thei birthright. But they were not educated to the law, and they di not always know what was the law of their native country. They were thoroughly conversant with the law of Moses; and they sometimes found it better suited to their condition than the law of England; and when it was so, they did not hesitate to adopt it. There were no lawyers, by profession or education, for many years; and it was not until 1671, that the law expressly authorized any party to employ one or two attorneys to manage his case, but on the express condition that they should do nothing "to deceive the Court or to darken the case;" a provision which, perhaps, might be adopted with profit at the present time.

In this respect, Massachusetts had a decided advantage over Plymouth. Her early emigrants were many of them either educated to the law, or at least conversant with it: all the laws and records show this. They adopted the substance, without the use of the technicalities, of the law at home. Their conveyances of land were in form, their laws clearly and properly drawn, and their judicial proceedings preserving the form and order practised at home. The leading men of Plymouth always sought the advice of the leading men of Massachusetts, and they were happy to follow it; and in nothing is the influence of Massachusetts more apparent than in the laws. Massachusetts was then the leading colony in New England, and her influence on all the other colonies is very striking; and it is not unusual to find her laws copied, word for word, and adopted by the other colonies. This influence was very much increased by the formation of the Confederacy in 1643, which brought the colonies into more intimate relations, and united them upon various matters necessary for their defence. The recommendations of the Commissioners of the United Colonies were generally treated with respect by the local legislatures, and oftentimes adopted by all of them at about the same time. These Commissioners did not confine themselves to the questions of peace and war, or of foreign commerce, but considered most matters connected with the prosperity of the colonies. If any one was lacking in the means of education, or in the support of a learned ministry, they did not hesitate to call attention to the fact, and to suggest a remedy. The influence of this Confederacy on the policy and fortunes of the several colonies would be an interesting subject of inquiry; and it would undoubtedly appear that this union was one of the important series of events, which not only sustained and protected New England in her weakness and infancy, but which finally led to the independence of the country, and the formation of our present national government.

In ecclesiastical matters, there was a difference between Massachusetts and Plymouth. The Plymouth colonists were Brownists, or Separatists. They had separated themselves wholly from the Church of England, and maintained the doctrine of Independency. The Massachusetts colonists had not, when they left home, wholly so separated themselves, but were connected with the mother church, though protesting against its service and ritual. But on finding themselves in a new country, they soon discovered that there was no material difference between them and the Independents at Plymouth. The Pilgrims at Plymouth assisted in the organization of the church at Salem, and Governor Bradford gave them the right hand of fellowship. In ecclesiastical matters, there is no doubt that the example of Plymouth exercised an important influence over the churches of Massachusetts: both, in a short time, became branches of one denomination, which has always been known as Congregational. Plymouth adhered to its system with great strictness, and Massachusetts substantially adopted it. The Plymouth churches sang from the Psalter of Ainsworth through their whole history, but Massachusetts prepared a version of the Psalms for herself, which was used very generally in her churches for more than a century, and was known as the New-England version.

The Plymouth colonists were zealous in establishing churches and in supporting public worship, but it was many years after the settlement before they supported their ministers by a general tax.

But in process of time there began to be some complaint that the ministers were not properly supported, and in 1655 the magistrates were ordered —

> "to use all gentle means to pursuade them to do their duty, but if any of them shall not be reclaimed thereby, but shall persist through plain obstinacy against an ordinance of God, that then it shall be in the power of the magistrate to use such other means as may put them on their duty."

These gentle means of persuasion did not answer the purpose; and, in a few years after, the legal obligation to support public worship throughout the colony was established by law, and pretty strictly enforced.

The Plymouth colonists were not so much wiser than the rest of the world, as to avoid all errors in political economy and legislation. They undertook much which modern experience has shown to be impracticable. In 1638 they fixed the wages of a laborer at twelvepence per day and board, or eighteen pence without board, allowing but sixpence a day for board. They also provided, that no single person who did not belong to the family should reside in it without the consent of the Governor and Council. They attempted to fix the price of corn and other grains, and to determine for what sum they should be received in pay. In 1669 the constables of every town were ordered to look after such as sleep or play about the meeting-house, in times of the public worship of God, on the Lord's day, and to report their names to the Court; and it is not unusual to find that persons were fined for these offences. At that time the men sat on one side of the meeting-house, and the women on the other, and the children by themselves with some one to keep them in order. In the church at Amsterdam, a deaconess was created to look after the children and sit among them with a birchen rod, ready to inflict summary punishment on any poor child who was so much of a mortal that he could not sit two whole hours, in that grave assembly, without seeing something which would render it impossible for him to suppress a smile. The wonder is, not that they laughed, but that they kept sober at all. In 1651 it was made penal for any one to neglect public worship, and subjected him to a fine of ten shillings. There was then about the same difficulty as to a license law as now, yet they had the good sense to make the owner of an estate, where an intoxicated man was found, liable, rather than the intoxicated man himself.

In 1646 a law was enacted which shows that there has been a great change in the business habits of our legislators. By this law, the General Court was required to meet in the morning at seven o'clock in summer, and at eight in winter, and to remain together till half-past eleven o'clock, when they adjourned for dinner, — that being then the usual dinner-hour. After dinner they were required to hold another session, till such hour as the Governor saw fit; and, in order to insure punctuality and constant attendance, each member was liable to a fine of sixpence for tardiness, and a like amount for each hour's absence during the session: a provision of law which we commend to all our legislators who desire a short session, if there are any such.

The organization of towns was substantially the same in the colonies of Plymouth and Massachusetts. They were organized for the transaction of such matters as related to their local interests, such as maintaining highways, supporting public worship, and, at a later period in the history of the colony, public schools. They were also required to support their own poor, and to train their own men in the art of war. The towns sent the deputies to the General Court, and recommended candidates for freemen. The selectmen held courts for the trial of small causes. In short, the towns were then, as now, small civil communities, exercising all the powers of self-government in all matters relating to their own local affairs.

Plymouth was far behind Massachusetts in the support of public schools. In 1663, the General Court advised the towns "to set up a schoolmaster to train up children to reading and writing." In 1673, the profits of the Cape fishery were appropriated to the support of a public school at Plymouth. In 1677, every town having twelve families was required to support a public grammar school. This is really the first act requiring the support of public schools. Yet, notwithstanding this, there is ample evidence that education was not neglected. This was a part of the religion of the Puritans, and in their indentures and wills they made provision for it so far as they could. In the infancy of the colony, they were ready to do, and did do, voluntarily what they afterwards required to be done by authority of law.

On the 24th of April, 1685, James II. was duly proclaimed at Plymouth. It soon became apparent, however, that he had no more regard for his subjects at Plymouth than at home. The charters granted by his predecessors offered no obstacle to the furtherance of his schemes. It made little difference with him whether the charter came from the Council at Plymouth, or was a direct royal grant. These charters had existed for more than half a century, and had been granted for the purpose of encouraging emigration to New England, and under them flourishing colonies had grown up. During the troublesome times in England, the people had enjoyed the favor of utter neglect from the home government. James looked with no favor on the people of New England or their institutions. They had from necessity established their own governments and laws, and these were not in accordance with his arbitrary schemes. He knew that they had no attachment to any of the Stuart race. Their charters were to him mere cobwebs; but still they were inconvenient, and must be swept away. So far as related to Plymouth, this was done in the most summary manner, and without any of the legal machinery used to annul the charter of Massachusetts Bay.

Sir Edmund Andros was appointed Governor of New England, and made the instrument for the subversion of their governments. And notwithstanding what has lately been said in his vindication, his conduct towards the people of the Plymouth colony was cruel, arbitrary, and unjust. For three years neither

General Court nor town meetings were permitted; land titles were deemed invalid; and all the powers of self-government which the Pilgrims and their descendants had claimed and exercised for three generations, were held in contempt, and totally subverted.

But there is a limit beyond which tyranny cannot go. That was soon reached by Andros, and the news of his overthrow and imprisonment by the patriotic people of Boston gave universal joy throughout the Pilgrim colony. They at once resumed their former government, and the Revolution in England gave them full faith in their ability to acquire a new charter, which would secure a separate and permanent government.

To accomplish this end, they appointed as their agents Sir Henry Ashurst, Rev. Ichabod Wiswell, of Duxbury, and Rev. Increase Mather, of Boston. Mather was then in England, having left Boston secretly for the purpose of laying the complaints of Massachusetts before the King. The result of the negotiations of these agents led to the suspicion that Mather acted for the interests of Massachusetts rather than of Plymouth. Such was the belief of Wiswell, who, in a letter to Governor Hinckley, says, —

> "All the frame of heaven moves on one axis, and the whole of New England's interests seems designed to be loaden on one bottom, and her particular motion to concentrate to the Massachusetts tropic. You know who were wont to trot after the *Bay* horse. I do believe that Plymouth's silence, Hampshire's neglect, and the rashness and influence of one who fled from New England in disguise by night, has not a little contributed to our disappointment."

Mather, however, always claimed to have acted in good faith, and to have prevented the annexation of Plymouth to New York, in whose charter it was at first actually included. And so far as we have any evidence on this subject, it appears that when Mather found it was impossible to procure a charter for the separate and independent existence of Plymouth, he made all laudable efforts to secure its union with Massachusetts. This was undoubtedly in accordance with the wishes of the people of Plymouth, who preferred a union with Massachusetts, if any union was to take place at all.

Upon the union of the two colonies under the province charter, it was provided that the local laws of each should remain in full force, — first, for six months, and afterwards indefinitely till altered by the province legislature. The institutions and laws of both were so nearly alike that it was no difficult matter to establish a uniform system over both portions. Some alterations were made by express enactment, and some by silent acquiescence. Of the latter class was the famous Massachusetts Ordinance of 1647 relating to the riparian ownership of flats on tide-waters, which has been adopted in that portion of our Commonwealth for more than a century.

It would hardly be just to speak of the colony of Plymouth, without referring to the charge of bribery against the captain of the "Mayflower." It is said that the Pilgrims intended to have settled near the Hudson River, but that the Dutch secretly bribed the captain of the "Mayflower" to bring them to Cape Cod. There is no doubt that such was their intention; but it is not necessary to account for the change in the place of settlement by making so gross a charge against the captain. It was first made by Morton, nearly fifty years after the event. He says he has late and certain intelligence of the fact,[1] but refers to no authority; and from that time to the present no record or other writing has been found which has the least tendency to sustain the charge. The charge is that the Dutch gave a bribe. It must of course have been known to several persons, who would have been likely to have left some official record or intimation of so important a fact; yet none has been found, though there has been, during the last twenty years, a most thorough examination of the Dutch as well as the English records relative to the Pilgrims, the absence of which is strong evidence that the charge is not true. The evidence of Morton must have been mere hearsay, and should not be received after the death of a man to destroy his character. We might perhaps rest our case on that ground alone. But as the story has been repeated a thousand times from that day to the present, and is now publicly taught in the schools of Boston as true, it may be well to consider some of the reasons which render it wholly improbable. In

[1] See Memorial, p. 34.

the first place, there was no motive for the act. The Dutch would have been glad to have had the Pilgrims settle at New York, and had actually had negotiations with them on the subject before they left Holland. None of the passengers of the "Mayflower" ever intimated or suspected such a crime in their captain, but had full faith in him, not only on the voyage, but through the first winter, and while he was employed by them some years afterwards. At that important council, while the "Mayflower" was in mid-ocean, when the great question was to be settled whether they should go forward or return, it does not appear that the captain did or said any thing to dissuade them from going forward, — a thing which he would have been likely to have done, had he then an intention to defeat their designs. But, on the other hand, Bradford's account of this event shows, that, while the seamen were almost in a state of mutiny, and the passengers in doubt what course should be pursued, the master did more than any other person to allay their fears, and to encourage them to proceed. In a fierce storm, he says, —

"One of the main beams in the mid-ship was bowed and cracked, which put them in some fear that the ship would not be able to perform the voyage. So some of the chief of the company, perceiving the mariners to fear the sufficiency of the ship, as appeared by their mutterings, they entered into serious consultation with the master and other officers of the ship, to consider in time of the danger, and rather to return than to cast themselves into a desperate and inevitable peril; and truly there was great distraction and difference of opinion among the mariners themselves. Fain would they do what could be done for their wages when being now half the seas over; and, on the other hand, they were loath to hazard their lives too desperately. But, on examining of all opinions, the master and others affirmed that they knew the ship to be strong and firm under water; and for the buckling of the main beam, there was a great iron screw the passengers brought out of Holland, which would raise the beam into his place; the which being done, the carpenter and master affirmed that, with a post put under it, set firm in the lower deck and otherwise bound, he would make it sufficient; and as for the decks and upper works, they would caulk them as well as they could; and though, with the working of the ship, they would not long keep stanch, yet there would otherwise be no great danger, if they did not overpress her with sails." (Bradford's Hist., p. 75.)

But there is still stronger evidence of the innocence of the captain, in Bradford's account of their approach to Cape Cod. He says, on seeing land, and having ascertained that it was Cape Cod,

"we were not a little joyful. After some deliberation had amongst themselves and with the master of the ship, they tacked about, and resolved to stand for the southward (the wind and weather being fair), to find some place about the Hudson's River for their habitation. But, after they had sailed the course about half a day, they fell amongst dangerous shoals and roaring breakers; and they were so far entangled therewith, as they conceived themselves in great danger; and the wind shrinking upon them withal, they resolved to bear up again for the Cape, and thought themselves happy to get out of those dangers before night overtook them, as by God's providence they did."

In Mourt's Relation, which Dr. Young supposes to have been the journal of Bradford and Winslow, it is said that, —

"By the break of day we espied land, which we deemed to be Cape Cod, and so afterward it proved; and the appearance of it much comforted us, especially seeing so goodly a land and wooded to the brink of the sea. It caused us to rejoice together, and praise God that had given us once again to see land, and thus we made our course south-south-west, purposing to go to a river ten leagues to the south of the Cape; but at night, the wind proving contrary, we put round again for the bay of Cape Cod."

The captain and the passengers undoubtedly all supposed that the Hudson River was some ten leagues south of Cape Cod, and by going there, they would reach their destined point. The whole statement is perfectly natural, and there was not then even a complaint of a mistake, or a suggestion of one. But very little was then known of the geography of the country. It was then, and for years afterwards, supposed, that New England was an island; and it will be recollected that the charter of Massachusetts Bay, granted ten years afterwards, conveyed all the land from sea to sea, without a suspicion that it extended thousands of miles across a continent. With their imperfect knowledge of our coast, it is no wonder that they did not reach the wished-for point. The real cause for wonder is, that they came so near as they did. We have no knowledge of the track of the "Mayflower" across the ocean. None of the journals or letters of the passengers give us any intimation of it. All they tell us is, that they started from Southampton; had favorable winds for several days; then were overtaken by storms, when they were compelled to beat about till, after a voyage of sixty-five days, they came in sight of Cape Cod. It has been commonly supposed that they had made some mistake, and were not in the position they intended; but if they followed the track of Smith, Gosnold, and other navigators who had, during the twenty years previous, visited the New-England coasts, as they probably did, by taking the northern route, then they were pursuing a direct course to the Hudson River; and a modern navigator, with a full knowledge of our coast, might with great propriety follow the same track, and go to New York through the Vineyard and Long Island Sounds. These statements of Bradford wholly rebut all suggestion of fraud or mistake on the part of the captain, and show us the real cause of cutting short their voyage, and landing at Cape Cod, instead of going to the Hudson River. They had been at sea sixty-five days; and when they saw Cape Cod, "they rejoiced to see so goodly a land." It was then the nineteenth of November, according to our present style. They were wholly unacquainted with the navigation of our coasts, and they fell in with "dangerous shoals and roaring breakers," by which they conceived themselves in great danger. It was these several causes united, that induced the passengers, and not the master, to turn about, and seek safety in the harbor of Provincetown; and they then regarded their ability to do so as a special favor of that Providence which had brought them safely across the ocean. This movement was not the result of any premeditated scheme, but sprang from sudden, unexpected, and overwhelming necessity. And who can now doubt that, under the circumstances, they acted wisely? and what folly and injustice to attribute an act to the machinations of the Dutch, or the fraud of the master, which can be fully and satisfactorily accounted for by the storms of winter, the dangerous shoals, the unknown coast, and the longing to leave the crowded vessel after so long a voyage! Thus much is due to the man whose name has been tarnished, and whose character has been most unjustly injured. It is due to the heroic commander of that frail bark, freighted as it was with the founders of an empire, to say that he acted his part most manfully, and that during the whole of that perilous voyage he did every thing which skill, care, and industry could do. In justice, there should be neither spot nor blemish upon his fame; but to him as well as to his passengers the world owes a deep and lasting debt of gratitude.

The colony of Plymouth, now happily incorporated into and made a part of our Commonwealth, has a history of its own, and it is a history that will never be forgotten. As a civil magistrate, Bradford, the father of the colony, and for twenty-one years its governor, would by his sound good sense and elevated patriotism have done honor to any age. To his wisdom and discretion, the colony owed much of its prosperity, and undoubtedly its prolonged political existence. Of the services of Brewster one can hardly make too high an estimate. For twenty-four years he was the spiritual father and guide of the colony. Of the intrepid and courageous Standish, — the leader in all military enterprises, whether against the Indians, the followers of Morton at Merry Mount, or their Dutch neighbors, — it was as true of him as of the Trojan, that success was never to be despaired of when he led the way. So the Winslows, Allerton, Alden, Hatherly, Prince, Howland, and Hinckley, were all good men and true, and their names are enrolled in letters of light in the history of the remarkable events which created this colony, and enabled it to do so much for the good of mankind.

Its duration was short. One or two of the passengers of the "Mayflower" may have survived it. Never was there a more successful experiment of popular government than it exhibited. During the whole seventy-one years there were but six governors, two of whom continued in office thirty-nine years. In their intercourse with the Indians, they present the same bright example of humanity and justice as in all their public acts. Not a foot of soil was taken from them without their consent, nor without the payment of an equivalent. The treaty with Massasoit was most scrupulously observed for half a century; and it was not their fault, nor that of that faithful sachem, that it was at last violated.

The Pilgrims belonged to that class of men of whom it has been said, that "God sifted a whole nation that he might send choice grain into the wilderness;" and their bright example will give new courage to the oppressed everywhere, and inspire in them new hope. Nor will the lustre of their fame diminish as time passes on, but will continue to grow brighter and brighter; and we may reasonably hope and expect, that the future generations which shall fill our continent, will regard the Fathers of this little colony as the founders of the free institutions which it will be their pride and joy to sustain and extend.

NOTE.

Since preparing the above, I have been able to examine the "Notes" of Sir Joseph Williamson, Under-Secretary of State, copied from the State Paper Office in England, at the request of the President of the Massachusetts Historical Society, and soon to be published in the Proceedings of that Society. They purport to have been written about 1663, just before the fitting out of the expedition against New Netherland, which led to its conquest. These Notes were evidently prepared as a justification of the English government in asserting their claim to the territory occupied by the Dutch; and take the ground that the Dutch claim was fraudulent from the beginning. In reference to the Pilgrims, they allege that they "hyred a ship at Tarnere in Zealand of 500 tunns to transport themselves, beinge the number of 460 persons to Hudson's river aforsaid. But the Dutch which transported the said English, brake faith with them most perfidiouslye, landing them, contrary to the agreement at their shipping, 140 leagues from the place N.E. in a barren country, since called Plymouth Colonie in New England."—This is undoubtedly the same story which Morton, six years after, published in another form in his Memorial; and his "late and certain intelligence" was probably derived from reports which the conquerors of New Netherland industriously circulated, with less regard to truth than as a justification of their acts. Morton may have received this intelligence from Plymouth men who had removed to Manhattan, among whom were Isaac Allerton and Thomas Willett. The whole statement is an utter perversion of the truth, and shows very plainly how, after a lapse of more than forty years, the false charge against the captain of the "Mayflower" originated.

SLAVERY

AS IT ONCE PREVAILED IN MASSACHUSETTS.

BY EMORY WASHBURN.

SLAVERY

AS IT ONCE PREVAILED IN MASSACHUSETTS.

THE subject of this evening's lecture is, *Slavery as it once prevailed in Massachusetts.* The inquiry will involve how far it was legalized here as an institution, and to what extent the people of the Commonwealth were responsible for its introduction and its continuance. As a thing of the past, its history is no otherwise interesting than as it is connected with the social and political condition of the colony and province, and as it awakens the inquiry how far the founders of the Commonwealth are obnoxious to blame for having tolerated it among them. To do justice to either of these, requires a further inquiry into the social and political condition of the world itself when the colony was planted. It would be difficult, without such a reference, to explain why and by what means an institution so hostile to every principle of human freedom should have been sustained in a colony of Christian men, whose object in coming here was to escape from oppression, and to found a Christian commonwealth. The facts of history, however, seem to establish this conclusion, that slavery never was in harmony with the public sentiment of the colony. It was sustained only by force of the policy and laws of the mother country, and was abolished by the people by the very first clause in the organic law of the State. One fact stands out on the very threshold of such an investigation; and that is, that history does not go back to a time when slavery was not sustained by civil society and enforced by law. No matter what may have been the form of its government or the character of its religious faith,—Pagan, Jewish, Hindoo, Moslem, or Christian,—every state, kingdom, and empire of which we have any account, has at some time cherished slavery as a social element. Nay, more: it has, in all these, been the basis on which rights and obligations have rested, which were in utter antagonism with that simple but sublime conception of revelation which regards mankind as brothers, the children of a common parent, and endowed with a common heritage of life and immortality.

An investigation, such as is here contemplated, might help to disabuse the Commonwealth of the reproach that many have been ready to cast upon her, by holding up to view, in the light of the present age, the events which characterized her history two centuries ago. Facts may often be so colored and arranged as to leave as false an impression upon the mind as if the picture had been false in all its parts. The existence of slavery in Massachusetts is, in itself, an historical problem which the association with which we are connected owes to itself to attempt to solve by applying the test of fair criticism and investigation. It is for such an effort, that an appeal is now made to your indulgence.

Let it not be supposed, however, that, to do this, we are to assume that slavery ever was a wise, a Christian, or a humane institution. Nor have we any occasion to arrogate perfection for the Fathers of Massachusetts. They were men, and, as such, had their weaknesses and their errors, as they had their virtues and their merits. They walked in the light of such moral and social science as they had, and it would be as obviously unjust to try them by the test of modern experience, as it would have been to condemn the philosophy of the days of Pericles, because it did not come up to the standard of the Sermon on the Mount.

A large proportion of the early colonists had come from the sturdy, strong-minded, middling classes of England. They had been trained in the school of Puritanism and the sharp contests of religious persecution, to think for themselves, and to judge of men rather by the intrinsic qualities which they exhibited than by the accident of birth. A man with them was a living soul, rather than a thing to wear the decorations of royal favor. They had grown up in those habits of thought which were then rife, which regarded the precepts of the Bible above the dogmas of political belief. And the laws of Moses had for them a higher sanction than any code of mere human legislation. Another circumstance connected with the period in which they lived ought to be constantly kept in mind, when undertaking to judge of them as the founders of a colony; and that is, the condition of the law of nations as it was then understood compared with the science as it is now practised and interpreted. It was still in its infancy. Customs, both in the prosecution of war and the treatment by one nation of the citizens of another, though utterly discarded in our day by every civilized state, were not only tolerated, but were recognized as a part of the code of Christian morality in the intercourse of nations. Grotius, who, more than any other writer, may be regarded as the founder of that system of international law which is now in force, and which changed the whole policy of civilized war, had published his great work on War and Peace, in Latin, only five years before the settlement of Boston. And the peace of Westphalia, which is regarded by many as the event from which the modern science of international law should date, was concluded eighteen years after the planting of the colony.[1]

Not only was Slavery then prevailing in England, and the trade in slaves held to be an established branch of commerce, but this had been true of every nation of whose affairs we have any certain knowledge. The Jews had their slaves, the Greeks theirs, and the same was true of the Romans and the Germans.

If we attempt to trace this custom, which had become so universal, to its origin or source, we find the most prolific of all to have been the incessant wars in which the nations of the old world were engaged. By the notion that long prevailed, prisoners taken captive in such wars were at the mercy of their captors, either to take their lives or sell them into bondage. And when this right of election on the part of captors was taken away, and the selling of captives into slavery superseded the right of taking their lives, it was regarded as a decided advance in the science of international law. The result was, that in some of the ancient states the slaves multiplied to an almost incredible extent. In Rome, in the time of the empire, single individuals, we are told, held from ten to twenty thousand

[1] Wheat. 55, 69

of these at a time. We are told, too, that the custom of ransoming prisoners of war did not originate till after the thirteenth century. And the present custom of exchanging prisoners was not known until after the sixteenth century.[1] Not only were prisoners of war thus early sold into bondage as slaves, but the right to do this was recognized as still existing by Grotius, Puffendorf, and Bynkershoek, the accredited oracles of the law of nations, long after Massachusetts was settled.[2]

And the circumstance which will hereafter be referred to again, may be mentioned in this connection, of the disposition by the English of their Scotch prisoners taken at the battle of Dunbar, a portion of whom were sent to the Massachusetts colony for sale, and sold as late as 1650. The language of C. J. Marshall, upon this subject, is this, —

> "From the earliest times war has existed, and war confers rights in which all have acquiesced. Among the most enlightened nations of antiquity, one of these was that the victor might enslave the vanquished. This, which was the usage of all, could not be pronounced repugnant to the law of nations, which is certainly to be tried by the test of general usage." (10 Wheat. R. 120.)

And as another illustration of the lax state of international law, we are told that, as late as the time of Cardinal Richelieu, one nation might arrest and imprison the citizens of another who should come into a country without a safe conduct from its government. And Richelieu died thirteen years after the settlement of the Massachusetts colony. In this connection, too, it should be borne in mind, that the enslaving of negroes in Africa was itself based upon the right of making slaves of captives taken in war.[3] And we have the authority of C. J. Marshall, in 1825, that —

> "Throughout the whole extent of that immense continent, so far as we know its history, it is still the law of nations that prisoners are slaves." (10 Wheat. R. 121.)

Though this was much the most prolific source of slavery, there were others recognized by the laws of different nations as well as by Grotius and Puffendorf; and one of these in use among the Jews was the selling of himself by one to another as

[1] 1 Kent, 15. [2] 20 How. St. Tr. 28. [3] Tayl. Civ. L. 414.

a slave.[1] Another ground upon which men were reduced to slavery was by the way of punishment for crimes. This prevailed also among the Jews, especially in case of theft. If the thief was unable to make recompense to the injured party, he might be sold.[2]

One of the incidents of slavery which ought to be kept in mind was, that the child of a slave was itself a slave. By the Roman civil law the *status* of the child as to being free or otherwise followed that of its mother. If she was a slave, her child was one also.

By the law of slavery, when a person became a slave in either of these modes, he became changed into a thing of property, to be used or sold at the beck of a master. Among the Romans, he might be cut up to feed the fish in his master's ponds; and even in the so-called Christian States, the law lent but the feeblest protection to a class so theoretically brutalized and debased.

But here, again, there grew up, in process of time, a distinction in favor of Christians, which ought not to be overlooked, when treating of this subject historically.

The notion began to be entertained at a pretty early period, that it was hardly becoming for one Christian to make another of his own faith a slave, merely because he had taken him captive in war; and it came in time to be a grave question in the English Courts, whether one could be held as a slave after he had been baptized: but for pagans and infidels no such scruple was entertained; and one of the salvos to the public conscience for engaging in the African slave trade was, that it was a means of converting infidels to Christianity. It is surprising, at this day, to know with what gravity such nonsense was listened to in the English courts. In 1677, nearly fifty years after our ancestors came to Massachusetts, the Court of King's Bench solemnly adjudged, "that negroes being usually bought and sold among merchants as merchandise, and being *Infidels*," there might be a property in them.[3] And seventeen years later, in 1694, the same Court held that "trover will lie for a negro boy, *for they are heathen*, and therefore a man may have property in them; and the Court, without averment made, will take notice

[1] Jahn Antiq. 77, 2 How. St. T. 28 n. [2] Jahn Sup., 20 How. St. T. 30.
[3] Lev. R. 201.

that they are heathen."[1] In other words, the law would presume a black man to be a heathen, until he could show to the contrary.

Negro slavery, moreover, which had been introduced by Spain into her colonies in 1508, became domesticated in England in 1553, when twenty-four slaves were imported directly from Africa. And in 1562 the slave-trade was inaugurated by Sir John Hawkins, who, for the atrocities which he committed in its prosecution, was knighted by Queen Elizabeth; and it became from that day a regular and recognized branch of English Commerce.

Such, in brief, was the state of public law, and such the condition of public sentiment among the Christian nations of Europe upon the subject of slavery and the slave-trade, when Winthrop and his colony set sail for America, bringing with them the royal charter, under which a settlement had already been begun at Salem.

Whatever may have been the individual motives of the colonists in planting themselves on these shores, their corporate powers were limited by the terms of their charter, which were rather those of a trading company than the organic law of a State. They might make such rules and regulations as would be necessary to carry on the business of the corporation, and maintain order and good government in the colony. But they were, in no measure, absolved from their allegiance as citizens, to the crown, or from the obligations they were under, as subjects, to the government at home; and the charter itself forbade them to make any laws or ordinances "contrary or repugnant to the laws and statutes" of the realm of England. And we are told by Judge Story that "the commercial intercourse of the colonies was regulated by the general laws of the British empire, and could not be restrained or obstructed by colonial legislation."[2] In nothing was the policy which this provision was meant to guard more persistently adhered to by the home government, than in that which had been inaugurated in 1562 in respect to the trade in slaves, and was subsequently continued for more than an hundred years after New England was colonized. It was regarded as an object of the first importance to the English government to acquire and maintain a command of this trade;

[1] 1 Raym. R. 147. [2] 1 Const. § 178.

and to that end, not only were the English colonies rigidly kept open as a market for this commerce, but efforts were made and treaties entered into, with a view of obtaining a monopoly of the traffic. Thus in 1713, by means of the "Assiento Treaty," so called, England obtained the exclusive right of supplying the Spanish islands and provinces in America with four thousand eight hundred negroes annually, for the term of thirty years.[1]

And that such was the purpose of the English government in respect to its American colonies, is illustrated in history, as well as conceded by the language of the highest judicial tribunals of that country.[2]

It was under circumstances like these, that the colony of Massachusetts Bay was planted and began its administration. At first, its affairs were carried on as a pure Democracy; and, after a few years, through delegates chosen for that purpose by the freemen in their several towns. In either form, therefore, whatever laws they did make are to be regarded as a reflex of the average sentiment and opinion of the freemen of the colony. So far as negro slavery was concerned, their power to act at all was exceedingly circumscribed. They could prohibit neither the importation nor the sale of slaves without clashing at once with the interests and wishes of government at home. Nothing seems to have been left open to them in respect to it, but simply to deal with all such as, by residence, were subject to their laws, independent of a prior jurisdiction, and to regulate the *status* of the children of slaves *born in the colonies.* This might be done without interfering, in terms, with what had once been the subject of sale or traffic, under the English laws of importation and trade. And, if denying to the owner of the parent the right to hold the child as a slave, was violating the spirit of the law under which the parent himself was held, it would go to show that the colonists were ready to break away from every thing but the *letter* of the law in favor of freedom. Laying aside then, for the present, so much as relates to the slavery of the African race, it might still exist in respect to such captives as were taken in war, such persons as sold themselves, and such as were reduced to slavery as a punishment for crime. It will be

[1] Wheat. 56. [2] 2 Hagg. Rep. 106.

necessary therefore to consider how far the laws of the colony authorized or tolerated either of these modes.

Unfortunately, for a full and precise understanding of the subject in all its possible bearings, it is difficult, if not impossible, to trace the course of legislation in the colony during the first ten years of its history. Many of its laws during this period are still preserved; but none of them were printed until 1648. If all had been preserved, it is believed, that, like some of those extant, they would be found to correspond, in many respects, with the provisions of the Levitical Code. This, however, we do know historically, that the freemen of the colony, as early as 1635, began to be restive, under the idea that the magistrates were clothed with too much *discretionary* power; and that a body of laws ought to be established by which the rights and duties of the citizen should be ascertained, and remedies provided for both public and private wrongs. The General Court, though somewhat reluctantly, came at last into the measure so far as to raise a committee to prepare a draft of such laws as should be agreeable to the word of God, and be the fundamentals of a Commonwealth.

Every thing, however, was done with great deliberation; and one reason for this, as we are told, was, that they might not pass any law which should transcend the power given them by the charter, by being repugnant to those of the mother country.[1] It was, besides, deemed desirable that the proposed body of laws should embrace, as far as possible, the prevailing sentiments and opinions of the freemen of the colony. And, to that end, an order was passed in 1638, calling upon them to come together in their respective towns, and prepare a statement of the heads of such laws as they desired. After this had been done, the whole were placed in the hands of the Rev. Mr. Ward of Ipswich, who, from having been bred a lawyer in England, it was supposed would be competent from these to put into form a body of laws to be reported to the General Court. The result was, that a collection of elementary rules declaratory of the duties, privileges, and restrictions which the people of the colony were to observe, was adopted in 1641, and took the name of the "Body of Liberties."[2] In some respects it answered to the

[1] Palf. Hist., vol. i. p. 443. [2] Ib. vol. ii. pp. 23–27.

English Magna Charta, but more nearly to the Declaration of Rights in our Constitution.

The object in having been thus minute in this detail was, to reach, if possible, the true state of public feeling in the colony, upon the subject of maintaining slavery, as it existed at the time of the adoption of this code. And it may be added, that, after all this precaution, provision was made in the code itself, that it should be read and revised at the three next annual sessions of the General Court.[1] It may, therefore, be assumed, that whatever found a place in the Body of Liberties, was in accordance with the judgment and wishes of the freemen of the colony.

Slavery was one of these topics; and the manner in which it was regarded is best judged of by the language of the code itself. This Body of Liberties consisted of ninety-eight articles, although generally spoken of as containing a hundred. In it there is no allusion to *color*, nor to any distinction of *race*, or *creed*, in the matter of rights or privileges. Unlike the English notion, the Christian and the Heathen, in this respect, stood upon the same level in the eye of the law. Among its criminal provisions, "man-stealing" was made a capital offence, resting for its authority, upon the 16th verse of the 21st chapter of Exodus. But it is the ninety-first article which bears more immediately upon the question under consideration. It is there declared that—

> "There shall *never* be *any* Bond Slavery, Villinage, or Captivity amongst us, *unless* it be lawful Captives taken in just Wars, and such strangers as willingly sell themselves, or are sold to us. And these shall have all the liberties and Christian usages which the law of God, established in Israel concerning such persons, doth morally require. This exempts none from servitude, who shall be judged thereto by authority." (Mass. Hist. Col., vol. xxviii. p. 231.)

It contemplates, it will be perceived, slavery as an institution already existing. Its purpose is not to introduce something new; but, obviously, to limit and restrict it *as it exists*, to *three* classes of persons, and declares that, beyond these, "there shall never be any Bond Slavery, Villinage, or Captivity" in the colony.

[1] Palf. Hist., vol. ii. p. 25.

And, what is most significant in the matter, the children of slaves born in the colony are thereby excluded from the classes that might be subjected to bond slavery. Around every human being in the colony, without regard to race or creed, not embraced in one of these classes, it throws the protection of the law, and declares the sanction of the death penalty for its violation.

The framers of such a law must have had some motive for such a declaration; and it is something more than a mere idle inquiry, to ascertain, if we can, what that motive was. A recent writer upon this subject has told the world, that this article in the Body of Liberties "sanctions the slave trade, and the perpetual bondage of Indians and negroes, their children and their children's children."[1] Whether this position is sought to be sustained by a fair review of the general facts of history, or by the writer's own construction of such as he has seen fit to select, can be better judged of, by a brief recurrence to the actual condition of the world, at the time of which he is speaking. Slavery, as we have seen, prevailed not only in England, but throughout Christendom; and, what is more, slavery existed, at that very moment, in the colony itself, by a previous importation of slaves under the sanction of the English government. Lord Stowell, the learned and illustrious Chief Justice of the English Court of Admiralty, tells us in an opinion given by him upon the subject, that —

> "Slavery was a very favored introduction into the colonies: it was deemed a great source of the mercantile interest of the country, and was, on that account, largely considered by the mother country as a great source of its wealth and strength. Treaties were made on that account, *and the colonies compelled* to submit to those treaties by the authority of this country."

With slavery, then, existing among them, under the sanction of a law which they could not repeal or gainsay, if it was in coincidence with the wishes of the colonists, what occasion was there for them to act upon the matter at all? And if it was their desire to perpetuate it as an institution in the colony, why limit and restrict it so that it must, from the nature of things, be certain

[1] Moore, Hist. of Slavery in Mass., p. 18.

to die out in a few years, unless kept alive by new importations?

These are questions which one might suppose would naturally occur to the mind of any one undertaking to fasten upon this colony the imputation of *sanctioning* "perpetual bondage." But the evidence does not stop here. If the colonists were actuated by the feelings and motives which were entertained by slaveholders generally, they would have manifested this by the slave *code* under which they were to regulate and perpetuate it; and a comparison of their legislation upon the subject, such as it was, with that of one or two of the other colonies may help us to form a judgment upon the matter. In 1664, a body of laws "collected," as the record shows, "out of the several laws now in force in his Majesty's American Colonies and Plantations," and, of course, including the Massachusetts colony, was adopted for the Duke of York's province, afterwards a part of New York. Under the head of "Bond Slavery," in that body of laws, there is a provision that "no *Christian* shall be kept in Bond Slavery, Villinage, or Captivity," except as therein stated, excluding from this exemption agreeably to the prevailing notion of some of the English courts, to which reference has already been made, all such as were *infidels* or *heathen*.[1] A law of Virginia of 1669 provides that —

> "If a slave resist his master or others, by his master's orders, correcting him, and by the extremity of the correction should chance to die, such death should not be counted a felony; but the master or other person appointed by his master to punish him, be acquit from molestation, since it could not be presumed that prepensive malice, which alone makes murder a felony, should induce any man to destroy his own estate." (1 Tuck. Black. pt. 2, 45.)

What a contrast is here presented between a law exempting a master, or any one employed by him, from punishment for whipping his slave to death, and that of this Body of Liberties which secures to the most friendless heathen that had ever endured the horrors of the "middle passage," "the liberties and *Christian* usages which the law of God, established in Israel" concerning those under bond slavery, morally required. And he might by

[1] N. Y. Hist. Col., vol. i. p. 322.

way of safeguard, even demand sureties of the peace against a violent and barbarous master.[1] With how much candor, then, can a writer not only charge the Body of Liberties with sanctioning the slave-trade and the perpetual bondage of Indians and negroes, their children and their children's children, but as entitling, in his words, "Massachusetts to precedence over any and all other colonies, in similar legislation."[2]

The subject of this Body of Liberties does not end here. It was not originally *printed*, and only nineteen copies were distributed, in manuscript, among the towns. An early transcript of one of these copies was discovered by the late Hon. Francis C. Gray, about forty years since, and was published by the Massachusetts Historical Society in 1843. The first printed edition of the colony laws was published in 1648. But no copy of that is known to be now extant. Another edition was printed in 1660, of which a few copies remain. In that edition, the ninety-first article of the original body stands by itself as a distinct law. The latter, however, omits, the words "such strangers" which are found in the original. Instead, therefore, of reading, that there shall be no bond slavery, unless it be lawful captives, &c., and *such strangers* as willingly sell themselves, it reads, "lawful captives taken in just war, as willingly sell themselves," &c., obviously showing that some words had been accidentally or intentionally omitted; for there was an inconsistency in speaking of captives taken in war willingly selling themselves. It required no such *sale* to make such persons slaves. We, accordingly, find that preparatory to a new edition of the laws which was published in 1672, a committee of the General Court was raised to examine those already published, and report such *errata* therein as required to be corrected. Among the *errata* reported by them, and passed upon by the General Court, was the mistake in the sentence above quoted. They supplied the omission by the words, "such as shall," which makes the clause read thus, "lawful captives taken in just wars, *such as shall* willingly sell themselves, or are sold to us," not limiting it to *strangers* who sell themselves, or are sold to us. But the change, even if it had any meaning or effect, left the matter of the *children* of slaves just where it was before,

1 4 Mass. Rep. 127. 2 Moore Hist., p. 18.

within the category of those of whom there should *never* be any *bond slavery.*

And that such is the true construction of the clauses referred to, has been settled by the repeated adjudications of the highest courts of Massachusetts, who have, again and again, held that no child born here since 1641, was ever, by law, a slave. Single judges may have dropped language, at times, that might be capable of another construction; but that of the courts, when speaking authoritatively upon the point, has all been one way, that freedom was the child's birthright.[1]

Starting with this early action of the freemen of the colony in their towns and by their representatives, we are next to trace the dealings of the *people* upon the subject of slavery, to see how, at any time, Massachusetts became implicated in its maintenance, and how far they had a right to claim the commendation of Edmund Burke of having refused to "deal any more in the inhuman traffick of the negro slave," the doing of which he pronounced to be "one of the causes of her quarrel with Great Britain."[2]

But before taking up this in detail, it may be well to inquire how far bond slavery, arising from either of the other sources, existed, at any time, in Massachusetts. No instance has been discovered of a sale by one man of himself to another, although the power of doing this was recognized in the Body of Liberties. But of sales by the way of punishment for crime, under a sentence of a court, there are several instances recorded. Thus we have one in Sandwich, in 1678, where three Indians were thus sold for having broken into a house and stolen. Being unable to make recompense to the owner, the Court authorized him to sell them.[3] That a measure like this would seem harsh in our day, is not to be denied. But to judge of it in its true light, we should place ourselves in the condition in which our Fathers stood, and see how far circumstances justified the measure. In the first place, they were justified in this policy by the respect they had for the Mosaic law, from which it was borrowed. In the next place, the idea of compelling the thief to make compensation to the

[1] 4 Mass. 128 n.; 16 Mass. 75; 13 Mass. 552; 10 Cush. 410; Quincy Rep. 29, Gray's note.

[2] Wheat. 590; Burke's Works, vol. ii. p. 44.

[3] Thach. Plym. 139.

injured party by his own labor is an obvious dictate of remunerative justice. The Hon. Mr. Lushington, of the British Parliament, in his examination before a committee of that body upon the subject of criminal law, in 1835, in answer to an inquiry involving the justice and expediency of obliging the guilty party to make restitution to the person injured, by his labor, said: "My own opinion is this, that, in every case where the offender is capable of indemnifying the person robbed for the loss he has sustained, he ought to be compelled so to do."[1] And a still more important consideration is, that the science of prison discipline and reform was, at that time, literally unknown. Hanging, drawing and quartering; whipping, maiming, and mutilating the person; or shutting up offenders in dungeons, in idleness, in cold, darkness, and pestilential filth, — were some of the punishments by which the public at that day sought to be *avenged* upon those who violated the law; so that, even upon the score of humanity as well as justice, the sale of a convict's services must have had much to commend itself to the judgment of a community situated as were the colonists of New England. But it ought to be added, that the instances in which this mode of punishment was adopted, appear to have been few, and under peculiar circumstances.

Of captives taken in war and sold into slavery by the colony, the number appears to have been larger, though it is not easy to ascertain in how many instances it was done. As a measure of policy, it was adopted in the case of such as were taken in the early Indian wars, and was justified, so far as such an act of severity could be justified, by the dread and alarm in which the colonists were held, while contending with a foe who recognized none of the laws of civilized warfare. It was chiefly confined to the remnants of the Pequod tribe, and to such as were taken in the war with King Philip, which, at one time, seemed to threaten extermination to the white race. As they could be bound by no treaty, the only measure of safety for the colonists was to hang or shoot their prisoners, shut them up and maintain them in jails or prisons, or put them in a situation not to again engage in burning the towns and murdering the inhabitants of the colony. And this could be done effectually by selling them

[1] 2d Rep. of Com. 53.

into bondage. The first was obviously too barbarous to be justified. The colonists were too few and too feeble to make the second possible. And the last alternative was resorted to as their only means of protection and intimidation. And this, at least, may be said in palliation, if not in approbation, of this policy, — it does not seem to have been dictated by considerations of gain or by mercenary motives; but rather as a measure of self-defence, justified, as we have seen, by the usages of Christian nations, and authorized by the best writers upon international law which were then accessible to the colonists, whose works they might have read in the light of their blazing dwellings.

The war with the Pequods was terminated in 1637. Nor was there any occasion to resort to this severe alternative again for the space of forty years, when the struggle with Philip began; and, even then, there were many in the colony who deprecated the principle upon which it rested. The Plymouth colony, immediately after Philip's war, forbade any one to buy the *children* "of those our captive salvages that were taken and became our lawful prisoners in our late wars with the Indians, without special leave of the government."[1] And a law of Massachusetts, as early as 1712, prohibited the importation of Indian servants into the colony.[2] There never was in fact a time when there were not earnest advocates and devout laborers in the colony for the conversion of these sons of the forest to the faith and habits of Christian civilization. Slavery was never their normal condition, and never reached beyond the individual who was personally subject to it.

If now we recur to negro slavery, it does not appear when it was first introduced into the colony. One thing is certain, that it did not come in with Winthrop's Company. When Josslyn was here in 1638, he found Mr. Maverick the owner of three negro slaves. He probably acquired them from a ship which brought some slaves from the West Indies in that year. And this is the first importation of which we have any account. But Maverick was not properly a member of Winthrop's Company. He came here before they left England, and had his establishment, and lived by himself, upon Noddle's Island. Nor was he in sympathy with them in church government or religious senti-

[1] Plym. Laws, p. 187. [2] 1 Holmes's Annals, p. 509.

ment. Governor Winthrop gives an account of the admission to the church, in 1641, of "a negro maid, servant to Mr. Stoughton, of Dorchester."[1]

The arrival of a Massachusetts ship with two negroes on board, whom the master had brought from Africa for sale, in 1645, four years after the adoption of the Body of Liberties, furnished an opportunity to test the sincerity of its framers, in seeking to limit and restrict slavery in the colony. And it derives an additional importance from the circumstance, generally overlooked, that it happened at a time when the colonists were more nearly at liberty to act out their own wishes in this respect than they had ever been before, or were at any time afterwards, by reason of the civil war in England, which had then begun, and the King's being in no condition to look after the conduct of his foreign subjects. Being, for the moment, in no fear of the home government, they must have acted as their own sense of right and sound policy dictated. Upon information that these negroes had been forcibly seized and abducted from the coast of Africa by the captain of the vessel, the magistrates interposed to prevent their being sold. But though the crime of man-stealing had been committed, they found they had no cognizance of it, because it had been done in a *foreign jurisdiction.* They, however, went as far towards reaching the wrong done as they could; and not only compelled the shipmaster to give up the men, but sent them back to Africa, at the charge of the colony, with "a letter," as it is said, "of the indignation of the Court thereabouts and justice thereof."[2] And they made this, moreover, an occasion, by an act of legislation of the General Court, in 1646, "to bear witness," in the language of the act, "against the heinous and crying sin of *man-stealing*, as also to prescribe such timely redress for what is past, and such a law for the future, as may sufficiently deter all others belonging to us to have to do in such vile and most odious courses, justly abhorred of all good and just men"[3] — an act of legislation to say the least, singularly at variance with the assumption, so confidently put forth, that the framers of the Body of Liberties (passed only four years previous to

[1] Life and Letters, vol. ii. p. 263. [2] Wint. Jour., vol. i. p. 245, Col L. 53.
[3] Col. 7, 53.

this) intended thereby to sanction "the slave-trade and the perpetual bondage of Indians and negroes."

In a few years, however, King Charles was again restored to his throne, and the legislation of the colony went on under its original restrictions and limitations.

In 1703, an act was passed which has subjected the General Court to some severe criticism, though evidently because the reasons and purposes of it were misunderstood by such as sought to cast censure upon their conduct. The substance of this act was, that no one should emancipate his slave, without giving bond to hold the town harmless from the expense of his support. And it has been assumed, that this was from a wish to check the facility of emancipating slaves. So far, however, is this from being true, that, while the act recognizes emancipation as being properly in use for freeing slaves, it simply attempts to prevent the gross injustice and inhumanity of a master holding his slave in bondage as long as his labor was profitable, and then turning him over, as a pauper, to be supported at the public charge. And the act itself holds such master or mistress chargeable for the slave's support.[1]

To show that no change in this respect had taken place in the policy of the government, we find that the General Court, in 1705, imposed a duty of £4 upon every slave imported into the province. And this law was renewed in 1728.[2] In 1767, a bill to restrain the importing of slaves passed the popular branch of the General Court, but failed in the Council. Nor would it have availed, if it had passed both branches, because it would have been vetoed by the Governor, acting under instructions from the Crown. This was shown in 1774, when such a bill did pass both branches of the General Court, and was thus vetoed.[3] These successive acts of legislation were a constantly recurring illustration of the truth of the remark of a modern writer of standard authority upon the subject, that —

"Though the condition of slavery in the colonies may not have been created by the imperial legislature, yet it may be said with truth, that the

[1] See 4 Mass. Rep. 130; Col. Law, 745. [2] Felt's Sal., p. 340; Statis., p. 203.

[3] Coffin's Newbury, p. 339; Felt's Statis., p. 205; Wheat. 588. See also Declaration of Independence.

colonies were *compelled* to receive African slaves by the home government." (1 Hurd, &c., 208 n.)

We have reached, in this review of the legislation of Massachusetts, the point at which the pressure of the royal power was taken from the action of the people, and the popular will began to have free play upon this, as well as other topics of public interest. The power of the Crown here ceased, for all practical purposes, in October, 1774. Nor was there any organized government in the Province, until the July following, except such as was furnished by what was called the *Provincial Congress*, composed of a convention of delegates from the several towns coming together for mutual consultation and advice. Committees of Correspondence, chosen in the towns and counties of the Province, shared with this Congress in giving a direction to public affairs. The subject of negro slavery was early agitated by these bodies, though they had no authority to act upon it. What they did, however, is an indication not to be mistaken, of what the feeling in the community upon that subject was. The slaves of Bristol and Worcester Counties addressed a memorial to a convention of these committees in Worcester in June, 1775. The response was in these words,—

"We abhor the enslaving of any of the human race, and particularly the negroes of this country; and whenever there shall be a door opened, or an opportunity present, for any thing to be done towards the emancipation of the negroes, we will use our influence and endeavor that such a thing may be brought about." (Lincoln, Hist. Wor. 110.)

The action of the government, when reorganized under the advice of the Continental Congress, was shown in September, 1776, in respect to several negroes, who had been taken in an English prize-ship, and brought into Salem to be sold. The General Court, having learned these facts, put a stop to the sale at once. And this was accompanied by a resolution on the part of the House,—

"That the selling and enslaving the human species is a direct violation of the natural rights alike vested in them by their Creator, and utterly inconsistent with the avowed principles on which this and the other States have carried on their struggle for liberty."

The result was, that the rights of prisoners of war were extended to such negroes as might thereafter be taken from the enemy during the war. In other words, the negro, though a slave to an English master, attained the attributes of a man when in a situation to be dealt with by the Commonwealth, though the law did not yet disturb the rights of private property in slaves, on the part of the citizen.

We have thus far had to do chiefly with the *acts* of *legislation* in the Colony and Province, in undertaking to trace the course of public sentiment, as well as the condition of slavery, up to the time of the Revolution. But there are other sources of evidence than legislation upon those subjects, which ought not to be overlooked, when undertaking to reach the truth, as it stands in history. Unfortunately, those sources are, at the best, meagre; and the facts derived from them are only fragmentary. It is to be remembered, that the Colony, while it remained such, never had a newspaper; and printing presses were almost unknown. Nor was there any newspaper in the Province until the beginning of the last century. The laws even were not printed till 1648; and not again till 1660. There are two or three sources from which may be drawn conclusions that will serve to indicate how slavery was regarded during the periods of the colonial and provincial history. One of these is the number of slaves who were held here, at any one time, as it tends to show whether the people were eager, or otherwise, to possess them; for, if they had wished for them, the English merchants were ever ready to supply such a desirable demand; it was a branch of English commerce. Another is the manner in which they were treated by their owners, as serving to show whether the motive in holding them was wholly a selfish one, for the sake of the labor which might be wrung out of them by harsh and cruel treatment; and, lastly, the expression which remains of individual and associate opinion, as it is contained in letters, pamphlets, and the records of religious and other associations. Nor should we forget, that, in the discussions to which the question of slavery gave rise, there were those in the Province who doubted the expediency of immediate emancipation; and that some went so far as to insist that the trade itself had better be regulated, than wholly suppressed. And this statement is due to fairness in undertaking to give the true measure of public sentiment upon the subject.

In respect to the *number* of slaves living here at any one time, no census seems to have been taken of them prior to 1754. And it is proper, in this connection, to meet a suggestion which has been industriously propagated by individuals, that the early settlers of Massachusetts engaged in, and prosecuted the *slave-trade* as a *regular business*. The writer already quoted, in the work referred to, indulges in this statement: "At the very birth of the foreign commerce of New England, the African slave-trade became a regular business."[1] The facts upon which a precisely opposite conclusion, so far as it relates to Massachusetts, has been arrived at by others, will enable one to judge whether such a sweeping charge is well founded. Mr. Felt says, that the first vessel that brought slaves to Massachusetts, in 1638, was only of one hundred and twenty tons burthen, and was freighted with cotton and tobacco; so that the number of these slaves was, probably, small.[2] He also refers to a statement of Governor Bradstreet in 1680, who expressly declares that there had not been a company of blacks or slaves brought into the country since the beginning of the plantation, except one smal vessel about two years before the time of making this statement, which brought between forty and fifty negroes, mostly women and children. And it is also stated by Governor Bradstreet, that these were sold here "for 10, 15, and £20 apiece," although they stood the merchant "in near £40 apiece,"[3] which must certainly have offered rather a poor encouragement to prosecute such a commerce, as "a regular business." And Governor Bradstreet adds, that, "now and then, two or three negroes were brought hither from Barbadoes, and other of his majesty's plantations, and sold here for about £20 apiece;" and he concludes, "that there may be within our government about one hundred, or one hundred and twenty."[4] Not a very extensive commerce certainly, after having been prosecuted for fifty years, as "a regular business"! But the evidence does not stop here. The Secretary of the Historical Society has a printed letter, bearing date November, 1690, addressed to a member of the then House of Commons, the title of which is, "That the trade to Africa is only manageable by an Incorporated

[1] Moore, p. 29.
[2] Hist. Salem, p. 109.
[3] Felt's Statis., p. 586.
[4] See Hist. Col., vol. xxviii. p. 337.

Company and a joint stock; demonstrated," &c. The letter goes on to show, that to carry on the trade requires ample funds and a well-regulated system, to make it profitable at all. One of its statements is in these words: —

"And as it could not then escape your observation, no more than it can now your memory, that the trade of Africa was, about twenty years ago, not only so abated, but sunk to such a degree that it became a matter of State, challenging the utmost wisdom and care of his then majesty; and of those of the profoundest prudence and of the largest mind, for the public good, who were, at the time, in the ministry, how to revive and restore it, so as to render it consistent with the honor of the government, useful to the American Plantations, and of ample advantage to the Nation."

And it adds, —

"Nor can any body of men, but an incorporated society acting by and upon a joint stock, gain and maintain such intelligence as may, upon so vast and extended a coast, either give life unto or procure an advantage by trade." [1]

If now we recur to the colonial statistics, they seem to establish two facts in connection with the circumstances already mentioned: first, that there was no such demand or desire for slaves on the part of the colonists, as to induce them to enter to any considerable extent, into the trade of supplying them; and, second, that if, as there appears to have been, there was an increase of the traffic after the year 1700, it was probably in consequence of the increased encouragement given to the trade, by the government *at home*, as recommended by the letter referred to, rather than of any action of the colonists, or any increased favor on their part, for the institution of slavery. We ought not to forget another fact in connection with the number of slaves, as given by Governor Bradstreet; that while, of the latter, there were only one hundred or one hundred and twenty, as late as 1680, the number of Scots, who had been captured by the English, and *sold into the colony* in 1651, was about two hundred and seventy-four, — all purchased in a single year, which showed,

[1] Confirmatory of this is the statement of Governor Dudley in 1708. "The African Company of England had not had any factory or ship here. Some traders on their own account, a long time since, have been upon the Coast of Guinea, and imported slaves." (Felt's Statis., p. 586.)

in some measure, the estimate at which our ancestors held the trade in African slaves.

In 1708, Governor Dudley estimates the whole number in the colony at five hundred and fifty; two hundred having arrived between 1698 and 1707.[1] Dr. Belknap thinks they were the most numerous here about 1745. And Mr. Felt, upon careful calculation, computes their number in 1754, at four thousand four hundred and eighty-nine. In 1763, the proportion of blacks, slave and free, to the whites in the province, as given by Dr. Belknap, was as one to forty-five.[2] While, at the same time, in Virginia, where slavery was in favor, there were ten blacks to eight whites, or one hundred thousand blacks to eighty-five thousand whites in that colony.

Nor was this because the colonists of Massachusetts did not wish for laborers. Labor is one of the great necessities of every new settlement. And we know, from various sources, at what cost and trouble they were to procure it. One means of doing it, was by some sort of contract with those who sold their service to the company, probably to pay for the cost of their transportation into the colony. In the Life and Letters of Governor Winthrop,[3] it is stated, that of the residents under Endicott, whom Governor Winthrop found here at his arrival, one hundred and eighty were bond servants of the planters who were to follow, all of whom were emancipated by him, on account of a scarcity of provisions in the colony, although they had cost them from 16 to £20 each.[4]

And the reason why the colonists preferred white to black servants was, not so much their profitableness, as that given by Governor Dudley, — they were "serviceable in war presently, and after, became planters," adding to the productive population and military strength of the colony; and Governor Bradstreet tells us in 1680, that of the Scots who were sold here in 1651, most of them had married and were then living, with about half as many Irish brought here, at several times, as servants.[5] They

[1] Felt's Statis., p. 586.

[2] Felt's Statis., p. 211; Hist. Col., vol. iv. pp. 198–199. [3] Vol. ii. p. 29.

[4] Felt's Salem, p. 42. This class of servants are described by Randolph in 1676, as being those "who serve for years for the charge of being transported thither by their masters" (Felt's Statis., 202.)

[5] Felts, Statis., p. 586.

seem to have passed from servants to planters, and to have acquired homes and families of their own.

If, now, we turn to the question of, how such slaves as they had were treated by their masters, the testimony seems to have been uniform throughout the colonial period. Dr. Belknap made a systematic business of ascertaining this point by an extended correspondence with many of the most intelligent men in the province. And among them were John Adams, Governor Sullivan, Dr. Holyoke, and others of that class; and the testimony he gives us is, that this treatment "was far from rigorous. No greater labor was exacted from them than of white people." "In the country, they lived as well as their masters, and often sat at the same table."[1] A large proportion of them were employed in domestic service in families in the larger towns. They could not have been worked in gangs, as was the case in the Southern States; for their number was so few, that, if equally divided among the families in the province, not more than one family in seven or eight could have had a single slave; and some judgment can be formed upon this subject, from the fact which many still can remember, that when the entire slave population of the State was emancipated by the adoption of the Constitution in 1780, many of them continued members of their masters' families, by preference, as long as they lived. The record has yet to be found of a slave woman ever being worked as a "field-hand" in Massachusetts. More than that, in many towns, and I know not but in all, the slave, if otherwise qualified, was admitted to the communion and fellowship of the church. For some years after 1652, negro servants were, moreover, enrolled in the militia. Nor is there any thing in the law, or, so far as history tells us, in usage, that excluded the children of slaves from the privileges of the free schools of Massachusetts. Marriages between slaves were celebrated by clergymen, and carried with them the legal incidents of such a relation.[2] That many of the children of slaves

[1] See also 4 Mass. Rep. 128.

[2] Col. L. 746; Quincy Rep. 30, Gray's note. J. W. Thornton, Esq., has in his possession the original of a form used by the Rev. Mr. Phillips, of Andover, who was ordained in 1710, in the marriage of slaves, in which he is careful to remind them that they remain still, really and truly, as ever, their master's property. The form seems to have been a special one of his own, and merely shows that, in 1756, when slavery was recognized in Massachusetts, there were minds constituted like

were brought up as slaves, and, when the affairs of their masters' families were settled, were inventoried as property, and disposed of as such, there is probably no reason to doubt. Nor is it difficult to imagine how such a state of things should more or less frequently have arisen.

A remark of Judge Cooley, of Michigan, in his recent work on Constitutional Limitations, applies with much force to the subject here referred to.

"A power," says he, "is frequently yielded to, merely because it is claimed; and it may be exercised for a long period, in violation of the constitutional prohibition, without the mischief which the Constitution was designed to guard against appearing, or without any one being sufficiently interested in the subject to raise the question." (p. 71.)

In the first place, nobody seems to have thought whether they were or were not slaves, until just before the Revolution. The number, at best, was too few to excite much attention. There was but here and there a lawyer to agitate the question, if it had been raised; and it was, obviously, for the policy of the towns, as well as a measure of humanity to the child, to have him brought up in his master's family, instead of being separated from his parents, and supported or bound out as a pauper. Such children grew up, unquestioning and unquestioned, as slaves *de facto*, without being, in any sense, slaves *de jure*. It was not, however, ordinarily, for the value they were of to their masters; for we are told by Dr. Belknap and his correspondents, that they were often given away in childhood. Nor does the fact that they were held as slaves, where the question as to their being such was never raised, militate with the position already stated, — that no child was ever born into *lawful* bondage in Massachusetts, from the year 1641 to the present hour. And when, at last, questions of this kind began to be raised, juries seem not to have been slow in vindicating the freedom of the

some in 1856, when it had ceased to be lawful there, who regarded the rights of the master to his human chattel, as more to be respected than the inborn rights of the slave himself as a human being. Judge Sewall, in his diary in 1700, speaks of a contemplated marriage between a negro servant-man of Mr. Wait and a negro servant-maid of Mrs. Thair, and adds, "and Mrs. Thair gave up the note of publication to Mr. Wait, for him to carry it to William Griggs Esq., town clerk, and to Williams, in order to have them published according to law."

slave. All they had wanted was an occasion to act. If we turn now to the third source of knowledge as to how slavery was regarded in the colony and province, — what was written and published and done by individuals and associations in respect to it, — we find a pamphlet by Judge Sewall, afterwards Chief Justice of the Superior Court, published in 1700, aimed directly at the unchristian character of slavery and the abominations of the slave-trade;[1] and, in 1716, he followed up this attack by a strenuous effort to change the form of valuing and taxing slaves, and to take them out of the list of chattels. In 1702, the people of Boston applied to their representatives in the General Court to have an end put to holding negroes as slaves. This may have been the moving cause of the act of 1705 already mentioned, which laid a duty upon all imported slaves; and the historian of Boston tells us, that, prior to 1727, those who were engaged in the traffic in slaves, and had occasion to advertise their human wares, often concealed their names, as people do now, who choose to keep dark as to what they think and say, by referring persons who wish for information to "the Printer."[2]

The record of how the people of Massachusetts stood in respect to the institution of slavery among them would be greatly imperfect if it omitted to mention the part which the Quakers of Nantucket took in the attempts made to suppress it. The venerable Nathaniel Barney, now of Poughkeepsie, has published an interesting account of their proceedings, and is in

[1] The account given by Judge Sewall, in his diary, of the circumstances under which this was written, is as follows: "Having been long and much dissatisfied with y[e] trade of fetching Negroes from Guinea, at last I had a strong inclination to write something about it; but it wore off. At last reading Bayne Ep[hs], ab[t] servants who mentions Blackamores, I began to be uneasy that I had so long neglected doing any thing. When I was thus thinking, in came Bro. Belknap, to shew me a petition he intended to present to y[e] Gen[l] Court for the freeing a negro and his wife who were unjustly held in Bondage. And there is a motion by a Boston Committee to get a law y[t] all importers of negroes shall pay 4£ per head to discourage y[e] bringing of y[m.] And Mr. C. Mather resolves to publish a sheet to exhort masters to labor y[r] conversion, which makes me hope that I was called of God to write this apology for them. Let his blessing accompany the same."

In a letter of Judge Sewall, in 1706, in speaking of this pamphlet, he says, "It is no small refreshment to me that I have the learned, reverend, and aged Mr. Higginson for my abettor. By the interposition of this breastwork, I hope to carry on and manage this enterprise with safety and success." (Letter-Book, p. 180.)

[2] Drake's Hist., p. 525.

possession of a manuscript copy of a tract against the making slaves of men, by *Elihu Colman*, written in 1729, and published in 1733. Following these as our guide, there can be little doubt that this body of Christians deserve the honor of being the first associated organization who made open war upon slavery in this country, or, so far as I have discovered, in the world. The Friends, at their Philadelphia yearly meeting in 1688, had begun the discussion without taking any decided action; but the Friends of Nantucket, moved and aroused by the fervid eloquence of a distinguished preacher of that denomination, a daughter of Tristram Coffin, and the wife of Nathaniel Starbuck, made a public protest and declaration, "that it is not agreeable to the truth for Friends to purchase slaves and hold them for the term of life." This was in 1716, and was followed in 1729 by an appeal from the same body to the Philadelphia yearly meeting, that —.

> "Inasmuch as we are restrained by the rule of discipline from being concerned in fetching or importing negro slaves from their own country, whether it is not as reasonable that we should be restricted from buying them when imported."

There is a peculiar significance in this language from the fact, stated by the venerable John Woolman, so kindly spoken of in the writings of Charles Lamb, that, when he was in Newport in 1760, he was pained to see slaves imported from Africa by a member of the society of Friends, then on sale there by the importer.

This movement by the people of Nantucket was followed by others of a similar character, which showed how generally the attention of the public was being aroused to the mischief and absurdity of tolerating such an institution in the midst of a people who professed a desire to be free.

And this feeling continued to gain strength, as the difficulties with the mother country became more threatening. In 1755, Salem applied to the General Court to suppress slavery.[1] Boston did the same in 1766, in 1767, and, as already stated, in 1772. In 1773, the action of the towns was more general and decided; and, without attempting to enumerate them all, it will be enough

[1] Felt's Salem, p. 204.

to mention, as representing different sections of the Province, the towns of Salem, Leicester, and Sandwich, which, in that year, specially and pointedly *instructed* their representatives to use their endeavors to put a stop to the importation of slaves.[1] The subject, too, found its way into the college; and, at the Commencement at Harvard that year, there was a public forensic disputation upon the question, "Whether slavery is in accordance with the law of nature?"

Pamphlets and newspapers began, as early as 1765, to discuss this question of slavery.[2] And, as the country approached the crisis of the Revolution, masters, in many cases, voluntarily emancipated their slaves; and appeals began to be made to the Courts, by those held in bondage, to be declared free. There were two such cases in Middlesex, between 1768 and 1770, in which judgment was rendered in favor of the parties suing for freedom; and another was decided in the same way in Essex, in 1773: which are referred to rather as examples, than to indicate the number or localities of these actions.[3]

There is a significant circumstance in the proceedings of the Courts of Massachusetts, in the fact, that, contrary to the uniform usage of other States where slavery has prevailed, slaves were here admitted to testify against white men, even in capital cases.[4]

It has sometimes been asked, Upon what ground, in the cases above referred to, the Courts pronounced in favor of the party suing for his freedom? Unfortunately the Records do not show this. If it was placed upon the circumstance of their being born in this Commonwealth, as seems to have been the case, from the language of C. J. Parsons,[5] it would be in accordance with the doctrine afterwards declared and maintained by the Courts. If it was because the jury saw fit, of their own accord, to render their verdict in such a way as to insure the negro his freedom,

[1] Felt's Salem; Freem. Hist. Barnst.; Hist. Leicester.

[2] Felt's Statis., p. 204.

[3] Coffin's Newb., p. 339.

[4] Quincy Rep. 30, Gray's note. The following is an extract of a letter from Judge Sewall, in 1719, "to Addington Davenport, Esq., going to judge Samuel Smith, of Sandwich, for killing his negro." — "The poorest boys and girls within the province, such as are of the lowest condition, whether they be English or Indians or Ethiopians, they have the same right to religion and life that the richest heirs have."

[5] 4 Mass. Rep., 127.

it serves, at least, to show how strong the sentiment then was in the community against the institution itself. We are told by John Adams, that "he never knew a jury, by a verdict, to determine a negro to be a slave. They always found him free." And he gives us to understand, that the arguments addressed to the Courts in favor of his liberty, were those "arising from the rights of mankind."[1]

Nor was the pulpit silent. The venerable pastor of the church in Newbury, as well as the late Mr. Coffin, the historian of that town, have given us interesting accounts of two spirited sermons preached in that pulpit, in 1774, by the Rev. Mr. Niles, afterwards a member of Congress from Vermont, and a judge of the Supreme Court. And, as evidence of their pertinency and effect, we are also told, that one of his parishioners, the next morning, called up the only slave he had, and gave him his freedom unsolicited.[2]

In this connection, moreover, a circumstance mentioned by the learned and faithful biographer of General Warren, ought not to be omitted, inasmuch as it shows how freely the feeling against the encroachments of the mother country was identified with that against slavery in every form. In November, 1772, the Committee of Correspondence of the town of Boston submitted to their constituents a statement of what they deemed to be the "Rights of the Colonies," and a list of the infringements of these.

It was unanimously adopted at a meeting in Faneuil Hall; and the selectmen of the town were directed to send copies of it to the selectmen of the several towns in the province. One of its positions is, — "The right to freedom being the gift of God Almighty, it is not in the power of man to alienate this gift, and voluntarily become a slave." And to show how the sentiments of this statement of the "Rights of the Colonies" chimed in with the feelings of the people of the towns, more than eighty of them sent in their cordial response in its favor, within the first five weeks after it had been issued.

The part which was taken by the black men of the Province in the struggle for our independence, has been admirably told by

[1] Original letter to Dr. Belknap, in possession of Mass. Hist. Soc.

[2] Dr. Withington's Letter; Coffin's Newbury, p. 340.

one fully competent to do it justice, in a work of our late associate, George Livermore; nor does any thing need to be added to show its bearing upon the subject now before us. Contemporary history is full of illustrations; and the language ascribed to Colonel Timothy Bigelow, of the Massachusetts Fifteenth of the Continental Line, was but an echo of the sentiment pervading this community everywhere, that, "while fighting for liberty, he would never be guilty of selling slaves."

With all this feeling, however, the events of that day show that it was tempered with prudence, and kept in subserviency to the great interests of the united colonies, in the common struggle for independence in which they were engaged. In 1777, a petition was presented to the General Court of Massachusetts by a number of Africans, for the abolition of slavery. A bill to that effect was reported and read twice, and then laid upon the table, for the purpose of consulting with the Continental Congress as to its expediency. In their letter, or petition, to Congress, the Legislature use these words: —

"Convinced of the justice of the measure, we are restrained from passing it, only from an apprehension that our brethren in the other colonies should conceive there was an impropriety in our determining on a question which may, in its nature and operation, be of extensive influence, without previously consulting your Honors."

They then proceed to —

"ask the attention of your Honors to this matter, that, if consistent with the union and harmony of the United States, we may follow the dictates of our own understanding and feelings; at the same time assuring your Honors, that we have such a sacred regard to the union and harmony of the United States, as to conceive ourselves under obligation to refrain from any measure that should have a tendency to injure that union which is the basis of our defence and happiness." [1]

[1] A writer in the "New-York Evening Post," of Jan. 28, 1869, informs the public, in a communication dated Jan. 25, 1869, including the letter referred to in the above text, that he had "*discovered* the draft of the letter to Congress, which is of sufficient interest to deserve publication." A copy of the original had been read before the Massachusetts Historical Society, at its regular meeting in September, 1868, by Charles Deane, Esq., its secretary; and the above extract had been taken from the *printed* sheets of the forthcoming volume of its Transactions, and had been delivered, forming a part of this lecture, on the 22d of the same January.

It is hardly necessary to add, that such a suggestion as the abolition of slavery could not have found favor among those who madly clung to an institution which was, even then, beginning to demoralize the coming republic. But the delicacy of Massachusetts in the manner of insisting upon it does not derogate from the sincerity with which she sought to procure it. And when the time came that she felt at liberty to act, it will be found that she did, by herself, what she had been disposed to ask permission of her sister States to do, — set open the doors of bondage, by an organic law of freedom; and, in 1780, echoed back the spirit of the Fathers of 1641, by declaring her slaves free.

To understand this measure, it should be remembered, that, in becoming a free State, she had no other form of government than the inadequate one under which her affairs had been administered under the Crown. It was, accordingly, attempted, in 1777, to frame a constitution, as had been done by some others of the colonies which had now become States.

But the instrument offered to the people contained no Declaration of Rights, and was otherwise so defective, that it was rejected, almost without a count of the votes. This was followed by the Constitution of 1780, the opening declaration of which serves as a key to the whole instrument, that "all men are born free and equal, and have certain natural, essential, and unalienable rights." Important as this clause was held to be in its practical bearing upon the condition of the slave, it contained no new thought, nor was it the enunciation of any new dogma in political science. It had come down from early times, having been advanced and maintained by a Tuscan writer as early as 1540; and had been often repeated, even by the politicians and statesmen of our own country. We read it, substantially, in the Declaration of our Independence of 1776. It had found a place, the same year, in the Bill of Rights of the Constitution of Virginia; and it was repeated in that of New Hampshire. But in its application to bodies politic, it seems to have borrowed its meaning and interpretation from the habits of thought on the part of the people by whom it was used. In New Hampshire, it seems to have been read, as saying, that all who should be born after its publication were to be free. While to the slave-holders of Virginia, and such as construe the Declaration of Independence in the same light, these words were nothing but a "glittering generality." But to the people of Massachusetts, these words were things. The framers of that constitution made no promise to the ear to break it to the hope. And when the highest judicial tribunal in the State was called upon to construe and apply this clause, they gave a response which struck off the chains from every slave in the Commonwealth; and Massachusetts was, at last, what she had so long been struggling to be, in all her dwellings, indeed the home of freemen.

The case in which this important decision was made, was that of a black man in the County of Worcester, by the name of Quork Walker.[1] And a similar case was soon after decided in Berkshire, where a black woman, by the name of Betty, was the subject. A case involving the same question is said to have arisen in Nantucket, about the same time, in which a like decision was had, when that staunch old Quaker, William Rotch, Sr., without waiting, as it is said, for any action of the Court, resolved to pay the *lay* of a black seaman, in a whaling voyage, to himself, instead of his master, on the ground that the Bill of Rights had made him free. And the Court sustained him in so doing. And what is worthy of notice, is the character and position of the men in the profession who were ready to engage in the cause of the slave. The counsel for Walker were Levi Lincoln, Sr., and Caleb Strong, whose very names are a part of our political history. And the counsel for the slave woman in Berkshire was Theodore Sedgwick, afterwards Speaker of Con-

[1] In June, 1781, Walker recovered judgment in the Court of Common Pleas against Jennison, for £50 damages; and Jennison appealed to the Superior Court. But, failing to prosecute his appeal, judgment was rendered for Walker, at the September Term of the Superior Court, 1781. At the same term of the Court of Common Pleas, Jennison's action against Caldwell for depriving him of the services of his servant, Walker, was tried; and a verdict was returned in favor of the defendant. The plaintiff appealed; but, at the September Term of the Superior Court, judgment was rendered for the defendant, Caldwell. At the same term of the Superior Court, September, 1781, an indictment was found against Jennison, for an assault upon Walker. It was tried before a jury, at the April Term, 1783; and the defendant was found guilty, and sentenced to pay a fine of $40 and costs. (Superior Court Records, Suffolk, 1781–2, p. 84; ib. 79, 1783, p. 85.)

gress, and Judge of our Supreme Court. To these we might add the names of Judge John Lowell and John Adams, to say nothing of Samuel Adams, and other prominent leaders in the politics of the State.

It ought not, however, to be kept out of sight, that there have been those who, to this day, cavil at the construction thus put upon this clause in the Constitution. And the writer already referred to, contests the idea that this clause in the Bill of Rights was intended "to annul the condition of servitude;" and adds, "We have made diligent inquiry, search, and examination, without discovering the slightest trace of positive contemporary evidence to show that this opinion was well founded."[1] He seems to have forgotten, that every member of the Court which pronounced this judgment, had been members of the Convention which formed this Constitution, and took part in its discussions; and two of them were of the committee who were appointed to prepare a draft of the Bill of Rights. Nor is this all: Judge Sullivan, one of these, and afterwards Attorney-General and Governor of Massachusetts, in a letter to Dr. Belknap, in 1795, declared, that "this decision put an end to the idea of slavery in this State." And the venerable Samuel Dexter, father of the still more eminent statesman of that name, sums up an account of this case with this brief declaration: "Thus ended slavery in Massachusetts." And here the subject might properly be left, so far as the truths of history and the good fame of Massachusetts are concerned. But there is that in the history of this subject which suggests a contrast between slavery as it existed here in 1660, and as we had occasion to witness it elsewhere in 1860.

It was a living organism in 1660, because, as we are told by Lord Brougham, when speaking of the abolition of slavery, "Every measure proposed by the Colonial Legislature, which did not meet the entire concurrence of the British Cabinet, was sure to be rejected in the last instance by the Crown."

In 1860, it owed its life to the persistent will of the States themselves in which it prevailed. It never, in Massachusetts, divided men socially into classes; nor did it build up a spurious oligarchy upon the roll-call of wretched beings under the ban of

[1] Moore, p. 203.

the law. It did not arrest the privileges or progress of free education, nor did it stifle the sense of faith and allegiance with which a generous mind regards the government that has protected and the country that has reared and cherished him. And when the time came for the emancipation of the black man, it found the master ready to offer the sacrifice upon the altar of liberty, or decorously yielding to the destiny that had made him free.

And the history of the Commonwealth for more than fourscore years has shown, that, in the relations of civil and political liberty, the black man and the white may live together in harmony under just laws, and a wise and liberal Constitution. And may we not hope that, with such a lesson before them, with slavery gone for ever, the men of our day may yet be wise; and with power restored, industry revived, and national harmony secured, our land may be the home of a free, a united, and a prosperous people?

RECORDS OF MASSACHUSETTS

UNDER ITS

FIRST CHARTER.

BY CHARLES W. UPHAM.

RECORDS OF MASSACHUSETTS

UNDER ITS

FIRST CHARTER.

THE design of the lecture this evening is to consider the Records of Massachusetts, under its first charter, from the point of view in which they illustrate the formation of a body-politic.

The organization of families and communities into some established order is demanded by the conditions of our nature. More than any other temporal concern, it merits and compels the attention of thoughtful minds; and the questions relating to it have always been acknowledged to rank in the highest department, as subjects of inquiry and meditation. Through the entire range of history, the greatest minds have been turned to it. But a glance at the condition of the nations of the earth shows how unsatisfactory have been the results. The experience of ages has effected little; and the theories of philosophers, not much more. The human race in all lands, and all ages, has groaned under the crushing weight of institutions constructed on false principles. Governments everywhere are upheld by military force; and depend for continuance upon ignorance and superstition. So far as we are an exception, it becomes us to inquire to what we owe the degree of our exemption.

Enlightened views on the subject of government are especially important to a people that governs itself. We can hardly expect to obtain them from treatises and essays, however ingenious and learned. There is, indeed, an inherent obstacle in the way of attaining to the truth by these means. Attempts to reason and speculate concerning it are thwarted by the influence on the mind of pre-existing usages and ideas. Every suggestion of reform is encountered by the necessity of adapting it to a surrounding state of things, and by well-grounded fear, that, however specious the theory, it may not work well in practice. The elements of motive, sentiment, and association, that actuate mankind, are so infinitely diversified that they cannot be calculated. Casual events, and complicated circumstances, not to be foreseen, may bring to naught the best considered schemes.

On this subject, the world craves and needs, not what theorists have conjectured, or philosophers propounded, but what has been tried, and found sufficient. The question is — Has a fair experiment ever been made, under favorable auspices, of laying the foundation, and building the fabric of a government of men? and, if so, let it be brought before us.

As answering this question, and meeting this demand, I cite the colony of Massachusetts, during its first half-century, as more to the purpose than any other instance in history.

In pursuance of the recommendation of Governor Clifford, in a special message of Feb. 12, 1853, the Legislature of Massachusetts ordered the first and second volumes of the "Records of the Governor and Company of the Massachusetts Bay in New England," to be printed, embracing the proceedings in London prior to the transfer of the patent; and continued after that event, under the style of "Colony Records," to 1649. The next year a resolve was passed, approved by Governor Washburn, February 17, for printing the third, fourth, and fifth volumes, carrying the record to 1686, and covering, altogether, the entire period of the government under the first charter. The form and manner in which they were printed do honor to the Commonwealth, and to the distinguished member of our society, intrusted with the responsible duty of editing them, Nathaniel Bradstreet Shurtleff. The copying was done, under his appointment, by David Pulsifer, whose thorough acquaintance with the chirography of early colonial times gives assurance of exactness.

These volumes supply the most important instruction anywhere to be found, on the formation of a civilized State. They are the text-book on the subject; and stand alone in their character, and the value of their contents, as I proceed to show.

On the 3d of November, 1620, James I. granted by letters-patent all that section of North America, between the fortieth and forty-eighth parallels of latitude, from sea to sea, to the "Council established at Plymouth, in the County of Devon, for the Planting, Ruling, Ordering, and Governing of New England in America."

The Council at Plymouth conveyed by a contract, indented March 14, 1628, so much of the territory, included in their aforesaid patent, as was between lines, three miles north of Merrimack River and three miles south of Charles River, running from sea to sea, to Sir Henry Rosewell and Sir John Young, Knights, Thomas Southcott, John Humphries, John Endicott, and Simon Whitcomb, their heirs, assigns, and associates.

One year afterwards, namely, on the 4th of March, 1629, in the fourth year of the reign of Charles I., letters-patent passed the seals, confirming to the above-named six persons, and twenty others, severally named, who had become associated with them, and their heirs, and assigns, "to their only proper and absolute use and behoof forevermore," the territory purchased from the Council at Plymouth. These twenty-six individuals thus came into complete possession, and were owners, so far as the crown of England could give title, of the continent within the limits described. The vocabulary of ordinary language, and of the law, was exhausted in expressing, in every possible iteration and reiteration, the fulness, absoluteness, and perpetuity of the feofment and jurisdiction thus conveyed. In three particulars only was any limitation imposed.

The company was forbidden, in ruling its vast American domain, to make regulations repugnant to the laws of England. But this was merely nominal, as no provision was made, or required to be made, for redress of any wrong done by the company to a planter, or to any outside party. There was, indeed, no way left open, through which the regulations of the company could be brought to adjudication on this point. No political powers, or rights whatever, were given by the patent to the people of the settlement; for the negative protection implied in the language, that no laws should be imposed upon them in conflict with the statutes of the realm, was a mere shadow of a shade, as events proved.

The company was required to pay to the crown one-fifth part of all ores of gold or silver found in the country. This amounted to nothing.

There was one other condition, which also, in practice, hardly amounted to any thing. The patent exempted the settlements, to be made by the company, from all duties of any kind, "inward or outward," for seven years; and, after that, for twenty-one years more, with this exception only, that, during the latter period, they were to be subject to a duty of five per cent upon goods shipped from the plantations to any other part of the dominions of England. But this had no sensible effect here, for the duty was to be exacted at the outer end of the voyage, in the port of discharge; and was there imposed upon all alike, foreigners as well as other colonists. Further, it was pledged by the crown, that on the re-exportation, at any time within thirteen months, of goods upon which this duty had been paid, to any country whatever, no further duty of any kind should be levied on them. The whole arrangement was justly to be regarded as the assurance of a privilege rather than the imposition of a burden. No provision was made relating to the subject, on the expiration of the twenty-one years, but the whole matter left, as between the crown and the company; for it must be noticed that there is no reference whatever, in the patent, to the authority, or even the existence, of Parliament, except as implied in the clauses requiring the regulations of the company not to be repugnant to the laws of England. The duty on goods was not in deference to any acts of Parliament, but carefully described, as "according to the ancient trade of merchants." In order that it might be made clear and certain, that the territories embraced in the patent should not be subject to Parliament, but exclusively connected with the personal private property of the crown, the device was adopted, as in the patent to the Council at Plymouth, of repeating over and over again, that they were appendages of the royal demesnes, "to be holden of us, as of our manor of East Greenwich." They were to be regarded as an enlargement of the grounds of one of the favorite residences of the sovereign. While thus protecting them from interference by any other parts of the government, the King bound himself, and his heirs and successors, to the end of time, not to encroach upon, but, on the contrary, to uphold the administration of the grantees in governing their territory; and enjoined the same upon all exercising authority, civil or military, throughout his dominions.

The persons to whom the patent was issued, were constituted a body-politic. They were to choose, annually, from among themselves, a governor, deputy governor, and eighteen assistants. Any seven or more of the assistants, together with the governor or deputy governor, were to hold a monthly court, for disposing of questions arising from time to time, and requiring immediate attention. There were to be quarterly meetings, held at specified times, by the whole body of the members, or "freemen," as they were called, of the company. These were for making laws or regulations, and the transaction of weighty business. They are spoken of in the patent as "great, general, and solemn assemblies," and termed the "four Great and General Courts" of the company. At the quarterly meeting, occurring in Easter term, that is, in the latter part of May, the annual elections were required to be made.

The King, in the patent, named the persons who were to fill the offices of the company, until the time fixed for an election should arrive. It is remarkable, that, although there were several knights among the grantees, he selected an untitled one for governor. "We do, by these presents, for us, our heirs, and successors, nominate, ordain, make, and constitute our well-beloved Matthew Cradock, the first and present Governor of the said company." Cradock was a London merchant of great wealth, and, as the Records show, of eminent practical ability, energy, and wisdom. He is said to have been connected by family ties, in some way, with Endicott, which accounts, perhaps, for his having been drawn in as an associate of the six original proprietors, and for the deep interest he took in the enterprise. It can hardly be doubted, I think, that he was the same Matthew Cradock, son of a wool merchant in Stafford, who, in the reign of James I., became the owner of the baronial estate in Staffordshire, called Caverswall. The castellated mansion, built as early as the Norman conquest, was reconstructed by him, under the superintendence of Inigo Jones. It is still standing in the form Cradock gave to it, and justly regarded as "one of the most striking, picturesque, and interesting remains of a distant age. A venerable and "solemn fortress-like structure," it demands special attention, as "presenting the ideal of the great architect of the transition from the ancient castle to the baronial mansion." To an American it has a deeper interest. If its possessor and occupant was the "well-beloved" Matthew Cradock, of the patent, it will appear, as we proceed, that to us that noble mansion will ever be invested with sacred memories and associations. Within its massive walls the thought, perhaps, was conceived which has made Massachusetts and our country what they are to-day. Cradock was returned to Parliament from the city of London, in 1640, and died not long after.[1]

It is important to bear in mind that the patent conferred upon the company, in the most emphatic language, all political power whatever, without any reservation that touched the substance of the grant. This is so vital to the case, as I am presenting it, that the expressions used may be quoted, —

"We do, of our further grace, certain knowledge, and mere motion, give and grant to the said governor or deputy governor, and such of the assistants and freemen of the said company, for the time being, as shall be assembled in any of their General Courts, or in any other courts to be specially summoned and assembled for that purpose, or to the greater part of them, that it shall and may be lawful to and for them, from time to time, to make, ordain, and establish all manner of wholesome and reasonable orders, laws, statutes, and ordinances, directions, and instructions, not contrary to the laws of this our realm of England, as well for settling of the forms and ceremonies of government and magistracy fit and necessary for the said plantation and the inhabitants there, and for naming and styling of all sorts of officers, both superior and inferior, and setting forth of the several duties, powers, and limits of every such office and place, and for impositions of lawful fines, mulcts, imprisonment, or other lawful correction, and for the directing, ruling, and disposing of all other matters and things."

Some dozen or two knights and gentlemen, more or less, sitting in the parlors of Matthew Cradock, in Swithen's Lane, within the ancient limits of London, by virtue of powers thus granted, held absolute sway over this part of America, from

[1] Baronial Halls and Ancient Picturesque Edifices of England, by S. C. Hall, F.S.A. London, 1858. Proceedings of Essex Institute, vol. i. p. 242: Memoir of Cradock, by David Roberts.

Massachusetts Bay to the Pacific Ocean; and they proceeded to administer their government by transporting settlers forthwith.

Very soon it was found expedient to send some one over to superintend affairs here on the spot, and John Endicott, an original purchaser of the country from the Council at Plymouth, was despatched accordingly. Some months after his departure, the company, on the 30th of April, 1629, elected him "Governor of the Plantation in the Massachusetts Bay," and a commission was duly forwarded to him with the form of an oath of office. This was, however, an arrangement, whereby no power was parted with by the company. It was a limited appointment. Endicott's office was to terminate in one year from the day when he took the oath, and the right was expressly reserved of removing him at any time within the year. His authority was limited by sundry conditions, and reports of all his doings were required to be transmitted to London for approval. He executed his functions with fidelity, energy, and ability. But, notwithstanding all his efforts and those of his employers, the affairs of the company were getting into embarrassment, and its operations threatened with ruin.

Cradock, a thorough business man, appreciated the condition of things. He saw the impending catastrophe; and, being of a bold and courageous spirit, with the comprehensive views of a statesman, proved himself competent to discover and apply the only remedy that could save the enterprise. That which had been fatal to colonial success in other attempts, was the difficulty in the Massachusetts plantation. It was managed by a distant administration. Deliberations and determinations by a body sitting in London could not meet the exigencies of a community, with an ocean between, and the interlapse of months in the transmission of orders and intelligence. Forming a plan by which all concerned might be extricated from the responsibilities in which they were becoming more and more involved, he was so fortunate as to secure the co-operation of parties competent to carry it through. A number of gentlemen of property, character, and influence, were found willing to join the company and assume its burdens, with the understanding that they would personally transport themselves and families to America, and make it their permanent home, provided they were allowed to carry the patent with them, hold its offices, execute its functions, and possess all its rights and powers. This was Cradock's proposal, and the arrangement was consummated.

John Winthrop, Thomas Dudley, and others, took their seats in the company, at a meeting, Oct. 15, 1629. At a meeting, five days afterwards, Cradock vacated the chair, and Winthrop was elected governor, with a new board of assistants, all to hold office for one year from that date. Early the next spring, he embarked for Massachusetts Bay, with the patent, and the frame and body of the government. Not a vestige of it was left in England.

There were undoubtedly great and daring irregularities in these proceedings, which could not have escaped notice, and would have been summarily arrested, had there been the slightest suspicion of their ultimate consequences. There is no pretence of authority in the patent for the removal of the company out of the realm, or for the relinquishment of his office by Cradock, in the time and manner. His stepping out of the chair, on the 20th of October, without even going through the ceremony of a resignation, and the election of Winthrop to serve an annual term, when by the patent he could only fill out an unexpired term, were equally without justification. Indeed, no provision is made in that instrument for the resignation of any office, and it is a procedure inadmissible by English usage. The transfer of the company to America brought with it another violation of the patent, inasmuch as they were on the passage across the Atlantic at the date fixed in express terms for the annual election, which was pretermitted in consequence altogether. These departures from and violations of the implied meaning and explicit requirements of the patent were necessities involved in the operation of the transference of it from England to America. Those engaged in it, faced the responsibilities of the occasion without shrinking. No stricture, or comment of any kind, appeared from any quarter; and the thing was done.

From the Records, Matthew Cradock alone appears as the originator and manager of this business; but from the nature of the whole proceeding, it is evident that Winthrop shared with him, as a principal co-actor. Let them each have the glory of the transaction. It is a glory that will become brighter through all time. History sheds no purer lustre upon any names than belongs to the men whose wisdom and statesmanship led to the bold and decisive step that enabled the colony of Massachusetts to bear its great part in teaching how a republic can be built up on a solid and permanent foundation.

The patent of Charles I. to the Massachusetts colony is what is called our First Charter; and, from this point, I shall speak of it under that appellation.

When Winthrop's fleet came to anchor in the harbor of Salem, he, and such members of the company as had accompanied or preceded him, found themselves in absolute and uncontrolled possession of the country, within the limits of their charter. Their jurisdiction and powers were complete; and had they been actuated by selfish motives, or a low ambition, and retained the character of a close corporation, the fortunes of the plantation, and their own fame, would have had the same fate, that of a brief duration and an ignoble end.

The charter gave to them, in express and repeated terms and without limitation, the right to admit new associates. Persons thus admitted became full partners and equal members of the company, called, as has been stated, Freemen. The exercise of this right was the magic by which they converted what was originally a royal act of incorporation for business and commercial purposes, into the constitution of a free and noble Commonwealth. In the year 1631, one hundred and twenty-six of the resident population were admitted, and in the next ten years twelve hundred more.

By this generous and enlightened policy, the PEOPLE here acceded to the rights and powers given in the charter. The Colony of Massachusetts became an independent State. Parliament could not touch it, and the crown had bound itself to keep its hands off.

The result of the proceedings thus far may be restated, at this point, in a few words: The charter gave to the Massachusetts Company sovereignty over its territory. The admission of the people of the plantation into the company gave that sovereignty to them. Having the charter in their possession, and rightfully holding under it, they claimed and exercised absolute self-government.

One hundred and forty-six years before the Declaration of the Independence of the United States, this was an independent government, and continued so for more than half a century, — more independent, in fact, than it has ever been since. Between the period of the First Charter and the war of the Revolution, it was a dependent province, its governors appointed by the British monarch, and the royal assent needed to give validity to its laws. Since the opening of the Revolutionary conflict, to this hour, it has been, in many respects and to a considerable extent, subject to the old Congress of the Confederation, and subsequently to the Government of the United States. But during the fifty-eight years of the First Charter, the people were as free to rule themselves as if they had been on another planet. They chose all their own officers, asked no approval of their laws, suffered no appeal in any case to the mother country, and bowed to no tribunals but of their own erection. This was, and ought to be considered, the first era of American independence.

In this respect, that is, in exemption from foreign interference, the situation of the original colonists of Massachusetts was all that could be desired; in other respects it was equally favorable. All the requisite conditions for the formation of a good government existed. A country lay before them, unoccupied, open, and free; sufficiently large to give room for the experiment, and comprising features and resources adapted to the uses of an industrious and intelligent people, with only here and there a solitary previous settler, or remnants of Aboriginal tribes in no way fastened to the soil. They had among them many persons of large experience in affairs, conversant with the laws and customs, not only of their own native country, but of the nations of Continental Europe, and well read in ancient history. Some of them had held eminent social position, and were of enlarged culture; and not a few, having enjoyed the advantages of the highest schools and seats of academic learning, and of Inns of Court, were remarkably qualified to act the part of statesmen. There probably was a greater amount of practical wisdom and energy among them than in any community, of equal numbers, ever brought together. What they had endured in the old country, and the sacrifices they had encountered in getting away from it, and in opening their wilderness homes, had given them an individual force and independence of character, and liberated their minds from the influence of all sentimental associations and traditional attachments to the usages, institutions, and social fixtures of all kinds in the old country.

An opportunity was thus given to solve the problem of government; to ascertain and determine the true method of forming a political organization in accordance with nature, reason, justice, and right, not to be paralleled elsewhere in the old or new world.

The colony of Plymouth, although dating ten years earlier than Massachusetts and extending its distinct history to the close of the era of our First Charter, cannot, in some respects, be regarded as standing on the same level. Its territory was not large enough to form the basis of a State, developed to its full dimensions and ramifications. Until after the process of political organization was under way here, the older colony could hardly give its attention to any thing else than the struggles required to extricate itself from financial entanglements with parties in England. It was long before they could feel that the houses they had built, and the lands they had cleared, were their own. The infant community springing from Plymouth rock demands, however, the sympathy, veneration, and imitation of the friends of freedom and virtue.

Before landing, on the 11th of November, 1620, the Pilgrims executed a written instrument, known as "The Compact," covenanting and combining themselves together "into a civil body politick," subscribed by forty-one persons. Among the names are those of several who were servants, some who were sailors, and one, at least, who could have had no pretensions to consideration on the ground of personal merit, for he is spoken of by Bradford as having been "shuffled into their company." From the first, he appears to have incurred censure for his "miscarriages." In 1621, he was tied together "neck and heels" for contempt of authority and "opprobrious speeches," and in 1630, hanged for murder.

In view of these facts we must consider the compact, drawn up in the cabin of the "Mayflower," as an instance of universal suffrage, announcing the cardinal principle of a government resting upon the whole people, and deriving its authority from the voices of all descriptions of persons, without distinction of rank, condition, or character, with a comprehensiveness which Massachusetts was long in reaching, and to which the United States could only have been brought by passing through the Red Sea of our recent intestine war.

The public documents and records of the colony of Plymouth have justly been regarded as among the chief historical treasures of the Commonwealth in which it was merged. In 1836, a resolve of the Massachusetts Legislature was approved by Governor Everett for the publication of the Laws of the Old Colony; and by his appointment they were prepared for the press and edited by our esteemed associate who, in a preceding lecture of this course, has done justice to the legislation of that colony. The result of his labors appeared in a valuable and interesting volume entitled "The Compact, with the Charter and Laws of the Colony of New Plymouth." In 1855, a resolve was passed, approved by Governor Gardner, to publish the "Records of the Colony of New Plymouth;" which was executed by printing them in the same beautiful shape as the Massachusetts Records, during the period of the First Charter. The work was performed under the superintendence of the same editor, Dr. Shurtleff. They show in detail the proceedings of a community, of a comparatively small population, on a limited area, conducting its affairs wisely and justly. Its institutions were simple and unpretentious, and administered by enlightened men, with as righteous purposes and free a spirit as the world ever saw. But when we consider government, as branching out in the directions demanded by a people in the exigencies of an expanding growth, requiring complicated arrangements and functions to meet its wants, it is obvious that such an opportunity to develop it was not afforded in Plymouth as in Massachusetts. It was not, for instance, until 1640 that any thing like a House of Deputies appeared, representing towns in a General Assembly in the older colony. In such respects it fell in our rear, even in the order of time.

Rhode Island originally consisted of several plantations, conflicting with each other, and carrying their contentions to the notice of the mother country, thereby keeping their affairs more or less within its jurisdiction. Its first General Court, in which towns were represented, was held in 1647. Nothing, however, can impair its glory, in having first planted and ever sacredly cherished the immortal principle of religious liberty.

What is now Connecticut consisted, for some time, of distinct jurisdictions. Their affairs, like those of Rhode Island, were dependent upon decisions looked for from the mother country; and finally, in 1665, they were consolidated, by the authority of the crown, extinguishing the colony of New Haven, into one government. The gallant rescue of the charter obtained at that time, from the grasp of Sir Edmund Andros, at Hartford in 1687, is justly regarded one of the most memorable incidents of American history. It continued in force to the time of the Revolution, and saved Connecticut from experiencing the fate to which Massachusetts was subjected, after the loss of its First Charter privileges, of a dependent province. It remained, in fact, the constitution of the State of Connecticut until 1818.

What are now Maine and New Hampshire were claimed by conflicting proprietors; a large part of the former, more or less, under a foreign jurisdiction, and both of them much of the time under that of Massachusetts.

As this colony was organized, and in full action, as a civil government, before the other New-England plantations; as it was central to them, to a great degree their common mother, and so much more populous than either, — its history is of larger significance and importance. In many instances, — indeed, for the most part, — they followed in its track and conformed to its practices.

New York was a Dutch dependency until 1664; and its first legislative Assembly was in 1683. New Jersey, Pennsylvania, Delaware, and the Carolinas were proprietary provinces. Maryland had a legislative Assembly in 1639; but remained a proprietary government. The early colonial condition of Virginia was much interrupted, and long in an unsettled state.

The records and memorials of all the colonies are, however, of great value, presenting many features worthy of study, and, in some particulars, severally having claims to special credit.

Massachusetts alone, was all along, for more than half a century, left unmolested to form a government, at her leisure, and as she saw fit. The Records that tell how she did it, possess, therefore, a value altogether unique. They exhibit precisely what a student of political science needs to know, and what can nowhere else be found. I proceed to note a few of the stages in the progress of eliminating the elements, and shaping the forms, of an effective, natural, and well-adjusted social and political organization, narrated in them.

After admitting the people to the freedom and power of the company, the founders of Massachusetts applied themselves slowly and cautiously, but with decisive measures, to their work. For some time, the company, at its meetings, which were all called Courts, took the entire management of affairs, however trivial, into its own immediate hands, acting directly on all matters whatsoever relating to person or property. At their first meeting, the governor and assistants were invested with the necessary powers to execute orders and decisions. At the next meeting, a beadle, afterwards dignified with the title of marshal, was sworn in, whose duty it was to attend the governor and execute his commands; also to be present at the Court, to maintain and enforce respect for its authority. The character and functions of justices of the peace were conferred upon the governor, deputy governor, and six of the assistants. Constables were appointed in the principal settlements.

It soon became apparent, that it was impracticable for assemblies of the whole body of the freemen, or for the Governor and assistants at their monthly meetings, to attend to the multifarious matters constantly demanding adjudication, in settlements as yet without known laws or established customs, and separated from each other by pathless forests. Cases could not reach the Court, with all the evidence required to decide upon them justly; and the Court, therefore, had to go to the cases. Certain persons were appointed in several localities, with limited jurisdiction, "to end small causes," as they expressed it. The body of the freemen, in General Court assembled, having thus begun to part with a portion of their power, and entered upon the path that separates judicial from legislative functions, carefully felt their way along, creating local tribunals in the towns, establishing counties with courts of trial within them, and gradually developing a comprehensive system of judicature.

In 1630, certain persons, their number not always being twelve, were appointed by the General Court to find and report to it the facts relating to particular cases, thus originating here the institution of a jury, as it has come down to us. The General Court continued, however, in most cases, to examine and decide matters directly. In 1635, grand juries were provided to present cases to the General Court.

The administration of estates, and the distribution of property, whether of testates or intestates, the General Court, for some time, kept in its own hands, heeding the law and practice in England, as far as it saw fit; but at a very early period, the policy was discussed, and finally carried into effect, of passing the whole business over to special functionaries. Probate officers were provided. Special care, however, was taken to divest this branch of the law of the ecclesiastical character given to it in the mother country. In arranging the judicial department, the General Court, consisting as it did, immediately or by representation, of the whole people, seems during the entire period of the First Charter, to have retained in its own hands an ultimate control. An appeal to its revising and final judgment was kept open from all tribunals and in all descriptions of cases. Although subsequent experience has shed great additional light upon the subject of the true position of the judiciary, the records, now under review, may well be studied, conveying, as they do, much pertinent instruction and matter for reflection.

As the plantations multiplied, and spread into the interior, it became inconvenient for the people to be fully present at the meetings of the General Court, and the transaction of business was embarrassed by an irregular and unreliable attendance. In 1632, the expedient was adopted of advising the appointment of two persons in each plantation to confer with the Governor and assistants, about the raising of a public stock. In 1634, it was made lawful for the freemen of the several settlements, to choose two or three of their number to attend the Court, to confer about public affairs generally, and to "have the full power and voices of all the said freemen derived to them for the making and establishing laws, granting lands," &c. The principle of representation was thus gradually introduced. All the plantations fell into the practice of appointing such delegates, who were called deputies. For a few years they sat with the assistants in the same room, the Governor or deputy governor presiding over the joint body. It seems to have become the custom for the deputies, to vote separately from the assistants; and a concurrence of the votes of the two portions of the assembly was required to carry a measure. Finally, it was concluded to have them sit in different rooms; and the deputies were organized as a distinct house, choosing their own speaker. In this way a double legislature was established. The fact that it has been adopted in all our States, and in the United States government, would seem to prove that it is founded on sufficient reasons, and essential to good legislation. In this, as in all things else, where the practice established here resembled that of the mother country, the resemblance was not the result of a spirit of conformity, or in deference to authority from that quarter, but solely because, in the natural progress of events, it was found expedient.

At an early day the General Court parted with a very considerable portion of its sovereignty to the several plantations, together with the fee of the lands within the limits of the same, thereby calling into existence what has always been regarded one of the chief elements of our political civilization, — Towns. John Adams declared, that to them, in a great degree, was to be attributed the preparation of this people to engage in, and carry through, the conflict of the Revolution. They are the nurseries of freedom, schools of universal education in popular rights, and alone can fit a people to make, obey, and execute the laws. No country can take the true start, or secure reliable progress in political reform, without them; and there is no race so degraded, as not to be redeemed to a capacity for self-government, if trained by such an institution to the exercise of control over affairs, by local communities in distinct neighborhoods.

Similar arrangements had existed for centuries in the mother country; and to them can be traced the characteristics which have made the English people competent to uphold a constitutional government. The encroachment upon these small local jurisdictions, — by modern Parliamentary interference and the establishment of central commissions or bureaus, — is regarded as having already lowered the character of the population of the rural districts of the kingdom. Towns were the basis of what are called hundreds; and in different sections of England, at different times, had different appellations, as thorp, now village, or hamlet; burgh, now borough; and town. The last, being probably the original name, was the prevalent one;[1] although when our fathers left England, it had become superseded, in some localities, by ville, and parish. But, under the latter designation, the institution had been perverted from its original character, which was purely secular, brought under the power of the Church, and made to receive an ecclesiastical impress.[2] The lawgivers of Massachusetts were too true to their British ancestry to call them villes, and their repugnance to associations, connected with the hierarchy at home, forbid their calling them parishes. They went back to the old Anglo-Saxon name. They made the jurisdiction of towns quite limited at first, gradually enlarging it, until it reached the dimensions still retained, embracing powers the most momentous, and constituting by far the greatest portion of what we feel to be the government under which we live.

When the public exigencies demanded it, a confederation of colonies was effected at the suggestion of the Connecticut plantations, but under the lead of Massachusetts. The entries contained in the Records on this subject, and the documents connected with its organization and operation, may be safely said to stand the test of comparison with the State papers of the originators of the Confederation of the Revolutionary age, and of the founders of our Federal Constitution, as showing the legitimate boundaries between the powers of separate States and of any general government that may be established among them.

The elements that give energy to a commonwealth, in peace or war, are strikingly disclosed and illustrated in the history of Massachusetts under the First Charter. A more efficient government for the preservation of order, security, and the common welfare, has never existed; and the rapidity with which the public resources were brought to bear in military movements, while it was repeated at the opening of the war of Independence, has never been surpassed, even in our day, which has witnessed

[1] A Restitution of Decayed Intelligence in Antiquities concerning our Nation, by Richard Verstigan, 1605, chap. ix. p. 295.

[2] The Parish, its Obligations and Powers; its officers and their duties, with illustrations of the practical workings of the institution in all secular affairs, by Toulmin Smith. London, 1854.

the uprising in their might of a great people to save the national life.

The early records of Massachusetts shed light upon all subjects that relate to the development of the moral as well as physical strength of a State, particularly the diffusion of knowledge, and of a public spirit ready to assume burdens and face danger; and to sacrifice ease, property, and life, for the common weal.

The promptitude, boldness, and impartiality of the internal administration of the government are particularly noticeable. Offences were rebuked and disorder suppressed by sure and decisive measures: no rank or station, no popular affection or habitual reverence for particular persons, however eminent or honored, could obstruct the course or embarrass the movements of even-handed power. The General Court, in the exercise of its sovereignty, treated all men alike, in as well as out of its own body. Sir Richard Saltonstall was fined; Endicott was admonished, disqualified temporarily for holding office, and committed for contempt of the authority and dignity of the Court; and even Winthrop, once in a while, was dropped from his high place.

In the administration of external affairs, the General Court was equally disregardful of all weak and timid considerations. Nothing can surpass the spirit, courage, ability, and success, with which it withstood and repelled attempts of encroachment from the mother country.

There was always a powerful party busily at work in the Court at London, bent upon the suppression of the Massachusetts colony; but by skilful diplomacy on the part of the Court and its able agents in England, following the policy comprehended by Winthrop in two words, — "Avoid and protract;" by standing tenaciously and resolutely upon their charter, particularly that feature of it which left no opening for an appeal to the mother country, and provided no process by which complaints could legitimately be brought against the company; by the opportune diversion of attention from colonial matters to occurrences in England, especially those connected with the controversy between the King and Parliament; and by the blessing of Providence, — every blow was warded off, until two generations had laid the foundations of the political fabric too deep to be moved.

It became, indeed, quite early a general feeling, among sensible people in England, that it was about as well to let the unmanageable and spunky little colony alone.

Collier, in his "Ecclesiastical History of Great Britain," quotes at length the Order in Council Archbishop Laud issued, June 17, 1634, to all places of trade and plantation where the English were settled, enjoining the establishment of the national church in them, and remarks, that, while that order was extended to all the four great divisions of the world, and generally received and obeyed in all colonies and settlements, "New England was somewhat of an exception. The Dissenters," he continues, "who transported themselves thither, established their own fancy."

Charles II., however, was prevailed upon by the enemies of the colony to send over, in 1664, Commissioners to reduce it to subordination; but they went back as they came, disconcerted by the firmness and outgeneralled by the strategy of the colonial authorities. The records containing the communications that passed between these gentlemen and the General Court, show the wonderful sagacity, wariness, and ability of the latter. The royal commissioners were allowed to gain no advantage in the encounter, but were drawn into false positions and exposed attitudes by the expert fencing of their adversary, until they were utterly discomfited and disarmed. The whole affair, as we read its particulars, becomes absolutely amusing, from the superior wisdom and adroitness of the Court. Every attempt to bring the administration here under the control of the mother country, ended in equally humiliating failure.

It cannot, indeed, be doubted, that, if matters had come to extremities at any time, even at the earliest period, when the population scarcely reached up into the thousands, they would have resisted in arms any hostile force that should have ventured to land on their shores, from whatever quarter it might come; relying on the justness of their cause, and the Divine aid, on which they cast themselves with prayer and faith, as no other people ever did. Winthrop informs us, that in January, 1635, in the prevalence of an apprehension that a General Governor was about to be sent over from England, the Court asked the ministers, convened on the occasion, what ought to be done in that event? and they replied, with one voice, that he ought not to be received. The fort at Castle Island was immediately built, and a large commission appointed, consisting of the principal inhabitants, of which Winthrop was at the head, for "military affairs," to organize and arm the whole strength of the country for either "offensive or defensive war." The idea was familiarly expressed by all, that they would no sooner relinquish their rights under the charter than their estates, that they would fight for both; and, if driven from their houses and lands on the seashore, they would withdraw deeper and deeper into the forests, carrying their charter, the ark of their covenant, with them. And finally, when James II. abrogated the charter and took ruthless possession of the country, with a design, as the colonial statesmen believed, in pursuance of a secret treaty, to cede it to France, the people of Boston and the vicinity rose in their wrath. Sir Edmund Andros found himself, the next morning, in the lock-up at Fort Hill. He was removed for safer keeping to Castle Island, which, by holding as a prisoner the deposed royal governor, fairly won a right to the title, subsequently given it, of Fort Independence. Finally, he was shipped back to England. In the mean time, old Simon Bradstreet, in his eighty-seventh year, who, fifty-nine years before came over with Winthrop, and was the first secretary and the last governor under the First Charter in Massachusetts, was recalled to his place by an insurgent people, and for three more years affairs were administered as in the days of the old charter. The bold procedure was acquiesced in at home and abroad, no one was called to account for it, and Andros got no redress. The First Charter history of Massachusetts thus closed in glory.

The study of these records will help us avoid errors into which the Fathers of Massachusetts were led. A large department of their legislation, that embracing sumptuary laws and police regulations, is now considered as passing beyond the boundaries of the legitimate power of government, and trenching upon the rights of private life, and the domain of personal freedom. The severities of their penal code are condemned by the sentiments of a more enlightened age; but, in reference to this point, allowance must be made for their circumstances. In the prevention and punishment of crime, they had not what we possess in philanthropic, reformatory, and penitentiary establishments.

In initiating and organizing a government, errors were committed, but they were readily rectified when discovered. In 1636 and 1637, the General Court was led into a measure singularly in conflict with its usual policy and the spirit of the people : a council for life was established, and Winthrop, Dudley, and Endicott elected to it. The prevalence of sounder views prevented any further proceedings, and the plan was dropped.

There is one branch of their administration exposed especially to stricture, and universally condemned, at the present day, which must not be overlooked; for their views and designs in relation to it are proved to have been fallacious and impracticable. They came here with a purpose most dear to their hearts, of establishing and enjoying a system of society and government in which all would be of one mind, in the reception of a particular theological creed and ecclesiastical order. This did not, in their view, involve any violation of the rights of conscience. The New World, as they reasoned, could accommodate persons of all persuasions. They had purchased and planted their territory, and cherished the hope of enjoying it in peace and unity. This idea had captivated their imaginations. The agitations and dissensions arising from conflicting religious theories were distasteful to their feelings. They had left the Old World to get rid of them, and thought it no wrong to ask those who desired to establish and propagate opinions in conflict with theirs, as there was room enough for all, to go elsewhere. To preserve peace, tranquillity, and order, they undertook to keep out Anabaptists, Antinomians, and Quakers. It was an error to expect to succeed in such a policy, and the attempt involved them in the follies and mischiefs of intolerance and persecution. As followers of the divine Word, and disciples of the Great Teacher, they ought to have known better. Tares will spring up with the wheat. LET THEM BOTH GROW TOGETHER UNTIL THE HARVEST. The Lord of the harvest, and he alone, has the right or the power to separate them. In this, then, — it cannot too emphatically be affirmed, — the founders of Massachusetts were in the wrong, and their example is to be held up as a warning. For having pursued the opposite policy, in opening a shelter for all sorts of opinions, and patiently enduring the turmoil of wrangling bigots and fanatical enthusiasts, rather than suffer the hand of the civil power to be lifted against them, the name of Roger Williams will be illustrious, and the peculiar honor of Rhode Island secure for ever.

At the very first meeting of the Massachusetts General Court, after the transfer of the charter, at which a governor and assistants were chosen, on the 18th of May, 1631, it was voted, that "no man shall be admitted to the freedom of this body-politic, but such as are members of some of the churches within the limits of the same;" and they suffered no churches to be gathered, but such as were sound in doctrine, according to the estimation of the General Court. Admitting that the policy announced in this vote was erroneous, and rejoicing, as we all do, that it has long ago been repudiated, it is but fair to give heed to what may be offered in its palliation. It was, in part, suggested by their peculiar situation. It was necessary, by all means, to keep their government from falling into the hands of persons who might appear among them with a disposition to win favor from the parties hostile to them around the royal court; and this seemed the most sure way to keep them out. Further, in spite of all precautions to prevent it, here, as in all first settlements, there were individuals of loose and profligate lives, wholly unfit to share in the government. It was an effectual bar against them. And, after all, it must be conceded, that there was one good feature in it. It ignored the distinction between high and low, rich and poor, bond and free; and was, as far as it went, in this view, a liberal measure. It is due to the Church, Catholic and Protestant, to give it the credit, in every age and every communion, whatever other barriers it has raised, of having welcomed to its bosom persons of all ranks and races, without reference to their position in the scale of society. It has been in advance of the State in this particular.

While we condemn the policy of the Fathers in reference to religious opinions, we must not charge them with having contemplated an established religion as a part of the frame of their government. To that they were utterly opposed. They often, it is true, sought the advice of the ministers concerning public affairs, appreciating their learning and wisdom, but never allowed them to participate in the government. They went further in this respect than we do. No minister, or church officer of any kind, not even a lay-elder, was permitted to hold any legislative, political, or civil appointment.

Increase Nowell, an original patentee and assistant, belonging to a high family at home, who came over with the charter, was a man of eminent gifts and graces, and all his life in distinguished public employment. When the church at Charlestown was planted, he was chosen a ruling or lay elder, and acted as such. The question was raised, whether he, being a magistrate, could hold office in a church. It was decided that he could not, and Nowell laid down his eldership.

Samuel Sharp was probably one of the best educated men of the first age of the colony. Bred to learning during his youth, and transferred at opening manhood to business as a merchant, he continued through life to cultivate his mind and gratify his literary tastes. He seems to have been a proficient also in military knowledge, as he was intrusted, from the first, with all that related to engineering, fortification, and ordnance, in the plantation. Colonial enterprise seems to have particularly attracted his interest. He was one of the company in London which managed the first settlement at Plymouth. The Records of the Massachusetts Company show the active part he took in its affairs, and the extent to which it availed itself of his business efficiency. When Endicott was elected temporary local governor, April 30, 1629, he divided the vote with him, was appointed one of his council, and authorized, in conjunction with Samuel Skelton, the first pastor of the Salem church, in the event of Endicott's death, to assume the government of the plantation. Although Matthew Cradock never came to America in person, he took lands, and shipped over successive cargoes of provisions, live stock, and other needful articles, selecting suitable persons to look out for their disbursement and distribution. Sharp was his chief agent, and enjoyed his full confidence. Henry Haughton was also concerned in the management of Cradock's affairs. The latter, at the formation of the Salem church, was elected its lay-elder; but, dying a few months afterwards, Sharp was chosen to his place, which he filled to his death in 1656. In consequence of holding this office, the great talents and capacity of Elder Sharp were lost to the civil service of the colony. His name, although consecrated by the memory of his various usefulness, Christian learning, and eminent piety, is seen no more on its records, except as having, with Endicott and others, been bound over to answer before the General Court, as representatives of the Salem church, for having denounced the proceedings of the Court against its minister, Roger Williams.

These instances sufficiently show how thoroughly the policy was carried out of not allowing any officers whatever of a church to hold political or civil appointments, or in any degree or shape to have share in the government.

The Fathers of Massachusetts have been ridiculed for the respect in which they held the Hebrew polity, and for bringing the authority of the Scriptures, particularly of the Old Testament, to corroborate their legislation. But it may be asked, Where else could they have gone? Not surely to precedents drawn from ancient despotisms, or European monarchies. References to the statutes of the Pentateuch were more to their purpose, and justly carried greater weight, than to feudal rolls of parliaments, basely obsequious to Tudors and Stuarts. The Hebrew government, for the ends it was designed to accomplish, was the most perfect ever contrived. It left a deeper imprint on national character than any government ever has. It gave to a people a national life which no power on earth has been able to extinguish. Subjugation, dispersion, and the scorn, hate, and persecution of all nations for two thousand years, have made no impression on it. The Jewish race has survived it all. In our day the proudest monarchs are bowing before its banking-houses, and it affords leading minds to parliaments and cabinets. Its perpetuity, as a distinct people, although scattered everywhere, and everywhere trodden down for ages, is the marvel of the world's history, and attests the greatness of Moses as a lawgiver.

The Massachusetts statesmen of the first age did not follow indiscriminately the details of the Jewish system; but, as the Records show, sought to discover and obey the requirements of eternal moral laws. They acted, in their secular administration, upon principles that will stand the test of all time; but found gratification and confirmation in the ancient Scriptures. It is wonderful to what an extent they were able to avail themselves of this resource. Any one who verifies, collates, and examines their references to the events, characters, and expressions of Holy Writ, will be surprised to find how apposite they are, and what a mine was thus opened. Verily, the volume containing the most ancient literature of the world, is worthy of being called the Book of Books. Not wholly unaware of the disparagement, in which some have indulged, of the Old Testament scriptures, I am constrained to say, that the longer I live, and the more I ponder them, the profounder is my admiration and veneration of the unapproached dignity and simplicity of style of their historical and narrative passages, and of the beauty, splendor, and sublimity of the conceptions and imagery that glorify their strains of eloquence, poetry, and prophecy, breathing an influence that expands and lifts up the soul, and is felt to be inspiration.

In support of what I have said, in reference to the legislation of the first colonial age, allow me to fall back upon the judgment of one whose name is among the ornaments of the Massachusetts Historical Society, and the memory of whose genius and scholarship is fresh in the hearts of the older members. Francis Calley Gray, in a notice of the compendium, made in 1641, of the laws of the Massachusetts colony, known as the "Body of Liberties,"[1] says, —

> "Our ancestors, instead of deducing all their laws from the Books of Moses, established, at the outset, a code of fundamental principles, which, taken as a whole, for wisdom, equity, adaptation to the wants of their community, and a liberality of sentiment superior to the age in which it was written, may fearlessly challenge comparison with any similar production, from Magna Charta itself, to the latest Bill of Rights that has been put forth in Europe or America."

The early lawgivers of Massachusetts were, indeed, in advance of their times. Before we ridicule or reproach their legislation, it becomes us to see to it that those whom we choose to make and administer law, are equally in advance of our times.

The just formation of a body-politic which these Records have now been used to illustrate, demands attention in our day. Much remains to be done, even in the most advanced and enlightened nations. Much is being done. All the light that can be obtained is needed. Men everywhere are crying out for it. Agita-

[1] Massachusetts Historical Collections, vol. viii. Third Series, p. 191.

tion and change rule the hour. The future is felt to be subject to unknown and indeterminable influences, and to depend upon the wills or fortunes or lives of individuals, or the fluctuating conflicts of parties. Who can predict what is in store for Spain, France, Italy, the German States, or the northern kingdoms of Europe? The current of events seems to be working radical changes in Great Britain and Ireland, and the dependencies of that empire. Although, in many respects the most advanced of the old forms of political civilization, it can hardly be doubted that it is doomed to pass through momentous crises; for the whole structure of its constitutional system rests upon fictions that must give way, sooner or later, to truth and right. It assumes that there are three estates essential to the composition of a nation, — king, lords, and commons. The last only has a legitimate and permanent existence. The people are the whole of a country, so far as its government is concerned, and must finally vindicate their rightful claim to power.

The framers of the Constitution of the United States are justly regarded as among the wisest statesmen of all times; but they failed, in some points, in contriving their scheme of government, to estimate aright the action of the principles of human nature, or calculate their forces. They did not foresee the operation or even the existence of what are called national parties. The arrangement they made for the election of a President was soon found utterly impracticable for the end designed. The Amendment of 1803, introducing the plan that has been subsequently followed, was only carried by the decision of the then Speaker of the House of Representatives, Nathaniel Macon, of North Carolina, who claimed the right, since conceded, of the presiding officer of that body, to vote when the House is not equally divided. His vote made the requisite two-thirds.

Indications are appearing that some further change may be demanded. The intermediate machinery of Electors is justly criticised; but great difficulty will be experienced, in contriving in any other way, to preserve the rights of the smaller States. So, also, on the elementary subject of suffrage, great enlargements have been recently made, but others are demanded. It is, indeed, evident that questions are impending that reach the foundations of political science. Let them be met, not with ridicule or reproach, but with intelligence and fairness. Having been brought to a higher stand-point, with a wider field of view than the Fathers, we ought to have a more liberal spirit; but for integrity of purpose, and independence of authority, for carefulness in deliberation, and firmness and courage in action, we may well study their example.

Pardon me for detaining you a moment longer, while summarily delineating the spectacle the early records of Massachusetts present.

Here, on a clear field, unoccupied by any organized society, with no pre-existent institutions to cumber the ground, but all as fresh as if never trodden by man before, the experiment of planting and constructing a civil government was fairly worked out. No external power was suffered to interfere, and no foreign precedents allowed to claim authority; no closet statesman or fanciful theorist formed the scheme; no lordly proprietor, or distant corporation, or board of trade, directors, or officials of any kind, dictated. The whole procedure was left, without let or hindrance, suggestion or influence, from any outside quarter, to the people on the spot. They were a select people for the work; — intelligent, thoughtful, brave, and devout. They were settled in families, and comprised all the elements of a State. Although emigrants from the Old World, they trailed none of its arbitrary, outgrown institutions or usages after them. Conversant with all the learning of ancient and feudal forms, they applied none of it here. Having a new country to dwell in, they resolved to establish nothing but what facts, as they occurred, should prove to be necessary or desirable. Oglethorpe planned a social system for Georgia, John Locke drafted a contrivance of government for the Carolinas, Lord Baltimore superintended Maryland, William Penn Pennsylvania, and other proprietors and patrons their several settlements. Not so in Massachusetts: the Fathers of this colony followed no far-off light; they moved only as experience opened the way; they tried every step as they advanced, indulged in no theories or speculations, and held fast only what was found, in their view, to be good, and thus accomplished the great end of a stable, prosperous, powerful, and permanent commonwealth. All the essential features of our present security and happiness were stamped into the fabric of society during the period of the First Charter.

The early growth of Massachusetts was natural; and the matured result as complete, as of every natural growth; but, unlike the growths of nature in other things, there was, in this, no element of decay. The institutions planted during our first fifty years withstood a century of immediately subsequent provincial endurance; and as another century under the flag of our Union is approaching its completion, they are striking their roots deeper every day. The foundation here laid can never be moved; and we owe it to the men who laid it, that, in education, arts, wealth, and power, we hold a rank second to none in the Republic. The path, here opened, other Colonies and States have travelled, and all must travel, to reach the fruition of liberty, order, justice, and the rights of man.

Of the grand Epic, Time is writing, of the Regeneration of Nations, the old charter history of Massachusetts is the First Book.

THE MEDICAL PROFESSION

IN MASSACHUSETTS.

By OLIVER WENDELL HOLMES.

THE MEDICAL PROFESSION

IN MASSACHUSETTS.

THE medical history of eight generations, told in an hour, must be in many parts a mere outline. The details I shall give will relate chiefly to the first century. I shall only indicate the leading occurrences, with the more prominent names of the two centuries which follow, and add some considerations suggested by the facts which have been passed in review.

A geographer who was asked to describe the tides of Massachusetts Bay, would have to recognize the circumstance that they are a limited manifestation of a great oceanic movement. To consider them apart from this, would be to localize a planetary phenomenon, and to provincialize a law of the universe. The art of healing in Massachusetts has shared more or less fully and readily the movement which, with its periods of ebb and flow, has been raising its level from age to age throughout the better part of Christendom. Its practitioners brought with them much of the knowledge and many of the errors of the Old World; they have always been in communication with its wisdom and its folly; it is not without interest to see how far the new conditions in which they found themselves have been favorable or unfavorable to the growth of sound medical knowledge and practice.

The state of medicine is an index of the civilization of an age and country, — one of the best, perhaps, by which it can be judged. Surgery invokes the aid of all the mechanical arts. From the rude violences of the age of stone, — a relic of which we may find in the practice of Zipporah, the wife of Moses,[1] —

[1] Exodus iv. 25.

to the delicate operations of to-day upon patients lulled into temporary insensibility, is a progress which presupposes a skill in metallurgy and in the labors of the workshop and the laboratory it has taken uncounted generations to accumulate. Before the morphia which deadens the pain of neuralgia, or the quinine which arrests the fit of an ague, can find their place in our pharmacies, commerce must have perfected its machinery, and science must have refined its processes, through periods only to be counted by the life of nations. Before the means which nature and art have put in the hands of the medical practitioner can be fairly brought into use, the prejudices of the vulgar must be overcome, the intrusions of false philosophy must be fenced out, and the partnership with the priesthood dissolved. All this implies that freedom and activity of thought which belong only to the most advanced conditions of society; and the progress towards this is by gradations as significant of wide-spread changes, as are the varying states of the barometer of far-extended conditions of the atmosphere.

Apart, then, from its special and technical interest, my subject has a meaning which gives a certain importance, and even dignity, to details in themselves trivial and almost unworthy of record. A medical entry in Governor Winthrop's journal may seem at first sight a mere curiosity; but, rightly interpreted, it is a key to his whole system of belief as to the order of the universe and the relations between man and his Maker. Nothing sheds such light on the superstitions of an age as the prevailing interpretation and treatment of disease. When the touch of a profligate monarch was a cure for one of the most inveterate of maladies, when the common symptoms of hysteria were prayed over as marks of demoniacal possession, we might well expect the spiritual realms of thought to be peopled with still stranger delusions.

Let us go before the Pilgrims of the "Mayflower," and look at the shores on which they were soon to land. A wasting pestilence had so thinned the savage tribes, that it was sometimes piously interpreted as having providentially prepared the way for the feeble band of exiles. Cotton Mather, who, next to the witches, hated the "tawnies," "wild beasts," "blood-hounds," "rattlesnakes," "infidels," as in different places he calls the unhappy Aborigines, describes the condition of things in his lively way, thus: —

"The *Indians* in these Parts had newly, even about a Year or Two before, been visited with such a prodigious Pestilence; as carried away not a *Tenth*, but *Nine Parts* of *Ten* (yea 'tis said *Nineteen* of *Twenty*) among them: so that the *Woods* were almost cleared of those pernicious Creatures to make Room for a *better Growth*."[1]

What this pestilence was has been much discussed. It is variously mentioned by different early writers as "the plague," "a great and grievous plague," "a sore consumption," as attended with spots which left unhealed places on those who recovered, as making the whole surface yellow as with a garment.[2] Perhaps no disease answers all these conditions so well as small-pox. We know from different sources what frightful havoc it made among the Indians in after years, — in 1631, for instance, when it swept away the aboriginal inhabitants of whole towns,[3] and in 1633.[4] We have seen a whole tribe, the Mandans, extirpated by it in our own day. The word "plague" was used very vaguely, as in the description of the "great sickness" found among the Indians by the expedition of 1622.[5] This same great sickness could hardly have been yellow fever, as it occurred in the month of November. I cannot think, therefore, that either the scourge of the East or our Southern malarial pestilence was the disease that wasted the Indians. As for the yellowness like a garment, that is too familiar to the eyes of all who have ever looked on the hideous mask of confluent variola.

Without the presence or the fear of these exotic maladies, the forlorn voyagers of the "Mayflower" had sickness enough to contend with. At their first landing at Cape Cod, gaunt and hungry and longing for fresh food, they found upon the sandy shore "great muscles, and very fat and full of sea-pearl." Sailors

1 Magnalia, book i. chap. 2.
2 Young, Chron. of the Pilgrims, p. 183, *note.*
3 Holmes's Annals, vol. i. p. 211, *note.*
4 Young, Chronicles of Massachusetts, p. 386.
5 Chronicles of the Pilgrims, p. 302.

and passengers indulged in the treacherous delicacy, which seems to have been the sea-clam; and found that these mollusks, like the shell the poet tells of, remembered their august abode, and treated the way-worn adventurers to a gastric reminiscence of the heaving billows. In the mean time, it blew and snowed and froze.[1] The water turned to ice on their clothes, and made them many times like coats of iron. Edward Tilley had like to have "sounded" with cold. The gunner, too, was sick unto death, but "hope of trucking" kept him on his feet, — a Yankee, it should seem, when he first touched the shore of New England. Most, if not all, got colds and coughs, which afterwards turned to scurvy, whereof many died.[2]

How can we wonder that the crowded and tempest-tossed voyagers, many of them already suffering, should have fallen before the trials of the first winter in Plymouth? Their imperfect shelter, their insufficient supply of bread, their salted food, now in unwholesome condition, account too well for the diseases and the mortality that marked this first dreadful season; weakness, swelling of the limbs, and other signs of scurvy, betrayed the want of proper nourishment and protection from the elements. In December six of their number died, in January eight, in February seventeen, in March thirteen. With the advance of spring the mortality diminished, the sick and lame began to recover, and the colonists, saddened but not disheartened, applied themselves to the labors of the opening year.[3]

One of the most pressing needs of the early colonists must have been that of physicians and surgeons. In Mr. Savage's remarkable Genealogical Dictionary of the first settlers who came over before 1692 and their descendants to the third generation, I find scattered through the four crowded volumes the names of one hundred and thirty-four medical practitioners. Of these, twelve, and probably many more, practised surgery; three were barber-surgeons. A little incident throws a glimmer from the dark lantern of memory upon William Dinely, one of these practitioners with the razor and the lancet. He was lost between Boston and Roxbury in a violent tempest of wind and snow; ten days afterwards a son was born to his widow, and with a

[1] Chronicles of the Pilgrims, p. 119. [2] Ib., pp. 138, 151. [3] Ib., p. 198.

touch of homely sentiment, I had almost said poetry, they called the little creature "Fathergone" Dinely. Six or seven, probably a larger number, were ministers as well as physicians, one of whom, I am sorry to say, took to drink and tumbled into the Connecticut River, and so ended. One was not only doctor, but also schoolmaster and poet. One practised medicine and kept a tavern. One was a butcher, but calls himself a surgeon in his will, a union of callings which suggests an obvious pleasantry. One female practitioner, employed by her own sex,—Ann Moore,—was the precursor of that intrepid sisterhood whose cause it has long been my pleasure and privilege to advocate on all fitting occasions.

Outside of this list I must place the name of Thomas Wilkinson, who was complained of, in 1676, for practising contrary to law.

Many names in the catalogue of these early physicians have been associated, in later periods, with the practice of the profession,—among them, Boylston, Clark, Danforth, Homan, Jeffrey, Kittredge, Oliver, Peaslee, Randall, Shattuck, Thacher, Wellington, Williams, Woodward. Touton was a Huguenot, Burchsted a German from Silesia, Lunerus a German or a Pole; "Pighogg Churrergeon," I hope, for the honor of the profession, was only Peacock disguised under this *alias*, which would not, I fear, prove very attractive to patients.

What doctrines and practice were these colonists likely to bring with them?

Two principal schools of medical practice prevailed in the Old World, during the greater part of the seventeenth century. The first held to the old methods of Galen: its theory was that the body, the microcosm, like the macrocosm, was made up of the four elements—fire, air, water, earth; having respectively the qualities hot, dry, moist, cold. The body was to be preserved in health by keeping each of these qualities in its natural proportion; heat, by the proper temperature; moisture, by the due amount of fluid; and so as to the rest. Diseases which arose from excess of heat were to be attacked by cooling remedies; those from excess of cold, by heating ones; and so of the other derangements of balance. This was truly the principle of *con-*

traria contrariis, which ill-informed persons have attempted to make out to be the general doctrine of medicine, whereas there is no general dogma other than this: disease is to be treated by any thing that is proved to cure it. The means the Galenist employed were chiefly diet and vegetable remedies, with the use of the lancet and other depleting agents. He attributed the four fundamental qualities to different vegetables, in four different degrees; thus chicory was cold in the fourth degree, pepper was hot in the fourth, endive was cold and dry in the second, and bitter almonds were hot in the first and dry in the second degree. When we say "cool as a cucumber," we are talking Galenism. The seeds of that vegetable ranked as one of "the four greater cold seeds" of this system. Galenism prevailed mostly in the south of Europe and France. The readers of Molière will have no difficulty in recalling some of its favorite modes of treatment, and the abundant mirth he extracted from them.

These Galenists were what we should call "herb-doctors" to-day. Their insignificant infusions lost credit after a time; their absurdly complicated mixtures excited contempt, and their nauseous prescriptions provoked loathing and disgust. A simpler and bolder practice found welcome in Germany, depending chiefly on mineral remedies, mercury, antimony, sulphur, arsenic, and the use, sometimes the secret use, of opium. Whatever we think of Paracelsus, the chief agent in the introduction of these remedies, and whatever limits we may assign to the use of these long-trusted mineral drugs, there can be no doubt that the chemical school, as it was called, did a great deal towards the expurgation of the old, overloaded, and repulsive pharmacopœia. We shall find evidence in the practice of our New-England physicians of the first century, that they often employed chemical remedies, and that, by the early part of the following century, their chief trust was in the few simple, potent drugs of Paracelsus.

We have seen that many of the practitioners of medicine, during the first century of New England, were clergymen. This relation between medicine and theology has existed from a very early period; from the Egyptian priest to the Indian medicine-man, the alliance has been maintained in one form or another. The partnership was very common among our British ancestors. Mr. Ward, the Vicar of Stratford-on-Avon, himself a notable example of the union of the two characters, writing about 1660, says, —

"The Saxons had their blood-letters, but under the Normans physicke begunne in England; 300 years agoe itt was not a distinct profession by itself, but practised by men in orders, witness Nicholas de Ternham, the chief English physician and Bishop of Durham; Hugh of Everham, a physician and cardinal; Grysant, physician and pope; John Chambers, Dr. of Physick, was the first bishop of Peterborough; Paul Bush, a bachelor of divinitie in Oxford, was a man well read in physick as well as divinitie, he was the first bishop of Bristol.[1]

"Again in King Richard the Second's time physicians and divines were not distinct professions; for one Tydeman, Bishop of Landaph and Worcester, was physician to King Richard the Second."[2]

This alliance may have had its share in creating and keeping up the many superstitions which have figured so largely in the history of medicine. It is curious to see that a medical work left in manuscript by the Rev. Cotton Mather, and hereafter to be referred to, is running over with follies and superstitious fancies; while his contemporary and fellow-townsman, William Douglass, relied on the same few simple remedies which, through Dr. Edward Holyoke and Dr. James Jackson, have come down to our own time, as the most important articles of the *materia medica.*

Let us now take a general glance at some of the conditions of the early settlers; and first, as to the healthfulness of the climate. The mortality of the season that followed the landing of the Pilgrims at Plymouth has been sufficiently accounted for. After this, the colonists seem to have found the new country agreeing very well with their English constitutions. Its clear air is the subject of eulogy. Its dainty springs of sweet water are praised not only by Higginson and Wood, but even the mischievous Morton says, that for its delicate waters Canaan came not near this country.[3] There is a tendency to dilate on these simple blessings, which reminds one a little of the Marchioness in Dickens's story, with her orange-peel-and-water beverage. Still more does one feel the warmth of coloring, —

[1] Diary of the Rev. John Ward, A.M., p. 117. London, 1839.

[2] Ib., p. 160.

[3] Chronicles of the Pilgrims, p. 129, *note.*

such as we expect from converts to a new faith, and settlers who want to entice others over to their clearings, — when Winslow speaks in 1621, of "abundance of roses, white, red, and *damask;* single, but very sweet indeed."[1] Most of all, however, when, in the same connection, he says, "Here are grapes white and red, and very sweet and strong also." This of our wild grape, a little vegetable Indian, which scalps a civilized man's mouth, as his animal representative scalps his cranium. But there is something quite charming in Winslow's picture of the luxury in which they are living. Lobsters, oysters, eels, muscles, fish, and fowl, delicious fruit, including the grapes aforesaid, — if they only had "kine, horses, and sheep," he makes no question but men would live as contented here, as in any part of the world. We cannot help admiring the way in which they took their trials, and made the most of their blessings.

"And how *Content* they were," says Cotton Mather, "when an Honest Man, as I have heard, inviting his Friends to a Dish of *Clams*, at the Table gave Thanks to Heaven, who *had given them to suck the abundance of the Seas, and of the Treasures hid in the Sands!*"[2]

Strangely enough, as it would seem, except for this buoyant determination to make the best of every thing, they hardly appear to recognize the difference of the climate from that which they had left. After almost three years' experience, Winslow says, he can scarce distinguish New England from Old England, in respect of heat and cold, frost, snow, rain, winds, &c. The winter, he thinks (if there is a difference), is sharper and longer; but yet he may be deceived by the want of the comforts he enjoyed at home. He cannot conceive any climate to agree better with the constitution of the English, not being oppressed with extremity of heats, nor nipped by biting cold: —

"By which means, blessed be God, we enjoy our health, notwithstanding those difficulties we have undergone, in such a measure as would have been admired, if we had lived in England with the like means."[3]

Edward Johnson, after mentioning the shifts to which they were put for food, says, —

"And yet, methinks, our children are as cheerful, fat, and lusty, with

[1] Chronicles of the Pilgrims, p. 234. [2] Magnalia, book i. chap. 5.
[3] Chron. of the Pilgrims, 369, 370.

feeding upon those muscles, clams, and other fish, as they were in England with their fill of bread."[1]

Higginson, himself a dyspeptic, "continually in physic," as he says, and accustomed to dress in thick clothing, and to comfort his stomach with drink that was "both strong and stale,"[2] — the "jolly good ale and old," I suppose, of free and easy Bishop Still's song, — found that he both could and did oftentimes drink New-England water very well, — which he seems to look upon as a remarkable feat. He could go as light-clad as any, too, with only a light stuff cassock upon his shirt, and stuff breeches without linings. Two of his children were sickly: one — little misshapen Mary — died on the passage, and, in her father's words, "was the first in our ship that was buried in the bowels of the great Atlantic sea;"[3] the other, who had been "most lamentably handled" by disease, recovered almost entirely "by the very wholesomeness of the air, altering, digesting, and drying up the cold and crude humors of the body." Wherefore, he thinks it a wise course for all cold complexions to come to take physic in New England, and ends with those often quoted words, that "a sup of New England's air is better than a whole draught of Old England's ale."[4] Mr. Higginson died, however, "of a hectic fever," a little more than a year after his arrival.

The medical records which I shall cite, show that the colonists were not exempt from the complaints of the Old World. Besides the common diseases to which their descendants are subject, there were two others, — to say nothing of the dreaded small-pox, which later medical science has disarmed, — little known among us at the present day, but frequent among the first settlers. The first of these was the scurvy, already mentioned, of which Winthrop speaks in 1630, saying, that it proved fatal to those who fell into discontent, and lingered after their former conditions in England; the poor homesick creatures in fact, whom we so forget in our florid pictures of the early times of the little band in the wilderness. Many who were suffering from scurvy, got well when the "Lyon" arrived from England, bringing store of juice of lemons.[5] The Governor speaks of another case in

[1] Chron. of Mass., p. 352, *note*.
[2] Ib., pp. 251, 252.
[3] Ib., p. 223.
[4] Ib., p. 252.
[5] Winthrop's New England, vol. i. pp. 44, 45.

1644; and it seems probable that the disease was not of rare occurrence.

The other complaint from which they suffered, but which has nearly disappeared from among us, was intermittent fever, or fever and ague. I investigated the question as to the prevalence of this disease in New England, in a dissertation, which was published in a volume with other papers, in the year 1836. I can add little to the facts there recorded. One which escaped me was, that Joshua Scottow, in "Old Men's Tears," dated 1691, speaks of "shaking agues," as among the trials to which they had been subjected. The outline map of New England, accompanying the dissertation above referred to, indicates all the places where I had evidence that the disease had originated. It was plain enough that it used to be known in many places where it has long ceased to be feared. Still it was and is remarkable to see what a clean bill of health in this particular respect our barren soil inherited with its sterility. There are some malarious spots on the edge of Lake Champlain, and there have been some temporary centres of malaria, within the memory of man, on one or more of our Massachusetts rivers, but these are harmless enough, for the most part, unless the millers dam them, when they are apt to retaliate with a whiff from their meadows, that sets the whole neighborhood shaking with fever and ague.

The Pilgrims of the "Mayflower" had with them a good physician, a man of standing, a deacon of their church, one whom they loved and trusted, Dr. Samuel Fuller. But no medical skill could keep cold and hunger and bad food, and, probably enough, desperate homesickness in some of the feebler sort, from doing their work. No detailed record remains of what they suffered or what was attempted for their relief during the first sad winter. The graves of those who died were levelled and sowed with grain that the losses of the little band might not be suspected by the savage tenants of the wilderness,[1] and their story remains untold.

Of Dr. Fuller's practice, at a later period, we have an account in a letter of his to Governor Bradford, dated June, 1630. "I have been to Matapan" (now Dorchester), he says, "and let some

[1] Holmes's Annals, vol. i. p. 168, *note*.

twenty of those people blood."[1] Such wholesale depletion as this, except with avowed homicidal intent, is quite unknown in these days; though I once saw the noted French surgeon, Lisfranc, in a fine phlebotomizing frenzy, order some ten or fifteen patients, taken almost indiscriminately, to be bled in a single morning.

Dr. Fuller's two visits to Salem, at the request of Governor Endicott, seem to have been very satisfactory to that gentleman.[2] Morton, the wild fellow of Merry Mount, gives a rather questionable reason for the Governor's being so well pleased with the physician's doings. The names under which he mentions the two personages, it will be seen, are not intended to be complimentary. "Dr. Noddy did a great cure for Captain Littleworth. He cured him of a disease called a wife."[3] William Gager, who came out with Winthrop, is spoken of as "a right godly man and skilful chyrurgeon," but died of a malignant fever not very long after his arrival.[4]

Two practitioners of the ancient town of Newbury are entitled to special notice, for different reasons. The first is Dr. John Clark, who is said by tradition to have been the first regularly educated physician who resided in New England. His portrait, in close-fitting skull-cap, with long locks and venerable flowing beard, is familiar to our eyes on the wall of our Society's antechamber. His left hand rests upon a skull, his right hand holds an instrument which deserves a passing comment. It is a *trephine*, a surgical implement for cutting round pieces out of broken skulls, so as to get at the fragments which have been driven in, and lift them up. It has a handle like that of a gimlet, with a claw like a hammer, to lift with, I suppose, which last contrivance I do not see figured in my books. But the point I refer to is this: the old instrument, the *trepan*, had a handle like a wimble, — what we call a brace or bit-stock. The *trephine* is not mentioned at all in Peter Lowe's book, London, 1634; nor in Wiseman's great work on Surgery, London, 1676; nor in the translation of Dionis, published by Jacob Tonson, in 1710. In fact it was only brought into more general use by Cheselden and Sharpe so late as the beginning of the last

[1] Chron. of Mass., p. 312. [2] Ib., p. 32. [3] Ib., p. 131.
[4] Winthrop's New England, vol. i. p. 33.

century.[1] As John Clark died in 1661, it is remarkable to see the last fashion in the way of skull-sawing contrivances in his hands, — to say nothing of the claw on the handle, and a Hey's saw, so called in England, lying on the table by him, and painted there more than a hundred years before Hey was born. This saw is an old invention, perhaps as old as Hippocrates, and may be seen figured in the *Armamentarium Chirurgicum* of Scultetus, or in the Works of Ambroise Paré.

Dr. Clark is said to have received a diploma before he came, for skill in lithotomy.[2] He loved horses, as a good many doctors do, and left a good property as they all ought to do. His grave and noble presence, with the few facts concerning him, told with more or less traditional authority, give us the feeling that the people of Newbury, and afterwards of Boston, had a wise and skilful medical adviser and surgeon in Dr. John Clark.

The venerable town of Newbury had another physician who was less fortunate. The following is a court record of 1652: —

"This is to certify whom it may concern, that we the subscribers, being called upon to testify against [doctor] William Snelling for words by him uttered, affirm that being in way of merry discourse, a health being drank to all friends, he answered, —

'I'll pledge my friends,
And for my foes
A plague for their heels
And,' —

[a similar malediction on the other extremity of their feet.]

"Since when he hath affirmed that he only intended the proverb used in the west country, nor do we believe he intended otherwise.

[Signed], WILLIAM THOMAS.
THOMAS MILWARD.

"March 12th 1651, All which I acknowledge, and I am sorry I did not expresse my intent, or that I was so weak as to use so foolish a proverb.

[Signed], GULIELMUS SNELLING."

Notwithstanding this confession and apology, the record tells us, that "William Snelling in his presentment for *cursing* is fined ten shillings and the fees of court."[3]

[1] British and For. Med. Rev., vol. xvi. p. 49.
[2] Thacher, Med. Biography, p. 222.
[3] Coffin, Hist. of Newbury, p. 55.

I will mention one other name among those of the Fathers of the medical profession in New England. The "apostle" Eliot says, writing in 1647, "We never had but one anatomy in the country, which Mr. Giles Firman, now in England, did make and read upon very well."[1]

Giles Firmin, as the name is commonly spelled, practised physic in this country for a time. He seems to have found it a poor business; for, in a letter to Governor Winthrop, he says, "I am strongly sett upon to studye divinitie: my studyes else must be lost, for physick is but a meene helpe."[2]

Giles Firmin's Lectures on Anatomy were the first scientific teachings of the New World. While the Fathers were enlightened enough to permit such instructions, they were severe in dealing with quackery; for, in 1631, our court records show that one Nicholas Knopp, or Knapp, was sentenced to be fined or whipped "for taking upon him to cure the scurvey by a water of noe worth nor value, which he solde att a very deare rate."[3] Empty purses or sore backs would be common with us to day if such a rule were enforced.

Besides the few worthies spoken of, and others whose names I have not space to record, we must remember that there were many clergymen who took charge of the bodies as well as the souls of their patients, among them two Presidents of Harvard College, — Charles Chauncy and Leonard Hoar, — and Thomas Thacher, first minister of the "Old South," author of the earliest medical treatise printed in the country,[4] whose epitaph in Latin and Greek, said to have been written by Eleazer, an "Indian Youth" and a member of the Senior Class of Harvard College, may be found in the "Magnalia."[5] I miss this noble savage's name in our triennial catalogue; and, as there is many a slip between the cup and lip, one is tempted to guess that he may have lost his degree by some display of his native instinct, — possibly a flourish of the tomahawk or scalping-knife. However this may have been, the good man he celebrated was a notable instance of the

1 Hist. Coll. 3d Series, vol. iv. p. 57.

2 Winthrop Papers in Hist. Coll. 4th Series, vol. vii. p. 273.

3 Mass. Col. Court Records, vol. i. p. 63.

4 "A Brief Rule to guide the Common People in Small-pox and Measles." 1674.

5 Book iii. chap. 26.

Angelical Conjunction, as the author of the "Magnalia" calls it, of the offices of clergyman and medical practitioner.

Michael Wigglesworth, author of the "Day of Doom," attended the sick "not only as a *Pastor*, but as a *Physician* too, and this, not only in his own town, but also in all those of the vicinity."[1] Mather says of the sons of Charles Chauncy, "*All* of these did, while they had Opportunity, Preach the Gospel; and most, if not *all* of them, like their excellent *Father* before them, had an eminent skill in physick added unto their other accomplishments," &c. Roger Williams is said to have saved many in a kind of pestilence which swept away many Indians.

To these names must be added, as sustaining a certain relation to the healing art, that of the first Governor Winthrop, who is said by John Cotton to have been "*Help* for our Bodies by *Physick* [and] for our Estates by Law,"[2] and that of his son, the Governor of Connecticut, who, as we shall see, was as much physician as magistrate.

I had submitted to me for examination, in 1862, a manuscript found among the Winthrop Papers, marked with the superscription, "For my worthy friend Mr. Wintrop," dated in 1643, London, signed Edward Stafford, and containing medical directions and prescriptions. It may be remembered by some present that I wrote a report on this paper, which was published in the "Proceedings" of this Society. Whether the paper was written for Governor John Winthrop, of Massachusetts, or for his son, Governor John, of Connecticut, there is no positive evidence that I have been able to obtain. It is very interesting, however, as giving short and simple practical directions, such as would be most like to be wanted and most useful, in the opinion of a physician in repute of that day.

The diseases prescribed for are *plague*, small-pox, fevers, king's evil, insanity, falling-sickness, and the like; with such injuries as broken bones, dislocations, and burning with gunpowder. The remedies are of three kinds: simples, such as St. John's wort, Clown's all-heal, elder, parsley, maidenhair; mineral drugs, such as lime, saltpetre, Armenian bole, crocus metallorum, or sulphuret of antimony; and thaumaturgic or mystical, of which the

[1] Cotton Mather's Funeral Sermon, preached Jan. 24, 1705.

[2] Ib., book ii. chap. 4.

chief is, "My black powder against the plague, small-pox; purples, all sorts of feavers; Poyson; either, by Way of Prevention or after Infection." This marvellous remedy was made by putting live toads into an earthen pot so as to half fill it, and baking and burning them "in the open ayre, not in an house," — concerning which latter possibility I suspect Madam Winthrop would have had something to say, — until they could be reduced by pounding, first into a brown, and then into a black, powder. Blood-letting in some inflammations, fasting in the early stage of fevers, and some of those peremptory drugs with which most of us have been well acquainted in our time, the infragrant memories of which I will not pursue beyond this slight allusion, are among his remedies.

The Winthrops, to one of whom Dr. Stafford's directions were addressed, were the medical as well as the political advisers of their fellow-citizens for three or four successive generations. One of them, Governor John, of Connecticut, practised so extensively, that, but for his more distinguished title in the State, he would have been remembered as the Doctor. The fact that he practised in another colony, for the most part, makes little difference in the value of the records we have of his medical experience, which have fortunately been preserved, and give a very fair idea, in all probability, of the way in which patients were treated in Massachusetts, when they fell into intelligent and somewhat educated hands, a little after the middle of the seventeenth century.

I have before me, while writing, a manuscript collection of the medical cases treated by him, and recorded at the time in his own hand, which has been intrusted to me by our President, his descendant. They are generally marked Hartford, and extend from the year 1657 to 1669. From these manuscripts, and from the letters printed in the Winthrop Papers published by our Society, I have endeavored to obtain some idea of the practice of Governor John Winthrop, Jr. The learned eye of Mr. Pulsifer would have helped me, no doubt, as it has done in other cases; but I have ventured this time to attempt finding my own way among the hieroglyphics of these old pages. By careful comparison of many prescriptions, and by the aid of Schröder, Salmon, Culpeper, and other old compilers, I have deciphered many of his difficult paragraphs with their mysterious recipes.

The Governor employed a number of the simples dear to ancient women, — elecampane and elder and wormwood and anise and the rest; but he also employed certain mineral remedies, which he almost always indicates by their ancient symbols, or by a name which should leave them a mystery to the vulgar. I am now prepared to reveal the mystic secrets of the Governor's beneficent art, which rendered so many good and great as well as so many poor and dependent people his debtors — at least, in their simple belief — for their health and their lives.

His great remedy, which he gave oftener than any other, was *nitre;* which he ordered in doses of twenty or thirty grains to adults, and of three grains to infants. Measles, colic, sciatica, headache, giddiness, and many other ailments, all found themselves treated, and I trust bettered, by nitre; a pretty safe medicine in moderate doses, and one not likely to keep the good Governor awake at night, thinking whether it might not kill, if it did not cure. We may say as much for spermaceti, which he seems to have considered "the sovereign'st thing on earth" for inward bruises, and often prescribes after falls and similar injuries.

One of the next remedies, in point of frequency, which he was in the habit of giving, was (probably *diaphoretic*) *antimony;* a mild form of that very active metal, and which, mild as it was, left his patients very commonly with a pretty strong conviction that they had been taking *something* that did not exactly agree with them. Now and then he gave a little iron or sulphur or calomel, but very rarely; occasionally, a good, honest dose of rhubarb or jalap; a taste of stinging horseradish, oftener of warming guiacum; sometimes, an anodyne, in the shape of mithridate, — the famous old farrago, which owed its virtue to poppy juice;[1] very often, a harmless powder of coral; less frequently, an inert prescription of pleasing amber; and (let me say it softly within possible hearing of his honored descendant), twice or oftener, — let us hope as a last resort, — an electuary

[1] This is the remedy which a Boston divine tried to simplify. See "Electuarium Novum Alexipharmacum," by Rev. Thomas Harward, lecturer at the Royal Chappell. Boston, 1732. This tract is in our Society's library.

of *millipedes*, — sowbugs, if we must give them their homely English name. One or two other prescriptions, of the many unmentionable ones which disgraced the pharmacopœia of the seventeenth century, are to be found, but only in very rare instances, in the faded characters of the manuscript.

The excellent Governor's accounts of diseases are so brief, that we get only a very general notion of the complaints for which he prescribed. Measles and their consequences are at first more prominent than any other one affection, but the common infirmities of both sexes and of all ages seem to have come under his healing hand. Fever and ague appears to have been of frequent occurrence.

His published correspondence shows, that many noted people were in communication with him as his patients. Roger Williams wants a little of his medicine for Mrs. Weekes's daughter; worshipful John Haynes is in receipt of his powders; troublesome Captain Underhill wants "a little white vitterall" for his wife, and something to cure his wife's friend's neuralgia (I think his wife's friend's husband had a little rather have had it sent by the hands of Mrs. Underhill, than by those of the gallant and discursive captain); and pious John Davenport says, *his* wife "tooke but one halfe of one of the papers" (which probably contained the medicine he called *rubila*), "but could not beare the taste of it, and is discouraged from taking any more;" and honored William Leete asks for more powders for his "poore little daughter" Graciana, though he found it "hard to make her take it," delicate, and of course sensitive, child as she was, languishing and dying before her time, in spite of all the bitter things she swallowed, — God help all little children in the hands of dosing doctors and howling dervishes! Restless Samuel Gorton, now tamed by the burden of fourscore and two years, writes so touching an account of his infirmities, and expresses such overflowing gratitude for the relief he has obtained from the Governor's prescriptions, wondering how "a thing so little in quantity, so little in sent, so little in taste, and so little to sence in operation, should beget and bring forth such efects," that we repent our hasty exclamation, and bless the memory of the good Governor, who gave relief to the worn-out frame of our long-departed brother, the sturdy old heretic of Rhode Island.

What was that medicine which so frequently occurs in the printed letters under the name of "rubila"? It is evidently a secret remedy, and, so far as I know, has not yet been made out. I had almost given it up in despair, when I found what appears to be a key to the mystery. In the vast multitude of prescriptions contained in the manuscripts, most of them written in symbols, I find one which I thus interpret: —

"Four grains of (diaphoretic) antimony, with twenty grains of nitre, with a little salt of tin, *making rubila*." Perhaps something was added to redden the powder, as he constantly speaks of "rubifying" or "viridating" his prescriptions; a very common practice of prescribers, when their powders look a little too much like plain salt or sugar.

Waitstill Winthrop, the Governor's son, "was a skilful physician," says Mr. Sewall, in his funeral sermon; "and generously gave, not only his *advice*, but also his *Medicines*, for the healing of the Sick, which, by the Blessing of God, were made successful for the recovery of many."[1] *His* son John, a member of the Royal Society, speaks of himself as "Dr. Winthrop," and mentions one of his own prescriptions in a letter to Cotton Mather. Our President tells me that there was an heirloom of the ancient skill in his family, within his own remembrance, in the form of a certain precious eye-water, to which the late President John Quincy Adams ascribed rare virtue, and which he used to obtain from the possessor of the ancient recipe.

These inherited prescriptions are often treasured in families, I do not doubt, for many generations. When I was yet of trivial age, and suffering occasionally, as many children do, from what one of my Cambridgeport schoolmates used to call the "ager," — meaning thereby toothache or faceache, — I used to get relief from a certain plaster which never went by any other name in the family than "Dr. Oliver."

Dr. James Oliver was my great-great-grandfather, graduated in 1680, and died in 1703. This was, no doubt, one of his *nostrums;* for *nostrum*, as is well known, means nothing more

[1] See also his epitaph in "Life and Letters of John Winthrop," by his descendant, Hon. Robert C. Winthrop.

than *our own* or *my own* particular medicine, or other possession or secret, and physicians in old times used to keep their choice recipes to themselves a good deal, as we have had occasion to see.

Some years ago I found among my old books a small manuscript marked "James Oliver. This Book Begun Aug. 12, (16)85." It is a rough sort of account-book, containing among other things prescriptions for patients, and charges for the same, with counter-charges for the purchase of medicines and other matters. Dr. Oliver practised in Cambridge, where may be seen his tomb with inscriptions, and with sculptured figures that look more like Diana of the Ephesians, as given in Calmet's Dictionary, than like any angels admitted into good society here or elsewhere.

I do not find any particular record of what his patients suffered from, but I have carefully copied out the remedies he mentions, and find them to form a very respectable catalogue. Besides the usual simples, elder, parsley, fennel, saffron, snakeroot, wormwood, I find the Elixir Proprietatis, with other elixirs and cordials, as if he rather fancied warming medicines; but he called in the aid of some of the more energetic remedies, including iron, and probably mercury, as he bought two pounds of it at one time.

The most interesting item is his bill against the estate of Samuel Pason, of Roxbury, for services during his last illness. He attended this gentleman — for such he must have been, by the amount of physic which he took, and which his heirs paid for — from June 4th, 1696, to September 3d, of the same year — three months. I observe he charges for *visits* as well as for medicines, which is not the case in most of his bills. He opens the attack with a carminative appeal to the visceral conscience, and follows it up with good hard-hitting remedies for dropsy, — as I suppose the disease would have been called, — and finishes off with a rallying dose of hartshorn and iron.

It is a source of honest pride to his descendant that his bill, which was honestly paid, as it seems to have been honorably earned, amounted to the handsome sum of seven pounds and two shillings. Let me add that he repeatedly prescribes plasters, one of which was very probably the "Dr. Oliver" that soothed my infant griefs, and for which I blush to say that my venerated ancestor received from Goodman Hancock the painfully exiguous sum of no pounds, no shillings, and sixpence.

I have illustrated the practice of the first century, from the two manuscripts I have examined, as giving an impartial idea of its every-day methods. The Governor, Johannes Secundus, it is fair to remember, was an amateur practitioner, while my ancestor was a professed physician. Comparing their modes of treatment with the many scientific follies still prevailing in the Old World, and still more with the extraordinary theological superstitions of the community in which they lived, we shall find reason, I think, to consider the art of healing as in a comparatively creditable state during the first century of New England.

In addition to the evidence as to methods of treatment furnished by the manuscripts I have cited, I subjoin the following document, to which my attention was called by Dr. Shurtleff, our present Mayor. This is a letter of which the original is to be found in vol. lxix. page 10 of the "Archives" preserved at the State House in Boston. It will be seen that what the surgeon wanted consisted chiefly of opiates, stimulants, cathartics, plasters, and materials for bandages. The complex and varied formulæ have given place to simpler and often more effective forms of the same remedies; but the list and the manner in which it is made out are proofs of the good sense and schooling of the surgeon, who, it may be noted, was in such haste that he neglected all his stops. He might well be in a hurry, as on the very day upon which he wrote, a great body of Indians — supposed to be six or seven hundred — appeared before Hatfield; and twenty-five resolute young men of Hadley, from which town he wrote, crossed the river and drove them away.[1]

HADLY May 30 : 76

Mr RAWSON S^r^

What we have rec^d^ by Tho : Houey the past month is not the cheifest of our wants as you have love for poor wounded I pray let us not want for these following medicines if you have not a speedy conveyance of them I pray send on purpose they are those things mentioned in

[1] Holmes's Annals, vol. i. p. 381.

my former letter but to prevent future mistakes I have wrote them att large wee have great want with the greatest hast and speed let us be supplyed

S[r]

Y[r] Ser[t]

WILL LOCKE

[1] Imp. Ung[t] Basilic	℔ ij	Oxycroceum	℔ j
[1] Liniment Arcei	℔ ij	Emp: Diachyl: Cum Gum	℔ j
Ung[t] Nervin:	℔ ij	De betonica	℔ j
Ol: Rosarum	℔ ij	Flor: chamemæli	℔ j
[2] Ol: terebinth:	℔ ij	Flor: meliloti	℔ j
Mithridat:	℔ j	Sal: prunellæ	℥ iiij
Diascordii	℔ j	pul: Aloes	℥ iiij
theriac: Andromac:	℔ ss	[1] Sem: Anisi Santonicæ an	℥ iiij
Licortiæ	℔ j	Aq: theriacalis	℔ ij
Hord: Gallic:	℔ iiij	Spt: Cinnamomi	℔ j
Empl: Diapal:	℔ iij	Syr: Gariophyllor:	℔ ij
Empl: De Minio	℔ iij	Syr: Rosarum Solut:	℔ ij
Empl: De Meliloti	℔ ij	Croci	ʒ ss
Empl: paracelsi	℔ j	Old linnin as much as you can get	

[Direction] for M[r] Edward Rawson
Secr[y]: wth hast & speed humbly
present These in
Boston

WILL: LOCKE

[Endorsed]

Mr Locke's Letter Rec[d] from the Governor 13 June & acquainted y[e] Council with it but could not obtaine any thing to be sent in answer thereto 13 June 1676

I have given some idea of the chief remedies used by our earlier physicians, which were both Galenic and chemical; that is, vegetable and mineral. They, of course, employed the usual perturbing medicines which Montaigne says are the chief reliance of their craft. There were, doubtless, individual practitioners who employed special remedies with exceptional boldness and perhaps success. Mr. Eliot is spoken of, in a letter of William Leete to Winthrop, Junior, as being under Mr. Greenland's mercurial administrations.[3] The latter was probably enough one of these specialists.

There is another class of remedies which appears to have been employed occasionally, but, on the whole, is so little prominent as to imply a good deal of common sense among the medical practitioners, as compared with the superstitions prevailing around them. I have said that I have caught the good Governor,

[1] Crossed out in the letter. [2] "The last was broken."

[3] Hist. Coll. 4th Series, vol. vii. p. 575.

now and then, prescribing the electuary of millipedes; but he is entirely excused by the almost incredible fact that they were retained in the *materia medica* so late as when Rees's Cyclopædia was published, and we there find the directions formerly given by the College of Edinburgh for their preparation. Once or twice we have found him admitting still more objectionable articles into his *materia medica;* in doing which, I am sorry to say that he could plead grave and learned authority. But these instances are very rare exceptions in a medical practice of many years, which is, on the whole, very respectable, considering the time and circumstances.

Some remedies of questionable though not odious character appear occasionally to have been employed by the early practitioners, but they were such as still had the support of the medical profession. Governor John Winthrop, the first, sends for East-Indian bezoar, with other commodities he is writing for.[1] Governor Endicott sends him one he had of Mr. Humfrey.[2] I hope it was genuine, for they cheated infamously in the matter of this concretion, which ought to come out of an animal's stomach, but the real history of which resembles what is sometimes told of modern sausages. There is a famous law-case of James the First's time, in which a goldsmith sold a hundred pounds' worth of what he called bezoar, which was proved to be false, and the purchaser got a verdict against him. Governor Endicott also sends Winthrop a unicorn's horn, which was the property of a certain Mrs. Beggarly, who, in spite of her name, seems to have been rich in medical knowledge and possessions.[3] The famous Thomas Bartholimus wrote a treatise on the virtues of this fabulous-sounding remedy, which was published in 1641, and republished in 1678.

The "antimonial cup," a drinking vessel made of that metal, which, like our quassia-wood cups, might be filled and emptied *in sæcula sæculorum* without exhausting its virtues, is mentioned by Matthew Cradock, in a letter to the elder Winthrop, but in a doubtful way, as it was thought, he says, to have shortened the days of Sir Nathaniel Riche; and Winthrop himself, as I think, refers to its use, calling it simply "the cup."[4] An antimonial

1 Hist. of N. England, vol. ii. p. 385. Appendix.

2 Hist. Coll. 4th Series, vol. vii. p. 156.

3 Ibid.

4 Hist. of N. England, vol. i. p. 394.

cup is included in the inventory of Samuel Seabury, who died 1680, and is valued at five shillings.[1] There is a treatise entitled "The Universall Remedy, or the Vertues of the Antimoniall Cup, By John Evans, Minister and Preacher of God's Word, London, 1634," in our own Society's library.

One other special remedy deserves notice, because of native growth. I do not know when Culver's root, *Leptandra Virginica* of our National Pharmacopœia, became noted, but Cotton Mather, writing in 1716 to John Winthrop, of New London, speaks of it as famous for the cure of consumptions, and wishes to get some of it, through his mediation, for Katharine, his eldest daughter.[2] He gets it, and gives it to the "poor damsel," who is languishing, as he says, and who dies the next month,[3]— all the sooner, I have little doubt, for this uncertain and violent drug with which the meddlesome pedant tormented her in that spirit of well-meant but restless quackery, which could touch nothing without making mischief, not even a quotation, and yet proved at length the means of bringing a great blessing to our community, as we shall see by and by; so does Providence use our very vanities and infirmities for its wise purposes.

Externally, I find the practitioners on whom I have chiefly relied, used the plasters of Paracelsus, of melilot, *diachylon*, and probably *diaphœnicon*, all well known to the old pharmacopœias, and some of them to the modern ones, — to say nothing of "my yellow salve," of Governor John, the second, for the composition of which we must apply to his respected descendant.

The authors I find quoted, are Barbette's Surgery, Camerarius on Gout, and Wecherus, of all whom notices may be found in the pages of Haller and Vanderlinden; also, Reed's Surgery, and Nicholas Culpeper's Practice of Physic and Anatomy, the last as belonging to Samuel Seabury, chirurgeon, before mentioned. Nicholas Culpeper was a shrewd charlatan, and as impudent a varlet as ever prescribed for a colic; but knew very well what he was about, and badgers the College with great vigor. A copy of Spigelius's famous Anatomy, in the Boston Athenæum, has the names of Increase and Samuel

1 Thacher's Medical Biography, p. 18.

2 Mather Papers in Hist. Coll. 4th Series, vol. viii. p. 420.

3 Ibid, *note*.

Mather written in it, and was doubtless early overhauled by the youthful Cotton, who refers to the great anatomist's singular death, among his curious stories in the "Magnalia," and quotes him among nearly a hundred authors whom he cites in his manuscript "The Angel of Bethesda." Dr. John Clark's "books and instruments, with several chirurgery materials in the closet,"[1] were valued in his inventory at sixty pounds; Dr. Matthew Fuller, who died in 1678, left a library valued at ten pounds; and a surgeon's chest and drugs, valued at sixteen pounds.[2]

Here we leave the first century and all attempts at any further detailed accounts of medicine and its practitioners. It is necessary to show in a brief glance what had been going on in Europe during the latter part of that century, the first quarter of which had been made illustrious in the history of medical science, by the discovery of the circulation.

Charles Barbeyrac, a Protestant in his religion, was a practitioner and teacher of medicine at Montpellier. His creed was in the way of his obtaining office; but the young men followed his instructions with enthusiasm. Religious and scientific freedom breed in and in, until it becomes hard to tell the family of one from that of the other. Barbeyrac threw overboard the old complex medical farragos of the pharmacopœias, as his church had disburdened itself of the popish ceremonies.

Among the students who followed his instructions, were two Englishmen: one of them, John Locke, afterwards author of an "Essay on the Human Understanding," three years younger than his teacher; the other, Thomas Sydenham, five years older. Both returned to England. Locke, whose medical knowledge is borne witness to by Sydenham, had the good fortune to form a correct opinion on a disease from which the Earl of Shaftesbury was suffering, which led to an operation that saved his life. Less felicitous was his experience with a certain *ancilla culinaria virgo*, — which I am afraid would in those days have been translated kitchen-wench, instead of lady of the culinary department, — who turned him off after she had got tired of him, and called in another practitioner.[3] This helped,

1 Thacher's Med. Biog., p. 222. 2 Ib., p. 18.

3 Locke and Sydenham, p. 124. By John Brown, M.D. Edinburgh, 1866.

perhaps, to spoil a promising doctor, and make an immortal metaphysician. At any rate, Locke laid down the professional wig and cane, and took to other studies.

The name of Thomas Sydenham is as distinguished in the history of medicine, as that of John Locke in philosophy. As Barbeyrac was found in opposition to the established religion, as Locke took the rational side against orthodox Bishop Stillingfleet, so Sydenham went with Parliament against Charles, and was never admitted a Fellow by the College of Physicians, which, after he was dead, placed his bust in their hall by the side of that of Harvey.

What Sydenham did for medicine was briefly this: he studied the course of diseases carefully, and especially as affected by the particular season; to patients with fever he gave air and cooling drinks, instead of smothering and heating them, with the idea of sweating out their disease; he ordered horse-back exercise to consumptives; he, like his teacher, used few and comparatively simple remedies; he did not give any drug at all, if he thought none was needed, but let well enough alone. He was a sensible man, in short, who applied his common sense to diseases which he had studied with the best light of science that he could obtain.

The influence of the reform he introduced must have been more or less felt in this country, but not much before the beginning of the eighteenth century, as his great work was not published until 1675, and then in Latin. I very strongly suspect that there was not so much to reform in the simple practice of the physicians of the new community, as there was in that of the learned big-wigs of the "College," who valued their remedies too much in proportion to their complexity, and the extravagant and fantastic ingredients which went to their making.

During the memorable century that bred and bore the Revolution, the medical profession gave great names to our history. But John Brooks belonged to the State, and Joseph Warren belongs to the country and mankind, and to speak of them would lead me beyond my limited subject. There would be little pleasure in dwelling on the name of Benjamin Church; and as for the medical politicians, like Elisha Cooke in the early part of the century, or Charles Jarvis, the "bald eagle of Boston," in its later years, whether their practice was heroic or not, their patients were, for he is a bold man who trusts one that is making speeches and coaxing voters, to meddle with the internal politics of his corporeal republic.

One great event stands out in the medical history of this eighteenth century; namely, the introduction of the practice of inoculation for small-pox. Six epidemics of this complaint had visited Boston in the course of a hundred years.[1] Prayers had been asked in the churches, for more than a hundred sick in a single day, and this many times. About a thousand persons had died in a twelvemonth, we are told, and, as we may infer, chiefly from this cause.[2]

In 1721, this disease, after a respite of nineteen years, again appeared as an epidemic. In that year it was that Cotton Mather, browsing, as was his wont, on all the printed fodder that came within reach of his ever-grinding mandibles, came upon an account of inoculation as practised in Turkey, contained in the Philosophical Transactions. He spoke of it to several physicians, who paid little heed to his story; for they knew his medical whims, and had probably been bored, as we say now-a-days, many of them, with listening to his "Angel of Bethesda," and satiated with his speculations on the *Nishmath Chajim.*

The Reverend Mather, — I use a mode of expression he often employed when speaking of his honored brethren, — the Reverend Mather was right this time, and the irreverent doctors who laughed at him were wrong. One only of their number disputes his claim to giving the first impulse to the practice in Boston. This is what that person says: —

> "The Small-Pox spread in *Boston, New England,* A. 1721, and the Reverend Dr. *Cotton Mather*, having had the use of these Communications from Dr. *William Douglass*" (that is, the writer of these words); "surreptitiously, without the knowledge of his Informer, that he might have the honour of a New fangled notion, sets an Undaunted Operator to work, and in this Country about 290 were inoculated." [3]

All this has not deprived Cotton Mather of the credit of sug-

1 W. Douglass's Diss. concerning Inoc., p. 25. Boston, 1730.

2 Magnalia, book i. "The Bostonian Ebenezer."

3 Diss. concerning Inoculation, p. 2.

gesting, and a bold and intelligent physician of the honor of carrying out, the new practice. On the twenty-seventh day of June, 1721, Zabdiel Boylston, of Boston, inoculated his only son for small-pox, — the first person ever submitted to the operation in the New World. The story of the fierce resistance to the introduction of the practice; of how Boylston was mobbed, and Mather had a hand-grenade thrown in at his window; of how William Douglass, the Scotchman, "always positive, and sometimes accurate," as was neatly said of him, at once depreciated the practice and tried to get the credit of suggesting it, and Lawrence Dalhonde, the Frenchman, testified to its destructive consequences; of how Edmund Massey, lecturer at St. Albans, preached against sinfully endeavoring to alter the course of nature by presumptuous interposition, which he would leave to the atheist and the scoffer, the heathen and unbeliever, while in the face of his sermon, afterwards reprinted in Boston, many of our New-England clergy stood up boldly in defence of the practice, — all this has been told so well and so often that I spare you its details. Set this good hint of Cotton Mather against that letter of his to John Richards, recommending the search after witch-marks, and the application of the water-ordeal, which means throw your grandmother into the water, if she has a mole on her arm; — if she swims, she is a witch and must be hung; if she sinks, the Lord have mercy on her soul!

Thus did America receive this great discovery, destined to save thousands of lives, *viâ* Boston, from the hands of one of our own Massachusetts physicians.

The year 1735 was rendered sadly memorable by the epidemic of the terrible disease known as "throat-distemper," and regarded by many as the same as our "diphtheria." Dr. Holyoke thinks the more general use of mercurials in inflammatory complaints dates from the time of their employment in this disease, in which they were thought to have proved specially useful.[1]

At some time in the course of this century, medical practice had settled down on four remedies as its chief reliance. When Dr. Holyoke, nearly seventy years ago, received young Mr. James Jackson as his student, he pointed to the labelled drawers and bottles all around his office, — for he was his own apothecary, —

[1] Memoir of Edward A. Holyoke, M.D., LL.D., p. 64. Boston, 1829.

and said, "I seem to have here a great number and variety of medicines; but I may name four, which are of more importance than all the rest put together; namely, Mercury, Antimony, Opium, and Peruvian Bark."[1] I doubt if either of them remembered, that, nearly seventy years before that, in 1730, Dr. William Douglass, the disputatious Scotchman, mentioned those same four remedies, in the dedication of his quarrelsome essay on inoculation, as the most important ones in the hands of the physicians of his time.

In the "Proceedings" of this Society for the year 1863 is a very pleasant paper by the late Dr. Ephraim Eliot, giving an account of the leading physicians of Boston during the last quarter of the last century. The names of Lloyd, Gardiner, Welsh, Rand, Bulfinch, Danforth, John Warren, Jeffries, are all famous in local history, and are commemorated in our medical biographies. One of them, at least, appears to have been more widely known, not only as one of the first aerial voyagers, but as an explorer in the almost equally hazardous realm of medical theory. Dr. John Jeffries, the first of that name, is considered by Broussais as a leader of medical opinion in America, and so referred to in his famous "Examen des Doctrines Médicales."

Two great movements took place in this eighteenth century, the effect of which has been chiefly felt in our own time; namely, the establishment of the Massachusetts Medical Society, and the founding of the Medical School of Harvard University.

The third century of our medical history began with the introduction of the second great medical discovery of modern times, — of all time up to that date, I may say, — once more *viâ* Boston, if we count the University village as its suburb, and once more by one of our Massachusetts physicians. In the month of July, 1800, Dr. Benjamin Waterhouse, of Cambridge, submitted four of his own children to the new process of vaccination, — the first persons vaccinated, as Dr. Zabdiel Boylston's son had been the first person inoculated in the New World.

A little before the first half of this century was completed, in the autumn of 1846, that great discovery went forth from the Massachusetts General Hospital, which repaid the debt of America

[1] Another Letter to a Young Physician, p. 15.

to the science of the Old World, and gave immortality to the place of its origin in the memory and the heart of mankind. The production of temporary insensibility at will—*tuto, cito, jucunde*, safely, quickly, pleasantly—is one of those triumphs over the infirmities of our mortal condition which change the aspect of life ever afterwards. Rhetoric can add nothing to its glory; gratitude, and the pride permitted to human weakness, that our Bethlehem should have been chosen as the birthplace of this new embodiment of the divine mercy, are all we can yet find room for.

The present century has seen the establishment of all those great charitable institutions for the cure of diseases of the body and of the mind, which our State and our city have a right to consider as among the chief ornaments of their civilization.

The last century had very little to show, in our State, in the way of medical literature. The worthies who took care of our grandfathers and great-grandfathers, like the Revolutionary heroes, fought (with disease) and bled (their patients) and died (in spite of their own remedies); but their names, once familiar, are heard only at rare intervals. Honored in their day, not unremembered by a few solitary students of the past, their memories are going sweetly to sleep in the arms of the patient old dry-nurse, whose "black-drop" is the never-failing anodyne of the restless generations of men. Except the lively controversy on inoculation, and floating papers in journals, we have not much of value for that long period, in the shape of medical records.

But while the trouble with the last century is to find authors to mention, the trouble of this would be to name all that we find. Of these, a very few claim unquestioned pre-eminence.

Nathan Smith, born in Rehoboth, Mass., a graduate of the Medical School of our University, did a great work for the advancement of medicine and surgery in New England, by his labors as teacher and author,—greater, it is claimed by some, than was ever done by any other man. The two Warrens, of our time, each left a large and permanent record of a most extended surgical practice. James Jackson not only educated a whole generation by his lessons of wisdom, but bequeathed some of the most valuable results of his experience to those who came after him, in a series of letters singularly pleasant and kindly as well as instructive. John Ware, keen and cautious, earnest and deliberate, wrote the two remarkable essays which have identified his name, for all time, with two important diseases, on which he has shed new light by his original observations.

I must do violence to the modesty of the living by referring to the many important contributions to medical science, by Dr. Jacob Bigelow, and especially to his discourse on "Self-limited Diseases," an address which can be read in a single hour, but the influence of which will be felt for a century.

Nor would the profession forgive me if I forgot to mention the admirable museum of pathological anatomy, created almost entirely by the hands of Dr. John Barnard Swett Jackson, and illustrated by his own printed descriptive catalogue, justly spoken of by a distinguished professor in the University of Pennsylvania, as the most important contribution which had ever been made to the branch to which it relates in this country.

When we look at the literature of mental disease, as seen in hospital reports and special treatises, we can mention the names of Wyman, Woodward, Brigham, Bell, and Ray, all either natives of Massachusetts or placed at the head of her institutions for the treatment of the insane.

We have a right to claim also one who is known all over the civilized world as a philanthropist, to us as a townsman and a graduate of our own Medical School, Dr. Samuel Gridley Howe, the guide and benefactor of a great multitude who were born to a world of inward or of outward darkness.

I cannot pass over in silence the part taken by our own physicians in those sanitary movements which are assuming every year greater importance. Two diseases especially have attracted attention, above all others, with reference to their causes and prevention; cholera, the "black death" of the nineteenth century, and consumption, the white plague of the North, both of which have been faithfully studied and reported on by physicians of our own State and city. The cultivation of medical and surgical specialties, which is fast becoming prevalent, is beginning to show its effects in the literature of the profession, which is every year growing richer in original observations and investigations.

To these benefactors, who have labored for us in their peaceful vocation, we must add the noble army of surgeons, who went with the soldiers who fought the battles of their country, sharing many of their dangers, not rarely falling victims to fatigue, disease, or the deadly volleys to which they often exposed themselves in the discharge of their duties.

The pleasant biographies of the venerable Dr. Thacher, and the worthy and kind-hearted gleaner, Dr. Stephen W. Williams, who came after him, are filled with the names of men who served their generation well, and rest from their labors, followed by the blessing of those for whom they endured the toils and fatigues inseparable from their calling. The hard-working, intelligent, country physician more especially deserves the gratitude of his own generation, for he rarely leaves any permanent record in the literature of his profession. Books are hard to obtain; hospitals, which are always centres of intelligence, are remote; thoroughly educated and superior men are separated by wide intervals; and long rides, though favorable to reflection, take up much of the time which might otherwise be given to the labors of the study. So it is that men of ability and vast experience, like the late Dr. Twitchell, for instance, make a great and deserved reputation, become the oracles of large districts, and yet leave nothing, or next to nothing, by which their names shall be preserved from blank oblivion.

One or two other facts deserve mention, as showing the readiness of our medical community to receive and adopt any important idea or discovery. The new science of *Histology*, as it is now called, was first brought fully before the profession of this country by the translation of Bichat's great work, " Anatomie Générale," by the late Dr. George Hayward.

The first work printed in this country on *Auscultation* — that wonderful art of discovering disease, which, as it were, puts a window in the breast, through which the vital organs can be *seen*, to all intents and purposes — was the manual published anonymously by " A Member of the Massachusetts Medical Society."

We are now in some slight measure prepared to weigh the record of the medical profession in Massachusetts, and pass our judgment upon it. But in order to do justice to the first generation of practitioners, we must compare what we know of their treatment of disease with the state of the art in England, and the superstitions which they saw all around them in other departments of knowledge or belief.

English medical literature must have been at a pretty low ebb when Sydenham recommended Don Quixote to Sir Richard Blackmore for professional reading. The College Pharmacopœia was loaded with the most absurd compound mixtures, one of the most complex of which (the same which the Reverend Mr. Harward, "Lecturer at the Royal Chappel in Boston" tried to simplify) was not dropped until the year 1801. Sir Kenelm Digby was playing his fantastic tricks with the Sympathetic powder, and teaching Governor Winthrop, the second, how to cure fever and ague, which some may like to know. Pare the patient's nails; put the parings in a little bag, and hang the bag round the neck of a live eel, and put him in a tub of water. The eel will die, and the patient will recover.[1]

Wiseman, the great surgeon, was discoursing eloquently on the efficacy of the royal touch in scrofula.[2] The founder of the Ashmolean Museum at Oxford, consorting with alchemists and astrologers, was treasuring the manuscripts of the late pious Dr. Richard Napier, in which certain letters (℞ Ris) were understood to mean Responsum Raphaelis, — the answer of the angel Raphael to the good man's medical questions.[3] The illustrious Robert Boyle was making his collection of choice and safe remedies, including the sole of an old shoe,[4] the thigh bone of a hanged man,[5] and things far worse than these, as articles of his *materia medica*. Dr. Stafford, whose paper of directions to his "friend, Mr. Wintrop," I cited, was probably a man of standing in London; yet toad-powder was his sovereign remedy.

See what was the state of belief in other matters among the most intelligent persons of the colonies, — magistrates and clergymen. Jonathan Brewster, son of the church-elder, writes

[1] Hist. Coll. 3d Series, vol. x.

[2] Several Chirurgicall Treatises, p. 245. London, 1676.

[3] Turner (William), Remarkable Providences, part i. chap. 2. Also referred to in Mather's MS. "The Angel of Bethesda."

[4] Medicinal Experiments, p. 105. 5th edition. London, 1712.

[5] Ib., p. 105.

the wildest letters to John Winthrop about alchemy, — mad for making gold as the Lynn rock-borers are for finding it.[1]

Remember the theology and the diabology of the time. Mr. Cotton's Theocracy was a royal government, with the King of kings as its nominal head, but with an upper chamber of saints, and a tremendous opposition in the lower house; the leader of which may have been equalled, but cannot have been surpassed by any of our earth-born politicians. The demons were prowling round the houses every night, as the foxes were sneaking about the hen-roosts. The men of Gloucester fired whole flasks of gunpowder at devils disguised as Indians and Frenchmen.[2]

How deeply the notion of miraculous interference with the course of nature was rooted, is shown by the tenacity of the superstition about earthquakes. We can hardly believe that our Professor Winthrop, father of the old judge and the "squire," whom many of us Cambridge people remember so well, had to defend himself against the learned and excellent Dr. Prince, of the Old South Church, for discussing their phenomena as if they belonged to the province of natural science.[3]

Not for the sake of degrading the aspect of the noble men who founded our State, do I refer to their idle beliefs and painful delusions, but to show against what influences the common sense of the medical profession had to assert itself.

Think, then, of the blazing stars, that shook their horrid hair in the sky; the phantom ship, that brought its message direct from the other world;[4] the story of the mouse and the snake at Watertown;[5] of the mice and the prayer-book;[6] of the snake in church;[7] of the calf with two heads;[8] and of the cabbage "in the perfect form of a cutlash,"[9] — all which innocent occurrences were accepted or feared as alarming portents.

We can smile at these: but we cannot smile at the account of unhappy Mary Dyer's malformed offspring;[10] or of Mrs.

[1] Hist. Coll. 4th Series, vol. vii. pp. 72, 77.

[2] Magnalia, book vii. art. 18.

[3] Two Lectures on Comets, p. vii. Boston, 1811.

[4] Magnalia, book i. chap. 6. Winthrop, Hist. of N. E., vol. ii. p. 328.

[5] Life and Letters of John Winthrop, p. 108.

[6] Winthrop, Hist. of N. E., vol. ii. p. 20.

[7] Ib., vol. ii. p. 330.

[8] Mather Papers in Hist. Soc. Coll. 4th Series, vol. viii. p. 614.

[9] Ibid.

[10] Winthrop, Hist. of N. E., vol. i. p. 261.

Hutchinson's domestic misfortune of similar character,[1] in the story of which the physician, Dr. John Clark of Rhode Island, alone appears to advantage; or as we read the Rev. Samuel Willard's fifteen alarming pages about an unfortunate young woman suffering with hysteria.[2] Or go a little deeper into tragedy, and see poor Dorothy Talby, mad as Ophelia, first admonished, then whipped; at last, taking her own little daughter's life; put on trial, and standing mute, threatened to be pressed to death, confessing, sentenced, praying to be beheaded; and none the less pitilessly swung from the fatal ladder.[3]

The cooper's crazy wife — crazy in the belief that she has committed the unpardonable sin — tries to drown her child, to save it from misery; and the poor lunatic, who would be tenderly cared for to-day in a quiet asylum, is judged to be acting under the instigation of Satan himself.[4] Yet, after all, what can we say, who put Bunyan's Pilgrim's Progress, full of nightmare dreams of horror, into all our children's hands; a story in which the awful image of the man in the cage might well turn the nursery where it is read into a madhouse?

The miserable delusion of witchcraft illustrates, in a still more impressive way, the false ideas which governed the supposed relation of men with the spiritual world. I have no doubt many physicians shared in these superstitions. Mr. Upham says they — that is, some of them — were in the habit of attributing their want of success to the fact, that an "evil hand" was on their patient.[5] The temptation was strong, no doubt, when magistrates and ministers and all that followed their lead were contented with such an explanation. But how was it in Salem, according to Mr. Upham's own statement? Dr. John Swinnerton was, he says, for many years the principal physician of Salem.[6] And he says, also, "The Swinnerton family were all along opposed to Mr. Parris, and kept remarkably clear from the witchcraft delusion."[7] Dr. John Swinnerton — the same, by the way, whose memory is illuminated by a ray from the genius

1 Winthrop, Hist. of N. E., p. 271.

2 Case of Elizabeth Knapp, Hist. Coll. 4th Series, vol. viii. p. 555.

3 Winthrop, Hist. of N. E., vol. i. p. 279.

4 Ib., vol. ii. p. 65.

5 Salem Witchcraft, vol. ii. p. 361. Boston, 1867.

6 Ib., vol. i. p. 140.

7 Ib., vol. ii. p. 495 (Supplement).

of Hawthorne — died the very year before the great witchcraft explosion took place. But who can doubt that it was from him that the family had learned to despise and to resist the base superstition; or that Bridget Bishop, whose house he rented, as Mr. Upham tells me, the first person hanged in the time of the delusion, would have found an efficient protector in her tenant, had he been living, to head the opposition of his family to the misguided clergymen and magistrates?

I cannot doubt that our early physicians brought with them many Old-World medical superstitions, and I have no question that they were more or less involved in the prevailing errors of the community in which they lived. But, on the whole, their record is a clean one, so far as we can get at it; and where it is questionable, we must remember, that there must have been many little-educated persons among them; and that all must have felt, to some extent, the influence of those sincere and devoted but unsafe men, the physic-practising clergymen, who often used spiritual means as a substitute for temporal ones, who looked upon a hysteric patient as possessed by the devil,[1] and treated a fractured skull by prayers and plasters, following the advice of a ruling elder in opposition to the unanimous opinion of seven surgeons.[2]

To what results the union of the two professions was liable to lead, may be seen by the example of a learned and famous person, who has left on record the product of his labors in the double capacity of clergyman and physician.

I have had the privilege of examining a manuscript of Cotton Mather's relating to medicine, by the kindness of the librarian of the American Antiquarian Society, to which society it belongs. A brief notice of this curious document may prove not uninteresting.

It is entitled "The Angel of Bethesda: an Essay upon the *Common Maladies of Mankind*, offering, first, the sentiments of Piety," &c., &c., and "a collection of plain but *potent* and *Approved* REMEDIES for the Maladies." There are sixty-six "Capsula's," as he calls them, or chapters, in his table of contents; of which, five — from the fifteenth to the nineteenth, inclusive — are missing. This is a most unfortunate loss, as the eighteenth capsula treated of agues, and we could have learned

[1] *Ante*, p. 292. [2] Winthrop's History, vol. ii. p. 203. The child recovered.

from it something of their degree of frequency in this part of New England. There is no date to the manuscript; which, however, refers to a case observed Nov. 14, 1724.

The divine takes precedence of the physician in this extraordinary production. He begins by preaching a sermon at his unfortunate patient. Having thrown him into a cold sweat by his spiritual sudorific, he attacks him with his material remedies, which are often quite as unpalatable. The simple and cleanly practice of Sydenham, with whose works he was acquainted, seems to have been thrown away upon him. Every thing he could find mentioned in the seventy or eighty authors he cites, all that the old women of both sexes had ever told him of, gets into his text, or squeezes itself into his margin.

Evolving disease out of sin, he hates it, one would say, as he hates its cause, and would drive it out of the body with all noisome appliances. "Sickness is in Fact *Flagellum Dei pro peccatis mundi.*" So saying, he encourages the young mother whose babe is wasting away upon her breast with these reflections: —

> "Think; oh the grievous Effects of *Sin!* This wretched *Infant* has not arrived unto years of sense enough, to *sin after the similitude of the transgression committed by Adam.* Nevertheless the *Transgression* of *Adam,* who had all mankind *Fœderally,* yea, Naturally, in him, has involved this Infant in the guilt of it. And the *poison of the old serpent,* which infected *Adam* when he fell into his *Transgression,* by hearkening to the Tempter, has corrupted all mankind, and is a seed unto such diseases as this *Infant* is now laboring under. *Lord,* what are we, and what are our children, but a Generation of Vipers?"

Many of his remedies are at least harmless, but his pedantry and utter want of judgment betray themselves everywhere. He piles his prescriptions one upon another, without the least discrimination. He is run away with by all sorts of fancies and superstitions. He prescribes *euphrasia,* eyebright, for disease of the eyes; appealing confidently to the strange old doctrine of *signatures,* which inferred its use from the resemblance of its flower to the organ of vision. For the scattering of wens, "the efficacy of a Dead Hand has been out of measure wonderful." But when he once comes to the odious class of remedies, he revels in them like a *scarabeus.* This allusion will bring us quite near enough to the inconceivable abominations with which he proposed to outrage the sinful stomachs of the unhappy confederates and accomplices of Adam.

It is well that the treatise was never printed, yet there are passages in it worth preserving. He speaks of some remedies which have since become more universally known: —

"Among the plants of our soyl, Sir William Temple singles out Five [Six] as being of the greatest virtue and most friendly to health: and his favorite plants, Sage, Rue, Saffron, Alehoof, Garlick, and Elder."

"But these *Five* [Six] *plants* may admitt of some competitors. The Quinquina — How celebrated: Immoderately, Hyperbolically celebrated!"

Of Ipecacuanha, he says, —

"This is now in its reign; the most fashionable vomit."

"I am not sorry that antimonial emetics begin to be disused."

He quotes "Mr. Lock" as recommending red poppy-water and abstinence from flesh as often useful in children's diseases.

One of his "Capsula's" is devoted to the animalcular origin of diseases, at the end of which he says, speaking of remedies for this supposed source of our distempers: —

"Mercury we know thee: But we are afraid thou wilt kill us too, if we employ thee to kill them that kill us.

"And yett, for the cleansing of the small Blood Vessels, and making way for the free circulation of the Blood and Lymph — there is nothing like Mercurial Deobstruents."

From this we learn that mercury was already in common use, and the subject of the same popular prejudice as in our own time.

His poetical turn shows itself here and there: —

"O Nightingale, with a Thorn at thy Breast; Under the trouble of a Cough, what can be more proper than such thoughts as these?" . . .

If there is pathos in this, there is bathos in his apostrophe to the millipede, beginning "Poor sowbug!" and eulogizing the healing virtues of that odious little beast; of which he tells us to take "half a pound, putt 'em alive into a quart or two of wine," with saffron and other drugs, and take two ounces twice a day.

The "Capsula" entitled "Nishmath Chajim," was printed in 1722, at New London, and is in the possession of our own Society. He means, by these words, something like the Archæus of Van Helmont, of which he discourses in a style wonderfully resembling that of Mr. Jenkinson, in the "Vicar of Wakefield."

"Many of the Ancients thought there was much of a Real *History* in the *Parable*, and their Opinion was that there is, DIAPHORA KATA TAS MORPHAS, A *Distinction* (and so a Resemblance) *of men* as to their *Shapes after Death*."

And so on, with Irenæus, Tertullian, Thespesius, and "the TA TONE PSEUCONE CROMATA," in the place of "*Sanconiathon, Manetho, Berosus*," and "*Anarchon ara kai ateleutaion to pan*."

One other passage deserves notice, as it relates to the single medical suggestion which does honor to Cotton Mather's memory. It does not appear that he availed himself of the information which he says he obtained from his slave, for such I suppose he was.

In his appendix to "Variolæ Triumphatæ," he says,—

"There has been a *wonderful practice* lately used in several parts of the world, which indeed is not yet become common in our nation.

"I was first informed of it by a Garamantee servant of my own, long before I knew that any *Europeans* or *Asiaticks* had the least acquaintance with it, and some years before I was enriched with the communications of the learned Foreigners, whose accounts I found agreeing with what I received of my servant, when he shewed me the Scar of the Wound made for the operation; and said, That no person ever died of the *small-pox*, in their countrey, that had the courage to use it.

"I have since met with a considerable Number of these *Africans*, who all agree in one story; That in their countrey *grandy-many* dy of the *small-pox:* But now they learn this way: people take juice of *small-pox* and *cutty-skin* and put in a Drop; then by 'nd by a little sicky, sicky: then very few little things like *small-pox;* and nobody dy of it; and nobody have small-pox any more. Thus, in *Africa*, where the poor creatures dy of the *small-pox* like Rotten Sheep, a merciful God has taught them an *Infallible preservative*. 'Tis a *common practice*, and is attended with a *constant success*."

What has come down to us of the first century of medical practice, in the hands of Winthrop and Oliver, is comparatively simple and reasonable. I suspect that the conditions of rude, stern life, in which the colonists found themselves in the wilderness, took the nonsense out of them, as the exigencies of a campaign did out of our physicians and surgeons in the late war. Good food and enough of it, pure air and water, cleanliness, good attendance, an anæsthetic, an opiate, a stimulant, quinine, and two or three common drugs, proved to be the marrow of medical treatment; and the fopperies of the pharmacopœia went the way of embroidered shirts and white kid gloves and malacca joints, in their time of need. "Good wine is the best cordiall for her," said Governor John, Junior, to Samuel Symonds, speaking of that gentleman's wife, — just as Sydenham, instead of physic, once ordered a roast chicken and a pint of canary for his patient in male hysterics.

But the profession of medicine never could reach its full development until it became entirely separated from that of divinity. The spiritual guide, the consoler in affliction, the confessor who is admitted into the secrets of our souls, has his own noble sphere of duties; but the healer of men must confine himself solely to the revelations of God in nature, as he sees their miracles with his own eyes. No doctrine of prayer or special providence is to be his excuse for not looking straight at secondary causes, and acting, exactly so far as experience justifies him, as if he were himself the divine agent which antiquity fabled him to be. While pious men were praying — humbly, sincerely, rightly, according to their knowledge — over the endless succession of little children dying of spasms in the great Dublin Hospital, a sagacious physician knocked some holes in the walls of the ward, let God's blessed air in on the little creatures, and so had already saved in that single hospital, as it was soberly calculated thirty years ago, more than sixteen thousand lives of these infant heirs of immortality.[1]

Let it be, if you will, that the wise inspiration of the physician was granted in virtue of the clergyman's supplications. Still, the habit of dealing with things seen, generates another kind of knowledge, and another way of thought, from that of dealing with things unseen; which knowledge and way of thought are special means granted by Providence, and to be thankfully accepted.

The mediæval ecclesiastics expressed a great truth in that say-

[1] Collins's Midwifery, p. 312. Published by order of the Massachusetts Medical Society. Boston, 1841.

ing, so often quoted, as carrying a reproach with it: "*Ubi tres medici, duo athei,*" — "Where there are three physicians, there are two atheists."

It was true then, it is true to-day, that the physician very commonly, if not very generally, denies and repudiates the deity of ecclesiastical commerce. The Being whom Ambroise Paré meant when he spoke those memorable words, which you may read over the professor's chair in the French School of Medicine, — "*Je le pensay, et Dieu le guarit,*" — "I dressed his wound, and God healed it," — is a different being from the God that scholastic theologians have projected from their consciousness, or shaped even from the sacred pages which have proved so plastic in their hands. He is a God who never leaves himself without witness, who repenteth him of the evil, who never allows a disease or an injury, compatible with the enjoyment of life, to take its course without establishing an effort,— limited by certain fixed conditions, it is true, but an effort, always, to restore the broken body or the shattered mind. In the perpetual presence of this great Healing Agent, who stays the bleeding of wounds, who knits the fractured bone, who expels the splinter by a gentle natural process, who walls in the inflammation that might involve the vital organs, who draws a cordon to separate the dead part from the living, who sends his three natural anæsthetics to the overtasked frame in due order, according to its need, — sleep, fainting, death; in this perpetual presence, it is doubtless hard for the physician to realize the theological fact of a vast and permanent sphere of the universe, where no organ finds itself in its natural medium, where no wound heals kindly, where the executive has abrogated the pardoning power, and mercy forgets its errand; where the omnipotent is unfelt save in malignant agencies, and the omnipresent is unseen and unrepresented; hard to accept the God of Dante's Inferno, and of Bunyan's caged lunatic. If this is atheism, call three, instead of two of the trio, atheists, and it will probably come nearer the truth.

I am not disposed to deny the occasional injurious effect of the materializing influences to which the physician is subjected. A spiritual guild is absolutely necessary to keep him, to keep us all, from becoming the "fingering slaves" that Wordsworth treats with such shrivelling scorn. But it is well that the two callings have been separated, and it is fitting that they remain apart. In settling the affairs of the late concern, I am afraid our good friends remain a little in our debt. We lent them our physician Michael Servetus in fair condition, and they returned him so damaged by fire, as to be quite useless for our purposes. Their Reverend Samuel Willard wrote us a not overwise report of a case of hysteria; and our Jean Astruc gave them (if we may trust Dr. Smith's Dictionary of the Bible) the first discerning criticism on the authorship of the Pentateuch. Our John Locke enlightened them with his letters concerning toleration; and their Cotton Mather obscured our twilight with his *Nishmath Chajim.*

Yet we must remember that the name of Basil Valentine, the monk, is associated with whatever good and harm we can ascribe to antimony; and that the most remarkable of our specifics long bore the name of "Jesuit's Bark," from an old legend connected with its introduction. "Frère Jacques," who taught the lithotomists of Paris, owes his ecclesiastical title to courtesy, as he did not belong to a religious order.

Medical science, and especially the study of mental disease, is destined, I believe, to react to much greater advantage on the theology of the future than theology has acted on medicine in the past. The liberal spirit very generally prevailing in both professions, and the good understanding between their most enlightened members, promise well for the future of both in a community which holds every point of human belief, every institution in human hands, and every word written in a human dialect, open to free discussion to-day, to-morrow, and to the end of time. Whether the world at large will ever be cured of trusting to specifics as a substitute for observing the laws of health, and to mechanical or intellectual formulæ as a substitute for character, may admit of question. Quackery and idolatry are all but immortal.

We can find most of the old beliefs alive amongst us to-day, only having changed their dresses and the social spheres in which they thrive. We think the quarrels of Galenists and chemists belong to the past, forgetting that Thomsonism has its numerous apostles in our community; that it is common to see remedies vaunted as purely vegetable, and that the prejudice against "mineral poisons," especially mercury, is as strong in many quarters now as it was at the beginning of the seventeenth century. Names are only air, and blow away with a change of wind; but beliefs are rooted in human wants and weakness, and die hard. The oaks of Dodona are prostrate, and the shrine of Delphi is desolate; but the Pythoness and the Sibyl may be consulted in Lowell Street for a very moderate compensation. Nostradamus and Lilly seem impossible in our time; but we have seen the advertisements of an astrologer in our Boston papers year after year, which seems to imply that he found believers and patrons. You smiled when I related Sir Kenelm Digby's prescription with the live eel in it; but if each of you were to empty his or her pocket, would there not roll out a horse-chestnut from more than one of them, carried about as a cure for rheumatism? The brazen head of Roger Bacon is mute; but is not "Planchette" uttering her responses in a hundred houses of this city? We think of palmistry or chiromancy as belonging to the days of Albertus Magnus, or, if existing in our time, as given over to the gypsies; but a very distinguished person has recently shown me the line of life, and the line of fortune, on the palm of his hand, with a seeming confidence in the sanguine predictions of his career which had been drawn from them. What shall we say of the plausible and well-dressed charlatans of our own time, who trade in false pretences, like Nicholas Knapp of old, but without any fear of being fined or whipped; or of the many follies and inanities, imposing on the credulous part of the community, each of them gaping with eager, open mouth for a gratuitous advertisement by the mention of its foolish name in any respectable connection?

I turn from this less pleasing aspect of the common intelligence which renders such follies possible, to close the honorable record of the medical profession in this our ancient Commonwealth.

We have seen it in the first century divided among clergymen, magistrates, and regular practitioners; yet, on the whole, for the time, and under the circumstances, respectable, except where it invoked supernatural agencies to account for natural phenomena.

In the second century it simplified its practice, educated many intelligent practitioners, and began the work of organizing for concerted action, and for medical teaching.

In this, our own century, it has built hospitals, perfected and multiplied its associations and educational institutions, enlarged and created museums, and challenged a place in the world of science by its literature.

In reviewing the whole course of its history we read a long list of honored names, and a precious record written in private memories, in public charities, in permanent contributions to medical science, in generous sacrifices for the country. We can point to our capital as the port of entry for the New World of the great medical discoveries of two successive centuries, and we can claim for it the triumph over the most dreaded foe that assails the human body, — a triumph which the annals of the race can hardly match in three thousand years of medical history.

EARLY RELATIONS WITH THE INDIANS.

By SAMUEL ELIOT, LL.D.

EARLY RELATIONS WITH THE INDIANS.

LAST New Year's, a general of the United-States army sends a despatch from the field to his commanding general, saying that the destruction of a Comanche village, on Christmas Day, had given the final blow to the Indian rebellion; that the tribes were in mourning for their losses, the people starving, their dogs eaten, and no buffalo remaining. Such is the soldier's view of the situation. The Indian's may be easily conceived. Could he read Tacitus, he would perhaps repeat the complaint of the British chieftain against the Romans: *Ubi solitudinem faciunt, pacem appellant.*

If these are our relations with the Indians within our borders; if a nation which has mastered a continent, absorbed emigrants from every civilized race, and from some races not civilized, which has driven slavery back into the past, and thrown open the future to liberty, is still doomed to struggle with a handful of savages, we shall not expect, in turning back the pages of our history two centuries and more, to find the early relations of our forefathers with their Indian neighbors all that they or their descendants could desire. The Indians, now a remote minority, were then a hard-pressing majority of the American population; the country, now ours, was then theirs; all that long settlement and immemorial possession can confer in the way of security, then inured to their advantage, as it now inures to ours; and he would have been a far-seeing prophet whose eye could pierce beyond the clouds then lowering upon the English frontier, and predict with any degree of assurance that successive suns would ever dispel them.

Of all the difficulties attending the colonization of these

shores, all the perplexities which the colonists brought with them, all their uncertainties of purpose, all their conflicts of jurisdiction; or, again, of all the difficulties they found here, whether arising from the loneliness and, in a human point of view, the helplessness of their position, whether caused by the hardness of the soil, the severity of the climate, or any other privation and anxiety inseparable from their lot, — the difficulty of dealing wisely, religiously, and successfully with the red men was the greatest. Could they have solved it, they would have been more than mortal. That they should even have attempted to solve it, and that the attempt should have been to any extent successful, implies a spirit and a power on their part which we have every reason to hold in reverent remembrance.

As seen from the mother country, the problem appeared comparatively simple. When King James issued the patent of Virginia in 1606, he foresees, or pretends to foresee, that the enterprise in which his subjects had engaged, might hereafter tend to the glory of God in propagating the Christian religion to people as yet in darkness and ignorance. It was much easier for a king like James to make a prediction than to contribute to its fulfilment. Missionary work of any kind lay far beyond his sphere of action; missionary work of such a kind as Virginia required lay far beyond his sphere of thought. It is as hard to conceive of him at the head of a mission to the Indians, as to imagine Dominie Sampson leading the British charge at Waterloo. His son, Charles I., was a monarch of a more missionary mould. Whatever his faults, they did not consist in a want of sincere reverence toward God, or of an equally sincere regard for the spiritual welfare of his fellow-beings. Could he have risen to the height of the work which he might have furthered in behalf of the Indians here, instead of plunging into the stormy contests of prerogative and the fathomless agonies of civil war, his reign might have had a different course, and his life a different end. But the conversion of the American Indian was an even more impracticable undertaking for Charles than the subjection of the English freeman. He was content to leave it to the colonists themselves; and we can find no deeper trace of his interest in the cause than in the words of the Massachusetts charter, where it is asserted that the conversion of the natives "in our Royal intention, and the Adventurer's free profession is the principal end of this plantation."

Fifteen years later, when Charles must have long since forgotten his royal intentions, or, at any rate, despaired of carrying them out, and at the height of the conflict between him and his subjects in England, in the year 1644, Master William Castell, parson of Courtenhall, in the County of Northampton, presents a petition to the "High Court of Parliament for the Propagating of the Gospel in America." After stating the necessity of the andertaking, he dwells upon the easiness of effecting it, and explains its long delay by showing how the English have placed themselves too much in the skirts of the Continent, as in New England; or how they have suffered from the want of "able and conscionable ministers," as in Virginia, where they are "more likely," as he thinks, "to turn heathen than to turn others to the Christian faith." The petition, drawn up in his name, is signed by Churchmen, Presbyterians, and Scotch Covenanters, for once united in a religious purpose, and that in the full violence of civil war. It was a beautiful omen; but no omens, however beautiful, are enough to bring to a successful issue a labor depending upon action long sustained, and sacrifice unmeasured to the last. Nor would the conversion of the Indians have followed as a matter of course, could the hindrances to which Master Castell alludes, have been removed, and the English settlers penetrating farther into the interior, or obtaining the assistance of better ministers, placed themselves in a situation where, according to his opinion, their success as missionaries would have been easy. In truth, there was no such thing as easiness in connection with the Indian missions, except as these were seen from across the seas.

Their aspect on this side was very different. The first view revealed the alarming fact, that the relations between the English and the Indians were not to originate in any course upon which the former could determine. The case was, so to speak, prejudged, at least to a considerable degree, by events which had occurred before the Pilgrims landed at Plymouth. As early as the year 1614, the master of a ship in Captain John Smith's expedition "stayed to fit for Spain with the dried Fish;" and, not content with this cargo, he took on board another, consisting of four-and-twenty "Poore Salvages," whom he carried to Malaga, and there attempted to sell into slavery. The greater part were rescued by some Spanish friars, who treated them as brethren, and taught them their faith. Some time after, and not long before the arrival of the "Mayflower," another English captain enticed a band of Indians on board his vessel, and there opened fire upon them, without any provocation, of which we can now learn. It seemed strange to the Plymouth colonists that more than three months should elapse after their arrival, before the Indians appeared. As soon as any came, they told the story of what had been done to their countrymen, and it was then clear why they had been so long in coming. "By all which, it may appear," says Governor Bradford, "how far these people were from peace, and with what danger this plantation was begun."

Two years later, Massasoit, then on his sick-bed, revealed to his visitors from Plymouth the existence of a conspiracy, by which it was proposed to sweep away the whole line of English settlements on the Massachusetts shore. This arose among the Indians at Wessaguscus, now Weymouth, where a party of adventurers had landed, a few months before, and presently sunk so low as to deserve not only the hatred but the scorn of the Indians near them. "So base were they," says Governor Bradford, as to become "servants to the Indians, and would cut them wood and fetch them water for a cap full of corn," while "others fell to plain stealing both night and day." Such was the effect of this reckless degradation upon the savages, that they resolved to destroy the settlement; and to take care that no revenge should follow from the English at Plymouth, the Weymouth Indians urged Massasoit to join them, and to strike the same blow against his neighbors that they were to strike against theirs. In disclosing the danger, he advised his friends at Plymouth to lose no time in seizing some of the Weymouth chiefs, whose capture would be followed by the submission of their tribe. Miles Standish was thereupon despatched with a party of soldiers, and, in an encounter with the Indians, seven of their number were slain, and the remainder driven into the interior; while the English there were assisted to embark and leave the spot where they had been so near to death. It was concerning the seven Indians who fell in this conflict, that John Robinson wrote the often-quoted words: "Oh, how happy a thing had it been, if you had converted some before you had killed any!" So Cotton said, afterwards, to the colonists of Massachusetts Bay: "Offend not the poor natives; but as you partake in their land, so make them partakers of your precious faith; as you reap their temporals, so feed them with your spirituals." But both Robinson and Cotton were where these things looked very differently from what they did here.

To establish such relations with the Indians as they desired, was not therefore in our fathers' power. The enemy was before them, and after them, with his tares. It was no fault of theirs that the natives had been carried into slavery, or put to death by English sailors; no fault of theirs that English adventurers should have stolen from the natives, or degraded themselves in the natives' eyes; and yet they suffered as much from these sad incidents as if they themselves had been the aggressors. The dragon's teeth were sown for them, not by them, but the armed men were just as sure to spring up. Oh that the pure principles of Plymouth or of Massachusetts could have reached the Indians without the intervention of alien crimes!

The circumstances upon which we have been dwelling are external; there are some internal to be remarked. From the moment that the Englishman landed upon our soil, the Indians were objects of apprehension; he knew nothing of their numbers, nothing of their situation, except that they bordered close upon his dwelling, and might at any time descend upon it with the war-whoop; he knew nothing of the country itself, of its extent, its divisions, or its resources; and his ignorance, both with regard to the inhabitants and their territory, must have made him feel as if they were very strong and he very weak in any human contrast. One of the four-and-twenty slaves taken to Spain, found his way back to his own land; and he was so forgiving as to help the Plymouth settlers in setting their corn, taking their fish and procuring other supplies. The incident is very suggestive; for it shows how much the English needed to make friends with the Indian, how much, therefore, they would be moved by selfish as well as unselfish considerations to live on friendly terms with him. A race of untold capacity for good or for evil could not but excite the anxiety of the New-England pioneers.

As time passed, and the Indians were found less formidable than they had at first appeared, the feeling of apprehension was displaced by another feeling, yet more threatening to the establishment of serviceable relations between the two races. The white man began to despise the red man: he found him treacherous, irresolute, incapable of industry, unequal to the shock of arms, a creature of inferior energies as well as of inferior aspirations to his own. He used harsh language in speaking of him; he put on a scornful manner in dealing with him; he thought him unworthy of the consideration which he gave to any other human being, and sometimes even unworthy of that which he gave to the brute. Daniel Gookin, for many years superintendent of the converted Indians in Massachusetts, speaks of them as "not many degrees above beasts." John Eliot, whose self-denying labors are familiar as household words, — whose life of sacrifice and endurance, in behalf of the truth, is like a pillar of fire by night amid many a dark passage of our early annals, whose heart knew no distinction between the Indian and the Englishman as followers of the Saviour, — can speak of the people for whom he labored unto death, "as the dregs of mankind." If men like Gookin and Eliot described the red men in such terms as these, what must the rude colonists, the men of war or of intrigue, have said to express the scorn with which they regarded their enemies or their victims among the Indians?

Thus while distance lent enchantment to the view of the American tribes, roaming in a sort of heroic simplicity through their native forests, and only waiting for a missionary to speak the word that should give them the Christian faith, nearness excited very different emotions; and the colonists passed from apprehension to contempt, and perhaps back again, in states of mind which boded any thing but good to the Indians. The hills we see in the distance, soft with haze and responsive to every passing shadow, are not more unlike the hills we climb with panting breast and weary foot, than were the natives of this soil, as seen from across the ocean, objects of tender sympathy and promise; but as seen on the soil itself, objects of terror and abhorrence. It is not strange that a Martha's Vineyard sagamore should have told the Missionary Mayhew, in the year 1646, "He wondered the English should be almost thirty years in the country, and the Indians fools still."

To make them wise, the first requisite was a willingness to teach them; and this, as we have seen, could not come without an effort. To convert the Indians, the English needed to convert themselves. But to turn one's own heart, is a far harder thing than to turn, or try to turn, another's; and so many of the colonists found it, in endeavoring to form any satisfactory relations between themselves and the Indians. "Those that labor in this harvest," says Daniel Gookin, "are first to endeavor to learn perfectly that first lesson in Christ's school, — I mean self-denial."

The teacher being ready, the next requisite was a proper mode of teaching. This, too, was no light thing to hit upon. For such instruction as the American savage required, the Englishman had never received a training, nor did he now see plainly where to seek it. Even the Bible, on which he leaned for support in all other emergencies, seemed to fail him in this, particularly if he turned to the Old Testament, as was the Puritan's wont, for any historical precedent.

"Like some watcher of the skies,
When a new planet swims into his ken,"

the colonist found himself in presence of a race whose peculiarities demanded peculiar, and in many respects original, treatment.

The earliest experiment was made, in a treaty between the Plymouth colony and Massasoit, in March, 1621. It was so far successful as to last for upwards of half a century; a long duration for treaties of that period, even between European States. But the experiment was not at all comprehensive. It aimed at benefiting the English rather than the Indians, for whose conversion or civilization it contained no provision.

From the treaty of 1621, we follow a gradual advance in the methods of dealing with the Indians, till we reach the legislation of Massachusetts, in 1646. On the 4th of November, in that year, a series, it might almost be called a code, of laws in relation to the natives, was adopted by the General Court. Among its provisions, is one assigning "parcels of lands," in order to encourage the natives "to live in an orderly way." Another enjoins that "those necessary and wholesome laws, which may be made to reduce them to civility of life, shall be once in the year (if times be safe) made known to them." After these enactments looking to their civilization, another follows, ordering that two ministers should be sent "to make known the Heavenly council of God among the Indians."

We have here a plan both large and wise. It shows more than legislative wisdom in the twofold purpose which it embraces. The social element had the first place, as was fit. In all ages of Christianity, its missionaries have felt the necessity of changing the outward, as well as the inward, life of their converts. For this the mediæval monks made their monasteries the schools of industry, as well as faith; for this the modern explorers, like Livingstone in Africa, insist that new occupations, as well as new doctrines, are essential to reclaim the heathen. "I confess," said John Eliot of his Indians, "I think no great good will be done till they be more civilized." Grave obstacles, too grave to be surmounted wholly, presented themselves at every turn. What the Englishman most liked, — his house, his farm, his trade, his studies, — the Indian seemed most to dislike. Governor Winthrop tells us, in his journal, of a question put by an Indian to "an honest, plain Englishman," concerning the first beginnings, or principles, of a commonwealth. The answer came after some thought, that the first principle was salt to preserve flesh or fish for use in time of need; the second, iron to cut down trees, build houses, and till the land; the third, ships to carry away what can be spared, and bring back what is needed. "Alas!" said the Indian, "then I fear we shall never be a commonwealth, for we can neither make salt, iron, or ships." Chief obstacle of all was the tribal organization: to do away with it, supposing that possible, was to rouse hostility; to leave it untouched, was to insure the continuance of barbarism. Eliot describes a collision between himself and the Sachem Cutshamoquin, of Dorchester, who remonstrated against the apostle's course, which, he said, all the sachems were determined to resist. "It pleased God," says Eliot, "to raise up my spirit, not to passion but to a bold resolution, telling him it was God's work I was about, and He was with me, and I feared not him nor all the sachems in the country." Notwithstanding all these difficulties, the working plan was seen to be right. The effort to civilize the Indian was not relaxed; the hope of converting him was not shaken.

Indeed, there was great encouragement at the outset. The volume of tracts relating to the Indian missions, reprinted by the Historical Society, thirty odd years ago, recalls the fond hopes with which this work of our fathers began. The titles run, — "The Day-Breaking, if not the Sun-Rising, of the Gospel," "The Clear Sun-Shine of the Gospel," "The Glorious Progress of the Gospel," "The Light appearing more and more towards the Perfect Day." These are but words, and yet they stand for deeds which move one's heart to a deep sympathy as he recalls the time when it was hoped that they would open the way to successful issues. For, as we now know too well, the sunshine was made only in some shady places, and the general darkness remained unbroken.

One of the earliest converts was Hiacoomes, "a man of a sad and sober spirit," says his teacher, Thomas Mayhew. He was born about 1620, and his conversion took place in 1643; when, as Mayhew writes, "this work had its first rise and beginning." A neighboring sagamore, railing at the convert for his submission to the English, struck him in the face; and when Hiacoomes told the story, he said: "I had one hand for injuries, and the other for God; while I did receive wrong with the one, the other laid the greater hold on God." A few years afterwards, Hiacoomes lost an infant child, at whose simple funeral there were no "black faces," no food or ornaments buried in the grave, no savage outcries, "but a patient resigning of it," says Mayhew, "to Him that gave it." Here evidently was a convert whose sincerity could not be questioned, nor could any one be more fitly employed in bringing his countrymen to the truth. His example must have been all-availing; and the patient labors in which he engaged as a teacher, are described as having been much assisted "for his own and their spiritual good and advantage." This early employment of a native missionary is another proof of the judicious system upon which the work for the Indians was carried forward. He could reach many an ear closed to the English preacher; he could overcome many a prejudice against which the white men, however earnest, were powerless.

Among the most touching narratives from these times is that which Eliot gives concerning the death-bed of Wamporas, " one of our first and principal men." He said, that God gives us three mercies in this world: the first, health and strength; the second, food and clothes; the third, sickness and death. And when, he added, " we have had our share in the two first, why should we not be willing to take our part in the third?" His last request to Eliot was, that the Englishmen with whom some of the Indian children had been placed should be strongly entreated to teach them "to know God." His last words were, " Lord, give me Jesus Christ." Instead of fleeing from him, as his countrymen were wont to flee from the dying, they flocked around him, eager to hear his counsels, and to witness the peace in which he died. " I think," says Eliot, "he did more good by his death than he could have done by his life."

Waaubon, in whose wigwam the apostle Eliot first preached to the Indians, offered his eldest son to be educated by the English, in the hope "that he might come to know God, although he despaired much concerning himself." It was a part of the missionary scheme, from the very beginning, that the sons and daughters of the Indians should receive special care. Like the children of every class to be reclaimed at any time, these excited greater hopes and encouraged greater exertions than their fathers did. Not many years after Eliot's apostleship began, an Indian college was founded at Cambridge, as a department of the still infant institution there. The building, large enough to hold twenty students, cost between three and four hundred pounds. One of its inmates was Joel, a son of Hiacoomes, who had nearly completed his academic course, when, returning from his home in Martha's Vineyard, he was wrecked on Nantucket, and murdered by the natives of that island. "Thus perished our young prophet Joel," says Gookin: "he was a good scholar and a pious man." The solitary Indian graduate of Harvard, Caleb Cheeshahteaumuck, died the year after he took his degree. Did the aboriginal Freshman suffer at the hands of the Puritan Sophomore? Was there any emphasis in the class-room on *Barbarus has segetes?* Alma Mater, at all events, was never more gracious or more maternal than in the nurture she gave to her Indian sons. If the lessons she taught them were of brief avail in life, they must have been a comfort in death.

> "The air is full of farewells to the dying,
> And mournings for the dead."

It seems as if learning could not touch the Indian without inflicting a mortal wound; as if his civilization were his extinction, and conversion a speedy release from a world of tribulation.

The Indian college was built by the Society for Propagating the Gospel in New England, established by the Long Parliament, in 1649, at the instance chiefly of New Englanders. As Gookin wrote afterwards, "There is always more occasion to disburse than there is money to be disbursed," — a remark not yet without force. The English Society proved of great service; its contributions came not only from the churches and the universities, but from the army of England, and it was unwearied for many years in aiding both the missionaries and their converts in New England. The Indian college, though soon bereft of the students for whom it was designed, continued to serve the natives, as the printing-house from which text-books and versions of the Scriptures, in their own tongue, were issued. As early as 1649, Eliot wrote of his desire to translate some parts of the Bible, for the use of his converts, which, he says, "I look at as a sacred and holy work." In 1651, he writes, "I have no hope to see the Bible translated, much less printed, in my days." But, with the help of the Society for Propagating the Gospel, and in the college which they reared, the work went on beyond his hopes, and was at length completed. It was the crowning labor, not only of his life, but of the lives of all who labored in the same cause; and the Indian Version on which their minds were employed, and in which their hearts were interested, served as the messenger of peace and good-will amid all the storms of passion by which the country and its races were distracted.

Such, so far as they can be described within these limits, were the early relations with the Indians. The results were never so considerable as had been anticipated, on either side of the ocean. About thirty years after Mayhew began his labors in Martha's

Vineyard, and Eliot preached his first sermon in the neighborhood of Boston, there were perhaps four thousand Praying Indians, so called, in Massachusetts; nearly one-half of whom belonged to the Vineyard and adjacent islands, rather more than one quarter to Eliot's churches, and the remaining quarter to Plymouth and other places. Mayhew writes to Gookin, in 1674, "The whole holds forth the face of Christianity: how sincere, I know not." The numbers just given show that the work had not been a colonial one, or it would have attained to much greater proportions. It was the individual rather than the community who took an interest in the Indians; it was only a man like Mayhew or Eliot who, —

> "With filial confidence inspired,
> Could lift to Heaven an unpresumptuous eye,
> And smiling say, 'My Father made them all.'"

Nor, on the other hand, was the work an Indian one collectively. Men like Hiacoomes and Wamporas entered into it with all their souls; but the great majority of their countrymen regarded it with indifference, if not positive aversion. The sketches of Christianity, as it extends among them, are all individual, like that of Mayhew's convert who told him, "When I walk in the woods alone, I have much talk with God, and great repentance for my sins, and now I throw behind me all my strange gods, and my heart goes right to God in prayer." This was the trail of one, not all, not even many.

The hindrances to general relations with the Indians have been touched upon: it remains only to account for the drawbacks to their conversion. We need not dwell on their accountability alone: they were unfit, both as savages and as heathens, to become facile or thorough converts; but were not their teachers unfit, in some respects, to convert them? The Englishman was too much preoccupied as a settler, to be an ideal missionary: he was laden with cares of his own, or of the colony; and the burden of another race was more than he could bear with ease or with efficiency. Nor were his missionary methods such as smoothed his way to the Indian. Eliot's first service, in Waaubon's wigwam, crowded with men, women, and children, consisted of a prayer in English, a sermon of one hour and a quarter, and "certain questions to see what they would say to them, that so we might screw, by variety of means, something or other of God into them." "After three hours' time thus spent with them," says the missionary, "we asked them if they were not weary, and they answered, 'No.'" Yet the not inappropriate name then given to these exercises, was "heartbreakings." The religious divisions of the teachers were another stumbling-block to their disciples. Mayhew's people were told, by some Quakers, that he was a priest of Baal. Two of Eliot's converts were taken to task, for his errors and theirs, by the Gorton sectaries at Warwick. It was difficult for the Indians to know which doctrine to believe, — indeed to feel that any doctrines, in such dispute, were worth believing at all.

But the one great hindrance to the conversion of the red men was the repeated outbreak of war, drowning the Christian's voice in the clash of arms. That meeting-house, which the Plymouth people built on Burial Hill, a casemate to their fort, with the sign not of the cross but of the cannon, is symbolic of all the Indian missions. The English came hither, as Bolingbroke to England, —

> "To ope
> The purple testament of bleeding war;"

and the drops from its pages blotted out the Scriptures of Peace. King Philip's war, in 1675, scattered the Christian Indians as sheep before a pack of wolves.

And yet the work, though broken up beyond the possibility of restoration, is not to be pronounced a failure. Had it saved but one soul; had Hiacoomes or Joel, or others of a higher rank in Indian eyes, like Wamporas or Waaubon, been the only gleanings, — the harvest would not have been vain. Even if it seems a failure, compared with the promises of the seed-time, it deserves to be classed with other failures, nobler than many a success; nobler, because their lines of light are broader; nobler, because their ideals are loftier: so that even a partial attainment of them is better than the perfect triumph of an inferior cause.

THE REGICIDES SHELTERED IN NEW ENGLAND.

By REV. CHANDLER ROBBINS, D.D.

THE REGICIDES SHELTERED IN NEW ENGLAND.

IF it were merely that a romantic interest attaches to the story of the Regicides sheltered in New England — however inviting on that account the theme might be — it would not have been selected as the subject of a lecture in the course now in progress. Its claim to this distinction rests rather upon the fact that it touches at various points the policy and the characters, the public and private life, of the Founders of Massachusetts. We cannot retouch the fading portraits of those stern puritan soldiers; we cannot review the stirring scenes in which they performed a prominent part; we cannot pass judgment upon their characters in connection with those transactions to which they owe both their celebrity and their sufferings; nor can we trace them in their long and dreary exile, — so far as it is possible to penetrate the mystery in which they were enveloped, — without throwing some light upon the pages of our early history, — upon persons, opinions, and movements, of greater importance than that which attaches to those ill-starred individuals.

And yet another reason influenced the friend to whom we are indebted for the arrangement of these lectures, in the selection and assignment of this topic. In preparing for publication in the Collections of the Massachusetts Historical Society a mass of manuscripts, originally belonging to the Mather family, and which afterwards formed a part of the Library of Rev. Thomas Prince, the Annalist of New England, I discovered that a large number related to the Regicides. Many of these proved to be in the handwriting of William Goffe himself; consisting of letters which he had written and received while in seclusion. He had employed secret characters to conceal the names of individuals and certain other particulars, in case the correspondence should be intercepted: but these were easily deciphered. The printing of these letters, which occupy nearly a hundred pages, has revived the interest which has always been felt in these refugees, and added a few particulars to the scanty information which history and tradition have heretofore supplied.

Our subject requires a preliminary glance at one of the most interesting and eventful periods in the history of England — I might say in the history of Liberty — that of the revolution which led to the overthrow of the British Monarchy and the establishment of a Commonwealth, in 1649.

Although the conflict between Charles I. and the Commons was provoked by circumstances peculiar to the period itself, and aggravated by the stubborn temper of the parties engaged in it, its real origin is to be traced back to principles which had been at work in the bosom of English society centuries before the accession of that misguided monarch to the throne. Whatever variety of motives and interests may have been accessory to the strife, and whatever prejudices and passions may have embittered it, it was, in the main, the renewal, only with unusual intensity, of the old struggle between despotism and liberty. Whether we regard it in its political or its religious aspects, — for both political and religious animosities were blended in it, in nearly equal proportions, — the ruling principle was the same. The King and his party were contending for absolute power both in the State and in the Church; the majority of the Parliament and its supporters in the army and in the nation for popular rights.

No just judgment can be formed of the character of this conflict without carefully distinguishing the prime cause from the collateral objects which became entangled with it, — the principles in controversy between the two great parties from the personal motives, exceptional designs, and incidental acts of the individuals and factions included in their ranks.

In respect to the cause itself, no loyal descendant of the Pilgrims can hesitate to give his sympathy to the side of the Commons. The tyranny against which they were struggling was the scourge which had driven our Forefathers from their pleasant land. The political and religious reform for which the best spirits among them were striving was the very same in which the members of the Massachusetts Company were engaged. The liberal movement which was going on with such fierce throes in the very heart of Old England, was simultaneously at work, with more quiet earnestness, because less actively resisted, in these distant Colonies. The men who were undertaking to build up a Christian Commonwealth on this side of the ocean were of one brotherhood with those who were engaged in demolishing the fabric of despotism on the other. Not only were they allied by the closest ties of personal friendship and political and religious sympathy, but in many instances by actual association in the enterprise that founded Massachusetts. Ten or twelve of the Massachusetts Company, including Cradock the Governor, and Vane a former Governor, were members of the Long Parliament. Hampden, Pym, and Fiennes, Patentees of Connecticut, were among its most influential Commoners.[1] Six or seven sat in judgment on the King; and a long list might be added of others connected with the civil war — some of them representing the best blood in England — who were more or less directly concerned with Winthrop and his Colleagues. Nothing but a prohibitory order from the King's Council had prevented Cromwell himself, with Hampden and Pym, who had actually embarked for the purpose, from transferring their persons and estates to America.[2] Who can tell what a different fate might have befallen Charles and England, had not tyranny, in gratifying its present malice, sharpened and laid up in store the weapons of its future destruction?

The Commons were mainly in the right. Their cause was the cause of liberty and justice. Many of the greatest and best men of the period, at home and in the Colonies, were on their side. The common heart of England was beating in unison with their purpose, so long and so far as they adhered to it with pure

1 Archæologia Amer., vol. iii.; Dr. Palfrey's History of N. E.

2 This fact has been questioned; but it appears to me that it is supported by sufficient authority. It is stated by Hume and several other historians. In "Cromwelliana," London, 1810, fol. p. 1, there is the following statement, — "In 1637, he," Cromwell, "had a design to remove to New England. Sir Matthew Boynton, Sir William Constable, Sir Arthur Haslerigg, Mr. John Hampden, and several other gentlemen were preparing to remove themselves with him, and were actually embarked for that purpose; but were prevented by a proclamation and order of Council."

patriotism, loyalty to justice, and unmixed devotion. And this they did — with due allowance for human imperfection — at least up to the moment when the sword was actually drawn. Nor does the responsibility for its unsheathing rest with them. The fatal challenge was given when the King with his armed retinue made his way to the Speaker's desk to enforce his demand that the five obnoxious members, with Hampden at their head, should be delivered up to his power. That infatuated act was virtually a declaration of war.[1] From that hour the grand struggle for liberty, which had hitherto been guided by wise and thoughtful statesmen, and pure and ardent patriots, began to pass over to the army, and while acquiring new force became subjected to new perils.

The elements of which that army was composed, while rendering it irresistible in the field, made it all the more dangerous in the State. It was made up not of ordinary soldiers who take up arms under the pressure of poverty, or from the love of fierce excitement and reckless adventure; but principally of respectable citizens, farmers, tradesmen, and rural gentlemen, of good estate and good education: not of mere human machines moving blindly at the beck of their commanders; but each one a thinking and reflecting individual, conscious of his power, and jealous of his independence; who regarded himself as a "chosen vessel in the hands of the Lord," specially ordained to fight his battles: many of them political zealots and religious enthusiasts, and not a few agitators, demagogues, levellers, and wild fanatics, breathing the ferocious spirit, and borrowing the vindictive language of the prophets and warriors of the Old Dispensation; men of austere morals, of iron will, of fiery temper, and desperate courage; a host of Titans, whom no difficulties discouraged, and no odds dismayed; who marched into battle with

[1] The question has been often debated whether the King or the Parliament began the civil war. There may be room for difference of opinion, as to which of the parties actually commenced the final struggle of arms; but there can be no dispute as to the fact that the "deplorable excesses by which it was so fatally provoked and embittered," mainly originated with the party of prerogative. The cruel persecutions, "imprisonments, fines, pilloryings, brandings, cutting off of ears," and other sanguinary punishments for opinion's sake, began with them. If it could be shown that the party of the Parliament first resorted to arms, it is clear that they were goaded to it beyond endurance.

exultation, determined to conquer and confident of victory, and never failed to crush and scatter the strongest force opposed to them.

Invariable success confirmed their conceit that they were the special favorites of Heaven. As hostile to the party of the Presbyterians as to that of the King, they sifted them more and more from their ranks as the war went on. That party, however, constituted the majority of the Parliament, and therefore, no sooner had the army broken the forces of the King than it directed its power against the Parliament itself. Thus, the war which had begun as a contest between royal usurpation and popular rights, ended in a struggle between Independency and Presbyterianism. The high and patriotic purpose for which Hampden and other kindred spirits had reluctantly unsheathed the sword was comparatively lost sight of; and the great national party, which had been united under their leadership by a common zeal for liberty and right, separated into two rival religious factions, contending with each other for supremacy with hardly less acrimony than they had together fought against the King. To secure his person and influence was an object of the first importance to both, and each resorted to intrigue to gain him over to their side. The Presbyterians desired a limited monarchy with their own particular system of church government; and offered to reinstate the King, if he would consent to its establishment as the religion of the State. The Independents preferred a Republic; but knew that if the King gave up Episcopacy, and combined with the Presbyterians, they should be defeated; and for this reason the leaders of the army offered to replace him upon the throne, on the single condition of liberty of conscience, and the security of the military power in their hands. The Parliament attempted to destroy the influence of the Independents and of Cromwell, their ruling spirit, by diminishing the army and forcing its officers to conform to the system of church government which they had established by an ordinance. The latter seeing that there was not a moment to be lost, if they would maintain their power, resolved, at a meeting in Cromwell's house, to seize the person of the King, and prepare to defend themselves against the votes of Parliament by force. The order was instantly executed; and the army, summoned to a general rendezvous, not only entered into a solemn engagement that they "would not disband nor divide, nor suffer themselves to be disbanded or divided," but passed a declaratory resolution that "the public welfare demanded the removal from credit and office of the men by whose counsels the army had been calumniated and oppressed."

The Parliament in alarm passed votes to pacify the army, which were read at the head of each regiment. The officers returned an evasive reply, and moved their headquarters nearer to the metropolis. Again Cromwell tried by every device to induce the King to throw himself upon the generosity of the army. He protested that "nothing was nearer to his heart than the restoration of Charles to his authority upon moderate and equal terms — that if he would co-operate with the Council of War, they would repay the obligation with interest."

Finding that the King was unyielding, — for he was as distrustful of their sincerity, as they were sure of his duplicity, — Cromwell and his associates plainly saw that nothing was left to them but either to relinquish their power, surrender the claims of the soldiers, give up all for which they had been fighting, and subject themselves to the penalties which surely awaited them, into the hands of whichsoever of the hostile parties the government should fall; or to resort to such desperate measures as would involve King, Parliament, and the Constitution itself, in common ruin.

Such a conclusion certainly did not enter into their original plan, although there may have been some zealots who looked forward to it in their wild dreams, or even suggested it in their ravings, but was a hasty result to which they were driven by a series of disappointments on their own part, and a train of mistakes on the part of the Prelatists and Presbyterians, together with the intense religious and political excitement to which the soldiers had wrought themselves up. They were not men who would hesitate long in such an extremity, or shrink from the path which necessity and Providence, as they believed, had marked out for them, however disastrous the consequences to which it might lead.

Their course was instantly decided upon. They seized the person of the King, and marched the army to London. "Now that I have the King in my hand," said Cromwell, "I have the Parliament in my pocket." A strong guard was placed over the two Houses. A demand was made that all the leading Presbyterians, and all who had adhered to them, and all the members who had recently voted in favor of pacification with the King, should be expelled from their seats. The demand was enforced by violence. The purged House became the tool of the army, which had now usurped the civil as well as the military power of the nation. At the beck of these grim soldiers, a small minority were compelled to resolve upon the impeachment of the King, and to pass an ordinance for his trial, by a special tribunal, which they called a High Court of Judicature. The Lords immediately rejected the measure, with a declaration that no resolution of the Lower House was valid without their concurrence. The indignant Commoners at first thought of accusing all the Peers of high treason; but instead of taking a step so absurd and reckless, concluded to cover their revolutionary design with a thin semblance of loyalty, by passing a resolution that, "as the people were, under God, the original of all just power, and the Commons were their representative, all the enactments of the latter had the force of law without the concurrence of King and Peers." Having now at one blow virtually overturned the Constitution and seized the supreme power, the way was cleared of every obstacle to the execution of their purpose.

The body of the people who were opposed to the tyranny of the army, and at heart attached to the Constitution, were the only quarter from which effective resistance could be apprehended. But the strong arm of the military could keep them down, at least for a time; and the stunning suddenness of the meditated blow would allow them no opportunity to rally. Meanwhile, the prime movers availed themselves of strange instruments to confirm their own zeal and warp the minds of the populace to their purpose. The revelations of visionary prophets, male and female, giving assurance of the sanction of Heaven upon their measures, were accepted with avidity and diligently reported. Cromwell himself declared that when he was lately praying for the restoration of the King, he had been favored with a preternatural sign that God had rejected him.

And, as "a fit prelude to the tragedy" about to be enacted, Hugh Peters, that wild enthusiast and crafty incendiary, was employed to preach to an audience of soldiers and citizens, with the fanatical eloquence of which he was a master. He took his text from the 149th Psalm, perverting the true application by a cunning change of the pronouns: "Bind *your* kings with chains and *your* nobles with fetters of iron." He compared the King to Barabbas, called the army the saviours of the people, and affirmed that there were in its ranks "five thousand saints not inferior to those who surround the throne of God." Then suddenly pausing, he closed his eyes, laid his head upon the cushion, and exclaimed, "I have had a revelation. The Slavery of the children of Israel and of the elect shall have an end by the extirpation of royalty in England, and in all other Kingdoms."

On the eighth day of January, 1649, only fifty-three out of the one hundred and thirty-three Commissioners sat for the first time in the Painted Chamber in Westminster Hall, — and sixty-seven was the largest number present on any subsequent day. The twelve Judges of the realm, who were at first appointed members of the Commission, having given their opinion that trial was illegal, were afterwards set aside, together with several of the Peers. Many others refused to take a part. Fairfax, the Commander-in-Chief of the Army, never appeared. Vane and St. John held themselves aloof. Algernon Sidney says, —

"I was at Penthurst when the act for the King's trial was passed, and coming up to town, I heard that my name was put in it. I presently went to the Painted Chamber where the Judges were assembled. A debate was raised, and I positively opposed the proceeding. Cromwell using these formal words, 'I tell you we will cut off his head with the Crown on it,' I replied, 'You may take your own course, I cannot stop you; but I will keep myself clear from having any hand in this business. Saying this, I immediately left them, and never returned."

One or two others who had the courage to attempt to stay the proceedings were summarily put down. A few of the weaker minded, who had no heart for the business, were intimidated into compliance. The remainder engaged in the work with a will: — Cromwell, who professedly, perhaps really, had entered upon it only after many struggles, and prayers specially answered, throwing himself into it with all his relentless resolution and indomitable energy, and at once assuming that lead, which in every enterprise his ambition prompted him to take, and his masterly powers fitted him to maintain: — others from a frenzied desire for a revolution which should level all prerogative, and all barriers to universal freedom: — and still others from a sincere and fervid conviction that they were serving God and their country in a holy and glorious cause.

Before this strange and terrible tribunal — not of Judges, not even of members of Parliament alone, but of grim soldiers also, and fierce partisans selected from among the people — constituted not for judgment, but for condemnation — implacable hostility stamped upon every face — Charles I. was arraigned.

The circumstances attending the trial are familiar to every reader of English history: — the charges brought against the King, of treason against the State, and of having been the cause of all the blood which had been shed, and of all the calamities which had afflicted the Kingdom since the commencement of the war, — the stern and rude manner of his treatment by Bradshaw, the President of the Court, — his persistent refusal, on three several occasions, to acknowledge the jurisdiction of the Court, — the insults of the mob and the clamorous demand of the soldiers for his execution, — the self-possession and dignity of his deportment, — and the final procedure of the Court, after an *ex parte* examination of a few witnesses, to pass the fatal sentence.

There are, however, a few incidents of the trial, related by one of the Judges, which appear to have escaped the notice of historians. They are interesting, not only as showing to what extent the Court was under the domineering influence of Cromwell, but from their incidental reference to one of the three individuals whom we shall have occasion, by and by, particularly to notice. They are copied here in a condensed form from a contemporary "broad-side" in the archives of the Massachusetts Historical Society.

When the President — after having refused to take any notice of the King's reiterated objection to the authority of the Court, and his earnest appeal to be allowed to speak to his Parliament, as he had "something to offer for the settlement of the nation that might be satisfactory to all" — had ordered the Clerk to read the sentence, John Downes, Esq. — who had been an adventurer to Virginia in 1620 — became so agitated, as he says, as to attract the notice of Cromwell, who occupied a contiguous seat, and who seeing him about to rise turned to him and said, "What ails thee, art thou mad, canst thou not sit still and be quiet?" The reply was, "No, Sir, I cannot be quiet." He then stood up and objected to the sentence, declaring that he had reasons to offer against it, and desired the Court to adjourn to hear them. The President decided that if any judge was dissatisfied the Court must adjourn, and ordered an adjournment to the inner Court of Wards. As soon as they had assembled in secret session, Cromwell called upon Downes to give an account why he had brought this trouble and disturbance upon the Court. When he had stated his objections, Cromwell in scornful wrath charged him with only pretending dissatisfaction out of servility to his old master.

"Surely," said he, "the gentleman doth not know that he has to deal with the hardest hearted man on earth. But, Sir, it is not the opinion of one peevish, tenacious man that must sway the Court, or deter them from their duty in so great a business; therefore, Sir, I pray you lose no more time, but return to the Court and do your duty."

Cromwell further whispered in his ear that he was convinced he "aimed at nothing but making a mutiny in the army and the cutting of throats." Another told him it was as much as his life was worth to make any disturbance; that it was not in the power of man, nor of this Parliament, to save the King's life; for "the whole army are resolved that if there be but any check or demur in giving judgment, they will immediately fall upon him and hew him to pieces, and the House itself will not be out of danger." The relater further says that he knew that "Mr. Dixwell amongst some others were dissatisfied."[1] Without fur-

[1] An authentication of this statement may be found in "A true Copy of the Journal of the High Court of Justice for the Tryal of King Charles I., as it was read in the House of Commons and attested under the hand of Phelps, Clerk to that infamous Court. Taken by J. Nalson, LL.D., Jan. 4th, 1683, London, 1684;" in Fellowes's Sketches: —

"27th Jan. 1648. The President ordered the Court to withdraw for a time. This he did to prevent the disturbance of their scene, by one of their own members, Colonel John Downes, who could not stifle the reluctance of his conscience when he

ther debate the Court resumed its session and proceeded to pass the sentence of death by beheading. This was on the 27th of January, 1649. On the 29th it was determined that the open street in front of the royal palace of Whitehall was a fit place for the execution, which was assigned for the following day. The warrant was immediately given.

But the last and most trying duty, that of affixing their individual signatures to the fatal order, still remained. It is no wonder that some of them should have shrunk from its performance. It was with difficulty the Commissioners could be got together for the purpose. Two or three of the most resolute took their station outside of the door to stop such of their colleagues as were passing towards the House of Commons. Cromwell sat within, boisterous, overbearing, and in high spirits, stimulating and even forcing the timid and reluctant. Some who had agreed to the sentence kept out of the way or utterly refused to sign.[1] At last fifty-nine signatures were obtained, and the death-warrant was complete.

Among the names affixed to this memorable instrument were those of the three individuals to a brief sketch of whose personal history it is high time to turn our attention.

EDWARD WHALLEY was descended from an ancient and highly respectable family. His father Richard, a member of Parliament, Sheriff of the County of Nottingham and the proprietor of large estates, had married a daughter of Sir Henry Cromwell, uncle

saw his Majesty press so earnestly for a short hearing; but declaring himself unsatisfied, forced them to yield to the King's request. The Court withdraws for half an hour into the Court of Wards. Their business was not to consider his Majesty's desire, but to chide Downes, and with reproaches and threats to harden him to go through the remainder of their villany with them. Which done they return."

[1] It is difficult to distinguish between what is true and what is false in the accounts which have been given by different narrators of Cromwell's behavior, — colored as they all appear to be, more or less, in accordance with the prejudices of the writers. There must, however, have been some foundation in his actual conduct for such stories as several highly respectable historians have credited and recorded as facts: for example, that after having signed himself, he smeared the face of the reckless wag Henry Martin with ink,— who immediately did the same to him; and that when his cousin, Colonel Ingoldsby, who had been appointed one of the Court, but never took his seat, came into the hall, he cried out, "This time he shall not escape," and laughing, seized hold of him, put the pen into his hand, and with the aid of one or two others forced him to sign.

to Oliver. The son was bred a merchant, but at the breaking out of the civil war, under the influence of his religious convictions, more than for any other reason, took up arms on the side of the Parliament, in opposition to the sentiments of his nearest relations. He distinguished himself as a soldier in many sieges and battles. At the battle of Naseby, in 1645, he charged and defeated two divisions of Horse, though supported by Prince Rupert who commanded the reserve: for which brilliant action the Parliament voted him a commission as Colonel of Horse. On the 9th of May of the following year, he received for his valiant service in taking Banbury by storm one hundred pounds to purchase two horses. He behaved soon after with great gallantry in the attack on the city of Worcester, which surrendered to him on the 23d of July. In 1647 the Commons granted him one of the manors of the Marquis, afterwards Duke, of Newcastle.

He enjoyed the full confidence of his cousin Cromwell, who appears to have had great influence over him, and while committing to him important trusts and conferring upon him high offices, to have sometimes used him, perhaps more than Whalley himself was aware, as a tool of his crafty policy.

He committed to his custody the person of the King during his confinement at Hampton Court. Of the manner in which he discharged the duties of this office, conflicting accounts are given, according as the prejudices of the writers who have referred to it lean to the side of the royalists or the army. The former charge him with coarseness and undue severity. But a letter subsequently addressed to him by the King is his sufficient exculpation. And yet he did not always avoid giving offence under circumstances so conducive to irritation. Clarendon tells us that, on one occasion, when Captain Sayers waited upon his Majesty to give back to him the ensigns of the Order of the Garter, which had belonged to the late Prince of Orange, and the two were walking forward and backward together, the suspicions of Whalley were aroused to such a degree that he stepped forward to interfere; whereupon the exasperated monarch pushed him away and indignantly raised his cane as if to chastise him for the affront.

It has always been supposed that the escape of the King from Hampton Court was not effected without the connivance of his guardian, who induced him to make the attempt by alarming him with the stories of a design to take his life. It is certain that on the very day of his flight Whalley read to him a letter which he said had been secretly delivered to him, intimating that the agitators in the army had formed a design to surprise and assassinate him. The authorship of the letter has been generally attributed to Cromwell, who is supposed to have written it for the purpose of working upon the fears of the King in order to induce him voluntarily to take a step which would remove him out of the custody of the Parliament, and bring him more completely into his own power.[1]

At the battle of Dunbar in 1650, he was associated with Monk in command of the Foot, and having greatly contributed to the rout of the Scottish army, he was left by Cromwell in Scotland with the rank of Commissary General and the command of four regiments of Horse.

After Oliver's elevation he was intrusted by him with the government of the Counties of Lincoln, Nottingham, Derby, Warwick, and Leicester, with the title of Major General; in which office he was so assiduous, that, as he himself says, he did not leave a single vagrant in a whole county. He was representative for Nottinghamshire in the Parliaments of 1654 and 1656, and raised by the Protector to his Upper House. He is said to have been so fond of this honor that he threatened to cane

[1] If those who have suggested this explanation had examined the curious and interesting book, entitled "Cromwelliana," they would have found an extract from Colonel Whalley's own statement in answer to a question put to him by the House of Commons, which places the authorship of the letter beyond a question, and confirms the suspicion as to the motives of the writer. "And whereas, Mr. Speaker," these are his words, "you demand of me what that letter was I showed the King the day he went away, the letter I will show you: but with your leave I shall first acquaint you with the author and the ground of my showing it to the King. The author is Lieutenant General Cromwell. The ground of my showing it is this: the letter intimates some murderous design, or at least some fear of it against the King. When I read the letter I was much astonished, abhorring that such a thing should be done, or so much as thought of, by any that bear the name of Christians. When I had shown the letter to his Majesty, I told him I was sent to safeguard, and not to murther him; I wished him to be confident no such thing should be done, I would first die at his foot in his defence; and therefore I showed it him, that he might be reassured, though menacing speeches came frequently to his ear, our General Officers abhorred so bloody and villainous a fact. Another reason was that I might get a nearer admittance to his Majesty that so I might better secure him," &c.

Colonel Ashfield in Westminster Hall for speaking derisively of this *quasi* House of Lords. The valiant Colonel, however, having set him at defiance, he prudently abstained from executing the menace; but went away and complained of him to the Protector Richard, who told the Colonel that unless he would ask pardon for the offence he would cashier him for using disrespectful language to his superior officers. The Colonel, no wise daunted, petitioned to have a fair hearing, — a demand which the Protector could not well refuse; but himself selected the officers to whom the case should be referred, and they, of course, decided that the fault should be humbly acknowledged and "my Lord Whalley's" pardon asked. To this sentence, however, the stubborn Colonel absolutely refused to submit.[1]

When a proposition was made in Parliament to make Cromwell king, Whalley, notwithstanding the great obligations which he was under to his powerful relative, and his dependence upon him for high and lucrative offices, strenuously opposed the measure.[2] His name appears among the signers of the Proclamation for the succession of Richard Cromwell to the Protectorate on the death of Oliver, the 3d of September, 1658. After the resignation of Richard he became an object of jealousy to the Parliament as having too much interest with the army, for which reason they took away his command; but this, it is said, only endeared him to the soldiers the more.

It deserves to be mentioned as an evidence of the high esteem in which the character of Whalley was held among men of discrimination and worth, that the celebrated Richard Baxter, author

1 Ludlow Memoirs, vol. ii. pp. 632, 633.

2 The fact is thus stated by several writers. I do not find any notice of Whalley's having opposed the measure in the Parliament itself. The account given by Whitelock is as follows: "Dec. 10, 1651, Cromwell called a meeting of divers members of Parliament, and some chief officers of the army, at the Speaker's house, and proposed to them that now, the old King being dead and his son defeated, he held it necessary to proceed to a settlement of the Nation." . . . "Cromwell discovered their inclinations for which he fished, and made use of what he then discerned. He said he really thought that a settlement of somewhat *with monarchical government in it* would be very effectual." . . . "Whalley said, I do not well understand matters of law; but it seems to me the best way not to have any thing of monarchical power in the settlement of our Government, and if we should resolve upon any, whom have we to pitch upon?" . . . "Cromwell put off the debate when it turned towards making the Duke of Gloucester, the King's third son, king."

of the "Saints' Rest," one of the ablest ministers and most voluminous writers of his age, who had been chaplain in his regiment, dedicated to him one of his practical works with expressions of sincere friendship and respect. It was at the time when he was enjoying the high offices to which he had been promoted by his Cousin Cromwell. How singularly must the closing words of this complimentary inscription have affected the mind of him to whom they were addressed, if they were ever recalled to his remembrance in the low estate to which he was subsequently reduced! How must they have impressed him with the uncertainty of earthly honors, as they brought forcibly to his thought the strong contrast between the prosperous career which his friend blindly predicted for him as the source of his trial, and the miserable and lonely condition from which his temptations actually arose! "Think not that your greatest trials are now over. Prosperity hath its peculiar temptations by which it hath foiled many that stood unshaken in the storms of adversity. The tempter who hath had you on the waves, will now assault you in the calm, and hath his last game to play *on the mountains*, till nature cause you to descend. Stand this charge and you win the day."[1]

WILLIAM GOFFE was a son of a puritanical clergyman, Rector of Stanmore in Sussex. The political and religious excitement of the times, acting upon an ardent and somewhat restless nature, led him to exchange the quiet duties of the business to which he had been brought up for the stirring life of a soldier. The influences of his early education determined the direction of his interest in the conflict between the Commons and the King. Enlisting with enthusiasm in the army of the Parliament, he rose by rapid gradations to a high rank. Though not liberally educated, he is mentioned in the Fasti Oxonienses as having received the honorary degree of Master of Arts. In the account

[1] Baxter's Practical Works, Orme's edition, vol. i. p. 453.

In Josiah Ricroft's "Survey of England's Champions and Truth's faithful Patriots, published by Authority, London, 1647," is the following tribute to Whalley: "I must not forget another of the valiant Commanders, Colonell Whalley, a man of honour and of trust, who deserves as much of the King and Parliament as the best of the Commanders in his Excellency Thomas Fairfax's army (now resident) one only excepted."

there given of him, it is said that he was "a frequent prayer-maker, preacher, and presser for righteousness and freedom, and therefore in high esteem in the army." He was a devoted partisan of Cromwell, and ever ready to execute his will. He assisted Colonel White in forcibly ejecting the members that were left behind of the "*Little*" or "*Barebones*" Parliament, in 1653. For this and other services he received from the Protector the honorable and lucrative post of Major General of Hampshire, Sussex, and Berks. He was a member for Great Yarmouth in the Parliament of 1654, and for Southampton in 1656, and was called up to the Protector's House of Lords. His name appears, together with that of Whalley, whose daughter he had married, in the order for proclaiming Richard Cromwell Protector after his father's death.

In Burton's "Parliamentary Diary," there is a brief and somewhat curious notice of one of Goffe's speeches in Parliament. "Jan. 19, 1656, Sir Gilbert Pickering said, on the question of voting an address to Cromwell, —

"If it were not against the orders of the House to call upon any man to speak, there was a very good pattern propounded to us as to the manner of addresses to his Highness, upon another occasion about three or four months ago. I wish we might follow that way. I remember very well what this speech was and who spoke it. It was Major General Goffe, upon the debate about the thanksgiving for the late victory from Spain. It was a long preachment, seriously inviting the House to a firm, and kind of corporal, union with his Highness. Something was expressed as to hanging about his neck like pearls, from a text out of Canticles." "Major General Goffe," says Burton, "tickled, I believe, by Sir Gilbert Pickering's call, stood up and expressed his favorable opinion of the proposed congratulation of Cromwell upon his great deliverance and desired the Speaker to express our sense of the former deliverances of his Highness, both public and private, upon whose preservation much of ours did depend. He then repeated something of his former preachment."

JOHN DIXWELL was a cadet of the Dixwells of Kent, an ancient and wealthy family, raised to the Baronetage. His elder brother, who died in 1643, left his large estate and his children, all minors, in his charge. A country gentleman, of independent means, and good education, who had nothing to gain, but much to lose by changes, every selfish interest would have induced him to withhold himself from the revolutionary party, if not to take sides against it. But his judgment and his conscience moved him to engage in what he believed to be the cause of freedom and of God. Enlisting in the Parliamentary army, he soon distinguished himself as a soldier and rose to the rank of a Colonel of Foot.

He was a member of all the Parliaments of the Commonwealth, with the single exception of that called the "Little" or "Barebones." It appears from a careful and thorough copy — now in the possession of his descendant, John James Dixwell, Esq. — of every entry in the Journals of the House of Commons in which the name of Colonel Dixwell occurs, that he was an active and distinguished member. The frequency of his appointment on important Committees and the nature of the questions submitted to his decision show the high consideration in which he was held as a man of sound judgment, firm purpose, and practical ability.

He was several times chosen a member of the Council of State from the year 1651 to 1659, and in the latter year was commissioned Lieutenant of Dover Castle.

On the 29th of May, 1660, Charles II. entered London, amidst the acclamations of the people, to take possession of the throne from which he had been so long excluded. In anticipation of this event, the three individuals whose career we have thus far sketched, hastily fled from the vengeance which they knew was in store for them if they remained in England; — Whalley and Goffe to America, and Dixwell first to Hanau, in Germany, and afterwards to New England.

The two former left Westminster on the 4th of May and arrived in Boston the 27th of July; bringing testimonials from various ministers in high esteem among their brethren here. By the same vessel which brought them over came the news of the King's accession. They attempted no concealment of their persons or characters; for the action of Parliament in regard to them had not yet been promulgated. Immediately on landing they called upon Governor Endicott who gave them a courteous welcome, and the same day proceeded to Cambridge, where it was their intention to reside. The high rank and social position which they had sustained in England, together with the gravity and dignity of their manners, secured for them general respect. They were admitted into the best society and met with marked attention. They attended public worship and lectures, took part in private devotional meetings, and were allowed to partake of the Communion.

Among those who treated them with such deference there were undoubtedly some who like Mitchell, the minister of Cambridge, were not fully aware, at the moment, of the exact relation in which they stood to the laws of their country. Writing, subsequently, in his own vindication, Mitchell says, "Since I have had opportunity, by reading and discourse, to look into that action for which these men suffer, I could never see that it was justifiable."

The Act of Indemnity, in which Whalley and Goffe were excepted absolutely as to life and estate, reached Massachusetts in November. It produced excitement and alarm; but was met by the members of the General Court with a divided feeling; some being inclined to protect the exiles at every hazard; a few doubtful whether it might not be their duty to secure their persons; and others disposed to give them opportunity to escape, so far as it could be done without openly conflicting with the royal government. On the 21st of February, 1661, the Governor summoned the Assistants to advise him as to the manner of dealing with them; but they came to no agreement. Four days after, the refugees themselves relieved the Magistrates from embarrassment by privately leaving Cambridge under an escort furnished by their friends, and making their way to New Haven.

On their journey thither, which occupied nine days, they stopped for a short time at Hartford, where they met with a kind reception from John Winthrop, Jr., Governor of the Colony of Connecticut, or Hartford, which had not at that time been consolidated with the Colony of New Haven. It is quite certain that their coming to New Haven was not wholly unexpected; at least by the Rev. John Davenport, one of the noble founders of that Colony, and one of the ablest and most influential of the ministers of New England,—who, it will be remembered, in his old age removed to Boston and became a minister of the First

Church.[1] About the time of their arrival, as if to predispose the minds of the people in their favor, he preached a sermon which is still extant in print, in the course of which he gave utterance to these bold and, under the circumstances, "almost treasonable" words: —

> "Withhold not countenance, entertainment, and protection from the people of God — whom men may call fools and fanatics — if any such come to you from other countries, as from France or England, or any other place. Be not forgetful to entertain strangers. Remember those that are in bonds as bound with them. Hide the outcasts, bewray not him that wandereth. Let mine outcasts dwell with thee. Be thou a covert to them from the face of the spoiler."

The Regicides themselves had special reason to expect friendly treatment in New Haven. It had long been the home of a sister of General Whalley, the amiable wife of Rev. William Hooke, for twelve years Mr. Davenport's colleague; and William Jones, whose father suffered death as one of the King's judges, had recently come from England, and taken up his residence there. Their reception was as cordial as they could have desired. They took up their abode in Mr. Davenport's house, and for several weeks held intercourse with the ministers and magistrates, with little or no reserve. Meanwhile the King's Proclamation for their arrest as traitors and murderers had been received at Boston, and news of its arrival followed them to New Haven. Aware of their peril and to mislead any who might be sent to apprehend them, they removed in open daylight to Milford, and there made themselves known; but returned covertly at night, and for more than a week lay secreted in Mr. Davenport's cellar, where what purports to have been their hiding-place is still shown.

But a more serious danger was imminent. One Captain Breedon, having carried to England information that he had seen

[1] In a letter from Davenport to John Winthrop, Jr., dated the eleventh day of August, 1660 (it will be remembered that the Regicides arrived in Boston, July 27th), he says, "The two gentlemen of great quality arrived in the Bay are Commissary General Whalley, Sister Hooke's brother, and his son in law who is with him is Colonel Goffe: boath godly men, and escaped persute in Engl. narrowly. I hope to see them here after the Commissioners are gone, if not before. I might hope to see them before, *upon my letter*, but I defer that on purpose that your chamber may be free for your reception and Mrs. Winthrope's when the Commissioners meete." The letter may be seen in Mass. Hist. Coll., vol. x., series 3.

them at Boston, a royal order was despatched to the Colonial government peremptorily demanding their arrest. Endicott, to whom it was transmitted, could do no less than appear to interest himself to put it in execution.[1] Without taking the advice of his Council, and, as it seems, not in full accordance with the feeling of some of the Deputies, he gave Commission to two young men who had recently come from England for purposes of trade, Thomas Kirk and Thomas Kellond, to search throughout Massachusetts; and furnished them with letters to the Governors of the other Colonies.

These two young royalists, strangers in the country, and sure to excite observation wherever they should go, started immediately on the track of the fugitives. At Hartford Governor Winthrop informed them that they had not long before passed out of that town on their way to New Haven. The pursuers, taking the same direction, on reaching Guilford, stopped at the residence of the Deputy Governor Leete. They showed him

1 Regard for truth compels the remark that there is reason to suspect the sincerity of more than one of the magistrates and principal men of the Colonies of Massachusetts and New Haven in their dealing with the Home government, and in their statements, respecting the Regicides. Colonel Temple, in a letter dated Boston, 20th August, 1661, to "Mr. Secretary Morice, about Goffe and Whalley," asserts, it may be with truth, that he "had used all the diligence and industry he was capable of in endeavors to discover and apprehend the Regicides"; but says that he "had been informed by Mr. Pinchin (Pynchon) and Captain Lord, residents of the Southern parts, that they are concealed there," and that he has "joyned himself" with them "in a secret designe, only knowne to us three, to secure their persons." It is possible that Mr. Pynchon was in earnest, but if he had been really so, it is not easy to understand how he could have failed to discover their place of concealment at Hadley, so near to his own residence.

Governor Bradstreet writes to the Lords of his Majesty's Privy Council, Boston, May 16, 1680, "I understand there have been misinformacons presented to his Majesty, and amongst others that the Inhabitants here have protected the murtherers of his Majesties Royall Father, in Contempt of his Majesties proclamation of the 6th of June 1660, which is manifestly untrue."

John Davenport writes to Temple, "19 day 6 m. 1661," that he had sent an Apology to the Deputy Governor of Massachusetts to be communicated to the General Court, in which he "will finde his innocency in reference to the two Colonels, and that of the this poore Coloney, of our Governor and Majestrates, who wanted neither will nor Industery to have served his Majtie in apprehending the 2 Collonells, but were Prevented and Hindered by god's overruilling Providence, which withheld them that they could not exciqute their true Purpose therein. I believe if his Majestie Rightly understood the Curcumstances of the Event he would not be displeased with our Majistrates, but to accquiesce in the Providence of the most high." (Mass. Hist. Coll. 3d series, vol. xviii. pp. 328–9.)

their warrant and demanded to be furnished with horses for their journey and "aid and power to search and apprehend" the refugees. A person told them that the Colonels were secreted in Mr. Davenport's house, "and that without all question Deputy Leete knew as much."[1] He put them off on various pretences till after the Sabbath, which occurred on the day succeeding the interview. Meanwhile a messenger was secretly despatched to give timely warning at New Haven. On Monday the two messengers set out on their journey; the Governor following them at a more moderate pace. On their arrival at the capital, he received them at the Court Chamber; when they informed him that they had reason to believe that those whom they sought were concealed in New Haven, and required assistance for their arrest. He replied that he "did not believe the story; that he could not and would not make them magistrates." They charged him with despising his Majesty's authority, and with his willingness to connive at the escape of his traitorous subjects. He then left them, and after a long consultation with the magistrates, broke up the Council; declaring that they "neither would nor could do any thing until they had called a General Court of the freemen."[2]

Thwarted at every point by the magistrates, whom they found, as they said, "obstinate and pertinacious in their contempt of his Majesty," and, in all probability, purposely put upon a false scent, the messengers started off for New Netherlands; and after a fruitless search returned by water to Boston.

There can be no doubt that intelligence of the appointment of these Commissioners, and of all their movements, had been secretly conveyed to the fugitives; for before they had left Boston, they had removed from the house of Mr. Davenport to that of William Jones, afterwards Deputy Governor; and during the conference with Governor Leete at Guilford, they were conveyed to a secluded mill, two miles to the north-west of New Haven. From thence, after two nights, they were conducted to a spot called Hatchet Harbor; and shortly after, to a rude covert of large stones on the eastern side, and near the summit of West Rock, still nearer to the town; "being supplied with food from a

1 Stiles's Judges. Hutchinson's Coll. Dr. Palfrey's Hist. of New England.

2 Report of Kellond and Kirk in Hutch. Coll. p. 334.

lonely farm-house in the neighborhood." Having remained in their hiding-place a few months, occasionally showing themselves in New Haven and elsewhere, from the honorable motive of relieving Mr. Davenport of the suspicion of concealing them, they took shelter in a house in Milford, where they stayed for two years in entire seclusion. At length, just as they were beginning to enjoy a feeling of comparative security, and to indulge themselves with occasional intercourse with their worthy neighbors, the tidings reached them of the expected arrival at Boston of Commissioners from England with extraordinary powers, whose coming might subject them, and their protectors also, to new dangers. This intelligence caused them once more to make a hasty retreat to their long since abandoned cave. But being discovered by a party of Indians, hunting in the woods, who might be induced by the offer of large rewards to betray them, they took their departure for the secluded town of Hadley, then far in the wilderness on the north-western frontier of New England, travelling only by night. Here a shelter had been prepared for them, under the roof of the worthy minister of the place, the Rev. John Russell. A considerable addition had recently been made to his house, which was now large and double, containing many rooms and closets. In one of the latter in the garret, having doors opening into two chambers, the floor boards could be slipped aside so as to admit of access to a dark under closet, near the old-fashioned chimney; from which, perhaps, there was originally a passage-way into the cellar. To this secure hiding-place they could retreat, in case a search should be made of the premises.

They reached Hadley on the thirteenth of October, 1664, no one in the place being aware of their arrival except the family of Mr. Russell, and one or two trusty persons among the principal inhabitants, from whom they received the kindest attention. They were enabled, through safe hands, to keep up a correspondence with their friends in Old and New England. Their letters dated from "Ebenezer," the name which they gave to their several places of refuge, were often conveyed to Boston by the representative from Hadley, Peter Tilton, — those for England being intrusted, as we have found, to Rev. Increase Mather, who transmitted them under cover in his own handwriting to some confidential correspondent who could forward them to their destination. Goffe wrote, occasionally, to Mather himself, upon religious and political topics, always expressing the highest esteem for his person and a deep sense of obligation for his favors.[1] They appear to have been kept well informed of all important public events in both countries, and to have been abundantly supplied with the means of subsistence. There is reason to believe that they were occasionally visited in their retreat by such men as Governor Leverett, Mr. Richard Saltonstall,[2] and their old friend Mr. Davenport.

It is certainly a matter of surprise that their secret could have been so well kept. The people of Hadley appear to have been ignorant of their residence among them, and it is probable that very few persons, even among the most intimate associates of their protectors, had any knowledge of their place of concealment. Governor Bradstreet in a letter to Randolph, in

1 Among the correspondents of Goffe was Rev. William Hooke. Several of his letters may be seen in the Mather Papers. He writes under the signature D. G. Goffe's wife and children were for a time in his family.

He was Master of Arts at Oxford in 1623, and after a short ministry in Devonshire, being persecuted for non-conformity, sought refuge in New England. He was minister of Taunton in 1637, soon after the settlement of that town, and subsequently settled at New Haven, as Mr. Davenport's colleague. After the elevation of Cromwell — cousin of his wife, who was Whalley's sister — to the Protectorate, and when his brother-in-law Whalley had been elevated to high office, he went back to his native country, not because he loved New England less, but Old England more. He probably thought that he could serve the land of his adoption better at the Court of England, and close to the ear of its powerful ruler. He embarked for home in 1656, and was received by Cromwell with such favor as to be appointed one of his domestic chaplains in the royal palace of Whitehall.

Several letters from his wife, Jane Hooke, are printed in the Mather Papers. She refers to the Regicides, to whom as well as to several poor ministers, she often sent contributions of money and clothing. Her correspondence proves her to have been a truly devout, amiable, and charitable woman. She deserves to be remembered among the benefactors of New England. The only fault to be found with her letters is the wretched spelling and punctuation.

2 Richard Saltonstall, Jr., son of Sir Richard, came to New England, with his father, in 1630, was admitted freeman of Massachusetts, Oct. 18, 1631, and the next year went back to England. He returned to Massachusetts in 1635, was Representative in 1636, and Assistant in 1637. He sailed again for England in 1649; again came back, and again sailed in 1672. He was once more in Massachusetts in 1680, and made Assistant; but left for England in 1682, and died in April, 1694. He left fifty pounds in the hands of Edward Collins, of Charlestown, for the Regicides, when he went to England in 1672. See the correspondence on this subject in the Mather Papers, pp. 134, 135.

1684,[1] says, that "Whalley and Goff were never hid or secured here, that ever I could heare of." It would seem not only that no one was willing to betray them, but that every one purposely endeavored not to know where they were. Such tender compassion, and such delicate and even sacred consideration for these hunted exiles, whose greatest crime was a desperate blow at oppression, and who had confidingly thrown themselves upon their protection, are among those noble traits in the character of our Fathers, which claim honorable commemoration from their descendants, and should never fail — as, thank God, they seldom have failed — to excite their generous emulation.

Several letters which passed between Goffe and his wife, the daughter of Whalley, were long ago printed by Governor Hutchinson; and others, found among the Mather Papers, have been published in the last volume of our Historical Collections. It is impossible for any who has a heart, to read them without almost tearful emotion. They are full of the tenderest expressions of endearment for each other, mingled with a sublime trust in Providence, and the most humble and docile submission. While they give evidence of bitter and unintermitted sorrow and loneliness, they betray no tremulousness of faith, no lack of fortitude, no disposition to repine. No token that love could desire of affection and longing is wanting in the language of either, and yet not a word passes from one to the other to weaken or dispirit, but rather to sustain and encourage. They abound in quotations from the Scriptures, especially from the prophetical writings, which they applied to themselves and their cause in a manner that strikes the modern reader as extravagant, and superstitious, if not hypocritical and almost absurd; but which was entirely in keeping with the custom of the class of religionists to which they belonged, and was adopted by themselves in perfect faith and guileless sincerity. They addressed each other, respectively, as son and mother, under the names of Walter and Frances Goldsmith. We recognize in him and Whalley the distinctive traits of the Puritans, — an impassioned piety, "a lofty air of manhood, deep thought and steady enthusi-

[1] Mather Papers, p. 533.

asm, — those same principles of stern fidelity and self-command which ennobled the better days of the Roman republic, and have made the men of every after era appear childish and frivolous in comparison." And in her we are struck with those qualities which every unprejudiced student of history admires and reverences in the characters of the Republican matrons of England. Making a slight deduction for a few peculiarities derived from their religious associations, we believe, that "no age has produced a more worthy counterpart to the Valerias and Portias of antiquity. In their high-minded feeling of patriotism and public honor, combined with the most dutiful and devoted conjugal attachment, their kindness and hospitality, their domestic virtue, their calm dignity, endurance, and self devotion, there is something that makes the Corinnes and Héloïses appear small and insignificant."[1]

If we may believe a tradition which has come down through the family of Governor Leverett, and which there is no good reason for discrediting, an opportunity was at length offered to the refugees, during their residence at Hadley, not only to repay the hospitality of their protectors, but to bring into action once more, though but for a moment, their military skill and prowess.

In the summer of 1676, while King Philip's war was raging, a powerful force of Indians made a sudden assault upon Hadley. The inhabitants at the time were assembled in their meeting-house observing a day of fasting and prayer; but, in apprehension of an attack, they had taken their muskets with them to the house of God. While they were engaged in their devotions, the younger of the solitary captives, who, perhaps, taking advantage of the absence of observers to enjoy a brief interval of comparative freedom, may have been seated at an open window, or walking near the house, discovered the approach of the wily foe, and hastened to give the alarm. With the air of one accustomed to command, he hastily drew up the little band of villagers in the most approved military order, put himself at their head, and by his own ardor and energy inspired them with such confidence, that, rushing upon the swarming savages, they succeeded, with the loss of only two or three men, in

[1] Jeffrey, Edinb. Rev., October, 1808. Review of Mrs. Hutchinson's Memoirs of her husband, Colonel Hutchinson.

driving them back into the wilderness. But when the confusion of the fight was over, the mysterious stranger had disappeared. It is hardly a matter of surprise that, in that superstitious age, there should have been some among the people who, in utter bewilderment as to the person of their deliverer and in devout gratitude for their strange preservation, should have regarded him as an angel sent from heaven with a divine commission for their rescue.[1]

General Whalley died at Hadley, probably in the year 1676, and was buried behind the front cellar-wall of Mr. Russell's house, where his bones have since been found. There is a tradition that General Goffe, after the decease of his father-in-law, disappeared from Hadley, going "westward towards Virginia," and ended his career in total obscurity. There are also some who insist, that though he may have died at Hadley, his remains, together with those of Whalley, were removed to New Haven, and deposited in two graves by the side of that of their fellow-exile Colonel Dixwell. To us it appears more probable that he ended his days in the quiet and hospitable place which must have seemed to him more like home than any other spot in this far country, and that beneath the same friendly soil on which he had found protection in life, his body — worn out with age and care, and laid down in secrecy and decent sorrow by the hands that had so long ministered to its comfort — has found even unto this day an undisturbed resting-place.[2]

1 There are several versions of this story. They differ somewhat in regard to details. That which I have followed seems as likely to be in accordance with the facts as either of the others. Holland's Hist. Western Mass.; Huntington's Cent. Address; Sir Walter Scott's Pev. of the Peak, &c.

2 There is a sentence in a letter from Goffe to Increase Mather, dated the 8th of September, 1676, in the Mather Papers, in Mass. Hist. Coll., vol. viii. 4th series, p. 158, which might lead to the inference that shortly before that time the writer had removed from Hadley to a new place of concealment. He says, "*I was greatly behoulding to Mr. Noell for his assistance in my remove to this town.*" This could hardly relate to the journey of the Regicides to Hadley so long before as 1664. Besides, had Whalley been with Goffe at the time of the removal to which he refers, he would not have said "*my* removal," but *our*. Although this sentence had not attracted my particular notice at the time of editing the Mather Papers, or when this lecture was written, it has since impressed me with a belief that after the death of Whalley — which for several reasons had been assigned to the year 1676 — Goffe *did* leave Hadley for some other town, — whether New Haven, or not, I know of no means of ascertaining.

In 1665, the year after their arrival at Hadley, Whalley and Goffe were joined by that old companion in arms and in the trial of the King, a brief sketch of whose life in England has already been given, — Colonel John Dixwell. When or how he had come to this country from Germany, his first place of exile, is not known. We can readily imagine with what strong emotions the exiles met, and with what deep and untiring interest they talked over, during the three or four years they remained in each other's neighborhood, the great events in which they had participated. At the end of that period, Dixwell removed to New Haven. As he had never been traced to America there was in his case less reason for fearing discovery. Assuming the name of Davids and carefully concealing his true character from the public, who regarded him as, for some unknown reason, obnoxious to the English government, he established his residence in a retired part of the town, and soon secured the respect of the inhabitants as a grave and quiet gentleman. He married twice; the first wife dying a few weeks after their nuptials. By the second he had several children; from one of whom are descended the highly respectable Boston family which bears the name of Dixwell. He early communicated to two or three ministers and a few other friends the secret of his history, and before his death took care to demonstrate his true name and character by his last will and other certified documents. He died in March, 1689, just before the welcome tidings of the downfall of the Stuart dynasty, which would have caused his aged heart to leap for joy, had reached America. A plain gravestone, with the simple inscription, "J. D. Esq, Deceased March ye 19th, in ye 82^{d} year of his age 1688–9," marked the place of his interment, in that part of the public square of New Haven which is flanked by the halls of Yale College, and which was the ancient burial-place of the town. In 1821, when the monuments in this ground were removed to the new cemetery in the north-west part of the city, this grave was left undisturbed. In 1849, his descendants, with a laudable feeling of veneration for their distinguished ancestor, by permission of the city authorities, caused a stately and graceful monument, with an appropriate inscription, to be erected to his memory; which is invariably pointed out by the citizens of New Haven to the stranger as an object of local pride, of antiquarian curiosity, and of universal interest.[1] It is worthy of notice that in one of the last papers subscribed by his own hand

[1] The monument is of marble, about six feet high, having inscriptions on its four sides. That on the east side is as follows: —

JOHN DIXWELL,
a zealous patriot — a sincere Christian,
an honest man,
he was faithful to duty
through good and through evil report
and having lost
fortune, position and home
in the cause of his country,
and of human rights,
found shelter and sympathy
here,
among the fathers of New England.
His descendants
have erected this monument
as a tribute of respect to his memory
and as a grateful record
of the generous protection
extended to him,
by the early inhabitants
of *New Haven.*
Erected A.D. 1849.

The inscription on the north side is as follows: —

J. D. ESQ,
DECEASED — MARCH YE
19TH, IN YE 82D YEAR OF
HIS AGE 1688-9.

Copied from the old gravestone.

Inscription on the west side: —

Here rest the remains of
JOHN DIXWELL, ESQ,
of the Priory of Folkestone
in the county of Kent, England,
of a family long prominent in Kent,
and Warwickshire, and himself possessing
large estates and much influence
in his country, he espoused the popular cause
in the revolution of 1640.
Between 1640 and 1660
he was colonel in the army,
an active member of four parliaments.
Thrice in the council of state
and one of the high court which tried
and condemned *King Charles the First.*
At the restoration of the monarchy,
he was compelled to leave his country;
and after a brief residence in Germany,
Came to *New Haven,*
and here lived in seclusion,
but enjoying the esteem and friendship
of the most worthy citizens,
till his death in 1688-9.

On the south side is the Dixwell coat of arms, with the motto,
ESSE QUAM VIDERI.

and placed upon record in the probate office, occurs this emphatic statement of his unabated attachment to the cause for which he had suffered, and his unshaken confidence in the justice of his acts in its behalf, — "Being confident that the Lord will appear for his people and the *good old cause for which I suffer*, and that there will be those in power again who will relieve the injured and oppressed."

We have been reviewing the history of eccentric but heroic men. Though we cannot justify the act for which they suffered, yet who of us is disposed to charge them with the intention, or even the consciousness, of crime? Nay, more, who of us can even wonder that, entranced as they were by the beautiful vision of universal liberty under the sceptre of Christ, ever floating before their imagination, and seeming to beckon to them from the far distant future, — which to the eye of their strong faith appeared so close at hand, — they should have rushed forward to realize it, forgetful of the lessons of history, regardless of precedent, scornful of danger, breaking through even lawful restraints, hewing down with sword and axe every obstruction that blocked the way, — thrones, tyrants, armies, hierarchies, constitutions, — pressing on with a terrible earnestness and a frenzied enthusiasm?

If there were any gigantic hypocrites, who had joined their ranks to make them their tools, to turn their nobler rage and invincible energy to the service of their towering ambition, the men whose lives we have been describing were themselves too sincere and self-devoting to connive at such deceit, or even to be suspicious of such motives. They never for one moment wavered in their loyalty to what they assuredly believed was the most sacred and glorious cause that could be committed by Heaven to human hearts and hands. To the day of their death they never faltered in the conviction that what they had done had received the august sanction of their God, and what they had suffered, they had suffered as martyrs to conscience, justice, and liberty.

It would be presumptuous and ungrateful in us who are enjoying the priceless blessings of freedom at the cost of others' sacrifices, — of the heroism, the sufferings, the virtues, yes, and the faults of our ancestors, — who are too luxuriously revelling in the harvest which they sowed in agony and watered with their blood, — to pass a cool and censorious judgment upon men like these. They should be tried only by a tribunal of their peers. Happy will it be for us if the worst fault that can be charged against us by the pen of man, or by the Recording Angel, shall be an overmastering hatred of oppression, and a too enthusiastic and impatient endeavor to hasten the fulfilment, before His own appointed time, of the sure and glorious promises of God.[1]

Our subject involves the interesting question of the attitude of New England towards the parent country during the eventful period to which it relates.

It is certain that the leading men in the colonies were not only deeply interested in the political movements on the opposite shore, but that they had no inconsiderable influence upon the party with which they were in sympathy. Besides the fact of their intimate personal relations and common interests, there is sufficient evidence that they were in frequent correspondence with the Republicans in England, and that their assistance with

1 There are traditionary anecdotes concerning Whalley and Goffe to which I have paid no attention, for most of them bear internal evidence of untruth; and with regard to the rest there is not sufficient ground to receive them into veritable history. There are also traditions that two or three other Regicide Judges were secreted in New England, in different localities, but they are undoubtedly erroneous. It is possible that there were several refugees from England, for other offences than connection with the King's death, who found shelter in our forests. There is a plausible account of a person who may have been an exile for some political cause, given in a speech by Rev. Frederic A. Whitney, at a dinner on the occasion of the celebration, in 1840, of the two hundredth anniversary of the incorporation of the town of Quincy, Mass. Mr. Whitney says, —

"Some years since I gathered from the lips of an aged citizen of Quincy, who was remarkable for his retentive memory and exceeding accuracy in all matters of fact, this tradition. His childhood he told me had been with those who had conversed with this lonely exile. Within his own memory there had stood on a hillock the humble abode of the old refugee. Here, as said tradition, under the assumed name of Revel, he lived and died; and his funeral was honored by the attendance of his Excellency the Provincial Governor, and of distinguished men from the neighboring metropolis."

Those who are curious in regard to such traditions will find many of them referred to in "Stiles's History of the Judges," together with much authentic information. Though over enthusiastic in his admiration of the Regicides, and extravagant in his attempts to justify and glorify their treatment of the King, and withal, somewhat credulous, the work of President Stiles shows ability, learning, and minute research, and is the principal source to which all who treat our subject are indebted for their material.

the pen, if not with the sword, was much relied upon and solicited. The Independents — who at the breaking out of the civil war were a small though vigorous minority struggling for existence, but who at its close held the destiny of the kingdom in their hands — early looked to New England not only for the ablest advocacy of their principles, but for the strong encouragement which the successful practical exemplification of them afforded.

In 1642, a letter signed by about forty persons, Peers, Commoners, and ministers, — Cromwell among the number, — was addressed to Cotton of Boston, Hooker of Hartford, and Davenport of New Haven, urging them to come over with all possible speed to give their help "for settling the affairs of the Church." Although neither of these ministers was persuaded to respond to the call in person, yet the writings of Cotton and other of the New-England clergy were published and circulated in England, and contributed a powerful element in support of the religious politics of their friends.

A large number of the most distinguished men in the colonies, — among them John Leverett, Edward Winslow, and Edward Hopkins, afterwards governors, respectively, of Massachusetts, Plymouth, and Connecticut, — and many ministers, subsequently went over to England to take a civil or military part in the ranks of the revolutionary party.[1] The sentiments of one, at least, of the most eminent and useful of the New-England clergymen, whose praise is on all our lips, the Apostle Eliot, were in entire accordance with those by which the Regicides professed to have been actuated. Goffe himself might have been the author of such sentences as the following, contained in an Epistle addressed "To the Chosen, Holy and Faithful, who manage the Wars of the Lord against Antichrist in Great Britain:" —

"The prayers, the expectation and faith of the saints in the Prophecies and Promises of Holy Scripture are daily sounding in the ears of the Lord for the downfall of Antichrist and with him all humane Powers, Politics, Dominions and Governments; and in the room thereof we wait for the coming of the Kingdom of the Lord Jesus. . . . Much is spoken of the rightful Heir of the Crown of England, and the injustice of casting out the right Heir: but Christ is the only right Heir of the Crown of

[1] Dr. Palfrey's Hist. of New England.

England, and of all other nations also; and he is now come to take possession of his Kingdom, making England first in that blessed work of setting up the Kingdom of the Lord Jesus: and in order thereunto he hath cast down not only the miry Religion and Government of Antichrist, but also the form of Civil Government which did stick fast to it."

This treatise was, by the author's permission, published in England in 1659, though written some six or seven years before, under the title of the "Christian Commonwealth." After the restoration of the monarchy, the magistrates of the colony, hearing that the book had excited much notice and given great offence, found it "full of seditious principles and notions in regard to all established Governments in the Christian world, and specially against the Government established in their native country;" but deferred proceedings against it in order that the author might have opportunity in the mean time to make a public recantation. This he did, "sincerely." The magistrates accepted his acknowledgment, and ordered the book to be suppressed.[1]

If the testimony of a witness in the trial of Hugh Peters for complicity in the murder of the King is to be credited, the Agency on which he was sent to England by Massachusetts, together with Thomas Welde of Roxbury, and William Hibbens

[1] Mass. Hist. Coll., 3d Series, vol. ix., where a reprint of the Christian Commonwealth may be seen; Palfrey's Hist. of New England; Chalmers's State Papers, &c.

"*Mr. Eliot's acknowledgment word for word.*

"Boston, this 24 of ye 3^{d} mo. 1661.

"Vnderstanding by an act of the honored Council, that there is offence taken at a booke, published in England by others, the copie whereof was sent ouer by myself about nine or tenn yeares since, and that the further consideration thereof is commended to this honnored Generall Court now sitting at Boston, Upon pervsall thereof I doe judge myself to haue offended & in way satisfaction, not only to the Authority of this Jurisdiction, but also vnto any others, that shall take notice thereof, I doe hereby acknowledge to this honored Court.

"Such expressions as doe too manifestly scandalize the Gouernment of England by King, Lords and Commons, as Antichristian, and justify the late Innovators, I doe sincerely beare testimony against, and acknowledge it to be not only a lawfull but an eminent forme of Gouernment.

"2. All formes of Ciuil Gouernment deduced from Scripture either expressly or by just consequence, I acknowledge to be of God & to be subjected vnto for Conscience sake.

"And Whatsoeuer is in the whole Epistle or booke inconsisting herewith I doe at once for all cordially disoune. JOHN ELIOT."

of Boston, in 1641, was not without reference to the promotion of "the interests of reformation by stirring up the war." There are circumstances also connected with that mission, besides the well-known conduct of Peters, which go to confirm such a suspicion. Dr. Palfrey intimates that "it is not owing to accident that the instructions to the Agents have not been preserved." All we know concerning those instructions is from the cautious language of Winthrop, who says, amongst other things, that they were sent to "congratulate the happy success there," of the Parliament in its early struggles with the King. The manuscript papers of Welde, of which a copy is in the Library of Harvard College, would lead to the conclusion that the ostensible objects of the Agents, especially of Hugh Peters, were not their only, if they were their principal, purpose.[1]

The tyranny of Charles I., and the hierarchy which was allied with it, were as hateful to the majority of the colonists here as to the friends of liberty at home. They heard with undisguised gratification of the first vigorous and promising efforts of the Parliament in their armed resistance to the encroachments of the Throne. To prevent the organization of a party in the royal interest, they passed an order that "what person soever shall by word, writing, or action, endeavor to disturb our peace, directly or indirectly, by drawing a party under pretence that he is for the King of England against the Parliament, shall be accounted as an offender of a high nature against this Commonwealth, and to be proceeded with either capitally or otherwise, according to the quality or degree of their offence."

But notwithstanding their sympathies were so strongly with the Commons, they were more than all jealous of their own political rights, and scrupulously careful not to compromise their independence by any appearance of subserviency to the Parliament, any more than to the King. When Charles I. had been brought to the block, no New-England colony expressed its formal approval of the act; nor have we any ground for believing that it met with general favor. It is probable that while some of the more passionate republicans were gratified, and justified the extreme measure, the more wise and considerate spirits regarded it with disapprobation and apprehension. When a Puritan

[1] See note on p. 584, vol. i., of Dr. Palfrey's Hist. of N. E.

Parliament came into power, Massachusetts "carefully abstained from any such solicitation for its favor as could be construed into an admission of its authority." When England made Cromwell virtually a monarch, she preserved a steady silence. When his son Richard was elevated to the Protectorate, no public notice was taken of the event, although the Council of State sent an order for his proclamation. And when Charles II. was restored to the throne, although intelligence of the fact reached Boston in July, 1660, no proclamation was made till August of the following year. It was the settled policy of our Fathers to act with a cautious neutrality, as it was from the first their sacred purpose to lay the foundations of an independent State, as far and as fast as it could be done consistently with a prudent regard to their temporary safety and interest, and a formal respect to their colonial obligations.

In giving a safe asylum to the Judges who had condemned and executed their lawful, but lawless King, they acted from the promptings of a compassionate and magnanimous spirit, which though it may have led them to violate the letter of their political bond, impelled them to the performance of that higher duty to humanity to which neither their hearts nor their consciences would suffer them to be faithless; and for their generous and resolute fidelity to which we are constrained to give them our honor and our love.

THE FIRST CHARTER

AND

THE EARLY RELIGIOUS LEGISLATION

OF MASSACHUSETTS.

By JOEL PARKER.

THE FIRST CHARTER

AND

THE EARLY RELIGIOUS LEGISLATION

OF MASSACHUSETTS.

IT has been regarded as a subject of complacency, that we know our origin, and can trace our history; that while other communities seek their early history in the mists of conjecture, or the myths of tradition, we can trace our own, in that documentary evidence which gives the greatest degree of certainty.

To a considerable extent, this is true. And yet there are particulars, essential to a right understanding of the principles upon which the original settlement of Massachusetts was made, respecting which there has been, and now is, such a diversity and discrepancy of opinion, after all the discussions of two hundred years, and after the labors of the Massachusetts Historical Society, for three quarters of a century, in collecting documents in regard to the subject, that the Ends and Aims of the first settlers of Massachusetts furnish the leading topic of the present course of lectures, in the hope that the errors which have prevailed on that subject may be corrected, and the purposes and objects of the founders of the Commonwealth may be more clearly and generally understood.

It is not surprising that there should be misconception upon this subject, when it is considered that the materials of the history of that time are widely dispersed, and often contradictory; malice manufacturing misrepresentations, prejudice engendering error, and mistake and carelessness causing fact and fiction to be so intermingled, that it is not seldom that the discovery of truth is a laborious task.

How many persons there are in the community, who, at this day, suppose that the celebrated so-called " Blue Laws of Connecticut" are the veritable legislation of the Puritan Colony there! The fact that one of them purports to provide, that "No one shall run on the Sabbath day, or walk in his garden or elsewhere, except reverently to and from meeting;" and another that "No woman shall kiss her child on the Sabbath, or on a fasting day," — might lead to a doubt;[1] but all this is deemed consistent with the spirit of the time, enforcing a strict observance of that holy day.

How few persons know that many of these "Blue Laws" are but the jokes of the wits and humorists of a subsequent age, for the purpose of sport and ridicule, having no enduring existence until Dr. Samuel Peters collecting, and probably adding to them, inserted, in what purported to be "A General History of Connecticut," a sketch, as he said, of laws made by the independent Dominion of New Haven, denominated "Blue Laws" by the neighboring colonies, and never suffered to be printed![2] The whole work has been shown to be so untruthful that the appearance of these so-called "Blue Laws" there, is of itself *primâ facie* evidence that they are fictitious.[3]

If we consider what a vast mass of contradictory material has accumulated within the last decade, to perplex the future historian of the late war, we shall cease to wonder that much may be done, even at the present day, by a diligent student of history, to elucidate the ends and aims of the Puritan Fathers of 1630.

It is because of the dispersion of material, and of the contradictory opinions which have been entertained respecting the rights, objects, and purposes of the founders of the Commonwealth, that I have deemed it not only a duty, but a pleasure, to answer the call made upon me to add a small contribution, such as it may be, to the present attempt of the Historical Society to illustrate the early history of Massachusetts.

The subject assigned to me is "the Religious Legislation of Massachusetts," — involving, of course, the inquiry how far any

[1] Another may furnish Congress with a model of brevity, in making up an "omnibus bill," near the close of a session: "No one shall read Common Prayer, keep Christmas or Saints days, make minced pies, dance, play cards, or play on any instrument of music, except the drum, trumpet, and jews-harp."

[2] See Gen. Hist. Conn. 63.

[3] See Prof. Kingsley's Hist. Discourse at New Haven, 1838. pp. 35, 56, 83, 104.

such legislation was lawful under the original charter, — and this, in turn, depending upon the question, to what extent the grantees had any right of legislation, properly so called, by the provisions of that instrument.

Upon this question the opinions have been much at variance, according as the charter has been regarded as instituting a corporation for trading purposes, or as the constitution and foundation of a government. That the grantees who settled here regarded it as the latter, and acted upon that construction, is apparent from their action at the outset, and throughout. But those opposed to them, contended at the time, that the former was its true intent and meaning, and historians have perpetuated that opinion. Minot, in his History of Massachusetts, says, —

> "This charter, from the omissions of several powers necessary to the future situation of the Colony, shows us how inadequate the ideas of the parties were to the important consequences which were about to follow from such an act. The Governor, with the assistants and freemen of the company, it is true, were empowered to make all laws, not repugnant to those of England; but the power of imposing fines, mulcts, imprisonment, or other lawful correction, is expressly given according to the course of other corporations in the realm; and the general circumstances of the settlement, and the practice of the times, can leave us no doubt that this body-politic was viewed rather as a trading company residing within the kingdom, than, what it very soon became, a foreign government exercising all the essentials of sovereignty over its subjects." [1]

He proceeds to speak of divers laws as having been made by the grantees, of their own motion and without any authority under the charter, and, after referring to the force of habits and prejudices, adds, —

> "But such was the force of these habits and prejudices, and so prone are mankind to place unlimited confidence in their government, when unprovoked by the usurpation and abuse of power, that the people of Massachusetts may be said to have submitted to a system of laws, by which the freedom of action was abridged, and to have voluntarily yoked themselves to an ecclesiastical authority, by which the rights of conscience lost, for a time, the very principles that their emigration had avowed."

Bancroft, who aspires to be the historian of the United States, writes, —

[1] See Minot, p. 19.

"The charter, which bears the signature of Charles I.,[1] and which was cherished for more than half a century as the most precious boon, established a corporation, like other corporations within the realm. The associates were constituted a body-politic by the name of the Governor and Company of the Massachusetts Bay in New England. The administration of its affairs was intrusted to a governor, deputy, and eighteen assistants, who were to be annually elected by the stockholders or members of the corporation. Four times a year, or oftener if desired, a general assembly of the freemen was to be held; and to these assemblies, which were invested with the necessary powers of legislation, inquest, and superintendence, the most important affairs were referred. No provision required the assent of the King to render the acts of the body valid; in his eye it was but a trading corporation, not a civil government; its doings were esteemed as indifferent as those of any guild or company in England; and if powers of jurisdiction in America were conceded, it was only from the nature of the business in which the stockholders were to engage." — "The charter designedly granted great facilities for colonization. It allowed the company to transport to its American territory any persons, whether English or foreigners, who would go willingly, would become lieges of the English king, and were not restrained 'by especial name.' It empowered, but it did not require the Governor to administer the oaths of supremacy and allegiance; yet the charter, according to the strict rules of legal interpretation, was far from conceding to the patentees the privilege of freedom of worship. Not a single line alludes to such a purpose; nor can it be implied by a reasonable construction from any clause."

He says further, — "The political condition of the colonists was not deemed by King Charles a subject worthy of his consideration. Full legislative and executive authority was conferred not on the emigrants, but on the company, of which the emigrants could not be active members, so long as the charter of the corporation remained in England. The associates in London were to establish ordinances, to settle forms of government, to name all necessary officers, to prescribe their duties, and to establish a criminal code. Massachusetts was not erected into a province, to be governed by laws of its own enactment; it was reserved for the corporation to decide what degree of civil rights its colonists should enjoy."

Again, — "The charter on which the freemen of Massachusetts succeeded in erecting a system of independent representative liberty, did not secure

[1] This, by the way, is a mistake in the outset. Charles Cæsar, the Master in Chancery, before whom Governor Cradock took the oath of office, and whose name is appended to a certificate of that fact, at the bottom of the charter, was not Charles I.

to them a single privilege of self-government; but left them, as the Virginians had been left, without one valuable franchise, at the mercy of a corporation within the realm. This was so evident, that some of those who had already emigrated, clamored that they were become slaves.[1]

"It was equally the right of the corporation to establish the terms on which new members should be admitted to its freedom. Its numbers could be enlarged or changed only by its own consent.

"It was perhaps implied, though it was not expressly required, that the affairs of the company should be administered in England; yet the place for holding the courts was not specially appointed. What if the corporation should vote the emigrants to be freemen, and call a meeting beyond the Atlantic? What if the Governor, deputy, assistants, and freemen should themselves emigrate, and thus break down the distinction between the colony and the corporation?[2] The history of Massachusetts is the counterpart to that of Virginia: the latter obtained its greatest liberty by the abrogation of the charter of its company; the former by a transfer of its charter, and a daring construction of its powers by the successors of the original patentees."[3]

Now I may remark that it is quite possible Charles I. was not very careful to scrutinize the effect of the powers which he assumed to confer by the charter.

The lands granted (with a vast extent of territory besides, claimed by the Crown) were, notwithstanding the glowing accounts of some navigators respecting the fisheries, deemed of such small importance that they came very near falling entirely under the jurisdiction of other governments, from the mere neglect of the English Government to take possession; and so far as any direct independent action of the Crown was concerned, such would have been their fate. The patent to the Great Council of Plymouth, procured by individuals, probably saved them as a British possession.

And along with this supposition of a lack of value in the territory, King Charles could not have been ignorant of the general character, political and religious, of the proposed emigrants, and might well have considered that it was quite immaterial what

1 These were the "old planters," — squatters, before the charter was granted.

2 If they might do so, it would appear that the charter did secure to them some privileges of self-government, and that they were not necessarily at the mercy of a corporation within the realm.

3 See Bancroft, vol. i. pp. 342–345.

powers were given to the grantees, to be exercised on the other side of the Atlantic, if thereby England would be rid of a class of people imbued with notions of republican freedom, and likely to be very troublesome as nonconformists, if they remained there.

If he could have cleared his kingdom of many more of a similar character, by a like process, he would have saved his crown and his life.

On the other hand, it is possible that the grantees were not fully aware of the extent of the powers conferred by the charter as they subsequently construed its provisions; but this admits of grave doubt. We may safely infer that the original draft was made by counsel employed by the applicants, and submitted to the crown lawyers for examination. It is not to be supposed that the crown officers would undertake the duty of preparing a document which had so much of a private character attached to it; and as it bears upon its face evidence that it was very carefully drawn up, apparently, so as to confer power without giving offence, we can hardly make a presumption that none of the grantees understood its full scope and effect. It is quite clear, however, that they did not anticipate such an influx of emigration that the very success of their experiment, so far as population was concerned, should have been its overthrow in some of its most important religious aspects.

But the question is not so much what the King, or other persons, may have supposed respecting the subject, as what provisions were contained in the charter.

Whatever rights the charter purported to grant, vested lawfully in the grantees.

The title to unoccupied lands belonging to Great Britain, whether acquired by conquest or discovery, was vested in the Crown. The right to grant corporate franchises was one of the prerogatives of the King. And the right to institute and to provide for the institution of colonial governments, whether by charter, proprietary grant, or commission, was likewise one of the prerogatives. Parliament had then nothing to do with the organization or government of colonies.

The confirmation, therefore, in the charter, of the grant of the lands from the Council of Plymouth (which derived title from the grant of James I., and which could grant the lands, but could not grant nor assign powers of government), with a new grant, in form, of the same lands, gave to the grantees a title in socage; substantially a fee-simple, except that there was to be a rendition of one-fifth of the gold and silver ores. The grant of corporate powers, in the usual form of grants to private corporations, conferred upon them all the ordinary rights of a private corporation, under which they could dispose of their lands, and transact all business in which the company had a private interest. And the grant of any powers of colonial government, embraced in the charter, was valid and effective to the extent of the powers which were granted, whatever those powers might be; the whole, as against the corporation, being subject to forfeiture for sufficient cause.

The grant and confirmation of the lands, and the grant of mere corporate powers for private purposes, were private rights, which vested in the grantees; and which the King could not divest, except upon some forfeiture regularly enforced. Upon such forfeiture, the corporation would be dissolved, and all of the lands belonging to it would revert, in the nature of an escheat. But this would not affect valid grants previously made by it.

The grant of power to institute a colonial government, being a grant not for private but for public purposes, may have a different consideration. Whether by reason of its connection with the grant of the lands and of ordinary corporate powers, it partook so far of the nature of a private right, that it could not be altered, modified, or revoked, except on forfeiture, enforced by process; or whether this part of the grant had such a public character, that the powers of government were held subject to alteration and amendment;—is hardly open to discussion. At the present day it is held, that municipal corporations, being for public uses and purposes, have no vested private rights in the powers and privileges granted to them, but that they may be changed at the pleasure of the government. That principle seems to be equally applicable to a grant of colonial powers of government; and the better opinion would seem to be, that it was within the legitimate prerogative of the King, at that day, to modify, and even to revoke, the powers of that character which had been granted by the Crown, substituting others appropriate for the purpose.[1]

If the King had assumed to revoke the powers of government granted by the charter, without substitution, or if he had imposed any other form of government, by which the essential features of that which was constituted under the charter would have been abrogated, it might have been an arbitrary exercise of power, justifying any revolutionary resistance which the Colony could have made. But the Crown, under the then existing laws of England, must have possessed legally such power over the Colony as the legislature may exercise over municipal corporations at the present day. The charter, so far as the powers of government were concerned, could not be treated as a private contract.

The charter was originally the only authority for the government of the territory embraced in it. The Council at Plymouth, in the county of Devon, never attempted to exercise powers of government over the Colony of Massachusetts; and there was no compact or agreement to form a government. The grantees professed, in all they did, to act under the charter, and, as they contended, according to the charter.

We are to look to the terms of the charter, therefore, and to a sound construction of its provisions, to ascertain what rights of legislation, religious or otherwise, were possessed by the grantees.

The charter bears date March 4, 1628 [29].

From a careful examination of it, I have no hesitation in maintaining five propositions in relation to it.

1. The charter is not, and was not, intended to be an act for the incorporation of a trading or merchants' company merely. But it was a grant which contemplated the settlement of a Colony, with power in the incorporated company to govern that

[1] If this distinction between public and private corporations, well settled at the present time, was not then recognized, it is not because there has been a change of principle since that period; but because the principles which govern these two descriptions of corporate rights were not then well developed; and hence the claim of the Crown to power over both public and private rights, and the claims of the colonists under their charter, without any distinction between the two. When a right application is made of this principle to the colonial history, it will show that the complaints of the colonists of infringement of their charters were not all well founded.

Colony. — This is shown from its whole structure, in the provisions relating to government, which I shall specify particularly under the other propositions, and moreover in the power given —

> "to the Governor and Company, and their successors," — "that it shall and may be lawful to and for the chief commanders, governors, and officers of the said company for the time being who shall be residents in the said part of New England in America by these presents granted, and others there inhabiting, by their appointment and direction, from time to time, and at all times hereafter, for their special defence and safety; to encounter, expulse, repel, and resist, by force of arms and by all fitting ways and means whatsoever, all such person and persons, as shall at any time hereafter attempt or enterprise the destruction, detriment, or annoyance to the said plantation or inhabitants, and to take and surprise by all ways and means whatsoever, all and every such person or persons with their ships, armor, munition, and other goods, as shall in hostile manner invade, or attempt the defeating of the said plantation, or the hurt of the said company and inhabitants."

Here is a complete grant of the power to make defensive war, without any order from, or recourse to, the Crown; and, of course, according to the judgment of the company and its officers.

2. The charter authorized the establishment of the government of the Colony within the limits of the territory to be governed, as was done by the vote to transfer the charter and government.

I am aware that Mr. Justice Story, in his Commentaries on the Constitution, says, "It is observable that the whole structure of the charter presupposes the residence of the company in England, and the transaction of all its business there."[1] But that position cannot be maintained. I venture to say, that there is no provision in the charter, which either expressly, or by implication, presupposes such residence. On the contrary, if it cannot be asserted that the whole scope of the charter contemplates the establishment of the government within the Colony, it will be found that it contains provisions which it would have been next to impossible to execute, except by a transfer of the charter and government to the place to be governed.

[1] 1 Story's Com. on the Const. § 64.

The charter provides that there shall, or may be, four general assemblies, which shall be styled and called the four great and General Courts of the company, in which, in the manner there provided, the Governor, or deputy, and such of the assistants and freemen of the company, as shall be present, "shall have full power and authority to choose, nominate, and appoint such, and so many others, as they shall think fit, and that shall be willing to accept the same, to be free of the said company and body, and them into the same to admit; and to elect and constitute such officers as they shall think fit and requisite, for the ordering, managing, and despatching of the affairs of the company."

Is it possible to believe that none of the emigrants, — the very men most interested in the administration of the affairs of the company, — were to be admitted as freemen, so as to have a voice? It would seem much more probable that it should have been intended they should form a majority. But how were they to attend the four General Courts, if these were held in England?

The clauses in relation to the election and removal of officers, and to the administration of the oaths of office, are still more significant.

"Yearly, once in the year," namely, the last Wednesday in Easter term, the Governor, deputy governor, and assistants, and all other officers of the company, were to be "newly chosen for the year ensuing," in the General Court, or assembly, to be held for that day and time, by the greater part of the company, for the time being, then and there present. And in case the Governor, deputy governor, any of the assistants, or *any other of the officers* to be appointed for the company, should die, or be removed (power being given to the company to remove for any misdemeanor or defect), it was made lawful for the company, in any of their assemblies, to proceed to a new election in the place of the officer so dying or removed; "and immediately upon and after such election," the authority, office, and power, before given to the officer removed, were to cease and determine.

By another provision of the charter, the Governor, deputy governor, assistants, and all other officers to be appointed and chosen, were required before they undertook the execution of their respective offices, to take an oath for the faithful performance of their duties. The Governor was to take the oath of office before the deputy governor, or two of the assistants; and the deputy governor, and assistants, and *all other officers chosen from time to time*, were to take their oaths before the Governor of the company.

It is readily seen that these provisions of the charter could be conveniently executed, if the company was within the Colony, and the government administered there. And a very slight examination shows how nearly impossible it would be to execute them, if the Colony was to be governed by a company in England. In the case of the death of the incumbent of an office, the duties of which were to be performed in the Colony, it would take a month for the intelligence of the decease to reach the company in England, and at least a month or six weeks more, ordinarily a much longer time, for a notice of the new election to reach the Colony; during which time, there would be no regular officer to perform the duties.

Is it answered that provision could be made by law, that in such case the duties should be performed by some other officer? That will not apply to the case of a removal, as it could not be known that the officer was removed, until a month or six weeks after the removal was made, and yet the office would be vacated at the time of the removal by the company in England; the officer performing acts supposed to be official, but which would be void.

The provision in relation to the oaths of office would be more nearly impracticable. All the officers, as we have seen, whether newly elected at an annual election, or to fill vacancies occasioned by death or removal, were to take the oath of office before they could execute the duties of the office; so that if the company remained in England, and the General Courts were held there, all the officers chosen for the managing and despatching of the affairs of the company, who resided in the plantation, and most of them must be there, would have to go to England to take their oaths of office, before they could execute their offices; or, the Governor would be obliged to be in the plantation to administer the oaths there, after notice who were elected; and after each annual election, the deputy governor, or two assistants, must first administer the oath to him, before he could go to the plantation, or if he were there, must go themselves to the plantation to find him, and administer the oath there, before he could administer the oaths to others. Such a state of things would furnish too great a temptation, in any but a Puritan community, to some other oaths than oaths of office.

It has been suggested that in the clause authorizing the General Court to make laws, there is a provision which would authorize a law, by which other persons than the Governor, deputy governor, or assistants, might administer oaths; and this may be true in relation to oaths to be administered to any officers, other than "all other officers to be hereafter chosen as aforesaid, from time to time," by the company, although the provision refers more particularly to laws prescribing the *forms* of oaths than to the administration of them, as will be seen by a reference to the provision itself.

If, however, it is assumed that it conferred power to make laws for the administration of oaths by such persons as the laws of the Colony should prescribe, it must be limited to officers other than those chosen by the company. It could not be construed to authorize a law providing for the administration of oaths to the Governor, deputy governor, assistants, or to "all other officers to be appointed and chosen as aforesaid" (that is, to all officers of the company), otherwise than according to the special provisions of the charter already considered prescribing before whom they should take their oaths; for, thus construed, it would give a power to make laws contradictory to the provisions of the charter itself, which would be a construction entirely inadmissible.

No general provision authorizing the making of laws, "for the settling of the forms and ceremonies of government and magistracy," "for naming and styling of all sorts of officers, both superior and inferior," for "setting forth the duties, powers, and limits, of every such office and place, and the forms of such oaths warrantable by the laws and statutes of this our realm of England, as shall be respectively ministered unto them," &c., can operate to abrogate the special provisions which precede it; — authorizing the election of officers, annual elections, appointments in case of death and removal, and providing that "the newly elected deputy governor, and assistants, and all other officers to be hereafter chosen as aforesaid, from time to time, shall take the oaths to their places respectively belonging before the Governor of the company for the time being."

Who, then, were the other officers to be hereafter chosen, as aforesaid, from time to time, respecting whom it was specially provided that they should take their oaths before the Governor? Certainly not merely the secretary, treasurer, and other persons, who should be directly connected with the meetings of the company. If the King had undertaken to plant a Colony, to prescribe the laws, and to appoint the officers; all the officers,—judges, sheriffs, attorney-general, &c., appointed by him, would have been officers of the Crown. When, instead of this, he committed the planting, ruling, appointing officers, &c., to the company; the judges, sheriffs, justices of the peace, and other officers appointed directly by the company, were officers of the company, as much so as the secretary and treasurer; and, as such, they were among the "other officers," who were required by the charter, to take their oaths before the Governor. Legislation providing for the administration of oaths to officers not appointed by the company might be valid; as would be provisions for the administration of oaths to jurymen, witnesses, &c.

If we infer that there was no supposition that the plantation would become so large as to require a great force of officers, it does not change the construction of the charter.

I admit that there were some proceedings which tend to show, that the requirements of the charter in respect to oaths were not fully understood by the members of the company generally. At the General Court in England, on the 30th April, 1629, Endicott, who had come over as governor of the plantation, before the charter was granted, was elected or confirmed as governor, and a deputy governor and council were appointed; and it was ordered, that the Governor, deputy governor, and council then in New England, should make choice of a secretary and other needful officers, and should frame and administer to them such oaths as they should think good. But this was very soon after the charter was procured, and while its provisions were imperfectly understood, as is evident from the fact that, at the same meeting, it was ordered, that Governor

Endicott, or his deputy, and the council, having taken their oaths, —

"shall have full power and authority, and they are hereby authorized, by power derived from His Majesty's letters patent, to make, ordain, and establish all manner of wholesome and reasonable orders, laws, statutes, ordinances, directions, and instructions, not contrary to the laws of the realm of England, for the present government of our plantation, and the inhabitants residing within the limits of our plantation, a copy of all which orders is to be sent to the company in England." [1]

It is quite clear, that those who passed this vote to confer upon the administrative government in the plantation — "by power," as they alleged, "derived from His Majesty's letters patent" — full authority to make laws, while the company to which the power was granted existed in England, had not an exact comprehension of the nature and character of the charter; for this vote assumed, that the power to make laws was assignable, or rather that it might be duplicated. Whether there were those who had a better knowledge, but thought that some such measure was necessary until the charter and government could be transferred, cannot now be known.

The attempt at two governments, in a modified form, continued some time afterwards.

"It was thought fit, in making the transfer, that the government of persons should be held in the plantation, and the government of trade and merchandise should be in England."

These proceedings occasioned the charge in the *quo warranto*, in 1635, that they held two councils, — one in England, and the other in America.

Authority was also given by the charter to the Governor, deputy governor, or any two assistants, to administer "the oath and oaths of supremacy and allegiance, or either of them, to all and every person and persons, which shall at any time or times go to or pass to the lands and premises" granted, to inhabit the same.

Persons, not subjects, might go with the assent of the company. Suppose there had been a disposition to administer these oaths, and all persons had been required, in conformity

[1] See Mass. Records, vol. i. pp. 38, 361, 386; Hazard's Coll., vol. i. pp. 256, 268.

with this authority, to take them: were persons proposing to emigrate, to seek, in England, for the officers authorized to administer them, and take the oaths before embarkation? Were strangers, — foreigners, — expected to do so?

The absurdity of provisions intended to operate in the manner stated, more especially in relation to removals and the administration of the oaths of office, furnishes plenary evidence that no construction was intended confining the company to England; and we are led, therefore, to the conclusion, that the transfer was not only beyond exception, but that it was perhaps contemplated by some of the parties interested, when the charter was granted.

The intrinsic difficulty of making laws for and governing such a colony by a corporation having its locality in England, would seem to be so apparent as to be evidence respecting the intent, and the true construction of the charter.

It was necessarily within the scope of the charter, that the grantees should occupy and cultivate the lands confirmed and granted by it, in the place where they were situated. It was equally, if not necessarily, within its scope, to exercise the private corporate privileges which related to those lands, in the place of their location, — and to institute and administer the political government, over the persons settled upon them, in the place which they inhabited.

There is also strong extraneous evidence to show, that there must have been a supposition, on the part of some of those concerned, that the charter and government would be transferred at an early day. Before the charter was obtained, and, it seems probable, during the time in which efforts were making to procure it, the grantees, under the grant from the Council of Plymouth, had adopted measures for the settlement of the plantation. Endicott embarked in June, 1628; arriving in September, with power to manage their affairs, and it appears with the title of Governor. A letter was addressed to him and others, April 17, 1629, informing them that the charter was obtained, confirming him as governor, and joining seven persons with him as a council. Then came the proceedings of April 30th already referred to. The experience of less than a year may have shown the necessity of having oaths of office administered in the plantation, and of having the laws made where they were to be administered, and thus have led to the orders of that date, without much study of the charter itself, by those members of the company who had not been actively engaged in procuring it; while those who better understood its provisions, in view of the probable transfer of the charter and government in a short time, did not deem it expedient to interpose objections.

At a General Court under the charter, May 13, 1629, Cradock was elected governor of the company for the year ensuing.[1] But at a court held July 28th, "Mr. Governor read certain propositions, conceived by himself; viz., that for the advancement of the plantation, the inducing persons of worth and quality to transplant themselves and families thither, and for other weighty reasons therein contained, to transfer the government of the plantation to those that shall inhabit there, and not to continue the same in subordination to the company here, as it now is." Those present were desired privately and seriously to consider of it, and produce their reasons at the next General Court, and in the mean time to carry the business secretly that it be not divulged.[2]

This was, doubtless, in connection with the negotiations with Winthrop and others, to come over and settle. But following so closely upon the grant of the charter, and taken in connection with its provisions, the inference is strong, I think, that the matter had been previously agitated among some of those interested.

At a General Court held August 29th, the reasons *pro* and *contra* having been heard, it appeared, by a hand vote, that it was the general desire and consent of the company, that the government and plantation should be settled in New England, and it was ordered accordingly.[3]

Other evidence is derived from the fact, that no objection appears to have been made by the King or his Council, which strengthens the inference that the crown lawyers, who examined the charter, must have supposed that such a movement was probable.

Mr. Justice Story says, "The power of the corporation to make the transfer has been seriously doubted, and even denied. But the boldness

[1] Mass. Records, vol. i. p. 40. [2] Mass. Records, vol. i. p. 49.
[3] Mass. Records, vol. i. p. 51.

of the step is not more striking than the silent acquiescence of the King in permitting it to take place." [1]

If, however, we suppose that some of his councillors, when the charter was examined, saw that this might be done, the wonder ceases.[2]

Upon petition of Sir Christopher Gardiner, Sir Ferdinando Gorges, and Captain John Mason, growing in part, doubtless, out of Gardiner's grievances, and in part, probably, out of the conflict of title in the others, but representing "great distraction and much disorder" in New England, the matter was referred to the Privy Council, and examined by a committee, who heard the complainants, and divers of the principal adventurers. Whereupon, without determining certain contested matters of fact, resting to be proved by parties that must be called from the Colony, the Council, Jan. 19, 1632, "not laying the fault or fancies (if any be), of some particular men, upon the general government or principal adventurers," [3] thought fit to declare "that the appearances were so fair, and hopes so great, that the country would prove both beneficial to this kingdom, and profitable to the particulars, as that the adventurers had cause to go on cheerfully with their undertakings; and rest assured *that if things were carried as pretended when the patents were granted, and accordingly as by the patent is appointed*, his Majesty would not only maintain the liberties and privileges heretofore granted, but supply any thing farther that might tend to the good government, prosperity, and comfort of his people there, of that place." [4] This shows, conclusively, not only that no objections were then taken by the Privy Council to the transfer of the charter and government, but that none were taken to the general exercise of the powers of a colonial government, in the manner in which the grantees were exercising them.

Winthrop, in his History of New England, referring to the first intelligence of this proceeding, says, "The principal matter

[1] 1 Story's Com., § 65.

[2] These matters are not material to the determination of the question whether the transfer was lawfully made. But the inference that it was originally contemplated seems so strong, that I have deemed it expedient to call attention to the facts.

[3] Hutch. Coll. Papers, p. 53.

[4] Hutch. Coll. Papers, p. 54; Chalm. Annals, vol. i. p. 155; Neal's Hist., p. 154.

they had against us, was the letters of some indiscreet persons among us, who had written against the church government in England."[1] But in a subsequent paragraph, having then, it is to be presumed, received a copy, he speaks of the petition, as "accusing us to intend rebellion, to have cast off our allegiance, and to be wholly separate from the church and laws of England; that our ministers and people did continually rail against the State, and church, and bishops there," &c. Sir Richard Saltonstall, Mr. Humfrey, and Mr. Cradock were called before a committee of the Council, and a hearing was had. Winthrop says further, that —

> "The king, when the matter was reported to him by Sir Thomas Jermyn, one of the Council, who spoke much in commendation of the Governor, both to the lords, and afterwards to his Majesty, said that he would have them severely punished, who did abuse his governor and the plantation; that the defendants were dismissed with a favorable order for their encouragement, being assured by some of the Council, that his Majesty did not intend to impose the ceremonies of the Church of England upon us, for that it was considered, that it was the freedom from such things that made people come over to us."[2]

There were subsequent complaints from two classes of persons, — those who had adverse territorial claims, and those who had experienced the discipline of the Colony. Mason was particularly active, insomuch that Winthrop appears to have been resigned to the providence of God, which, in 1635, "in mercy, taking him away," terminated his efforts to overthrow the government.[3]

In February, 1633–34, on the understanding of the transportation of great numbers to New England, among them "divers persons known to be ill affected, discontented not only with civil, but ecclesiastical government here, whereby such confusion and distraction is already grown there, especially in point of religion, as, beside the ruin of the said plantation, cannot but highly tend to the scandal both of Church and State here," there was an order of the King in Council to stay divers ships then in the Thames, ready to set sail, with an order that the masters and freighters should attend the Council, and a

[1] Winthrop's Hist., vol. i. p. 100. [2] Ib., p. 103. [3] Ib., p. 187.

further order, "that Mr. Cradock, a chief adventurer in that plantation, now present before the board, should cause the letters patent for the plantation to be brought before this board."[1]

The ships were permitted to sail, on representations respecting the commercial interests which would be affected by their detention; and it would seem from what followed, that Cradock answered, that the charter was in the hands of Winthrop.

Laud became Archbishop of Canterbury in 1633; and his influence may perhaps be traced in this action of the Privy Council. Winthrop attributes it to "the archbishops and others of the Council;" and supposes that the intention was "to call in our patent."[2]

Shortly afterwards, on the 28th of April, 1634, a commission for regulating plantations, was issued to the Archbishop of Canterbury, the Lord Keeper, and others, most, if not all, of them members of the Privy Council, giving them, among other things, power of protection and government over the colonies planted and to be planted, "power to make laws, ordinances, and constitutions, concerning either the *State public* of the said colonies, or utility of private persons, and their lands, goods," &c.; "and for *relief* and *support of the clergy;*" "and for *consigning of convenient maintenance unto them by tithes*," &c.; power to inflict punishment on offenders by imprisonment and other restraints, or by loss of life, or members; power to hear and determine all complaints, whether against the whole colonies, or any governor, or officer. And then comes a clause, the intent of which may readily be discovered from what followed.

"And we do, furthermore, give unto you, or any five or more of you, letters patents, and other writings whatsoever, of us or of our royal predecessors granted, for or concerning the planting of any colonies, in any countries, provinces, islands, or territories whatsoever, beyond the seas; and if, *upon view thereof*, the same shall appear to you, or any five or more of you, to have been surreptitiously and unduly obtained, or *that any privileges or liberties therein granted, be hurtful to us, our Crown or*

[1] Hutch. Hist., vol. i. p. 33. From the order in which these proceedings are stated in Hubbard and Hutchinson, it would appear, that the King's expression of satisfaction was at the close of this hearing in 1633; but the dates in Winthrop's History show that to have been the year previous. Hubbard's dates in regard to these matters are not trustworthy.

[2] Winthrop, vol. i. p. 135.

prerogative royal, or to any foreign princes, to cause the same, according to the laws and customs of our realm of England, to be revoked; and to do all other things which shall be necessary, for the wholesome government and protection of the said colonies and our people therein abiding."[1]

It appears from a recital in a subsequent order, made in 1638, that the Commissioners, in 1634 or 1635, gave an order "to Mr. Cradock, a member of that plantation, to cause the grant or letters patent of that plantation (alleged by him to be there remaining in the hands of Mr. Winthrop) to be sent over hither."

In pursuance of the project for a general governor for the whole of New England, Gorges was directed to confer with the Council at Plymouth, to resolve whether they would resign their patent; and in April, 1635, the Duke of Lenox and others of that company, supposed to be acting in Gorges' interest, presented to the Lords of the Council[2] a petition, proposing to surrender; but praying, among other things, that the patent for the plantation of the Massachusetts Bay might be revoked.

Under the direction of the Commissioners, Sir John Banks, the Attorney-General, brought a *quo warranto* to enforce a forfeiture, in 1635. The process seems to have been founded upon an assumption, that the company had no rights whatever. There were fourteen allegations of usurpation; denying the defendants' claim of title to land, their claims to be a corporation, and to have the sole government of the country, &c.; and alleging that they made laws and statutes against the laws of England. There was no allegation that they had unlawfully established the government within the colony; but among the usurpations set forth was, —

"to keep a constant council in England of men of their own company and choosing, and to name, choose, and swear certain persons to be of that council; and to keep one council, ever resident in New England, chosen out of themselves, and to name, choose, and swear whom they please to be of that council."

Also, to have several common seals.[3] There was no service in the Colony;[4] but service was made upon several of the grantees

1 Hutch. Hist. (App.) vol. i. p. 502.

2 The Commissioners for Foreign Plantations are often so called, and there is danger of confusion, unless care is taken to distinguish their acts from those of the Privy Council.

3 Hutch. Coll. Papers, p. 101.

4 Hutch. Hist., vol. i. p. 86.

who were in England, each of whom, except Cradock, pleaded severally that he never usurped any of said liberties, and disclaimed. Against them, there was judgment that they should not for the future intermeddle with any of said franchises, but should be for ever excluded from the use of the same. Cradock appeared, and then made default; upon which there was judgment that he should be convicted of the usurpation charged, and that the liberties, privileges, and franchises should be taken and seized into the King's hand. The process was pending about two years, and there was judgment of outlawry against the rest of the patentees.[1] But this judgment availed nothing. Jones and Winnington, attorney and solicitor general, in 1678, concurred in an opinion, "that neither the *quo warranto* was so brought, nor the judgment thereupon so given, as could cause a dissolution of the charter."[2] The particular reasons were not stated. But we may well suppose the reason to have been, that there was no service on the corporation, nor on any of the members in Massachusetts, nor any legal outlawry as against them, and judgment of seizure was rendered against Cradock only. The reason for this probably was, that the process of the Court of King's Bench did not run into the Colony, because the Court had no jurisdiction there; and there could, of course, be no legal service there.

April 4th, 1638, the Lords Commissioners, taking into consideration that complaints grow more frequent "for want of a settled and orderly government in those parts;" and, calling to mind their former order to Mr. Cradock, about two or three years since, to cause the patent to be sent over; and, being informed by the attorney-general that judgment had been entered in the *quo warranto*, ordered that the clerk of the council, attendant upon them, should, in a letter from himself to Mr. Winthrop, convey their order; in which, "in his Majesty's name, and according to his express will and pleasure," as they said, they strictly required and enjoined him, or any other who had the custody, that they fail not to transmit the patent by the return of the ship; —

"it being resolved, that, in case of any further neglect or contempt by them showed therein, their Lordships will cause a strict course to be

[1] Hutch. Coll. Papers, p. 103. [2] Chalmers's Annals, vol. i. pp. 405, 439.

taken against them, and will move his Majesty to reassume into his hands the whole plantation."[1]

The General Court replied, that they were much grieved that their Lordships should call in the patent, there being no cause known to them, and no delinquency or fault of theirs expressed in the order; asking to know what was laid to their charge, and to have time to answer; assuring their Lordships that they were never called to answer the *quo warranto;* and if they had been, they doubted not that they should have put in a sufficient plea; and representing that, if the patent should be taken from them, they should be looked on as "runnigadoes" and outlaws, enforced to remove to some other place, or to return to their native country, either of which would put them to unsupportable extremities; and that (among other evils enumerated) the common people would conceive, that his Majesty had cast them off, and that they were freed from their allegiance, and thereupon would "be ready to confederate themselves under a new government, for their necessary safety and subsistence, which will be of dangerous example to other plantations, and perilous to ourselves of incurring his Majesty's displeasure."[2]

These repeated calls for the patent were in fact demands for its surrender, and they so understood.

Hutchinson says, "It was never known what reception this answer met with. It is certain that no further demand was made."[3] But he is mistaken.

It appears from Winthrop's History, vol. i. p. 298, that in 1639 — the precise date is not given —

"The Governor received letters from Mr. Cradock, and in them another order from the Lords Commissioners, to this effect; that, whereas they had received our petition upon their former order, &c., by which they perceived, that we were taken with some jealousies and fears of their intentions, &c., they did accept of our answer, and did now declare their

[1] Hutch. Coll. Papers, vol. i. p. 105. Hutchinson appends to a copy of the order this note: "Whether the intent of this order was, that the patent should be sent over, that the government of the colony might be under a corporation in England according to the true intent of the patent, or whether it was that the patent might be surrendered, is uncertain." But the *quo warranto* might have solved that doubt.

[2] Hutch. Hist. App., vol. i. p. 507; Winthrop, vol. i. p. 269.

[3] Hutch. Hist., vol. i. p. 88.

intentions to be only to regulate all plantations to be subordinate to their said Commission; and that they meant to continue our liberties, &c.; and therefore did now again peremptorily require the Governor to send them our patent by the first ship; and that, in the mean time, they did give us, by that order, full power to go on in the government of the people, until we had a new patent sent us; and withal they added threats of further course to be taken with us, if we failed!"

The next paragraph of the History is a curiosity, and I cannot resist the temptation to copy it in full. It shows why Hutchinson never heard of the reception, and the further demand:—

"This order being imparted to the next General Court, some advised to return answer to it. Others thought fitter to make no answer at all; because, being sent in a private letter, and not delivered by a certain messenger, as the former order was, they could not proceed upon it, because they could not have any proof that it was delivered to the Governor; and order was taken, that Mr. Cradock's agent, who delivered the letter to the Governor, &c., should, in his letters to his master, make no mention of the letters he delivered to the Governor, seeing that his master had not laid any charge upon him to that end."

The Lords Commissioners frankly admit their object, in this last order. They intended to bring all the plantations into subjection under their commission. The charter stood in their way. They called for it, and it did not come. Process to enforce a forfeiture of it had failed. There was a very good reason for this thrice-repeated demand by the Commissioners. Their commission purported to give it to them, with authority to revoke it, if, upon view of it, they found any thing hurtful to the King, his crown, or prerogative royal. The possession of it was thus made necessary to a revocation by the Commissioners. A view of a copy was not sufficient. No reason is apparent why this might not have been made otherwise. Perhaps it would have been, if there had been apprehension of difficulty in obtaining possession. But so it stood. Therefore the repeated attempts to obtain a surrender, with the threats if it was not forthcoming. It was important to exhibit a semblance of a legal revocation. There were too many complaints of the exercise of arbitrary power in England, to render it expedient to add others in relation to the colonies.

We have seen how the General Court disposed of the last

demand; and the King and Laud soon found other matters to occupy their attention.

Now in all these proceedings, the character of which I have stated in detail, I find no trace of an allegation, that "the true intent of the patent" was, that the government of the Colony should be under a corporation in England; and I submit, that the omission of such an allegation was a moral impossibility, if it had been so understood, especially as the transfer of the charter caused the main obstacle to the efforts of the Commissioners to revoke it.

The first appearance of an official objection which I have found, against the transfer, was in July, 1679, in the course of the difficulties in which Randolph was so conspicuous; "when," as Chalmers says, "the King wrote to the General Court, and required that other agents should be sent over, properly instructed; giving as a reason, which struck at the foundation of its power, that, since the charter by its frame was originally to have been executed within the kingdom, otherwise than by deputy, it is not possible to establish perfect settlement till those things are better understood."[1] This objection is among the articles of high crimes and misdemeanors presented by Randolph to the Committee of the Council, in 1682.[2] But it finds no place in the process in Chancery, in 1684, in which a decree was entered, that the charter be vacated, and cancelled.[3]

Chalmers, in another place, states, that the Attorney-General, Sawyer, gave it as his official opinion, "that the patent having created the grantees *and their assigns* a body corporate, they might transfer their charter and act in New England." The reason thus stated, is certainly not satisfactory. Chalmers adds, that "the two Chief Justices, Rainsford and North, fell into a similar mistake, by supposing that the corporate powers were to have been originally executed in New England,"[4] — an opinion which I have endeavored to sustain, by the terms of the charter, before I was aware of the high authority by which it was supported.

Usage is permitted to give a construction to an ancient charter or deed, where there is an ambiguity. Here was a use of the powers of government under the charter, — holding

[1] Chalmers's Annals, vol. i. p. 408.
[2] Ib., p. 462.
[3] Mass. Hist. Coll. 4th Series, vol. ii. p. 246.
[4] Chalmers, p. 173.

General Courts, and transacting all the business of the corporation within the Colony, which, if unlawful, rendered all the acts done under it during the time legally invalid, — with no objection on the part of the Crown in that particular, although other objections were made that the corporation had transcended its powers.

If this is not strictly a "usage" within the general rule, it is a contemporaneous construction by all parties, which is as strong, and even stronger, evidence than usage, to give the true interpretation of an instrument. When we add to this the fact, that in two processes to enforce the forfeiture of the charter, there is an entire omission of any allegation that wrong had been done in this respect, the evidence is sufficient to overcome any, even a very grave, ambiguity. But the fact, that there is here no ambiguity, explains the absence of all objections.

I am referred to "A copy of the docquet of the grant to Sir Henry Rosewell and others, taken out of the Privy-seal-office, at Whitehall," authorizing the draft of the charter; to show that it was the intention of the Crown or Council that the corporation should have its residence in England. It runs thus: —

"A grant and confirmation unto Sir Henry Rosewell, his partners, and their associates, to their heirs and assigns for ever, of a part of America, called New-England, granted unto him by a charter from divers noblemen and others, to whom the same was granted by the late king James, with a tenure in socage, and reservation of one-third part of the gold and silver ore: Incorporating them by the name of the governor and company of the Massachusetts-Bay, in New-England, in America, with such other privileges, for electing governors and officers here in England for the said company; with such other privileges and immunities as were originally granted to the said noblemen and others, and are usually allowed to corporations here in England. His majesty's pleasure, signified by Sir Ralph Freemen, upon direction of the lord-keeper of the great-seal; subscribed by Mr. Attorney-general; procured by the lord viscount Dorchester; February, 1628. Memorandum. Their charter passed 4th March following." [1]

I will admit that this is explicit enough to show that there was an intention when that minute was made, that the corporation should have a local habitation in England.

But I remark first, that by the plainest rules of evidence, this memorandum of the proceedings of the Council, prior to the

[1] Chalmers's Annals, vol. i. p. 147.

grant of the charter, cannot be admitted as evidence to control or vary the provisions of this instrument, as actually drawn up, formally executed, with the great seal annexed, and made matter of record; or to show the intention at the time of the final execution. In the absence of all ambiguity, the intention is to be derived only from the instrument itself.

My next remark is, that this "docquet," taken in connection with the charter itself, and other admitted facts, furnishes most plenary proof that the intention thus appearing, was in fact changed when the charter was afterwards drawn and authenticated. There would be no need of another "docquet" to show this, as the charter itself would and did show it.

The palpable difference between the terms of this memorandum and the charter itself, in the omission of an express provision in the charter assigning a residence in England to the corporation, can be accounted for only on a change of intention upon that point. It was not a matter which could have slipped out accidentally, and the omission have escaped the scrutiny to which the charter must have been subjected after it was prepared, and before it passed the great seal.

Further, the docquet shows an intention at that time, to grant such other privileges and immunities as were originally granted to the said noblemen and others (the Council at Plymouth), and are usually allowed to corporations in England. Here again, the great difference between the charter itself, and the intention shown by the minutes, is palpable evidence of a change of intention in this respect, also. It is sufficient to specify the difference in two or three particulars.

The Council consisted of forty members, each of whom were to be presented to the Lord Chancellor, or the Lord High Treasurer, or the Lord Chamberlain of the Household, to take his oath. Power was given to the President, deputy, or any two councillors, to administer the oaths of allegiance and supremacy to all persons who should go to the Colony of New England; and it was made *lawful* for them to minister oaths as well to persons employed by them, for the faithful performance of their service, as to other persons, for the clearing of the truth; but there was no clause requiring officers other than those who were councillors to take any oath of office; and their laws, as we have seen, were to be as near as conveniently might be to those of England. The difference between the Council at Plymouth, and the Governor and Company of Massachusetts Bay, was substantially between an aristocratic corporation, composed of forty noblemen and gentlemen, which was to exercise its powers at a specified place in England, and make laws like the laws of England, as near as conveniently might be, and which might or might not administer oaths to persons in its employment; and a democratic corporation of an indefinite number, which was to hold General Courts, and might enact such laws as should be found expedient, so they were not contrary to the laws of the realm; which was required to administer oaths to all the officers, in a particular mode, for the faithful discharge of their duties; and which was not restricted as to place, so that it might set up its government either in England or on the Plantation, as it should see fit. Assuredly the docquet did not govern the provisions of the charter.

After setting out the copy of the docquet, Chalmers proceeds, —

"In the same papers, bundle 5, page 322, there is a sketch, drawn by Mr. Blathwayt, stating 'the clauses in the charter, shewing, that it was intended thereby that the corporation should be resident in England.' And, indeed, the whole tenor of the patent, as well as the subsequent conduct of the corporation, evinces the truth of that important fact. But the following extract of an agreement, entered into at Cambridge, the 26th of August, 1629, between Saltonstall, Dudley, Winthrop, and other chief leaders of Massachusetts, demonstrates that truth. From a collection of papers, made by Mr. Hutchinson, relative to the history of Massachusetts, p. 25–6: —

"'We sincerely promise, to embark for the said plantation, by the first of March next, to the end to pass the seas (under God's protection), to inhabit and continue in New England. Provided always, that, before the last of September next, the whole government, together with the patent for the said plantation, be first, by an order of Court, legally transferred and established, to remain with us and others, which shall inhabit upon the said plantation.'"

Blathwayt was contemporary with Randolph. It seems, therefore, that this specification of clauses was made about the time Randolph was alleging that the government was unlawfully established in Massachusetts; that is to say, some forty or fifty years after its establishment there. What these clauses were, I am unable to say. Chalmers does not state them, and, unfortunately, I do not find them in the charter.

But the most wonderful evidence of an intention that the corporation should be resident in England, is that derived by Chalmers from the agreement of Winthrop and others, which he copies, and which he says demonstrates its truth. His conclusion is to be accounted for, perhaps, by the supposition that he understood the words, "by an order of Court," in this agreement, to refer to the Court of his Majesty, at Whitehall; whereas, the contracting parties had reference to an order of the General Court of the Company, such as was passed three days afterwards.

Chalmers concedes that this docquet "evinces, that what was so strongly asserted, during the reign of Charles II., to prove that the charter was surreptitiously obtained, is unjust."

I have considered this proposition at length; not only because the transfer has sometimes been regarded as sharp practice on the part of the grantees, but for the reason, already suggested, that, if the transfer was unlawful, the whole legislation of the company afterwards was unwarranted. The company had power to make laws for, and to govern, a Colony. But their authority to do this was as a corporation; and a corporation, having a fixed locality, cannot hold corporate meetings, make by-laws, elect officers, and do other acts necessary to be done by the corporation itself, except in the place where it has its legal residence. In the absence of prohibition or limitation, it may hold property, may trade, and perform other acts which can be done by agents, elsewhere.

3. The charter gave ample powers of legislation and of government for the Plantation, or Colony, including power to legislate on religious subjects, in the manner in which the grantees and their associates claimed and exercised the legislative power.

It granted power to the General Courts —

"from time to time to make, ordain, and establish, all manner of wholesome and reasonable orders, laws, statutes, ordinances, directions, and instructions, not contrary to the laws of this our realm of England, as well for settling the forms and ceremonies of government and magistracy, fit and necessary for the said plantation, and the inhabitants there, and for naming and settling all sorts of officers, both superior and inferior, which they shall find needful for that government and plantation, and the distinguishing and setting forth of the several duties, powers, and limits of every such office and place, and the forms of such oaths warrantable by the laws and statutes of this our realm of England as shall be respectively ministered unto them, for the execution of the said several offices and places; as also for the disposing and ordering of the elections of such of the said officers as shall be annual, and of such others as shall be to succeed in case of death or removal, and ministering the said oaths to the newly elected officers, and for impositions of lawful fines, mulcts, imprisonment, or other lawful correction, according to the course of other corporations in this our realm of England; and for the directing, ruling, and disposing of all other matters and things, whereby our said people, inhabitants there, may be so religiously, peaceably, and civilly governed, as their good life and orderly conversation may win and incite the natives of the country to the knowledge and obedience of the only true God and Saviour of mankind, and the Christian faith, which, in our royal intention and the adventurer's free profession, is the principal end of this plantation."

"Willing, commanding, and requiring, ordaining and appointing," that all such orders, laws, statutes, and ordinances, instructions and directions, as should be so made by the Governor, deputy governor, assistants, and freemen, and published in writing under their common seal, should be carefully and duly observed, kept, performed, and put in execution; the letters patent to be to all officers a sufficient warrant therefor, against the King himself, and his heirs and successors.

But there was a restriction upon their legislation, religious as well as civil. They were to make no laws contrary to the laws of the realm; and the question arises, What was the character and what the extent of this restraint?

We may safely conclude that the meaning of the provision is not that they are to make no laws different from the common law of England, for much of that law was entirely inapplicable to their condition, so that they were under the necessity of making different laws. Laws different from, contrary to, the laws of feudal tenure could not come within the prohibition. The same may be said of laws relating to the peerage, and divers other matters of more common concern.

So we may be assured that it was not a prohibition to make laws different from the statutes of England, for it was known that it was to escape from some of those laws that they emigrated. If they could make no law which provided for a different form of worship than that which was established in England, — if they must establish that with all its concomitants, they would hardly have crossed the Atlantic for the privilege of voluntarily subjugating themselves by their own acts, to the pains and penalties, and violation of conscience, to which the acts of others would have subjected them if they had remained. Moreover, they had no bishops, — could not consecrate any, — and no one proposed to do that for them when the charter was granted. Laud would doubtless have been pleased to do them that favor three or four years afterwards; but their right of legislation, or the restraints upon it, or the removal of restraints, did not depend upon that.

The true construction of the clause is, that they shall make no laws contrary to, — antagonistic to, — in contravention of, the laws of the realm which extended or should extend over them, as inhabitants of the Colony, and which were to be their paramount law.

We are thus brought to the question, whether any, and what laws of the realm were in force in the Colony at the time of the charter and emigration. Happily we can settle this question by authority. It is agreed that the law of the conqueror does not extend over the conquered country, until the conqueror pleases to put it in force there. And although we now hold that the title of the Crown to the greater portion of this country was by right of discovery, it was held by the Courts of England, long subsequent to the reign of Charles I., to be a title by conquest. Chief-Justice Holt, in the Court of King's Bench, in the 4th of Anne, said, " The laws of England do not extend to Virginia! being a conquered country, their law is what the King pleases."[1] And Blackstone, lecturing as late as 1756, says, " Our American plantations are principally of this latter sort [conquered or ceded countries], being obtained in the last century, either by right of conquest, and driving out the natives, (with what natural justice I shall not at present inquire), or by

[1] Salkeld's Reports, vol. i. p. 666.

treaties. And, therefore, the common law of England, as such, has no allowance or authority there." He adds, that they are "not bound by any acts of Parliament, unless particularly named."[1]

Mr. Justice Story, it is true, says of the doctrine of Mr. Justice Blackstone, "It is manifestly erroneous, so far as it is applied to the colonies and plantations composing our Union. In the charters, under which all these colonies were settled, with a single exception [Pennsylvania], there is, as has been already seen, an express declaration, that all subjects and their children inhabiting therein, shall be deemed natural-born subjects, and shall enjoy all the privileges and immunities thereof; and that the laws of England, so far as they are applicable, shall be in force there; and no laws shall be made, which are repugnant to, but as near as may be conveniently, shall conform to the laws of England."[2]

But here is a great mistake, so far as it relates to Massachusetts. There is no provision, either in the Colony or in the Province charter, that the laws of England, so far as they are applicable, shall be in force there; nor that the laws of the Colony or Province shall, as near as conveniently may be, conform to the laws of England.

He says farther, "Now, this declaration, even if the Crown previously possessed a right to establish what laws it pleased over the territory, as a conquest from the natives, being a fundamental rule of the original settlement of the colonies, and before the emigrations thither, was conclusive, and could not afterwards be abrogated by the Crown."

And in the next section, "The universal principle (and the practice has conformed to it) has been, that the common law is our birthright and inheritance; and that our ancestors brought hither with them, upon their emigration, all of it which was applicable to their situation."

1 Blackstone's Com., vol. i. p. 108.

2 Story's Com. on the Constitution, § 156. — The principle that the laws of the discoverer extend over the discovered country, without any action for that purpose, if sound to any extent, must be subject to grave limitations. One of the reasons given why the laws of the conqueror do not extend over the conquered country is, "because, for a time, there must want officers, without which our laws can have no force." (Salkeld's Reports, vol. i. p. 412.) That would certainly apply with its full force to the discoveries in America. If the colonists had found the common law here, or had brought it with them, it must have been packed away, until the machinery was provided to put it in operation. Another reason, viz., that the laws of the conqueror may not be suited to the state and condition of the conquered, is applicable, to a great extent, in the case of settlement, under title derived from discovery.

This allegation may be found repeated again and again, — in judicial decisions, even, since the time of the Province charter, — but it must be taken with some grains of allowance. Applied to the early emigrants and their proceedings, it cannot be supported. As to them, there is better and more satisfactory evidence that they did not bring the common law with them as a part of their law, than can be derived from any inference respecting the general principle which would govern the case, either as an acquisition by conquest, purchase, or discovery.

James I. having the right to govern the country either directly or through a local government established by him, granted the charter of the Council at Plymouth, in the county of Devon, giving the grantees power to correct, punish, pardon, govern, and rule, the inabitants —

"according to such laws, orders, ordinances, directions, and instructions, as by the said Council aforesaid shall be established; and, in defect thereof, in cases of necessity, according to the good discretions of the said governors and officers respectively, as well in cases capital and criminal as civil, both marine and others; so always as the said statutes, ordinances, and proceedings, as near as conveniently may be agreeable to the laws, statutes, government, and policy of this our realm of England."

The Puritans claimed title to their lands under this charter, but not their corporate authority and privileges. Their charter gave them power to pass laws, without any provision for the introduction of the common law, and not even requiring that their laws and proceedings should be as near as conveniently might be to the laws of the realm; but providing that they should make none contrary to the laws of the realm. The grantees neither claimed nor recognized the common law as a part of the laws by which they were governed. There is nothing in their records, nor in their statutes, nor in their declarations, to show any recognition of it as their law. It neither regulated the rights of persons or things, nor did it furnish the rule of judicial decision. Where a discretionary power was vested in the magistrate, he consulted the common law with an inquiry how the case would be determined by that law, and it is quite probable that he usually adopted it, because it is said to be founded in right reason; and for reasons of a prudential character, it was desirable that their proceedings should be, in the language of the charter of the Council at Plymouth, as near as conveniently might be, agreeable to the laws and policy of the realm. But the magistrate was not bound by it, being at perfect liberty, if he thought fit, to act on what he deemed a better opinion of his own.

The claim of the colonists, that the common law was a part of their birthright, and formed a part of their laws, came in at a later period, after their controversies with the Crown had assumed grave proportions. It was interposed as a shield against arbitrary power, and was doubtless founded upon the clause in the charter securing to them the privileges and immunities of natural-born subjects, perhaps also upon a general principle to that effect in the absence of special provisions. It may be a matter of curious inquiry to ascertain the precise circumstances of its introduction and reception.

The Puritans claimed the right to pass their own laws, with the Bible, and not the common law, as their fundamental law.

This is conclusively shown by the answer of the General Court, in 1646, to the petition of Dr. Child and others, complaining, among other things, that they could not, according to their judgments, discern a settled form of government according to the laws of England. To this complaint the answer is, —

"For our government itself, it is framed according to our charter and the fundamental and common laws of England, and carried on according to the same (taking the words of eternal truth and righteousness along with them, as that rule by which all kingdoms and jurisdictions must render account of every act and administration, in the last day), with as bare allowance for the disproportion between such an ancient, populous, wealthy kingdom, and so poor an infant thin colony, as common reason can afford. And because this will better appear by comparing particulars, we shall draw them into a parallel. In the one column we will set down the fundamental and common laws and customs of England, beginning with Magna Charta, and so go on to such others as we had occasion to make use of, or may at present suit with our small beginnings. In the other column, we will set down the sum of such laws and customs as are in force and use in this jurisdiction, showing withal (where occasion serves) how they are warranted by our charter. As for those positive laws or statutes of England which have been from time to time established upon the basis of the common law, as they have been ordained upon occasions, so they have been alterable still upon like occasion, without hazarding or weakening the foundation, as the experience of many hundred years hath given proof of. Therefore there is no necessity that our own positive laws (which are not fundamental) should be framed after the pattern of those of England; for there may be such different respects, as in one place may require alteration, and in the other not."[1]

Then follows, in lengthened columns, divers provisions of Magna Charta and the common law, on the one side, and the corresponding "Fundamentals of Massachusetts," on the other, showing their similarity.

To the same effect is the statement of Edward Winslow, in his "New England's Salamander Discovered," published in London, 1647, in answer to Dr. Child's "New England's Jonas cast up at London:" —

"As for the law of England, I honor it, and ever did, and yet know well that it was never intended for New England, neither by the Parliament, nor yet in the letters patents, we have for the exercise of government under the protection of this State; but all that is required of us in the making of our laws and ordinances, offices and officers, is to go as near the laws of England as may be:[2] which we punctually follow, so near as we can. . . .

"And however we follow the custom and practice of England so near as our condition will give way, yet as the garments of a grown man would rather oppress and stifle a child, if put upon him, than any way comfort or refresh him, being too heavy for him, so, have I often said, the laws of England, to take the body of them, are too unwieldy for our weak condition. Besides, there were some things supported by them which we came from thence to avoid; as the hierarchy, the cross in baptism, the holy days, the Book of Common Prayer," &c. . . .

"As for our trials between man and man, he knows we go by jury there as well as here. And in criminals and capitals we go by grand jury and petty jury. And where the death of any is sudden, violent, or uncertain, the crowner sits upon it by a quest, and returneth a verdict, &c., and all according to the commendable custom of England, whom we desire to follow. But their main objection is, that we have not penal laws exactly set down in all cases? 'Tis true, I confess, neither can they find any Commonwealth under heaven, or ever was, but some things were reserved to the discretion of the judges; and so it is with us, and no otherwise, our General Courts meeting together twice a year, at least, hitherto,

[1] Hutch. Coll. Papers, p. 199.

[2] Referring, it seems, to the charter of the Council at Plymouth, which granted to Bradford the charter of the Plymouth Colony.

for that very end, and so continuing so long as their occasions and the season will permit: and in case any misdemeanor befall where no penalty is set down, it is by solemn order left to the discretion of the bench, who, next to the Word of God, take the law of England for their precedent before all other whatsoever. And as I said before, if I would enter into particulars, I could here set down in a line parallel, as I received it,[1] in answer to the petition of Doctor Robert Child, &c., mentioned in their book, 'the fundamentals of the Massachusetts concurring with the privileges of Magna Charta and the common law of England at large.'"[2]

Chief-Justice Hutchinson, also, is a competent authority upon the point, that the first emigrants did not claim the common law as a part of their law, nor acknowledge it as having authority with them. In a charge to the grand jury, March term, 1767, he said, —

"I don't know a nation in the world, that makes the distinction between murther and manslaughter, which the English do. It was not made in this country before the charter [Province charter]; for our forefathers founded their laws upon the law of Moses, which makes no such distinction."

In another charge, March term, 1768, while he repeats the statement — at that time, and since, quite common — respecting the introduction of the common law, he is even more explicit in his declaration, that the first emigrants did not consider themselves bound by it, and did not regard it as their law.

"Our ancestors, gentlemen, when they came over to this country, brought with them the common law of our mother country (which is with great propriety so called); and although their first charter bound them down to make no laws contrary to the law of England, yet, from the situation they were then in, and from their peculiar circumstances, they then apprehended they had a right to adopt the judicial laws of Moses which were given to the Israelites of old. They at that time considered, not how crimes affected the peace and harmony of society, but almost always adapted their punishment to the real guilt of the criminal. . . . .

"Upon a judgment given against the old charter, the people could never obtain so great a boon, as they thought their old charter: since, you are sensible, they appointed all their officers, made all their laws, without any control from home. . . . . We stand, therefore, upon quite a different

1 He was agent for Massachusetts at the time.

2 See Mass. Hist. Coll. 3d Series, vol. ii. pp. 137–140.

footing from our forefathers, and the principle of our laws is very variant from that which governed them under the old charter. There were several attempts made, since our present charter, to enact laws upon the old charter principles; but they all failed, and the laws were disallowed in Great Britain."

"The principle of law which now governs us, is to punish crimes, only as they affect society."[1]

But all this is not necessary to the support of my position, that the common law, and the statute law of England in amendment of the common law, were not the laws of the realm, contrary to which the colonists were to make no laws; for their power to pass statutes contrary to both, has been exercised without question ever since the common law has been recognized as in force in the Colony and in the Province; subject, after the Province charter, to the negative of the Crown, as provided in that instrument.

Chalmers interprets the restraint, — "You shall make no ordinances inconsistent with the connection between the territory and the country of which it is a member;" and says further, "so a colony may adopt new customs; may abrogate that part of the common law which is unsuitable to its new situation; may repeal the statute law wherein it is inapplicable to its condition. All it may change, except only the principles of its coalition with the State, or the special regulations of the supreme power, or great body-politic of the empire with regard to it." — With this exposition of the clause of restraint, it would be quite unimportant whether or not the common and statute law of the realm extended over the Colony. Any law of the Colony inconsistent with either would abrogate or repeal it, without any violation of the clause of restraint.[2]

It may be said that the King was restrained by Magna Charta and the Petition of Right, as well in his colonial possessions, as in England itself.

The colonists were subject to the lawful legislation of the mother country; and so far as that legislation was extended over them by the force of the legislation itself, or by the legiti-

[1] Quincy's Mass. Reports, 1761–1772. Published 1865. Pages 235, 258–260.

[2] Chalmers's Annals, vol. i. p. 140.

mate power of the Crown, so far they could make no laws, civil or religious, in contravention of it. The navigation acts extended over them; and their legislation, contrary to those acts, was one of the allegations in the *scire facias*, on which the charter was vacated and cancelled. But it was held, that the *habeas corpus* act, passed 31st, Charles II., did not extend to the colonies, because they were not named in it.

After the clause authorizing legislation, follows a provision that the Governor and company "and all the chief commanders, captains, governors, and other officers and ministers" as should by said orders, laws, &c., from time to time be employed in the government of the said inhabitants and plantation, or in the way by sea thither or from thence, according to the nature and limits of their offices, —

"shall, from time to time, hereafter for ever," — "have full and absolute power and authority to correct, punish, pardon, govern, and rule all such the subjects of us, our heirs and successors, as shall from time to time adventure themselves in any voyage thither or from thence, or that shall at any time hereafter inhabit within the precincts and parts of New England aforesaid, according to the orders, laws, ordinances, instructions, and directions aforesaid, not being repugnant to the laws and statutes of our realm of England as aforesaid."

The power to pardon is conclusive evidence of a grant of political government, no such power being known in an ordinary corporation.

It hardly seems to be within the power of language, more completely to negative the idea that the charter constituted a corporation mainly for the purpose of trade and traffic; or, more clearly, to grant powers of legislation and government, whereby the inhabitants of the Colony might be "religiously, peaceably, and civilly governed."

Whatever Charles II. may have said about general liberty of conscience, of which he personally made a very large exhibition in some particulars, Charles I. and his ministers could not but form a reasonable judgment respecting the mode and manner in which the Colony would be religiously, as well as civilly, governed under his charter, whether he ever read it or not.

4. The charter authorized the exclusion of all persons whom the grantees and their associates should see fit to exclude from

settlement in the Colony; and the exclusion of those already settled, by banishment as a punishment for offences.

They were the owners of the soil; and, in the absence of conditions or limitations, the owner of such a title has an exclusive right of possession. They were the grantees of a charter of incorporation; and such grantees, unless there is some special provision or circumstance controlling them, may determine who shall be admitted to a participation in their corporate rights.

There was, here, nothing of condition or limitation in relation to their title to the territory; and their right to judge whom they would admit did not depend upon the general principle merely, but was express. They were to admit such persons as they thought fit, to be freemen.

Persons who came on their invitation, or through inducements held out by them, or with their consent in any way, could not in justice be sent away arbitrarily, or for any fancied dislike. In that respect they stood like other governments; and the proprietorship of the soil, which they held out for occupation and settlement, would not give them the right of removal as if such parties were trespassers. Coming by consent, and obeying the laws, they would be entitled to protection. But aside from considerations of this kind, the power of exclusion, on fair notice not to come, could not be made more perfect.

The King desired to limit their power of *admission*, so that persons especially obnoxious or dangerous to him, should not be harbored there, and he retained the power of exclusion to himself, by an express provision, which, however, was so limited that he could exclude only persons who were designated by name.

It has been supposed that the provision, that all subjects of the King and his successors who should go to, and inhabit within, the lands granted, should have and enjoy all liberties and immunities of free natural subjects, might be regarded as evidence of a restriction upon the right of exclusion by the grantees. But this cannot be maintained, for two reasons. — First, because this can be applied only to persons rightfully there, or going to, or returning from, the territory. It could not, of course, apply to any one whom the King had excluded by name from going there; and if there be this implied limitation upon it, in relation to persons excluded by the King, the same limitation must be implied in regard to persons excluded by the colonial government, which, as we have just seen, aside from this provision, had, from its title, as perfect a power of exclusion as the King had by the clause for that purpose in his favor. It would be a gross violation of sound rules of construction, to say that this clause was a clause of protection to persons who had no lands, and no interest in the charter, and who were, moreover, prohibited from coming and remaining there, by the owners of the land and the grantees of the charter; for if it might so apply to *any*, it would apply to *all* who should go, and the right to the land and the corporate privileges would soon be rendered a nullity.— Second, this clause, rightly understood, is a limitation upon the royal authority, to the extent of its operation, and not upon the authority of the colonists. The King will not put persons out of the pale of English subjects,—deprive them of the privileges of English subjects,— because they go and inhabit there. They shall be Englishmen still. Let us see this a little more clearly, by a citation of the provision itself.

> "And, further, our will and pleasure is, and we do hereby for us, our heirs and successors, ordain and declare, and grant to the said governor and company, and their successors, that all and every the subjects of us, our heirs or successors, which shall go to and inhabit within the said lands and premises hereby mentioned to be granted, and every of their children which shall happen to be born there, or on the seas in going thither, or returning from thence, shall have and enjoy all liberties and immunities of free and natural subjects within any of the dominions of us, our heirs or successors, to all intents, constructions, and purposes whatsoever, as if they and every of them were born within the realm of England."

You perceive that it is confined to *subjects*, and does not include strangers. It provides that these subjects, and their children born there or on the passage to and from, shall have the liberties and immunities of free natural subjects within any of the King's dominions, as if they were born within the realm. What were the liberties and immunities of such subjects? Certainly, not to go and inhabit the crown lands against the will of the King, or any lands which the King had granted, against the will of the persons to whom the grant had been made. Certainly, not to intrude themselves into any corporate rights which had been granted to others. Persons who should go and inhabit lawfully, should have the general rights of Englishmen as secured by "Magna Charta," and the customs of the realm. But this did not exempt them from any legislation, otherwise lawful, under the charter.

5. The charter authorized the creation and erection of courts of judicature to hear, try, and determine causes, and to render final judgments and cause execution to be done, without any appeal to the courts of England, or any supervisory power of such courts.

To the express provision authorizing the establishment of all manner of wholesome laws, statutes, and ordinances, for settling the forms and ceremonies of government and magistracy, fit and necessary for the Plantation, — for the settling of all sorts of officers which they shall find needful for that government and Plantation, and for setting forth their several duties and powers, — and also to that giving full and absolute power and authority to correct, punish, pardon, govern, and rule, I have already referred.

There is no provision in the charter for any original jurisdiction of the courts of England, over the Colony, nor for an appeal, in any shape, to those courts. And there was no custom of the realm, no common law, which gave any such jurisdiction. If it were supposed that the King had power to confer jurisdiction upon the courts of England, original jurisdiction in those courts would have been a denial of justice. And an appellate jurisdiction, afterwards deemed oppressive in the days of the Province, would, in the infancy of the settlement, have been next to impossible. The fact that there was no service of the writ, *quo warranto*, in 1635, within the Colony, shows very clearly that it was understood that process did not run there.

The Lords Commissioners seem to have been careful not to attempt a regular service of their orders within the Colony. They were sent in letters from Mr. Meautis, their clerk, and from Mr. Cradock, to the Governor.

Hutchinson, in stating the proceedings in 1691, when the grant of a Province charter was under consideration, remarks, —

"By the old charter, it was said, they had power to imprison or inflict punishment, in criminal cases, according to the course of corporations in England, but that, unless capital cases be expressly mentioned, the power would not reach them; that no power was given to erect judicatories, or courts for probate of wills, or with admiralty jurisdiction, nor any power to constitute a house of deputies or representatives, nor to impose taxes on the inhabitants, nor to incorporate towns, colleges, schools, &c., which powers and privileges had been, notwithstanding, usurped."[1]

But this construction, limiting all the powers under the charter, "according to the course of corporations in England," is utterly unwarrantable. That expression occurs but once in the charter, and follows immediately after a provision in relation to elections. If it is not confined to "fines, mulcts," &c., in relation to that subject, no reasonable construction can extend it to other provisions which I have cited. It would be absolutely impossible to govern a colony in America, according to the course of corporations in England constituted for trading or even for municipal purposes.

Hutchinson inserts in a note the opinion of Mr. Hook, who was consulted by Hampden in relation to the Province charter, among other things, that the grantees under the old charter had "no power to keep a prerogative court, prove wills, &c.; nor to erect courts of judicature, especially chancery courts."[2] This is very astonishing, unless we suppose that Mr. Hook, in considering the express powers which should be inserted in the new charter, accepted the objections which had been made to the old, by Gardiner and others, without any critical examination. Certainly, the old charter was intended to be complete for its purposes. No addition was contemplated to be made, either by King or Parliament. How were the people to be civilly and peaceably governed, without courts? Was the power to punish and pardon to be exercised without any judgment of conviction? What is meant by the power granted to make laws, "as well for settling of the forms and ceremonies of government and *magistracy*, fit and necessary for the said plantation," — "and for naming and settling of *all sorts of officers*, both superior and inferior, which they shall find needful for that government and plantation"? The idea of a colony to be settled and governed without courts would be preposterous.

It would seem, therefore, that the propositions which I have stated are fully sustained without any resort to the express pro-

[1] Hutch. Hist., vol. i. p. 415. [2] Ib., p. 111.

vision in the charter, which embodies a general principle of law now well understood and applied in cases of doubt, to deeds of private persons, that the charter should be construed, reputed, and adjudged in all cases most favorably for the benefit and behoof of the grantees.

If any thing were needed to fortify the foregoing positions, it may be found in the fact, that, in the process and proceedings in the latter part of the reign of Charles II. to enforce a forfeiture of the charter, or to annul it, there was no allegation of a usurpation of power in any of these particulars; nor any alleged grounds of forfeiture founded upon either of them.

The causes of forfeiture, as set forth in the Court of Chancery, were, that the Governor and company assuming on themselves, under color of their letters patent, power to assemble to make good and wholesome laws and ordinances, not repugnant to the laws of England, but respecting only their own private gain and profit, assumed the unlawful and unjust power to levy money of the subjects of the King, and, in prosecution of that power, made laws for levying poll taxes, and duties on merchandise and tonnage; that they had passed a law providing for a mint, and the coining of money; and another, requiring an oath of fidelity to the government of the Colony.[1]

Undoubtedly, the absence of other allegations of abuse of power under the charter is not conclusive evidence of a belief on the part of the crown lawyers, that there were none others which could be sustained; but there is no good reason why more should not have been enumerated, if it was supposed that others of a grave character existed, and a transfer of the charter and government, or an exclusion of his majesty's roystering subjects from inhabitancy, or any religious legislation whatever, if supposed to be unlawful, would hardly have been omitted.

I have no means at hand to determine with certainty, why this process was instituted in the Court of Chancery, which, ordinarily, has no jurisdiction of proceedings *quo warranto*, and

[1] The power to coin money being, at that time, not an ordinary legislative power, but one of the King's prerogatives, the value of unusual pieces to be ascertained by proclamation, it might well be held that the charter did not confer it. And some of the legislation of the Colony may have been contrary to the navigation acts of the realm. To that extent, the complaints seem to have been well founded; perhaps somewhat further.

relieves against, rather than enforces, forfeitures. In a "Brief Relation of the Plantation of New England," by an unknown author, written at London, in 1689, it is stated, —

"that, in the year 1683, a *quo warranto* was issued out against them," — that "the Governor and company appointed an attorney to appear and answer to the *quo warranto*, in the Court of King's Bench. The prosecutors not being able to make any thing of it there, a new suit was begun by a *scire facias* in the Court of Chancery." [1]

Chalmers says of the *quo warranto*, "Randolph's was the ominous hand which carried it across the Atlantic. And to give weight to the messenger who, in Massachusetts, had little in himself, and to the proceeding, which was equally obnoxious, a frigate was ordered to transport him thither." He says further, "After a variety of obstructions, arising from the distance, *the novelty*, and *real difficulty* of the business, a judgment was given for the King by the high Court of Chancery in Trinity term, 1684, against the Governor and company in Massachusetts, that their letters patents, and the enrolment thereof, be cancelled."

The validity of the proceedings was afterwards "questioned by very great authority." [2]

The reason why the prosecutors could not make any thing of it in the King's Bench may have been that suggested in relation to the former writ, that, as the process of the court did not run into the Colony, there could be no service there.[3] It may have been that the writ did not issue against "the Governor and company." The colonists instructed counsel to take that exception. But if that was the main objection, it might readily have been obviated by the issue of another writ. If so issued, however, it would have been an admission of the existence of the corporation, which was challenged by the allegations of usurpation in the process in 1635.

It may be conjectured that the *scire facias* was brought in Chancery on the ground, that chancery might annul the charter, though out of its jurisdiction, on the same principle that it now sometimes compels a man within its jurisdiction to give a

[1] Mass. Hist. Coll. 3d Series, vol. i. p. 96. [2] Annals, vol. i. pp. 414, 415.

[3] "The sheriff's" [of Middlesex, England] "principal objection why he did not return a summons was, the notice was given after the return was past. *He did also make it a question whether he could take notice of New England, being out of his bailiwick.*" — *Letter of Attorney-General Sawyer*. See Palfrey's Hist. New England, vol. iii. p. 391, *note*.

deed transferring a title to lands lying within another government. But the cases are not alike.

No judgment of forfeiture was entered, nor any decree ordering any person to bring in and surrender the charter, or to do any other act in relation to it. The court adjudged, that the letters patent, "and the enrolment thereof, be vacated, cancelled, and annihilated, and into the said court restored, there to be cancelled;" but there was no attempt to enforce the latter part of the decree.

The proceedings may have been instituted in that court, upon the ground of an ancient jurisdiction of the chancellor to repeal grants of the King, which had been issued improvidently. But the assumption to enter a decree, that a charter granting lands, and corporate powers, and powers of government, and which had existed more than half a century, should "be vacated, cancelled, and annihilated," on account of usurpations, which, in case of ordinary corporations, may be a subject for proceedings by writ of *quo warranto* in the King's Bench, — and especially to do this upon a writ issued to the sheriff of Middlesex, in England, under such circumstances that there could be neither service nor notice, — would be of itself a usurpation. And this seems to be its true character, whatever might be the reason alleged.

If the colonial government was exercising power inconsistent with the charter, or with colonial dependence, the true remedy would at this day appear to have been, not by process to enforce a forfeiture, or to vacate the charter, which, if effective, would leave the inhabitants without any legal government; but by an enforcement or amendment of the charter, in regard to its public powers and character, by the Crown, from which it was derived, or by an act of Parliament making the requisite provision for that purpose.

The better opinion may be, that meeting with technical difficulties in the court of law, resort was had to Chancery, *because of a better assurance of speedy success.*[1]

The proceeding appears to have been no more effective in its character, than might have been a judgment of seizure, in a process at law; and, in fact, little better than would have been an order of the King in Council, that the charter was forfeited, with a revocation of its powers. However, the decree an-

[1] See Palf. Hist., vol. iii. 391–394.

swered its purpose. The colonists were not in a situation to contest it.[1]

Certain differences between this charter and the charter of the Council established at Plymouth in the county of Devon, have already been considered.

It may be noticed farther, as fortifying the position, that the powers granted in the charter of Charles included a power of exclusion, that the Great Patent to the Council provided, expressly, that the territories granted should not be visited, frequented, or traded unto, by any other of the King's subjects, with a provision prohibiting all the King's subjects from visiting or trading there, unless it be with the license and consent of the Council, upon pain of the King's indignation, and imprisonment of their bodies during his pleasure, with forfeiture besides. And the King condescended and granted, that he would not grant any liberty or license to any person to sail, trade, or traffic there, without the good-will and liking of the Council.

The provisions of the charter of Charles were so comprehensive that there was no necessity for such express exclusions.

A comparison of the provisions of the charter, with the subsequent proceedings of the Puritans, relieves them from the charges which have been so persistently urged against them.

It has been said, that "the charter did not include any clause providing for the free exercise of religion, or the rights of conscience." But this is a mistake. It is true that there is not, in express terms, any such provision. It would have been most surprising, if the King had made proclamation of any such liberty, by a formal grant. But the power of legislation, which included the power to legislate on religious matters, was as plenary for that purpose, as an express grant would have been. The "letter from King Charles II. to Massachusetts," in 1662, asserts that "the principle and foundation of that charter was, and is, the freedom of liberty of conscience."[2] And a letter prepared for the royal signature, by the lords of the committee for plantations, in October, 1681, not only recites that the charter granted "such powers and authorities as were thought

[1] See the Exemplification of the judgment. Mass. Hist. Coll., 4th Series, vol. ii. p. 246.

[2] Hutch. Coll. Papers, vol. i. p. 378.

necessary for the better government of our subjects, at so remote a distance from this our kingdom;" but adds, "nothing was denied, which you then deemed requisite for the full enjoyment of your property, and the *liberty of your conscience*, so you would always contain yourselves within that duty which the bonds of inseparable allegiance bind you to."[1]

They did not come here to establish or provide for any general liberty of conscience. In his very full and complete exposition of this fact, the reverend and learned gentleman with whom I am associated, Dr. Ellis, stated that they placed a restraint — the restraint of the Bible — upon *their own* liberty of conscience. This depends upon the signification which we give to the term conscience, which, as you know, is sometimes used to designate the faculty by which we have ideas of right and wrong in reference to actions, without regard to, and perhaps in ignorance of, the precepts of the Bible, occasionally called natural conscience; and it is sometimes used to designate the same faculty, instructed in the Bible, receiving it as the word of God, by which to test right and wrong, incorporating its restraints into, and making them part of itself, — not unfrequently termed an educated or enlightened conscience. In the former signification, which is plainly the sense in which Dr. Ellis uses the word, the Puritans did not seek to establish liberty of conscience even for themselves.

The charter in giving power to make orders, laws, &c., for directing, ruling, and disposing of all other matters and things, by which the inhabitants might be religiously governed, clearly contemplated government in matters of religion; and government in matters of religion, in those days, meant any thing other than liberty for every man to do what his notion of right and wrong dictated in that matter. The grantees meant and understood it, as government according to the laws of the Bible. In the other sense of the term, conscience, that is, the faculty of distinguishing between right and wrong, instructed by the Bible, and according to its precepts, as they understood them, — liberty of conscience for themselves was precisely what they intended to secure. In other words, their great object was to secure for themselves and those who, with their principles, should associate

[1] Chalmers, vol. i. p. 444.

with them, the liberty to worship God according to the dictates of their own consciences, — enlightened by the Bible.

The key to their enterprise, as thus presented, unlocks the repository of their ends and aims, intents and purposes; and you have the explanation and the justification of their religious legislation.

They founded a civil State, upon a basis which should support the worship of God according to their conscientious convictions of duty; and an ecclesiastical State, combined with it, which should sustain, and be in harmony with, the civil government; excluding what was antagonistic to the welfare of either.

Some one may inquire, If such was the design of the Puritan Fathers in the establishment of their government here, why was it not more distinctly stated and proclaimed at the time, leaving no room for misconception afterwards? The ready answer is, that, if a public development of all their purposes had been made, there might have been danger of some measures to defeat their designs, and to extinguish their hopes. The King and his ministers must have known the general character of the enterprise. There was no necessity that there should be a public proclamation of their intentions beyond what was made. It is sufficient that there was no stratagem and no deception in the matter. Doubtless, as the enterprise proceeded, some measures were adopted, which were not originally contemplated.

Is it asked, How it is possible that the Puritan Fathers, who were not recluses, but many of them men of education, — men of great intelligence in their day, — men mixing with the world, — could entertain the idea of establishing a Commonwealth, where religion should outwardly be brought to a rigorous test of uniformity, when they themselves were non-conformists to the Church of England?

It may quite as well be asked, Why, with their deep religious convictions, they should have had any doubts of success? Theirs was a religious as well as a civil State. The Jewish government, which was their pattern so far as it might be applicable, existed for ages. The Papacy had, for centuries, claimed the implicit reception of its dogmas, and unhesitating obedience to its mandates. The Reformation denied the infallibility of the Church of Rome, and exposed its errors; but the political government of England, as soon as it gave support to it, exercised a similar right of requiring conformity to the new doctrines, and the established ordinances. The Puritans loathed the corruptions of the Hierarchy, and sought for purity of doctrine and simplicity of worship. They had unwavering faith that God would regard their enterprise, — their government, — and their Church, in its unhesitating reception of His revealed truth, in its sincere desire to learn His will, and do what was pleasing in His sight, in its simple forms of adoration and worship, — with especial favor. Why should they not, in the full assurance of that faith, devoutly believe that God Himself had not only opened to them a way of escape from impending persecution; but that He had reserved this wilderness to that time, as the place for the establishment of that faith and that worship on an enduring foundation? In point of fact, the government which they established, did last for more than one generation, on the distinctive principles of their foundation; and left its impress on the future, in a more wide-spread liberty, not only for our day, but for after ages.

With the design and purpose by which they were actuated, with the deep conviction of the truth of their principles, of the importance of their enterprise, of the sacredness of the trust committed to them, and of their duty to use all lawful means to secure its success, — all their legislation may be said to have been religious legislation. They legislated in the fear of God, and with a profound sense of their responsibility to Him; which is more than can be said of the greater portion of the legislation at the present day.

If, however, we take a more restricted signification, it may well be maintained that all their legislation, which had a direct tendency to aid in the accomplishment of their great purpose to build up a true Church and a righteous State, each supporting the other, was religious legislation. All the legislation for the enforcement of good morals, of good order in the community, was in aid of this great object, and therefore in subservience to religion.

More especially may the legal provisions for the promotion of education be regarded as of that character. One great purpose of their polity was to raise up a diligent and faithful ministry; and the college which they founded, and to which our present Massachusetts turns with such pride, had that for one of its objects.

It is, however, of the legislation having a more direct bearing upon the interests of religion, that I am to speak. We know from the character of their enterprise, what it must have been. We know from their records, what it was.

Of course, it had reference, in the first instance, to the support of the ministers who were settled over the different churches; who were participators in the hardships, hopes, and labors of the enterprise, and contributed so largely to its success.

At the first court, held Aug. 23, 1630: "*Impr.*, it was propounded how the ministers should be maintained."

"Mr. Wilson and Mr. Phillips only propounded. It was ordered that houses be built for them at the public charge. Sir Richard Saltonstall undertook to see it done at his plantation for Mr. Phillips, and Mr. Governor at the other plantation for Mr. Wilson. It was propounded what should be their present maintenance. After specifying the quantity of meat, malt, money, &c., it is added, 'all this to be at the common charge, those of Mattapan and Salem only excepted."[1]

Benedict, in his History of the Baptists, page 368, speaks of this, as "the first dangerous act performed by the rulers of this incipient government, which led to innumerable evils, hardships, and privations to all who had the misfortune to dissent from the ruling powers, in after times." And again, he says, "This was the *viper* in *embryo;* here was an importation and establishment, in the outset of the settlement, of the odious doctrine of Church and State, which had thrown Europe into confusion, had caused rivers of blood to be shed, had crowded prisons with innocent victims, and had driven the Pilgrims [he means Puritans] themselves, who were now engaged in this mistaken legislation, from all that was dear in their native homes."

This is certainly very unwarrantable language, in reference to the subject-matter. Whatever we may think, or say, of subsequent events, it is a grievous misuse of the vocabulary, to term this a "dangerous act," and a "viper in embryo." On the contrary, it was the most natural, consistent, and just proceeding that could be imagined.

[1] Mass. Records, vol. i. p. 73.

The people who adopted this measure were a small company, who had come here with their families, their religious teachers, and their household goods, to form a settlement. We will leave out of our consideration here, their expatriation, their desire to enjoy the worship of God unmolested, and their sacrifices for the accomplishment of their purposes. They were religious persons, deeply impressed with the importance of supporting the institutions of religion. They revered their teachers, looked to their wisdom for advice in temporal as well as spiritual things, and were bound to provide for them a support. If they had not done so, they would have been worse than the infidels. What more just, what less exceptionable, measure could they have adopted, than to assess, in such manner as to them seemed best, a tax upon themselves for that purpose? If they were content, there were no others who should object.

We have, I think, in the character thus ascribed by this historian to this simple and just provision for the support of their religious teachers, the key to the difficulties which afterwards arose between them and others, who, with different religious views, instead of founding other settlements in the wilderness, where they could enjoy *their* liberty of conscience, after their own modes and forms, chose rather to claim a right to participate in the privileges of the Puritans, at the same time that they placed themselves in a very obnoxious antagonism to some of their most cherished principles. They intruded themselves into the Puritan Commonwealth, set up their standard of opposition to the principles and laws which they found there, and then complained, because the Puritans were not inclined to change their laws for the especial accommodation of their antagonists.

I will consider this measure, as it developed itself afterwards, when I come to the question of their right of exclusion, and the manner in which they exercised it; my object being, just now, to rescue this first act of religious legislation from the viperous metaphor, which, without sufficient provocation, attempts to fasten its fangs into it.

One of the chief accusations against the Puritans, — perhaps the greatest of all, — one which comes with a curl of the lip, or a toss of the head, or some other significant manifestation to make it emphatic, arises out of the connection of their churches with the politics of the State, — a union of Church and State, as it has been called. At an early day, they passed a law by which none but church-members were to be admitted as freemen, so that the right of voting in the affairs of the company, and of the government, as established by and in the corporate body, — the right of suffrage, — was confined to persons who were members of the Church.

Persons who care very little how many Quakers and Ranters were hung, are very sensitive respecting the safeguards with which the Puritans surrounded the ballot-box. Had they not some reason for the adoption of a sure rule?

Dr. Ellis, in his first lecture, stated that there is not in Boston, at the present day, any conceit, notion, fancy, or opinion, which did not exist soon after the settlement of Massachusetts; but I doubt, whether, among all the mischievous persons and all the preposterous notions of that day, there were any persons who maintained that there was such a thing as a *natural right of suffrage;* that is, a right *by nature*, in every body, to participate in the government of all others, as well as of themselves; that being the character of suffrage in a republican government. If there were any such, certainly the Puritans were not of their community.

Well, undoubtedly, we should not select church-membership as a criterion by which to determine who should have the right of suffrage at the present day. It behooves us, however, to be very careful that we do not adopt something much worse.

The law itself is in these words, " *To the end the body of the freemen may be preserved of honest and good men:* It is ordered, That henceforth no man shall be admitted to the freedom of this Commonwealth but such as are members of some of the Churches within the limits of this jurisdiction."

Can we lay our hands upon our hearts, and say, that all our laws regulating suffrage have as wise and honest an object and purpose as that disclosed in this enactment?

Why should the enlightened people of this day and generation denounce or censure the Puritans, because they regulated the right to participate in the government which they founded upon that basis? — upon a basis which, in their estimation, gave the suffrage to honest and good men, — exceptions, of course.

Thank God, being a church-member is not evidence that a person has a *bad* character, even in New York; although there may be exceptions which serve to show that such membership is not *conclusive* evidence of a good character, even in Massachusetts.

Had not the Puritans the legal right to limit participation in their government, in that manner? Was it morally wrong in them to do so? Was it unjust? Was it inexpedient? Unless we can answer some one, at least, of these questions emphatically in the affirmative, we convict ourselves, and not the Puritan Fathers, when we set ourselves up as censors, and condemn their legislation.

As to the legal right, in the first place! If the exposition which has been given of the provisions of the charter has been satisfactory, I need not add any thing upon this subject. Nothing can be more clear than their right to judge and determine whom they would admit to the participation of the privileges under their charter. They were expressly authorized to admit freemen; they were not to admit all comers. They must exercise a right of selection in some manner.

Was it morally wrong to adopt their principle of selection? With a concession of the principle that all rightful government should be for the greatest good of the community over which it is exercised, and that in a republican State, the question what measures will produce the greatest good must be determined by the majority of voices having the right of decision, I think I might venture the proposition, that any rule of suffrage which such majority should conscientiously determine to adopt, as that best calculated to promote the welfare of the whole, whatever else might be thought of it, could not be censured as morally wrong. But some enthusiastic advocate of universal suffrage might, perhaps, wish to be heard on that proposition; so we will confine ourselves to the Puritan Commonwealth.

Was it morally wrong in the grantees of the charter to determine, that the greatest good of their organization would be best promoted by a limitation of that character? I certainly do not suppose, that any one who has a reasonable sense respecting moral right and wrong, will be disposed to argue that question with me.

They profess to have done it, "to the end the body of freemen may be preserved of honest and good men." They are, at least, entitled to the credit of the motive on which they professed to act until that motive be disproved, and there is not the first particle of proof that they were not actuated by it. Admit that this rule did not assure to them the association of all the good and honest men in the community. Will any of you tell me what criterion they should have adopted, in their circumstances, which would have given higher assurance of the accomplishment of the worthy end which they proposed to themselves? If I should pause for a reply, I think none would be forthcoming.

Was this rule unjust? Who at that day should impeach it on this score? It was made by the grantees of a charter, and those whom they had admitted as associates, prescribing for themselves a limitation on which alone they would admit other associates.

The charter was, as we have seen, in form, and partly in fact, an act incorporating a company to which a large grant of land had been made, and to which was given the power to purchase and hold property, and the power also to plant and govern a colony upon the territory thus granted. The charter gave them expressly, what at this day follows as a corporate right, without any express words, the right to admit whom they pleased as freemen of the corporation; that is, as associates entitled to a participation in all their rights and privileges equally with themselves. They might have required a price for the privilege of an ownership in the lands and a participation in the franchise of the corporation, if they had thought proper. But money was no part of their object in the admission of freemen, or in voting for officers. They had not even arrived at that knowledge of the science of government which teaches that legislators may sell their votes in a caucus for the nomination of candidates for an office to which they hold the power of election, and then say that there was no bribery in that, because the nomination of the caucus was not an election. They might have required any other condition of membership which to them seemed just and right. Under these circumstances, who should advance a claim to thrust himself into a participation of their rights and privileges? The question answers itself. No one, unless he could say, that they had held out to him a prospect of participation, and then refused it. No one said that this had been done, even by implication. The rule was adopted very soon after the settlement, and was known and understood. If there was any such individual case, it would not affect the principle.

Was the rule inexpedient? — is the remaining question. We might inquire here, on what principle of right it is that we are to judge and condemn them upon such a question. We may judge and express our opinion whether they acted wisely for their own interests, without assuming to censure them for their judgment respecting a matter which, as it was then presented, was one affecting their rights, property, and duties. — But let us try this question also. In considering the three preceding questions, I have treated them mainly as questions of right and of business in relation to a civil corporation. This presents itself in the same aspect; but we must also take into consideration the religious character of the enterprise.

And here there seems to be no possible room for doubt. It is true that it offered some temptation to persons to join the Church from sinister motives. Few persons, however, would venture, for secular reasons, to enter the pale of a church so strict in its observances; and the sure support which the churches would receive from the legislation of a General Court composed of their own members, would greatly overbalance any danger from hypocritical members.

This restriction of the privilege of freemen to persons who were members of the churches, is not to be regarded as evidence of intolerance or bigotry. Of itself, it required no profession of faith, — no creed.

For the purpose of admission to a church, a person must have assented to the creed of that church very much as at the present day, so far as the Church has a creed. And so, through the operation of this rule, any person who was admitted to the privileges of a freeman, must have given his assent to the creed. But this assent to the creed, merely, was not the reason why he was admitted to the franchise. Somewhat more than assent to the creed was required, in order to admission to the Church. The candidate must be a person of good character, honest, and of a blameless life. It was to secure a body of men, of such a character, that this rule was adopted. And, moreover, church-membership was not of itself the sole qualification.

The Plymouth Colony undertook to secure the same result in a different mode. It was enacted there, that the deputies should propound candidates to the court, being such as have been also approved by the freemen of the town where such persons live. Then it was required that they be propounded at a June court, and stand propounded one whole year. And in the Revision of the Laws of that Colony in 1671, we find that none should be admitted as freemen but such as were, at least, twenty-one years of age, had the testimony of their neighbors that they are of sober and peaceable conversation, orthodox in the fundamentals of religion, with twenty pounds ratable estate, and to stand propounded a year, unless it was some person well known, or of whom the court might make present improvement.[1]

Which would best satisfy the candidate for suffrage at the present day, — the Puritan, or Pilgrim rule, — Massachusetts, or Plymouth? — more especially when there was another law of Plymouth by which freemen might be disfranchised, — a provision which, if it existed at the present day, and were enforced, would cause a great exodus among the voters. — Even Rhode Island would not admit persons whom they considered turbulent and unruly, to ownership, or to exercise the privileges of freemen.

Of itself, the rule did not prohibit immigration into the Colony. Whoever chose might come, notwithstanding the adoption of this rule. Persons ambitious of participating in the government might be influenced by it not to come; but it would be their ambition which prevented them in such case. Persons might not desire to live under a government, with a religious legislation such as might be expected from such legislators; but it would be the desire for a larger license which prevented them. The rule itself might be the remote cause; but another, operating more directly upon them, would intervene, and a maxim of the law teaches us to look to the near, and not to remote, causes, as the ground for complaint, if there be any. The rule denied to no one a participation in the protection which the government offered to persons and property.

[1] Plym. Col. Laws (Ed. 1836), p. 258.

But, still farther, all the alteration which Charles II., or his ministers, required, in respect to the right of suffrage, when, in 1662, he or they undertook to regulate the affairs of the Colony was, that "all the *freeholders*, of *competent estates*, not *vicious* in *conversation*, and *orthodox* in *religion* (though of different persuasions in church government) may have their votes in the election of all officers, civil and military."[1] Would this rule satisfy us better than church-membership? The duty of making up the list of voters, on this basis, would not be an enviable one, at this day; and an action for exclusion from the list might open a wide field of inquiry.

The laws having for their object the conversion of the Indians to Christianity, were part and parcel of the religious legislation of the Colony.

The laws for the observance of the Lord's day were very strict, and provision was early made for instructing the Indians on that subject.

There were penalties for neglecting the worship of the churches, disturbing the order thereof, and for reproaching the ordinances.

The law against *Heresy* provided, that "if any *Christian* within this jurisdiction shall go about to subvert and destroy the Christian faith and religion, by broaching and maintaining any damnable heresies," of which there followed a very respectable catalogue, commencing with, "denying the immortality of the soul," "every such person continuing obstinate therein, after due means of conviction, shall be sentenced to banishment."

Persons above sixteen years of age professing the Christian religion, might be punished for denying the inspiration of any of the books of the Old and New Testaments.

But the introduction to the law against Heresy disclaimed all power over the faith and consciences of men.

And in the proceedings respecting the celebrated Cambridge Platform, the General Court declared that they could not see light to impose any forms, as a binding rule, but gave their testimony to it.

The Antinomian controversy was not merely a difference of opinion upon a speculative doctrinal question, but an open attack upon what was regarded as sound doctrine, in such a manner as

[1] Hutch. Coll. Papers, p. 379.

to cause a commotion in the State, as is shown by the disarming of the followers of Wheelwright; a measure which would not have been resorted to, but in fear of an outbreak.

Another part of the religious legislation of the Puritans, upon which much vituperation has been expended, and many sneers wasted, is that regarding witchcraft.

Are we all quite sure, that there was actually no witchcraft in the days of the Puritans?

We have, at this day, not only our rappings and tippings, our rope-tyings and our planchettes, but we summon spirits from the vasty deep, and, unlike those of Hotspur, they do come, bringing with them communications from the spirit-world, which must give us a very poor idea of heaven, if we suppose them to have come from that quarter.

Is not the difference between this age and the former mainly in the fact, that witchcraft with us does not come on accusation; but that our witches volunteer their manifestations, are quite willing to display their powers, and are thus far more kindly disposed than their predecessors, not having, as yet, taken to sticking pins into people?

For my own part, my imagination could just as easily mount an old woman on a broomstick, and set her careering through infinite space, as it could get up a conversation with General Washington about fly-traps, or with John Adams on the respective merits of hair-dyes, or some other subject of even less significance. And when I give credence to all the supernaturals of our present time, I intend to believe also, unreservedly, in the Salem witchcraft!

But, suppose we hold a little longer to the belief that the witchcraft of the former time was trickery and delusion; upon what sound basis are we to single out the Puritans for condemnation?

The legislation of the Puritans in regard to witchcraft was but the legislation of the age in which they lived, and with their respect for the Jewish law, they, of all people, must have had such legislation.

In England, the law against witchcraft was enforced with as little doubt of its existence, and of its being a proper object of criminal cognizance, as prevailed in Massachusetts; and the executions there were much more numerous.

Even the Plymouth Colony had its legislation against it; and if the witches had not thought that that small community offered too limited a field in which to exercise their vocation, I know no reason for believing that the good people there would not have enforced their laws against them. How should they have done otherwise?

Only a small portion of the people of Massachusetts, however, had any active participation in the prosecutions, and many made grave objections to them.

The General Court appointed a special court for the trials; and one at least of the judges of this court, and several of the justices, were much dissatisfied with the proceedings.[1] Of the majority of the judges who were present, it may be said, that they had the belief in witchcraft, which that most eminent and upright judge, Sir Matthew Hale, entertained as firmly as they did; and that they had quite as much evidence as was introduced in cases before him, in which he was instrumental in procuring convictions, on which he gave sentence of death, with a conscientious belief that he was doing good service to God and the State. He seems not to have wavered in this belief, to the day of his death.

It has been suggested, that there was one physician in Massachusetts who, if his life had been spared, might, either by his professional skill or by his wise counsels, have done something to prevent or stay this lamentable delusion. It is a subject of profound regret that he should have died a year before his labors would have been so exceedingly useful. Those who were living "gave countenance and currency to the idea of witchcraft in the public mind, and were very generally in the habit, when a patient did not do well under their prescriptions, of getting rid of all difficulty by saying that 'an evil hand' was upon him."[2] Very convenient, indeed!

Roman Catholic priests and Jesuits were forbidden to come within the jurisdiction.

The right of the colonial government to exclude persons actually settled in the Colony, existed from the power to make

[1] Thomas Brattle's Letter, Mass. Hist. Coll., 1st Series, vol. v. p. 75. Bentley's Description of Salem, ib., vol. vi. p. 266.

[2] Upham's Witchcraft at Salem Village, vol. ii. p. 361.

laws, constitute courts and magistrates, and punish offences. Banishment was a recognized mode of punishment; and this was their common penalty for grave offences against their religious polity. It was peculiarly adapted to a Commonwealth which was to be governed on religious principles, and to suppress the promulgation of religious doctrines inimical to its welfare. The Puritans desired to remove the disturbers of their peace; and many, if not most of these, were religious controversialists.

Difficulties, which ended in sentence of banishment, for offences against their religious legislation, arose in various ways.

You will not be shocked, I trust, if I venture the supposition that there is nothing in the whole world on which conscience is so sensitive, or by which it is so grievously violated, as the compulsory payment of money to be appropriated towards any thing connected with religion.

A man pays taxes, which he knows will be appropriated to the support of an unrighteous war for the acquisition of territory belonging to the Indians, or to some weaker nation; for wasteful expenditure on public buildings, or corrupt purchases for the benefit of contractors, or for the transportation of patent medicines in the mail under the franks of members of Congress, — he shrugs his shoulders, but his conscience is quiet. Let him understand, however, that his tax is appropriated to the support of a minister of the gospel, who preaches some doctrine to which he does not assent, — be the difference but

> "the division of the twentieth part
> Of one poor scruple, — nay if the scale do turn
> But in the estimation of a hair,"—

his conscience immediately takes the alarm, and he becomes the subject of persecution.

The Puritans being satisfied with the mode of supporting ministers by a tax, which we have seen was originally adopted at the first meeting of the Court of Assistants in the Colony, continued it by subsequent enactments. All inhabitants were assessed, proportionably to all charges in Church and Commonwealth. If all the inhabitants had been as closely united in their religious sympathies as were the first emigrants, there could have been no objection to this, at least none of a conscientious character. But this was impossible in the nature of things. Other emigrants came, with different tenets. It was, of course, impracticable to exclude all such, however great the caution might have been. Change of opinion must, also, have caused more or less of dissent. Difference of views caused opposition to the tax. The government disclaimed any right to interfere with the consciences of men, but insisted upon obedience to the law as a civil duty. The recusants denied the authority of the magistracy to enforce the commands of the first table, and made speeches against it. The magistrates alleged that this was not only unsound in doctrine, but endangered the authority of the civil State. The recusants preached. The magistrates banished. The recusants insisted that they were persecuted for their principles. The magistrates averred that they were punished for their practices.

Two questions may arise here. First, — Whether this was a tax for the support of religious doctrines, or one for the support of the civil State through the agency of religious teaching. If the first, then, by its enforced collection, conscience was violated. If the latter, then, by a refusal of payment, a rightful civil law was defied. Second,—Whether the speeches which were made, were the dictates of conscience, which required a testimony of that character against the enormities of the law, — or the utterances of the mere human will, determined to gratify its own wilfulness, and, if possible, to retain the money in its own pocket.

These questions, as the lawyers would say, may be regarded as exceedingly nice, — questions about which men may argue; and, like the village schoolmaster, "e'en though vanquished," they may "argue still."

As I am not one of those who can

> "distinguish and divide
> A hair, 'twixt south and south-west side,"

I must leave it to the casuists of the next two centuries to determine whether or not the institutions of religion may be such a support to the civil State, that a tax, by the State, to sustain them, can be regarded as a mere civil regulation, violating no man's conscience, even if the money be applied to the maintenance of teachers who differ from him, — whether or not the religious doctrine and the civil support may be regarded as so far distinct, that the civil magistrate may tax on the ground of the civil right, and the party pay without interference with the religious right. Whatever opinions may be entertained, the Puritans, I think, took, substantially, that distinction, and their rule, thus stated, survived the Colony, lived through the Province, was incorporated into the Constitution of 1780, withstood the efforts of two Constitutional conventions for its abrogation, and yielded at last, more than two centuries after its first introduction.

It is a matter of recent history, that a republic founded upon a substratum of infidelity has but a short existence. The duration of one which shall disclaim the support of religious teachings, and rely upon the intelligence attendant upon universal suffrage, and the purity derived from a universal scramble for office, is a problem which has not yet received its solution.

But to leave the Puritans here would not be doing them justice on this subject. They have been charged with inconsistency, and persecution, in reference to these proceedings.

Mr. Benedict, just quoted, says further of the original order for the maintenance of the ministers, —

"From these resolutions on board this floating vessel, which by subsequent acts became a permanent law, subjecting every citizen, whatever was his religious belief, to support the ministry of the established church, and to pay all the taxes which the dominant party might impose for their houses of worship, their ordinations, and all their ecclesiastical affairs, proceeded the great mistake of the Puritan Fathers. And from the same incipient measure grew all the unrighteous tithes and taxes, the vexatious and ruinous lawsuits, the imprisonment and stripes of the multitudes who refused to support a system of worship which they did not approve."

After other remarks of a similar character, he adds, p. 369, —

"The most charitable exposition we can give of this unpleasant subject is, that good men with bad principles were led astray; that although they were driven by persecution from their native land, and here intended to form an asylum for the oppressed who should fly to them for shelter, of every nation and of every creed; yet from the strength of habit, and the general opinions of mankind, in that age, they dare not leave the sacred cause to its own inherent influence; and the spirit of the times, rather than the disposition of the men, hurried them forward to those persecuting measures which have fixed an indelible stain on their otherwise fair name."

Assuming the matter to be one involving a question of conscience, this might be true, if they intended to form an asylum for persons of all creeds, to come and promulgate all doctrines, even to denunciation of their own most cherished principles. But the fact being shown to be just the reverse of all this, the allegation of persecution fails, along with that of inconsistency.

A man persecutes nobody, by defending his own from encroachment. The lands within their chartered limits were theirs. The government was theirs. The faith and modes of worship were theirs. Under their grant from the Council at Plymouth and their charter from the Crown, they secured to themselves, as we have seen, substantially, a fee-simple in their lands, which they could protect against all encroachments. They endeavored to secure to themselves, also, a theologic fee-simple, so to speak, or at least a life-estate, and they were exceedingly tenacious of this, and more sensitive to trespasses upon it than to trespasses upon property, in the proportion that the concerns of religion held a higher place in their estimation than mere temporal affairs. There was little temptation to commit trespasses upon their temporal fee. But there were other zealots besides themselves, who were quite desirous of becoming tenants in common, at least, if not disseisors, of their ecclesiastical fee. The attempt was promptly met, first by warning off; and when that failed, by an ecclesiastical action of trespass, resulting in a fine; and when that failed, by a process of ejectment, called a sentence of banishment.

It would be but upon a very superficial view of the subject, to say, that they had no right to do this, and that it was inconsistent with their position in England. The Puritans in England, like others there who dissented, were mostly natives of the soil: they had natural rights there, — a right to form their opinions upon religious subjects, equally with all other inhabitants of that country; an equal right to express them peaceably; a right to adopt their creed and forms of worship, according to the dictates of their consciences (even if the government might tax them); and a right to the protection and support of the government, in the enjoyment of their rights and liberties. That was their country, their home: there were their families, and their relatives, friends, all their associations. They had no other place in which to enjoy their rights. Members of the Church of

England had the same natural rights, and no more. Other dissenters from her doctrines had the same rights, and no less. The Church of England, claiming to be established by law, required conformity to her creed and usages and forms, in matters deemed by others essential errors; and hence violation of conscience, and persecution.

It was open to all who might be able, to escape from this persecution. It was natural that those who attempted it should associate for the purpose. The Puritans did so, — provided for themselves a place of refuge in the wilderness, and obtained a charter of government. This was emphatically for themselves and those who sympathized with them, and not for others. The creeds, modes, and forms of others who dissented, were as obnoxious to them as those of the Hierarchy. They were not required by any principle of religion, or morals, or comity, or benevolence, to provide for a theologic warfare against themselves and their cherished opinions on the western shore of the Atlantic; and they did not do it. They did not profess toleration. Why should they? With a perfect conviction that they were right, of course others were wrong. And error was fatal! We have as little of toleration at the present time, in relation to some other things, and with less excuse. Others who came were bound to respect their religious, equally with their civil, institutions. There was no persecution in their attempt to maintain them, by the exclusion of those who could be restrained in no other way. No one had a right to come and set up an opposition, and plead "conscience." That plea was open to a general demurrer. "What of that!" You have no right to bring such a conscience here.

I submit that the argument is unanswerable, and a full justification of the general principle upon which the Puritans acted. We may think their creed too narrow. There was, doubtless, mistake, anger, error, excess, wrong, in individual cases. I seek not to justify such things. All I claim is a vindication of the legal and moral right of the Puritan Fathers to govern their own Commonwealth, the child of their labors, of their prayers, of their hopes, and of their fears also; and to exclude others, who could not join in fellowship with them, from the enjoyment of their privileges, without being accused of persecution.

Whether their ecclesiastical right could stand on this foundation for more than one or two generations, is another and a different question. It would, certainly, not be a very long period before those who had been born on the soil would have as great a right of non-conformity to the existing state of things, as the Puritans had in England, and upon similar grounds. They had, in fact, no theologic fee-simple, and could not transmit an inheritance in any exclusive right. They had nothing more than a life-estate, in this respect.

But the matter was not suffered to develop itself in that way. The theologic trespassers brought it to a more direct and speedy issue.

The members of the Church of England seem to have left the Puritan Fathers in the undisturbed enjoyment of their rights. They neither sought nor were involved in any controversy with them here, in the early settlement, unless the controversy respecting the charter had that aspect.

With the exception of the Quakers, the Anabaptists were the most prominent in this religious aggression.

In 1639, several persons were fined for attempting to gather a small company of believers.

A law for the banishment of Anabaptists was passed in 1644, with a preamble giving them a very bad character.[1]

"The heart-rending sufferings which were inflicted on John Clark, Obadiah Holmes, and others" (so Benedict characterizes the affair), in 1651, may serve to illustrate the spirit of the times. Clark, Holmes, and John Crandall, "representatives of the church at Newport," Rhode Island, came to Lynn and held a meeting at the house of a brother, on the plea that he was too old to go to Newport. Benedict says, "The circumstance of these men being representatives, leads us to infer that something was designed more than an ordinary visit." Undoubtedly! They came to do what they knew was a violation of the laws of Massachusetts. — The constable came, as might have been (probably was) expected, broke up the meeting, arrested, and took them to the ale-house, or ordinary, and being, evidently, a man zealous in the faith, and doubtless supposing that the meeting-house was a more suitable place than the ale-house for such people, — wishing also,

[1] Mass. Records, vol. ii. p. 85.

probably, that they should hear a little sound doctrine, — he proposed, at dinner, if they were free, to take them to the meeting. They replied, " We are in thy hand; and if thee will take us to the meeting, thither will we go." But they informed him further, " If thou forcest us into your assembly, then shall we be constrained to declare ourselves, that we cannot hold communion with them." The zealous constable did not care for that, and so to the meeting they went. Taking off their hats at the threshold, when they were seated they put them on again, and Clark opened his book and fell to reading. The constable, by order of a magistrate, took off their hats. When the preaching and praying were over, Clark, as a stranger, stood up and desired to say a few things to the congregation. The preacher said, we will have no objections to what has been delivered. But Clark must explain his gesture of dissent (putting on his hat); and the explanation being, substantially, that to conjoin and act with them would be sin, and that he could not judge that they were gathered together and walked according to the visible order of the Lord, he was told he had said and done that which he must answer for, and was silenced. Shortly after, they were tried; and, according to the account, his defence embarrassed the judges. Clark says, —

" At length the Governor stepped up and told us we had denied infant baptism, and, being somewhat transported, told me I had deserved death, and said he would not have such trash brought into their jurisdiction; moreover he said, you go up and down and secretly insinuate into those that are weak, but you cannot maintain it against our ministers. You may try and dispute with them."

They were fined, and refusing to pay were imprisoned. But Clark caught at the last remark of the Governor, as if it were a challenge to a debate, and the next morning sent a formal acceptance, with a request that a time might be named; shrewdly prefacing it with, " Whereas it pleased this honored court yesterday to condemn *the faith and order*, which I hold and practise," — so that the dispute might be upon his faith and order. The magistrates were not to be caught in that way, but inquired whether he would dispute upon the things contained in his sentence, &c. " For," said they, " the court sentenced you not for your judgment and conscience, but for matter of fact and practice." Clark replied, " You say the court sentenced me for matter of fact and practice; be it so. I say that matter of fact and practice was but the manifestation of my judgment and conscience, and I make account, that man is void of judgment and conscience, that hath not a fact and practice suitable thereunto."

The magistrates saw, doubtless, that the debate would involve his faith and his conscience, and, if allowed, that he would gain the opportunity which he desired, of promulgating his doctrines under their permission, and therefore protection, and declined to allow it. Clark's friends paid his fine, and he was discharged.

But Clark, as Benedict says, "knowing that his adversaries would attribute the failure of it [the debate] to him," immediately on his release drew up an address, reciting, that through the indulgency of tender-hearted friends, without his consent, and contrary to his judgment, the sentence had been satisfied and a warrant procured by which he was secluded the place of his imprisonment, by reason whereof he saw no call but to his habitation; yet, lest the cause should suffer, he signified that if it should please the magistrates, or the General Court, to grant his former request, he should cheerfully embrace it, and come from the island to attend to it.

The magistrates replied, that they conceived he had misrepresented the Governor's speech in saying he was challenged to dispute, adding, —

"Nevertheless, if you are forward to dispute, and that you will move it yourself to the court or magistrates about Boston, we shall take order to appoint one who will be ready to answer your motion, you keeping close to the questions propounded by yourself; and a moderator shall be appointed also to attend upon the service; and whereas you desire you might be free in your dispute, keeping close to the points to be disputed or without incurring damage by the civil justice, observing what hath been before written, it is granted; the day may be agreed if you yield the premises."

Clark took exception to the answer, and repeated his former motion, saying, if the General Court should accept it, and, under the secretary's hand, should grant a free dispute without molestation or interruption, he should be well satisfied. Benedict says, "Mr. Clark all along kept in view the law which had been made seven years before, which threatened so terribly any one who should oppose infant baptism. This was the reason of his requesting an order to dispute in legal form." And he adds, "Mr. Clark, therefore, left his adversaries in triumph." Again, "So completely was he at home in the baptismal controversy, that he was evidently as desirous for the public discussion, as his opponents were to avoid it."

Thus it was that Mr. Clark returned to his habitation, a "persecuted" man, who had endured "heart-rending sufferings."[1] Judging from the fact that he came willingly and knowingly; that he was nothing loath to be forced to go to a meeting where he should be constrained to declare his dissent; that he used the trial to make an open defence of his doctrines; that he was so anxious to debate the matter afterwards with the ministers, if he could have a clear field without danger of the law; and that he finally left his adversaries in triumph; — it is at least an open question, whether the *persecution* was not more in the avoidance of the public free debate, than in the fine, and imprisonment for non-payment. He seems in all this to have had an eye to the things temporal, in regard to his controversy with Mr. Coddington, perhaps quite as much as to things spiritual.[2]

Clark carried his complaints to England;[3] and Sir Richard Saltonstall wrote to Cotton and Wilson, the ministers at Boston, —

"It doth not a little grieve my spirit to hear what sad things are reported daily of your tyranny and persecutions in New England, as that you fine, whip, and imprison men for their consciences. First, you compel such to come into your assemblies, as you know will not join you in your worship; and when they show their dislike thereof, or witness against it, then you stir up your magistrates to punish them for such (as you conceive) their public affronts. . . . We pray for you, and wish you prosperity every way; hoped the Lord would have given you so much light and love there, that you might have been eyes to God's people here, and not to practise those courses in a wilderness, which you went so far to prevent. These rigid ways have laid you very low in the hearts of the saints. I do assure you, I have heard them pray in the public assemblies, that the Lord would give you meek and humble spirits, not to strive so much for uniformity, as to keep the unity of the spirit in the bond of peace."

1 Benedict, pp. 371–375; Backus's Hist. of New England, vol. i. pp. 214–228.

2 See Palfrey, Hist. N. E., vol. ii. p. 359.

3 Ill News from New England, Mass. Hist. Coll. 4th Series, vol. ii. pp. 3, 27.

Mr. Cotton, answering "for Brother Wilson and self," said of Holmes, "As for his whipping, it was more voluntarily chosen by him than inflicted on him. His censure by the Court, was, to have paid, as I know, £30, or else be whipt; his fine was offered to be paid by friends for him freely, but he chose rather to be whipt; in which case, if his suffering of stripes was any worship of God at all, surely it could be accounted no better than will-worship." . . .

To the other paragraph above quoted, he replied, "You know not, if you think we came into this wilderness to practise those courses here, which we fled from in England. We believe there is a vast difference between men's inventions and God's institutions; we fled from men's inventions to which we else should have been compelled; we compel none to men's inventions. If our ways (rigid ways as you call them) have laid us low in the hearts of God's people, yea, and of the saints (as you style them), we do not believe it is any part of their saintship. Nevertheless, I tell you the truth, we have tolerated in our churches some Anabaptists, some Antinomians, and some seekers, and do so still at this day. We are far from arrogating infallibility of judgment to ourselves, or affecting uniformity; uniformity God never required, infallibility he never granted us." [1]

These proceedings serve well to illustrate not only the religious legislation and civil administration of that period, but the spirit and temper of all parties. The Bible was the guide of the Puritans, and their law. Their legislation was founded upon it. Compelling men, therefore, to conform to their laws, was compelling them to conform, not to men's inventions, but to God's institutions.

The proceedings in reference to the "Quakers and Ranters" come under consideration, as a part of the religious legislation of the Puritan Commonwealth; and notwithstanding the matter has been discussed with great ability and research by Dr. Ellis, in the third lecture of this course, it may be proper for me, as it comes also within the scope of my subject, to say a few words upon it, instead of passing it by with a mere recognition.

Polonius, along with other very good advice to his son, Laertes, counselled him to —

"beware
Of entrance to a quarrel: but, being in,
Bear't, that the opposed may beware of thee."

[1] See the letters entire, Hutch. Coll. Papers, pp. 401–407.

The people of Rhode Island happily acted upon the first part of this maxim, in reference to the Quakers who came among tnem. Had the Puritans done the same, it is probable that the nuisance would have been equally harmless in Massachusetts. But such a forbearance would have been wholly at variance with their principle of excluding disturbers of their peace, and with their practice of rigidly enforcing their laws. They entered, therefore, upon the quarrel sought to be fixed upon them, with an energy that made it apparent they were not unmindful of the principle embodied in the latter part of Polonius's advice.

With a commendable moderation in the outset, they evinced a rigid determination to maintain their authority. They warned, they sent away, they fined, they whipped, they imprisoned, and branded. When these more usual punishments failed, ears (not many of them) were cut off. This cruel, but in England, at that day, not very unusual, punishment was inefficient also. Then came banishment, with a condition annexed, that a return without permission was on pain of death. And when all else was utterly ineffectual, the penalty of death was inflicted.

The Federal Commissioners of the four colonies (Massachusetts, Plymouth, Connecticut, and New Haven), at their annual meeting in 1656, had recommended that such persons, if any come, should be forthwith secured or removed out of all the jurisdictions. When, two years afterwards, it was found that punishments of the milder character were of no avail, the Federal Commissioners propounded and seriously commended to the several General Courts to make a law of the precise character of that under which Massachusetts inflicted the extreme penalty.[1] In other instances, prior to this time, parties had been banished with a like condition, and there had been no instance of a violation of it. So it was believed would be the case in this instance. But here was a different class of offenders,— fanatical, or self-willed, — self-devoted to their will. We may call it conscience, but it was conscience as defined by the Indian, "Something here [laying his hand on his breast], which says, 'I won't.'" We may call it insanity; but, if insanity, it was of the same self-willed character.

[1] Palfrey, Hist. of New England, vol. ii. p. 469. John Winthrop, of Connecticut, attached a qualification to his subscription.

It is quite possible that something of human passion may have been excited in the magistrates of the Colony by this wanton contempt of their right and their authority. But mischief arising from mere contempt, — still less, resentment and passion consequent upon such contempt, — could furnish no justification for proceeding to the last extremity. In that view the most that could be said in extenuation would be, that there was a successful courting of martyrdom by a series of persistent efforts, and under circumstances which rendered it next to impossible for the government to refuse the crown. That the Quakers, supposing them to be sane, richly deserved any suitable punishment for disturbing the peace, is not to be doubted.

The cry of persecution of the Quakers by the Puritans has been long and often repeated. It is within a few days, that I saw, in a notice of a sombre work, entitled "New-England Tragedies," this paragraph: "They [the Puritans] persecuted the Quakers with immense zest and activity; but it cannot be denied that the Quakers gave great provocation."

Now I take a direct issue with the first part of this allegation, and with all other averments that the Puritans of Massachusetts persecuted the Quakers. Let us bear in mind that it was not for non-conformity that the Quakers were prosecuted; and let us understand the significance of the terms we use. What is *persecution?* If we turn to the great work of our late learned and most worthy associate, Dr. Worcester, we shall find a satisfactory definition; and tried by that standard, or by any other entitled to regard, I maintain, without hesitation, that so far from the Puritans persecuting the Quakers, it was the Quakers who persecuted the Puritans. Pardon me, if I consider this somewhat in detail.

There was no pursuit either "with malignity or enmity" in the proceedings of the magistrates, even if anger occasioned by such persistent annoyance may have been excited. The Puritans did not "harass" the Quakers "with penalties." The Quakers harassed the Puritans, and the Puritans inflicted penalties for the transgression of their laws, as other communities inflict penalties for transgressions. There must be something more than this to constitute persecution, or the tenants of our state prisons may cry out, persecution! So again, it was not the Puritans who "afflicted," "distressed," "oppressed," and "vexed," the Quakers, on account of their opinions; but the reverse of all that.

Wenlock Christison, the last person upon whom sentence of death was passed, is reported by Sewell, in his History of the Quakers, to have said to the court, "If ye have power to take my life from me, God can raise up the same principle of life in ten of his servants, and send them among you in my room, that you may have torment upon torment, which is your portion; for there is no peace to the wicked, saith my God." That states the truth of the matter, so far as persecution is concerned. The Puritans had no peace, but "torment upon torment" from the Quakers.

The only reasonable question which can arise, is, Were the Puritans justified in the infliction of the extreme penalties? That the Quakers harassed, afflicted, distressed, oppressed, and vexed them, may not be a sufficient justification for that.

Was there danger to the Puritan Commonwealth, — danger of its overthrow, — danger of the subversion of the principles upon which it was founded? Every other expedient to rid themselves of the nuisance had been tried in vain; and this punishment was denounced as the penalty for a return from banishment, in the hope and expectation that its terror would be effectual, and render its infliction unnecessary.

When this proved otherwise; when their principles were denounced, their authority derided and defied, their peace disturbed, and they were dared to carry into execution their own decrees, — if there was danger to their institutions, what course ought the magistrates to have adopted?

The Quakers courted death, if the Puritans dared to inflict it. They despised and rejected the mercy which would have saved them. Assuming that they were sane, however much we may lament the occurrence, why should we waste our sympathies on them, if, by their proceedings, they endangered the Commonwealth into which they intruded? It is said now, that they were more fit subjects for an insane hospital than for any of the punishments which were inflicted. If they were insane, we cannot hold the Puritans responsible because we have discovered that fact two centuries afterwards. There was no such supposition at the time, neither was there an insane hospital.

Great odium has been cast upon the law and its administration, in the infliction of those extreme punishments, and upon the clergy, so far as they participated. I submit, whether the responsibility is not chargeable rather upon the lamentable state of medical science at that time, which, while busying itself with catnip and elecampane, millipedes and powder of baked toads, had not discovered that there was any other form of mental disease than that which manifested itself in a furious derangement. How should lawgivers, judges, and jurors, or clergymen even, ascertain the fact of insanity, — a matter so foreign to their ordinary studies, — when the studies and diagnosis of the physician failed to perceive it. Medical science at a much later day, under the lead of jurisprudence, has redeemed its character. The medical profession having left the investigation of the virtues of baked toad-powder for that of the phenomena of mental disease, the law seeks information on that subject, in aid of its administration.

Medical testimony is heard on the question, sane or insane? Medical experts give their opinions, and the interests of humanity are subserved, and the cause of justice often promoted; though it must be acknowledged, that the notion of mental derangement is carried to an extreme, when a jury finds a defendant sane the moment immediately before, and sane again the moment immediately following, the commission of a very deliberate homicide, but insane at the precise moment when the deed was committed. I admit that the Bench deserves censure, when it fails to rebuke such a perversion of principles. But it would be unreasonable to expect too much from a judiciary elected by a popular vote, and whose tenure of office is for a short term of years.

Upon the question whether their institutions were endangered by the Quakers, the Puritans are entitled to be heard.

In a humble petition and address of the General Court, presented to the King in February, 1660, it is, among other things, said, —

"Concerning the Quakers, open, capital blasphemers, open seducers from the Glorious Trinity, the Lord's Christ, our Lord Jesus Christ, &c., the blessed Gospel, and from the Holy Scriptures as the rule of life, open enemies to government itself as established in the hands of any but men of their own principles, malignant and assiduous promoters of doctrines directly tending to subvert both our churches and state; after all other means, for a long time used in vain, we were at last constrained, for our own safety, to pass a sentence of banishment against them, upon pain of death. Such was their dangerous, impetuous, and desperate turbulency, both to religion and to the state, civil and ecclesiastical, as that, how unwilling soever, could it have been avoided, the magistrate at last, in conscience both to God and man, judged himself called, for the defence of all, to keep the passage with the point of the sword held toward them. This could do no harm to him that would be warned thereby; their wittingly rushing themselves thereupon was their own act, and we, with all humility, conceive a crime bringing their bloods upon their own head."[1]

Assuming this representation to be true, the colonists must stand excused.

Dr. Palfrey says, — "Imprudently calculating on the effect of their threats, the Court had placed themselves in a position which they could not maintain without grievous severity, nor abandon without humiliation and danger. For a little time there seemed reason to hope that the law would do its office without harm to any one."

Again, — "Whether or not their imaginations had exaggerated the original danger, it could no longer, after an experiment of more than three years, be justly considered great."

And again, — "But among the colonies of New England, it is the unhappy distinction of the chartered — and therefore at once more self-confident and more endangered — colony of Massachusetts, to have been the only one in which Quakers who refused to absent themselves were condemned to die. Her right to her territory was absolute, deplorable as was the extreme assertion of it. No householder has a more unqualified title to declare who shall have the shelter of his roof, than had the Governor and Company of Massachusetts Bay to decide who should be sojourners or visitors within their precincts. Their danger was real, though the experiment proved it to be far less than was at first supposed. The provocations which were offered were exceedingly offensive. It is hard to say what should have been done with disturbers so unmanageable. But that one thing should not have been done till they had become more mischievous, is plain enough. They should not have been put to death. Sooner than put them to death, it were devoutly to be wished that the annoyed dwellers in Massachusetts had opened their hospitable drawing-

[1] Mass. Records, vol. iv. part i. p. 451.

rooms to naked women, and suffered their ministers to ascend the pulpits by steps paved with fragments of glass bottles."[1]

But if the danger of the civil Commonwealth was not extreme, that of the religious government connected with it was imminent. If the Quakers might contravene and defy the laws which protected the religious institutions and worship of the Puritans, all others might do the same. Their peculiar religious government was thus in extreme peril. With regard to that, the controversy was preservation or destruction; and the result was the latter.

The infliction of the punishment of death did not avail. The Quakers had an indomitable perseverance, and much encouragement to continue the contest. The law inflicting this penalty had passed but by a majority of one. There was much opposition to its execution. The military guard shows the fear which existed of an outbreak. The opposition was such that the government gave up any farther attempt to execute the extreme penalties. The Quakers came in greater numbers, and committed greater extravagancies. The government mitigated the penalties, and finally submitted to the intrusion. The Quakers triumphed; — and the experiment of the Puritans, — the theologic freehold, — the Commonwealth which was to exclude unsound doctrine and practice, — failed then and there, — and, so far as we can perceive, from that time forth, for evermore.

The civil government did not fail, the religion did not fail; but the principle of the legal exclusion of error received a fatal blow.

The failure was not merely because the Quakers had conquered, but by reason of the causes through which they had conquered.

I quote from Dr. Palfrey once more, p. 482, —

"It was settled that the Governor and Company of Massachusetts Bay were not to have the disposal of their home. They had bought it, and paid dear for it. They had on their side that sort of rigid justice which accredited writers recognize, when they lay down the rule that a perfect right may be maintained at any cost to the invader. But trespassers had come who would not be kept away, except by violent measures, which had

[1] Palfrey's New England, vol. ii. pp. 474, 476, 484.

produced only a partial effect, and which the invaded could not prevail upon themselves any longer to employ. The feeling of humanity, which all along had pleaded for a surrender, at length uttered itself in overpowering tones."

And Sir Ferdinando Gorges, in his "Brief Narration of the Original Undertakings of the Advancement of Plantations into the Parts of America," published in 1658, speaking of the charter, says, —

"By the authority whereof the undertakers proceeded so effectually, that in a very short time numbers of people of all sorts flocked thither in heaps, that at last it was specially ordered by the King's command, that none should be suffered to go without license first had and obtained, and they to take the oaths of supremacy and allegiance. So that what I long before prophesied, when I could hardly get any for money to reside there, was now brought to pass in a high measure. The reason of that restraint was grounded upon the several complaints, that came out of those parts, of the divers sects and schisms that were amongst them, all contemning the public government of the ecclesiastical state. And it was doubted that they would, in short time, wholly shake off the royal jurisdiction of the Sovereign Magistrate."[1]

We can see now that it was impossible that their peculiar religious institutions, — "God's institutions," as Mr. Cotton called them, — should be maintained for a long period against the influx of population "contemning the public government of the ecclesiastical state" here: we can see that it would have been better, (to use a common form of speech), infinitely better, had they voluntarily yielded to the pressure, at an earlier day, and quietly submitted to a modification of their religious establishment, giving greater liberty for dissent, and more tolerance to opposition. The civil state can hardly be said to have been in danger of overthrow. It may not have been wise, it may not have evinced sound statesmanship, for them to attempt to maintain their experiment against the intrusion of the Quakers, considering the opposition which was made to it.

If, under the existing circumstances, they saw the impending inevitable consequences, they cannot be held excused in sacrificing life to the end that their church polity might be vigorously enforced for a little time, only to be overthrown within a short

[1] Mass. Hist. Soc. Coll., 3d Series, vol. vi. p. 80.

period. Anger and passion, under great provocation, can afford at best but palliation.

But, assuming that there was no danger to their civil government, the principle which lay at the foundation of their whole government, civil as well as ecclesiastical, — the principle of excluding what they deemed fundamental error in religion by the civil arm, — was on trial; and if, on the other hand, they might well believe, and did believe, that God's institutions committed to their charge could be sustained, error excluded, their peace preserved, and their peculiar Commonwealth maintained, by the rigid enforcement of their laws, even unto death, the danger which menaced their institutions from the proceedings of the Quakers must hold them excused. On what authority shall we pronounce that they must have seen the first, and could not have acted upon the last, of these propositions?

Their Commonwealth was one of small beginnings. If it could have been kept a small Commonwealth, — distinct and independent, its religious legislation enforced as it might have been under such circumstances, — it would, doubtless, have preserved its original constitution much longer; and with their knowledge of the mutability of human affairs, they could not have anticipated that it was to endure for all generations. They were authorized originally, by the circumstances to which I have referred, to anticipate for it a reasonable duration, and they were men who could commit to God's providence the ordering of the future. The extract from Sir Ferdinando Gorges' "Brief Narration" shows that they did not anticipate that the example of their emigration would be followed by such a numerous company of men, who, of divers sects and with divers schisms, "contemning the public government of the ecclesiastical state," claimed liberty, not so much to worship God according to the dictates of their consciences, as liberty not to worship Him at all.

There is a grave question, I think, not as yet sufficiently considered, how far writers of fiction, whether of prose or poetry, are at liberty to represent historical personages otherwise than on the basis of historical truth.

If the fiction be like Irving's Knickerbocker's New York, — a burlesque so transparent that no one is for a moment misled, — there is no harm done. But if the tale or poem be of that character that no one but an expert in history can distinguish between the true and the false, the fact and the fiction, very serious injury may be, in many instances will be, done to the reputation of those who have bequeathed that reputation to posterity, in the hope that it may be preserved untarnished. More especially is this true, if, the prologue says,—

> "the author seeks and strives
> To represent the dead as in their lives."

It is well for the author of the "New-England Tragedies" that the Puritan laws are no longer in force, else he might be called to answer, not only for that he did—

> "perchance misdate the day and year,
> And group events together by his art,
> That in the Chronicles lie far apart,"

but that he did, moreover, interpolate matter which had neither day, nor year, nor chronicle, in point of fact, thereby giving false impressions respecting the truth of history.

The relation of events in their order is one of the first of the requisites of history. Not only the year, but sometimes the very day in which a thing is done, is of the utmost importance to a right understanding of the character of men, and of their acts also.

It is not an immaterial matter, whether the Puritans forbore, at last, to proceed capitally against the Quakers from their own conviction that such a course would cause a great sacrifice of life, and would finally fail of accomplishing their object; or whether, thirsting for blood still, they were stopped by a "mandamus" from Charles II.,—who, by the way, had no power to issue such a judicial writ, even if he might amend the charter.

It may not be amiss, therefore, to state, that the last execution, that of William Leddra, took place March 14, 1661; that Wenlock Christison, or, as the record has it, Wendlock Christopherson, who had been banished and threatened with death if he should return, confronting the judges on Leddra's trial with, "I am come here to warn you, that you shed no more innocent blood," was arrested, and, after three months, brought up for trial. Dr. Palfrey says,—

"There was an unprecedented division among the magistrates, and they are said to have been no less than two weeks in debate." — "Christison was condemned to die; but the dreadful sentence could not again be executed. In the mean time, the General Court had met; and the evidences of opposition to any further pursuance of this rigorous policy were unmistakable. The contest of will was at an end. The trial that was to decide which party would hold out longest, had been made; and the Quakers had conquered." [1]

It may be proper for me to add, that Christison, concluding that, if he might have his liberty, he had freedom to depart, was discharged from prison in June, 1661; that King Charles's letter, directing "that, if there were any of those people called Quakers amongst them, now already condemned to suffer death or other corporal punishment, or that were imprisoned and obnoxious to the like condemnation, they were to forbear to proceed any further therein," and should send such persons to England for trial, was dated Sept. 9th, of that year, and received in November. Dr. Palfrey says further: —

"The command, however, produced little effect. The resolution to abstain from further capital punishments had been taken some months before; though the magistrates perhaps were not indisposed to appeal to the King's injunction, rather than avow a change of judgment on their own part." [2]

And it is of some importance to know farther, that, after a representation from the government of the colony to the King on this subject, his Majesty, in a letter dated June 28th, 1662, after saying, that "the end and foundation of the charter was and is the freedom and liberty of conscience," and charging and requiring that freedom and liberty be duly admitted and allowed, so that the "Book of Common Prayer" might be used, and all persons of good and honest lives and conversations be admitted to the sacraments and their children to baptism, adds, —

"We cannot be understood hereby to direct or wish that any indulgence should be granted to those persons commonly called Quakers, whose being ∧ inconsistent with any kind of government. We have found it necessary, by the advice of our Parliament here, to make sharp laws against them, and are well contented that you do the like there."

[1] Palfrey, vol. ii. p. 481. [2] Palfrey, vol. ii. pp. 519, 520.

This is the King's final judgment on the matter.[1]

A few days since, a leading newspaper in a neighboring State appended to a courteous notice of this course of Lectures, a very uncourteous paragraph respecting the founders of Massachusetts, saying, that —

> "They were simply a band of narrow-minded sectaries, animated by no broad nor generous motives; but aiming to establish a morose and exclusive community, from which every one of broader sympathy and more tolerant spirit should be rigorously shut out."

And then, naming three of the principal men among them, it was said, —

> "that, so far from being the promoters of a great movement, they prove, on examination, of very moderate calibre. They were designed for village deacons, rather than for founders of states."

One cannot, and has no disposition to, repress a smile at language like this.

It is neither my duty nor my privilege, at this time, to enter into a discussion respecting the statesmanship of the founders of Massachusetts. But it lies within my province to say here and now, that, but for the religious legislation of the founders of Massachusetts, many persons would have come here, who, like some of those who went to Rhode Island, were not fit for village deacons, nor for any other honest and honorable position.

A clerical friend of mine, in a sermon last Thanksgiving Day, referring to the Puritan Commonwealth and the disturbances by Roger Williams and others, happily remarked, that "every Utopia ought to be supplemented with a Narragansett."

Their experiment of founding and maintaining a civil state upon a basis which should support the worship of God according to the dictates of their conscientious convictions of duty, and an ecclesiastical state combined which should be in harmony with it, and of excluding whatever was antagonistic to its welfare, failed in its exclusiveness; but the change was only in the admission of the element of a more extended liberty of conscience; and of what is dignified by that name without its

[1] Mass. Records, vol. iv. part ii. p. 165; Hutch. Coll. Papers, p. 379.

vitality; with greater liberty also of action. Their failure was partial only; their success, great and enduring.

With an intelligent appreciation of its true principles, they laid here the foundation of civil liberty upheld by law and restrained by law, and of a system of impartial justice.

In the "Body of the Liberties," enacted in 1641, is a prefatory declaration, that—

"We do, therefore, this day, religiously and unanimously, decree and confirm these following Rights, liberties, and privileges, concerning our Churches, and Civil State, to be respectively, impartially, and inviolably enjoyed and observed throughout our jurisdiction for ever."

The first and second declarations following this, are, of themselves, a Massachusetts Magna Charta.

"1. No man's life shall be taken away, no man's honor or good name shall be stained, no man's person shall be arrested, restrained, banished, dismembered, nor any ways punished, no man shall be deprived of his wife or children, no man's goods or estate shall be taken away from him, nor any way indamaged under color of law or Countenance of Authority, unless it be by virtue or equity of some express law of the Country warranting the same, established by a General Court and sufficiently published, or in case of the defect of a law in any particular case, by the word of God. And in Capital cases, or in cases concerning dismembering or banishment according to that word to be judged by the General Court."

"2. Every person within this jurisdiction, whether Inhabitant or foreigner, shall enjoy the same justice and law that is general for the plantation, which we constitute and execute one towards another, without partiality or delay."[1]

The main principle of these declarations is recognized in the constitutions of the States, and of the United States. If it shall be abandoned, and the theory substituted that the general government is to be administered according to the will of the people, as ascertained, from time to time, by the action of Congress, civil liberty in the United States will receive a shock, from which it will never recover under that government.

With a profound conviction of the truth and of the vital importance of their religious principles, they achieved and secured to themselves liberty to worship God according to the dictates

[1] Mass. Hist. Society's Coll. 3d Series, vol. viii. p. 216.

of their consciences. They disclaimed again and again power over the faith and consciences of others. If they were pertinacious in their determination that those who could not join at least in attendance upon their religious worship, and especially that those who placed themselves in hostility to their principles and practice, should find their liberty elsewhere, — their efforts to secure liberty for themselves have resulted in a larger liberty to all others.

With the rod of a persevering industry, they smote the rock of Massachusetts, literally lying in the wilderness; and if the elements of prosperity existing within did not gush forth in immediate profusion, they have since flowed in copious streams to sustain and enrich their descendants.

Let not the conclusion that the Puritans founded their State in order that they might worship God according to the dictates of their own consciences, without admitting others to disturb their worship by contention about doctrines and ordinances, detract from the high estimation in which they have been held, heretofore.

Let us not even presume to believe that they would have effected a better work, had they attempted to provide entire liberty for what every man, woman, and child deemed the dictates of their several consciences.

We are not authorized to say that it would have been better if they had founded a colony on the shores of Massachusetts, with what we call liberty of conscience, — liberty for every one not only to think as he pleases, which the Puritans allowed, but liberty for every one to preach, and harangue, and vituperate, and denounce every other one who differs and dissents from his or her particular notion, — liberty to women to hold conventions, and make pretty invectives against government, and liberty to others to denounce the Constitution which is, or should be, the organic law. All this is supposed to be safe for us. Would it have been safe for them? On what premises shall we maintain such a position? Nay, upon what data shall we persuade ourselves that, forming their infant settlement upon such a foundation, their Patmos would not have been turned into a Pandemonium, — that their experiment would not have proved a disastrous failure in its very inception?

Above all, let us not stultify ourselves by the superlative folly of regarding the Puritans as "a band of narrow-minded sectaries, animated by no broad nor generous motives," who aimed "to establish a morose and exclusive community, from which every one of broader sympathy and more tolerant spirit should be rigorously shut out." Exclusion of the promoters of contention is not the exclusion of persons of the broadest sympathy and the widest toleration.

Let us have a correct understanding of what the Puritans were in their day, which will lead us to very different conclusions.

They were non-conformists. It was their non-conformity, religious and civil, which brought them hither, to establish the principles of their non-conformity, in a colony to be based on the very foundations of their non-conformity.

Thirty years after the death of John Wycliffe, the Council of Constance condemned his opinions and writings; and decreed that his memory should be pronounced infamous, and that his bones, if to be distinguished from those of the faithful, should be removed from the consecrated ground, and cast upon a dunghill. Thirteen years subsequently, in pursuance of this sentence, his remains were taken from their place and burned; and the ashes were cast into the Swift, a brook which empties itself into the Avon.

"The Avon to the Severn runs,
The Severn to the sea,
And Wycliffe's dust shall spread abroad,
Wide as the waters be."

Many of you recollect those beautiful lines. You know who repeated them, with a reference to the blood of Kossuth, if it should be shed by the Emperor of Russia.

Who was John Wycliffe? A non-conformist,—"The morning star of the Reformation,"—the original and type of the non-conformists who, denying the supremacy of King and bishops, as he denied that of the Pope, kindled the spark of civil and religious liberty in England; who cherished and fostered it in the wilderness, until, increasing and extending its beneficent warmth, it shot forth such a light, that the fires of persecution paled before its radiance.

Sneers about village deacons cannot tarnish the reputation of such men. Detractors may think to cast their dust upon the waters; but, like that of Wycliffe, it "shall spread abroad, wide as the waters be."

If the liberty which they claimed and secured, was, in their day, confined in a great measure to themselves and their institutions; after generations have had the benefit of an expansion of its principles into a more extended freedom.

We may reject their creed. We may regret their austerity. But they will live in history, as they have lived, the very embodiment of a noble devotion to the principles which induced them to establish a colony, to be "so religiously, peaceably, and civilly governed," as thereby to incite the very heathen to embrace the principles of Christianity.

PURITAN POLITICS

IN

ENGLAND AND NEW ENGLAND.

By EDWARD E. HALE.

PURITAN POLITICS

IN

ENGLAND AND NEW ENGLAND.

I AM to treat in an hour, as I can, a subject which could be scarcely entered upon, had the whole of this course of lectures been devoted to it. It is a subject, as I believe, for which we are now but beginning to collect the materials. For the religious and political prejudices of England did a great deal, in two centuries, to shroud in England the motives and even the acts of the men to whom is due the English liberty of to-day. And, on our side of the water, the complete change of scene and circumstance has swept away most of the traditions, and all the prejudices of the politics of the Fathers. It is not seventy years, I think, since Oliver Cromwell's portrait still hung as a tavern sign in Boston; and, quite up to our own times, such names as Newbury Street and Worcester Street ought to remind the children what kings fled before their fathers, in the fights of Newbury and Worcester. But, in fact, I am afraid such memorials have availed but little. For most of us who are men and women, while we were taught in our childhood to weep over the sorrows of the exiles in the "Mayflower," drank in at the same time, from fountains fed by David Hume and Walter Scott, the notion that King Charles was a martyr, and that his judges were crazy men. I should say it was only within the last twenty years, that there had been fair chance for an honest verdict as to Puritan politics, whether in this country or in England. In that time, the service for King Charles the martyr has been omitted by authority from the English prayer-book. The opening of the English State papers has given us more light than we had before. Not that we have even yet the complete materials for history, but the graves are giving up their dead; and from hour to hour the lies of Clarendon and the rest are exposed.

I can only attempt the outline of the political movements of the founders of Massachusetts, and the Puritans of New England, — the great men who have been wisely called "the greatest geniuses for government that the world ever saw embarked together in one common cause."

I shall be guided all along by the studies and by the philosophy of our own great historian Dr. Palfrey, from whose crowded chapters, I find, I took unconsciously even the title which the lecture bears. I have been indebted to his thoughtful kindness or to his counsel, from the first moment of my life; and it is no new experience to me, that in my enterprise of this evening I find him my constant guide. And I have, also, the constant advantage of the exquisite care, the range of observation and the profound discrimination, of Mr. Haven, who, as the members of the Historical Society well know, is far better fitted than I to enter on this theme.

I think the key to the whole story may be found in the ominous words which King James's first House of Commons addressed to the House of Lords immediately after he had been lecturing them on his own prerogative, and on his intolerance to the Puritans. "There may be a people without a King, but there can be no King without a people." This was comfortable doctrine for a monarch, who, in his escape from Scotland, had promised himself the privileges of unrestricted tyranny. Fortunately for civil liberty in England and America, in all countries and in all times, none of the Stuarts ever learned in time what this ominous sentence means, — not James I., the most foolish of them; nor Charles I., the most false; nor Charles II., the most worthless; nor James II., the most obstinate. For eighty-six years, however, it was the business of the Puritans of England, counselled and led in large measure, as I shall show, by the Puritans of New England, to teach the Stuarts, and to teach the world, that lesson. And they taught it, — that the people is stronger than the King, and can tie the King's hands.

The state-craft jugglery of the closet shall not undo the knots; the trenchant sword of battle shall not cut the cords. If the King will learn the lesson in no other way, he shall learn it when he sees the headsman's axe flashing before his eyes. The people is stronger than the sovereign; and from the people's power his power comes. That is the lesson. There may be a people without a King; there can be no King without a people.

I must not enter on the history of Elizabeth's reign, though the name of Puritan in English history belongs as far back as the year 1550.

King James, at the age of thirty-five, came to the crown in 1603. On his journey from Scotland to London, just half way from the frontier to the city, he passed through Sherwood Forest, and entertained the day, under good conduct, in hunting there, — the last huntsman mentioned, I think, in the series where Robin Hood is first. In that day's sport, he passed the manor house of Scrooby, where William Brewster lived, — afterwards our old Plymouth Elder. At that very time our Pilgrim Fathers met privately to worship in that house every Sunday. James took, very likely, a mug of ale from William Brewster's hands, he lunched in the open air, on the bank of a stream a little further on, and in such sylvan amusement came on to Worsop, where he slept.[1] The manor of Scrooby, Brewster's home, belonged to the Archbishop of York. It attracted the King's attention, so that he thought he would like it for a royal residence, whenever he might hunt again in Sherwood Forest. It is a little curious now to see, that the first letter written by this Presbyterian King to the Archbishop of York, after his arrival at his capital, was, not a discussion of theology, but a proposal to the Archbishop to sell to him the manor house in

1 Nichols's Progresses of King James I. The whole passage is this: —

"The 20th day being Wednesday, his Majestie rode toward Worksop, the noble Earle of Shrewsbury's House, — at Bawtry, the High Sheriff of Yorkshire took his leave of the King, — and there Mr. Askoth (Ayscough) the High Sheriff of Nottinghamshire received him, being gallantly appointed both with horse and man, and so he conducted his majestie on, till he came within a mile of Blyth, where his Highness lighted and sat down on a banke side to eat and drink."

Here Nichols's note is, "Bawtry is a small market town, situated partly in the parish of Scrooby, in Yorkshire, and partly in that of Blyth, in Nottinghamshire. The division of the two counties is marked by a small current of water in the yard of the Crown inn."

which the Pilgrim Fathers were then secretly meeting, on the Lord's day, for their weekly worship; and in which they continued to meet till this same Presbyterian King "harried them out of the kingdom." The incident, trifling in itself, illustrates very perfectly the relation between the three parties then in England. The extreme Puritans, represented by no man better than William Brewster, were meeting in private houses for their worship. They were expecting grace and help from a Presbyterian monarch. The Bishops and Archbishops were doubting and dreading what might come to them and theirs, from a King who had been nursed in the school of John Knox and Jane Geddies. And this King — who was to arbitrate between the parties, and to meet the hopes of one and the fears of the other, — was thinking more of himself and his own comfort than of the consciences of either. All this, I say, is typified, when James I. asks Archbishop Hutton, to turn William Brewster out of his home, that he may have a convenient hunting-lodge.[1]

In five years more, Brewster and the Fathers, who met to worship in the Archbishop's manor house, were harried out of England. James and the Church, of which the Archbishop was the second officer, were in absolute accord, — hunting the same game!

The first incident of his reign, around which the politics of the time took form, was the conference of the clergy at Hampton Court for the revision of the Liturgy, in which the Puritan and the High Church party were both represented. The King showed at once, that he meant to throw himself into the arms of the party which would give him most power in the State, and could do most to place him in the position of the absolute monarchs of the Continent of Europe. Any pretensions of his Scottish reign were swept away, like other pettinesses and inconveniences of his Northern home. He silenced the Puritan doctors by entering himself into the arena.

"If you aim at a Scottish presbytery, it agrees as well with monarchy as God and the devil." These words show the spirit of the King's contributions to the discussion, of which Archbishop

[1] The King's letter to the Archbishop comes to light in the Calendar of Domestic Papers of his reign, edited by Mrs. Green.

Whitgift was pleased to say, that "undoubtedly his Majesty spake by the special assistance of God's Spirit." It was in this Conference that his favorite axiom, "No Bishop, no King," first appears on the royal lips. Perhaps it suggested the more ominous axiom, which I have quoted from his first Parliament,— "There can be no King without a People."

That Parliament was not summoned till the King had been on the throne more than a year; a pestilence in London delaying its assembly. The celebrated gunpowder plot — in which twenty resolute men, who kept a secret for a year and a half, expected to destroy the King, his family, the Lords, and the Commons, and in which they came so near success — was detected just as the session began. The reaction from that plot might have given to James that hold on the people which, I think, he never gained. But he did not enter into the rage against the Roman Catholics, to whose church the conspirators belonged; and the terrible experience prolonged only a little the "inevitable conflict" between him and his subjects.

If we trace the history of the Court, the chapters of this reign are the histories of favorites, Carr and Villiers; of the death of Prince Henry; of the matches proposed for Prince Charles; and of the fortunes of the Princess Elizabeth, at one moment the object of Protestant idolatry. The episodes in that court history are such as closed poor Raleigh's life. If we trace the history of the people, we find the steady growth of resistance to other authority than the authority of the law. We find the luxury of wider and wider study of the Scripture, passing sometimes into the fanaticism and folly of a novelty. We trace the growth to manhood of Eliot and Hampden, Winthrop and Vane and Cromwell. Shakspeare died in 1615, midway in the King's reign. The Colony of Virginia was planted under the old system of colonization, 1607; and, in the same year, the Pilgrim Fathers were driven out of England, little knowing that they were to be the great exemplars of the success of the new system of colonization.[1] The received version of

[1] It took near a hundred years for our Fathers to learn again how to establish permanent colonies. The effort, for the sixteenth century, was made, almost always, by sending men alone; and in almost every instance it failed. When England borrowed from Greek experience, and from Spanish experience, and sent women with the

the English Scriptures was made by a commission appointed by the King, and came into common use in England. The two things in history which preserve the reign of James from contempt are the translation of the Bible and the settlement of America. And I can give no better illustration of the way in which history has been written in the past, than by saying that in the two great English histories of this reign, by Hume and by Lingard, the translation of the Bible is not so much as mentioned, and that Lingard does not give a word to the planting of America. Hume only squeezes out for it a wretched page in the midst of chapters devoted to the disgusting intrigues of Rochester and the Countess of Essex and Buckingham and the rest, none of whom are of any worth but for this, that they were busily destroying the last relics of the regard which men had for the institutions of feudal times.

The intrigues of the Court and the deep determination of the people of England can be put face to face, however, by dragging out from history the contemporary revelations. William Brewster, telling of old times around his pine-knot fire in Plymouth, filled his stage with such actors as Mary Queen of Scots, Queen Elizabeth, King James, Raleigh, Essex, Southampton, all of whom he must have seen, as I suppose he must have seen William Shakspeare. On that Christmas season of 1620, at the moment when John Carver and Edward Winslow were cutting the timber for the first store-house of Plymouth, building better than they knew indeed, King James was entertaining at his palace the embassy which first proposed the ill-fated marriage between Charles I. and Henrietta of France. Of the masque prepared for that royal entertainment, all that is known is that the humor consisted in the ridicule of a Puritan.[1] From the building of the store-house grew the old Colony, the Colony of Massachusetts, the New-England confederation, the union of the United States and the republican government and the civil liberty of America. From the policy which united

men, homes were founded for the first time, and the nature of colonization changed. Jamestown and Sagadahoc were the last experiments on the old theory; Plymouth, the first on the new. The settlement at Manhattan was not so much a colony as a trading-port.

[1] The authorities may be found at length in Mrs. Green's Calendars. I have quoted them in detail in an article in the "Galaxy" magazine for January, 1868

Charles and Henrietta grew the English rebellion and the English revolution, from that marriage came Charles II., James II., and Queen Mary. The two lines of history which are thus suggested lead out from the contrast between the history of the Court and the history of the people in the reign of King James.

But in King Charles's time, people and King come closer, and the history of the politics of the people is the history of the politics of the King. Charles quarrelled with his first Parliament; and if he could have had his way, he would never have had another. Our associate, Mr. Sabine, reminds us that the very first question on which King and Commons broke was an American question, — a question of the fisheries.[1] For eleven years Charles reigned as absolutely as Philip II. ever reigned in Spain. He and his would have been glad to reign so until now, and might have done so but that there was an English church and an English people. Nay: do not let me, even in the accident of expression, imply that between the church and the people there was any distinction, if you speak of the real church and the real people. Of that great crisis of English history, the secret is this, that the real people of England were religious men and women to the very bottom of their hearts; that what they did in matters politic they did as matter of religious duty; not as what poor James called a piece of state-craft, but as a part of their religious allegiance to the King of kings. I believe this profound conviction of religious duty has been the secret of all the successful politics of the men of that race from that day to this day. But it was a divine mystery which it was not given to politicians like Wentworth, or formalists like Laud, or liars like King Charles, to understand. None the less was there a fire beneath the whole, of which the tokens were sometimes fearful and sometimes awful. Its presence there gives to the study of the politics to which it lent the heat, an interest, which to the intrigues of courtiers like those of Louis, or even to the rivalries of statesmen like those of Elizabeth, is all unknown.

It is, of course, impossible to measure by any statistics the extent or the depth of this religious feeling or of any religious

[1] Sabine's Report on the Principal Fisheries, Washington, 1853, p. 45.

feeling. It is to be observed, however, that a long series of non-conformity on the one hand, and of what the English Church calls pluralism on the other, left but two thousand clergymen in the service of the ten thousand livings of England, in Queen Elizabeth's time. Of these two thousand clergymen, nearly one thousand marked themselves as Puritan by joining in the petition[1] which, at James's accession, begged him to amend the rubrics in favor of puritan consciences. These figures show, that, while there were ten thousand congregations or churches in England, but little more than one thousand of her clergy gave even a silent acquiescence to such extravagant pretensions as those of Whitgift and Bancroft, who, in such matters, were the predecessors of Laud. In Charles's time, the fact is incidentally stated, that, in the mere dead-weight of property, the Puritan House of Commons was three times as rich as was the House of Lords. And of the House of Lords, a very considerable part held with the people as against the King. Be it always remembered, too, that on the side of the King also, as soon as you leave the rank of mere soldiers and mere courtiers, you are surrounded by men and women of the purest conscience. You meet such men as George Herbert and Owen Feltham. When they came to the arbitrament of arms, the misfortune to the King was that five-sixths of England were against him. And, as I said, that which gives the terrible reality to the history, is the truth which I think no man will question, that, on both sides, a large proportion of the combatants were actuated by profound religious conviction. And what saved England and America in that crisis, was that the monarchs who wished to play the tyrant there, found the English Church and the English people on the other side.

The first years of Charles's reign gave no hope to the people of England. I speak of the people in contrast from the men and women of the Court, who were trying to hold to the methods of feudal rule. The marriage of the King with a Roman Catholic princess had offended and affronted the Protestantism of England. When he made war with France under the pretext

[1] Thence called "the millenary petition." The spelling is important. It will be remembered that it asked for an exemption from the surplice and other customs considered "Popish."

of coming to the defence of the hard-pressed Huguenots, he conducted the war under such lead as Buckingham's; collected his revenue under such systems as Louis and Philip would have used; and, by the method, disgusted the English people, who might have been interested in the cause of the war. Two years after his reign began, Charles wanted the help of the Archbishop of Canterbury. The Archbishop was in disgrace already, because he had refused the aid of the Church in the disgusting intrigue — with which I will insult no man's ears — in which Somerset and the Lady Essex were the actors. Now, in his retirement, he refused to license the printing of a sermon, in which a court chaplain, Sibthorpe, had laid down the doctrine that a king might do what he pleased; and no man might say, "What dost thou?" For this refusal, King Charles suspended him, — the highest officer of the Church beneath himself. The act, at this day, would disgust the most ardent lover of the Episcopacy, as much as it then disgusted the most eager Puritan. Buckingham's disgrace on the coast of France soon followed. The King's third Parliament was summoned, and Charles strove to govern it by buying Wentworth, — afterwards known as Lord Strafford, — "the first Englishman," says Macaulay boldly, "disgraced by a peerage." Laud was placed at the head of the High Commission Court. Parliament defied the King, and the King defied them. He dissolved them; and, as I said, began to reign for years as an absolute monarch. The Star Chamber was in its glory, and such men as Eliot and Holles were in the Tower.

Such were the first five years of this young King's reign, — one steady insult to the best feeling of his people. In those five years, Rev. John White, minister of Dorchester, the founder of Massachusetts, was, in his way, encouraging this man, who had heard of New England, and teaching that to whom the name had never come before. "There was a land of refuge," White was saying to all men. And a larger and larger company of the merchants of London, of the merchants of the other cities, and gradually of the country gentlemen of England, were learning that, if their battle were lost at home, it might be won in a land where there was no bishop and no King. I make no question that White, and those who acted with him, appealed to every motive that was honest, that would swell the number of those who would engage in the colonization movement. I have myself, in my poor way, in later times, acted with those who were promoting emigration to the west of the Missouri River, when we thought that on that emigration great principles for all time depended. And I think therefore, that, unless men are very different now from what they were then, men entered into the great emigration from which we have grown with a large variety of motive. Only I am sure, no man came here because he loved King Charles, or because he believed in Laud's Court of High Commission. And I am sure, that John White and Matthew Cradock and Isaac Johnson and Richard Saltonstall and our great leader, Winthrop, meant that the enterprise should be controlled by men who would never give in to the tyrannies of Charles or to the pretensions of Laud. How well those intentions were carried out, I have next to show.

England "grows weary of her inhabitants; so as man, who is the most precious of all creatures, is here more vile and base than the earth we tread upon." These are the words which Winthrop uses, in the "Nine Reasons" which justify the new plantation. These reasons are passed from hand to hand among the men most saddened by the oppressions of the Star Chamber, and most determined to find freedom somewhere. As soon as Mr. Forster published his larger life of Sir John Eliot, our President, Mr. Winthrop, in correspondence with him, discovered that the paper on Emigration there spoken of, sent by Eliot in the Tower to Hampden in his house, was a copy of Winthrop's "Nine Reasons." Eliot had transcribed Winthrop's paper, and sent it to Hampden for his study. These men, the great leaders of the English Puritans, were thus personally interested in the enterprise here. We knew already that it had the support of Lord Brooke and Lord Warwick and Lord Say and Sele. It is now certain that John Hampden is not the Hampden who spent an early winter with our Plymouth friends; but it is equally certain that he and Eliot were interesting themselves in our Massachusetts Colony when it sailed, and were among those who saw how essential was this beginning to the success of their great cause. Under such auspices, the government and charter were transferred from England to New England, — the boldest change of base in history. In its success, as I believe, the history of constitutional liberty begins. That change was made by men who meant that their new-born State should not be dependent, if they could help it, on the powers which were ruling England to her ruin.[1]

On their arrival here, they settled the great question of bishop or no bishop, which was one of the elements of strife at home. They settled it by an arrangement of their churches, in the face of all that had been asserted by Whitgift and Bancroft and Laud. So far as the forms of government went, they swore their magistrates, their freemen and their people to be faithful to the government of the Commonwealth of Massachusetts Bay; but they alluded no more in that oath to their allegiance to King Charles than to allegiance to King Louis or to the Pope of Rome. The Governor and assistants only, for the first twelve years, were sworn to be faithful to King Charles; but, so soon as he took up arms against the Parliament, his name disappears from the oath, long before it was disused by any one in England. Four years only after the foundation of Boston, a rumor came from England, that a governor-general was to be appointed by the King. The magistrates took counsel with the ministers; and the ministers advised, that, if a governor-general were sent, "we ought not accept him; but defend our lawful possessions, if we were able; otherwise, to avoid and protract." Two years later, some English ship captains in our harbor intimated, that they should be glad to see the royal colors displayed on the fort in the harbor. They were answered, that we had not the King's colors to show. The shipmasters offered to lend them, but it cost a day's discussion and evident heart-burnings before they could be displayed there; and this was done only on a nicely drawn distinction on the King's authority in the fort and the King's authority in the Colony. Early in the history, Endicott cut the cross out of the colors; and from that moment till the

[1] I may be thought to speak of this "change of base" with the prejudice of a New-Englander. I am glad to quote Mr. John Forster's language, therefore. In his letter to Mr. Robert C. Winthrop, forwarding a copy of the Eliot manuscript, he says, "There is a new and striking interest contributed to a transaction which, more largely than any other in history, has affected the destinies of the human race."

The Eliot draft and a draft from the State-paper office were printed in our "Proceedings," at the date of July, 1865. Another copy is in Hutchinson, and another in "The Life and Letters of Winthrop."

Restoration, I think, the Commonwealth of Massachusetts had a flag of its own. On a new rumor, that the King or the Star Chamber proposed to extend their authority thus far, the chronicler, who had left his home to establish here his tabernacle, undoubtedly expresses the determination of all the leaders when he says, they would rather remove again, and establish themselves in a "vacuum domicilium," — a home which no sovereign claimed, — this side the King of kings. To the valley of the Mohawk, perhaps, or, if God guided, further west, — to some Salt-Lake Valley, if it were needed! They meant that men should know whether Charles's authority could go farther in America than the shores which the guns of his ships could command.

But there was no danger for Massachusetts. The bow had been bent too far, and it broke. The little history which had thus been rehearsed by a handful of zealous men, on the little stage of Massachusetts, was to be acted out by a larger company, to whom they sent many teachers, in the England which they feared. William Vassall, one of the Massachusetts Company, Lord Say and Sele and John Hampden, both patentees of Connecticut, determined to bring the question of ship-money to trial. Once more, as Mr. Sabine reminds us, the turning question is a question of the fisheries. The ship-money built the fleet which drove off Dutch intrusion of the English fishing privileges. Sir John Eliot, meanwhile, Hampden's friend and ours, had died in the Tower. Laud had tried his hand on the reformation of Scotland. Charles had followed up the experiment with an army; and Alexander Leslie, with his other army of ministers, — an army which was within itself a church, of which every corps possessed a presbytery, — drove Charles and his army back to England. So passed the ten years while Winthrop and Dudley and the rest were organizing New England into an independent State. The King had no choice left. By his own folly, he had wriggled himself to the corner of his board. He called, at last, a Parliament, and dissolved it. Then he was forced to call the Long Parliament; and then, though he did not know it, the game was done. "*Shah-mat*," says the Persian, as he finishes on the chess-board the game of simulated war, and the words have passed into all languages. Sometimes you take the bit of crowned ivory from the board, sometimes you leave it there. That is nothing. The game is ended. Shah-mat, — check-mate. The King is dead!

In Charles's case, the King, with his knights and bishops, hopped from square to square on their little board, for eight short years, hoping to avoid the inevitable. But the people of England had the power in their hands. The Great Remonstrance, at the end of 1641, showed that the Long Parliament understood its duty, and could do it. "If the vote had been lost," said Cromwell, as they left the House that night, "I would have sold all I had to-morrow, and would never have seen England more." He meant he would have come to New England.

"O'er the deep
Fly, and one current to the ocean add;
One spirit to the souls our fathers had;
One freeman more, America, to thee."

This was not the time when Charles stopped the ships on the Thames, when, it is said, Hampden was on board ready to emigrate. It is fairly doubted, whether Cromwell had joined that earlier emigration. This was four years later, — at the end of 1641. Had Cromwell come, he would have arrived here just before the first Commencement of Harvard College; he would have arrived, just as the General Court was striking the name of King Charles out of the oath; he would have arrived, just as the short-lived standing council was disarmed; he would have arrived, just as the position of the Lower House first came into discussion; he would have arrived, just as the four colonies were arranging their confederation. At the election day of that year, John Winthrop was chosen governor for the first year of his third term. Would he perhaps have yielded his seat the next year to Oliver Cromwell? Would Oliver Cromwell have been the sixth governor of Massachusetts? or would he have led a company to Strawberry Bank, to the Connecticut or to the Mohawk, and become himself the Protector of an infant Commonwealth?

It was not so written. The King tried war, — under the impression that has more than once deceived the cavaliers of a waning chivalry, that people who believe in precedents and principles, who trust in prayer because they trust in God, will not prove quick at fighting. At the stronghold of Nottingham, in the Sherwood Forest, where James had hunted, Charles displayed his banner. Two years of skirmishing advanced the final settlement but little; and the death of Hampden and Pym took from the Parliament the men who seemed their ablest guides. These two leaders were almost American except in name, both early friends of Massachusetts, both grantees of the charter of Connecticut. If Lord Nugent is to be believed, Hampden was actually on shipboard once on his way hither. Meanwhile our Earl of Warwick, who had really secured for us the Massachusetts charter, showed that his training for maritime adventures stood him well in stead, in his command of the Parliament fleet, which cut off from the King any foreign resources.

At this point, the Independents of England began more distinctly to study the methods of Massachusetts. Unterrified by the shock of arms, Parliament attempted the difficult question of church administration. The celebrated Westminster Assembly was convened, — hated, with good reason, by most children of recent generations, — but, for the first years of its existence, second only to the Long Parliament itself in its influence in England. To this assembly, Cotton, Hooker, and Davenport, the ministers of the first churches of Boston, Hartford, and New Haven, were earnestly invited by leading men in England, who dreaded the Presbyterian influence of that body. They were strongly tempted, I suppose, but they did not go. Hooker, for one, felt sure that he could arrange the church system of America. He believed in the independence of America too thoroughly to compromise our system by any failure in England. And, as it proved, the plans of Cotton have worked well here to this hour.

On the question of Presbyterian Church Government, or Independency, or Congregationalism, as Cotton preferred to call our form of it, a great deal seemed to depend. Among other things, the alliance with Presbyterian Scotland seemed to depend upon it. At the outset of the civil war, there seemed no doubt that the Presbyterian influence prevailed both in the Parliament and the Westminster Assembly. We are to remember all along, as Lord Nugent says, that nothing has more tended to cloud this history, than the use of the one word Puritan to represent Presbyterians and Independents. When we speak of the Puritans, as proclaiming religious liberty, in the trumpet tones of Milton, — we mean not the Presbyterians, but the Independents. Looking back upon history, we can see that the Presbyterians were tempted to hold that mid-way position, or position of compromise, which seldom triumphs in revolutions which involve a principle, — the position which the Girondists held in France in the first revolution, and which the Parliamentary opposition in the French Chambers held in the last. The little company of Independents steadily gained force in Parliament and in the Assembly, which their numbers at the outset did not seem to promise. What is of vast importance at such a crisis, it proved that, with such leaders as Cromwell, they were gaining the sway of the army, while the simplicity and democracy of their system gained, for the moment at least, the confidence of the great body of the people. In all their argument, they had always the great advantage of showing our working example of their theory. A working example is what the Englishman or American, of Saxon lineage, always respects as he respects no untried theory. The New-England churches were Independent Churches; and Cromwell and Vane and Fiennes and St. John used the tracts of Cotton and Hooker and Norton and the other New-England ministers, as being for a thousand reasons the best weapons in their arsenal.

In the arrangement of the churches of England, the theory of the New-England Independents triumphed over the theory of the Presbyterians. I do not claim that it triumphed because of their advocacy. I think it more safe to say, that it triumphed, because it was an extreme opinion, and those were extreme times. It triumphed without any formal vote. On the other hand, the formal votes of the Westminster Assembly arranged the Presbyterian order, and the Presbyterian machinery was established in London and in Lancashire. But no enactment of Parliament carried it out through England; and the more simple statement, which made each congregation an independent church, was the statement which for the period of the English Commonwealth prevailed in practice.

But the times had swept men beyond any mere question of

ecclesiastical arrangement. It was now a question between half-way men and men who, in President Lincoln's phrase, would "put it through." Cromwell and his friends among the Independents had found out what I suppose the leaders of the people find out in the beginning of all civil wars. They found out that, in their own army, the Essexes and the Manchesters were afraid of beating the King too well. The question of Independent *versus* Presbyterian, which was at first a question of church discipline, became a question of strategy in the field, of diplomacy in negotiation, of stern practice in Parliament, and at last in the Palace Yard. It became at last the question between the army and the Parliament. And, in that question, the Independents, — who ruled the army, — as we know, prevailed. The army purged the Parliament. The purged Parliament created the High Court of Justice, for the trying and judging of Charles Stuart. The High Court of Justice found him guilty of treason and beheaded him. There may be a people without a King, — there cannot be a King without a people.

I should like to discuss the question, whether their success were the success of might, or of right, or of both together. I believe the right conquered, when the might conquered. The Fathers of New England thought so: I think with them. I must not discuss that question now. I must leave it where Cromwell left it in his letter to Hammond. Two lawful powers in England disagree as to the disposition to be made of the King. One is the army, lawfully called, and consisting of thousands of Christian men, who have risked, and still risk, their lives, as witness for their sincerity. The other is the Parliament, chosen eight years since by the clumsy borough system of England; of which a majority believes that the King's word may still be taken. These two are at issue. Cromwell says that the army is the truer representation of the people of England. I think he is right. As to the question decided, whether Charles could be believed for an instant, when his interest required him to be false, all men know now that the decision of the army was the true one.

If I know myself, I can speak without prejudice here. Personally, I am proud to run back the lines of my own ancestry to Adrian Scrope who voted for the King's death, and afterwards, trusting in Charles II.'s amnesty, lost his own head for trusting it. By another line, I am proud to trace my ancestry to Mary Dyer, the Quaker, who, at nearly the same time, was hanged by the Massachusetts Puritans here on Boston Common, because she, too, thought she ought to obey God rather than man. I am proud of both these ancestors. I am as proud of one of them as I am of the other. They teach me very distinctly the lesson of the narrowness of Puritan presumption. But while I learn that lesson, I learn also the lesson of the Puritan's unfaltering loyalty to the King of kings. I think no man studies history fairly, who does not learn one of those lessons, while he learns the other; and, speaking for myself, if I had been called upon to make the great decision between the people of England and him who had had a fair chance to prove himself their king, — I hope I should not have been daunted by the terrors which then surrounded the mere name of Royalty. I hope I should have meted to him justice for his every act of falsehood and of treason. I hope I should have treated him as fairly as I would have treated the meanest soldier in his army. So tried, I have no doubt that Charles I. deserved death, if it were ever deserved by man from the hand of man.

That work was the work of the English Independents. The same men who established the Commonwealth of Massachusetts, in this act established the Commonwealth of England. Not that the Independents voted, without distinction, for the execution of the King; but they did mean, without distinction, to give to the people the rule of the Commonwealth. I have no desire to overstate the share which New-Englanders, who had recrossed to England, had in the great issue. I say simply that New England did, on a small scale, what England then did on a large scale; and that the same men directed there, as had sympathized here. Here, were but ten thousand men, all told: there, were at least a million. The population of England was at least five millions, of whom one-fifth, I suppose, were men. To the assistance of England, the ten thousand here lent such men as Stephen Winthrop, Edward Winslow, John Leverett, and Robert Sedgwick, who took the highest military rank; such men as Desborough, Peters, Downing, and Hopkins, who took high civil rank. And you remember it is said that of the first graduates of Harvard College, the abler part always returned to England to give there the service of their lives.[1]

The words "Independence" and "Independent" are now favorite words in America. I have observed in later days that they have found especial favor in connection with the word "Sovereignty" in those States of this Union which fancy they are descended from the cavaliers of England. "Independent and Sovereign States," they say. Favorite words in America, since a Continental Congress of the United States, led by the children of Roundheads, proclaimed the United States to be "free and independent." It is well, therefore, to remember how those words came into the English language. They are not in the English Bible. They are not in Shakspeare's plays. You read there of Dependence. Yes. But not yet of Independency. The word "Independency" was born when the hated Brownists separated themselves from the Church of England. The word "Independent" was borrowed from their vocabulary to designate the men who triumphed with Cromwell; and from that dictionary of the Church the word was borrowed again in 1776, when the United States of America became an independent nation.

I must not attempt any further details of the triumphs of the Commonwealths of England and of New England. I have attempted to show that their politics were at heart the same. The leaders of the Commonwealth of England were the friends of New England. The leaders in New England came here, with omens which seemed unpromising, to win a success which was denied at home. I know no self-sacrifice in history more loyal and gallant than that of our great governor, when he was asked to go back to England, to take place of honor and command, in their hopeful beginnings; and when he held to the little State in the wilderness, rather than return to the delights

[1] Johnson's Memoranda are in the following words, at the date 1672: "Ministers that have come from England, chiefly in the ten first years, ninety-four; of which returned, twenty-seven; died in the country (New England), thirty-six; yet alive in the country, thirty-one. Ministers bred in New England, and (excepting about ten) in Harvard College, one hundred and thirty-two, of which died in the country, ten; now living, eighty-one; removed to England, forty-one." (Chronological Table in New-England's Rarities, Archæol. Amer. vol. iv. p. 233.) [p. 103 of the edition of 1672.] The Triennial Catalogue gives only one hundred and one ministers up to 1672 in Harvard College. But all that Johnson names did not necessarily take the degree of A.B.

of home and the certainty of distinction. It was that little State, of perhaps 30,000 people, which treated almost as an equal with the Parliament of England. In speaking of that State, the Long Parliament speaks of commerce between "the kingdom of England" and "the kingdom of New England." To that independent State the Parliament yielded the privilege of universal commerce, which to all *colonies* of England was denied. And that independent State, in the next session of the General Court of Massachusetts, returned the international civility; and, by the first reciprocal treaty, gave to the kingdom of England like privileges to those which to "the kingdom of New England" had thus been granted. To the navigation laws of that Parliament and of Cromwell, England owes this day the commerce which whitens every sea. To that first reciprocal treaty, New England owed the early maritime development which has sent her ships to every ocean.

As time has passed by, the Parliament of England has learned that Oliver Cromwell was never sovereign in that island. In the line of statues of English sovereigns in Parliament House, the eye first rests upon the vacant space between the image of Charles I. and Charles II. There is no Cromwell there! Yet, if he were not sovereign of England for the ten years after the royal traitor died, it would be hard to say who was. He was not the sovereign of New England in those years. In those years, New England knew no sovereign but her people. But he was the friend of New England, and the friend of her rulers. They loved him, they believed in him, they honored him. He represented the policy which, for ten years, triumphed in Old England, and which has triumphed in New England till this time. Massachusetts is about to acknowledge her debt to Winthrop, which she can never pay, by erecting his statue in the National Capitol. There it is to stand, first among the founders of America; first, where Virginia Dare and John Smith and George Calvert, and even Roger Williams and William Penn, are second. When that obligation is thus acknowledged, Massachusetts may well erect in her own capitol, face to face with Chantrey's statue of George Washington, the statue which England has not reared, of Oliver Cromwell. It may bear this inscription: —

OLIVER CROMWELL.

This man believed in Independency.
He was the sovereign of England for ten years.
He was the friend of New England through his life.

This statue stands here till the England which we love, and from which we were born, shall know who her true heroes were.

EDUCATION IN MASSACHUSETTS.

LEGISLATION AND HISTORY.

By GEO. B. EMERSON.

EDUCATION IN MASSACHUSETTS.

LEGISLATION AND HISTORY.

THE subject assigned to me by the Committee of the Historical Society, is Education in Massachusetts,—Legislation and History. I shall endeavor to show, as far as I can do it in a single lecture, what Massachusetts has done for the advancement and diffusion of education, and how she has done it.

In 1636, three, or, at the utmost, four thousand emigrants, mostly from the mild southern counties of Old England, were dwelling in sixteen towns and hamlets, on the sandy shores of Massachusetts Bay. They were not yet hardened to the fierce extremes of a New-England climate, and had suffered and were suffering terribly from the heats of summer, the blustering chilly winds of spring, and the cold and snow-storms of winter, in their hastily built log-cabins, and wretched huts and hovels, no better, often, than the wigwams of the savage Indians. They were the most religious people under heaven; yet their only place of worship in Boston was built with mud-walls and a roof thatched with straw. They had been exposed to scarcity of all kinds, sometimes nearly approaching to absolute famine. When the large colony led by Governor Winthrop reached Salem, in June, 1630, they found that, during the previous winter, more than a fourth part of their predecessors had died, and many of the survivors were ill; and, of the new-comers, a fifth part fell victims to disease before the end of autumn.

Yet, in the first volume of the Records of the General Court, we read,—

"At a Court holden Sept. 8, 1636, and continued by adjournment to the 28th of the eighth month, October, 1636, the

Court agreed to give £400 towards a school or college; £200 to be paid next year, and £200 when the work is finished; and the next Court to appoint where and what building." At a General Court held at Newtown, on the 2d of the ninth month, 1637, "The college is ordered to be at Newtown."

The people of Massachusetts at that time were poor, with all the hardships of new settlers in a savage country, clearing up the forests, building houses and barns and churches, enlarging their pastures, and bringing the earth into cultivation.

Four hundred pounds sterling, then, would correspond to $2,000. This would be a grant of fifty cents for each individual of the four thousand inhabitants, equal to a grant, at the same rate, for each individual of the present population, say one million two hundred and fifty thousand, of $625,000. But it must be remembered that a dollar then was equivalent to several dollars now; and that Massachusetts then was one of the poorest States in the world, and is now one of the richest, — its valuation in 1865 being more than one thousand millions. Considering these things, we may well conclude with Dr. Dwight, "It is questionable whether a more honorable specimen of public spirit can be found in the history of mankind."[1] The name of the town was soon afterwards changed from Newtown to Cambridge, "a grateful tribute to the transatlantic literary parent of many of the first emigrants, and indicative of the high destiny to which they intended the institution should aspire."[2]

"In the year 1638," says President Quincy, "while they were only contemplating its commencement, John Harvard, a dissenting clergyman of England, resident at Charlestown, died, and bequeathed one-half of his whole property, and his entire library, to the institution. An instance of benevolence thus striking and timely, proceeding from one who had been scarcely a year in the country, was accepted by our Fathers as an omen of divine favor. With prayer and thanksgiving they immediately commenced the seminary, and conferred upon it the name of Harvard."[3]

What was done in the endowment of Harvard College has been imitated a thousand times since. The beneficence of the State has been enlarged and multiplied by the beneficence of

[1] Dwight's Travels in New England, vol. i. p. 481, as quoted by President Quincy, in History of Harvard University, vol. i. p. 8.

[2] Quincy's Hist. H. U., vol. i. p. 9.

[3] Id., pp. 9, 10.

individuals. The State gives £400 for the founding of a school at Cambridge; John Harvard adds £800. The towns throughout the colony contribute according to, or far beyond, their means; individuals with wonderful munificence. In the course of eight years, £269 18*s.* 8*d.* were given by the towns in the four colonies,[1] for the benefit of the officers and students in the college. Of this sum, Boston gave nearly £85; Charlestown, £37 16*s.* 2*d.*; Lynn, £1. In 1654, Rev. Mr. Allen, of Dedham, gave two cows, valued at £9. In 1656, Richard Dana, in cotton cloth, 9*s.*; a widow in Roxbury, £1; Richard Saltonstall, £104. The inhabitants of Eleuthera, one of the Bahama Islands, "out of their poverty, in testimony of their gratitude towards the inhabitants of Massachusetts, for necessaries sent them in their extreme want," £124. This shows that charity to strangers began early in Massachusetts. The island of Eleuthera was then farther off than Ireland or Crete is now.

In 1669, of £2,697 5*s.* paid by the inhabitants in contributions for erecting a new college building, the town of Portsmouth gave £60 a year, for seven years; of which Richard Cutts subscribed £20 per annum; and Boston £800, of which Sir Thomas Temple gave £100, and Benjamin Gibbs £50; Salem, £130 2*s.* 2*d.*, of which Rev. Mr. Higginson subscribed £5, Mr. William Brown £40, Mr. Edmund Batter £20; the town of Hull, £3 18*s.*; Scarborough in Maine, £2 9*s.* 6*d.*:[2] so universal was the generous feeling towards the college.

The amount of donations in money during the seventeenth century was £6,134 16*s.* 10*d.* Then there were large gifts in land and books. The poor gave according to their ability; Richard Harr, one great salt, and one small trencher salt; Mr. Vane, a fruit-dish, sugar-spoon, and silver-tipped jug; Mr. Wilson, one pewter flagon; Sir Thomas Temple, one pair of globes; John Willet, a bell; Edward Page, one silver goblet; the farmers, gifts in corn, from many bushels down to a single peck.

One of the most remarkable things in the history of Harvard College is the fact that, in all the constitutions of the college, there is nothing illiberal or sectarian, nothing to check the freest pursuit of truth in theological opinions, and in every thing else;

[1] Plymouth, New Haven, Connecticut, and Massachusetts.

[2] Quincy's H. C., Appendix, vol. i. p. 508.

and this, too, while the founders of the college were severely and strictly Orthodox, often exclusive in their own opinions, and that their object was unquestionably to provide for the thorough education of ministers of the gospel of like views with themselves. Whether it was that they had confidence that free inquiry would lead others to the same conclusions it had led themselves; or that there were differences of opinion among them, which prevented the framing of a declaration of faith that should satisfy all; or that they were beginning to find that a declaration of faith, while it excluded those who honestly differed, could never exclude hypocrites; or that they had a profound and reverent belief that the living God would, in all future time, be near the souls of all true and earnest men, to enlighten and guide them; or whether it was by a special providence that we have been secured from what has been elsewhere a plague and a snare, — we know not: we only know that no subscription or declaration of faith has ever been required from any officer of the college. The device on the first seal was three open books, with VERITAS upon them: Search for THE TRUTH everywhere; for a college or school, the noblest and best motto possible. This was succeeded by *In Christi Gloriam*, — to the glory of Christ; and this soon after by the present motto, *Christo et Ecclesiæ*, — to Christ and the Church.

How earnest and sincere our Puritan Fathers were in doing all that could be fairly done to secure soundness in the faith, is shown by the uniform character of their legislation.

In the Records of the Court for May 3, 1654, we read, —

"Forasmuch as it greatly concerns the welfare of this country that the youth thereof be educated not only in good literature but sound doctrine, this Court doth therefore commend it to the serious consideration and special care of the officers of the college and the selectmen of the several towns, not to admit or suffer any such to be continued in the office or place of teaching, educating, or instructing of youth or children, in the college or schools, that have manifested themselves unsound in the faith or scandalous in their lives, and not giving due satisfaction according to the rules of Christ."

The conditions for admission at Harvard College, established by President Dunster, for the year 1642 and onward, are as follows: —

1. "Whoever shall be able to read Cicero, or any other such like classical author, at sight, and, correctly and without assistance, to speak and write Latin, in prose and verse, and to inflect exactly the paradigms of Greek nouns and verbs, has a right to expect to be admitted into the college; and no one may claim admission without these qualifications."

And, throughout their course, the scholars were not, within the college limits, upon any pretext, to use the vernacular, unless when called to deliver an oration, or some other public exercise, in English.[1]

From this it appears that the standard for admission was higher than it has been since. I believe that, not comparatively, but absolutely, boys were better fitted for college then than they are now. They had better teachers. Few teachers at present are able, by their own example and usage, to teach boys to speak the Latin language readily and correctly. Few are themselves able to read Cicero or Tacitus at sight. A great mistake, one of the greatest possible, has been made, in relinquishing the mode of teaching the Latin language at that time prevalent, I believe, in England and throughout Germany, as well as in this country. For, unquestionably, the only sure way of learning a language rapidly, pleasantly, satisfactorily, and so as to be a permanent acquisition, is the natural way; that is, as a spoken language. In consequence of this change, the character of the

[1] Scholares vernaculâ linguâ intra collegii limites, nullo pretextu, utuntor, nisi ad orationem, aut aliud aliquod exercitium publicum Anglice habendum evocati fuerint. (President Dunster's Laws and Rules, 1642–46, in Quincy's Hist., vol. i. p. 578).

"The learned and excellent Henry Dunster," says Dr. Palfrey, "when he accepted this great charge" (of the Presidency of the college), "had just arrived from England, having been there a non-conformist minister, after receiving an education at Emmanuel College, Cambridge." (Palfrey, vol. ii. p. 49.) He drew up the Laws and Rules of the college, and probably settled the course of study, according to the practice of the English Universities at that time. It consisted, in a large degree, of Latin, Greek, and English, with something of Hebrew, Syriac, and Chaldee, and also of divinity. It included Arithmetic, Geometry, Physics, Logic, Ethics, Politics, and Rhetoric. In the Saturday afternoons of summer, lectures were given on the nature of plants; in winter, on history. Much time was spent in discussion, and still more in composition. ("New-England's First Fruits," in Mass. Hist. Coll., vol. i. pp. 245–6.)

Few persons, if any, have done so much for education and discipline, in America, as President Dunster. See many curious particulars of his life, opinions, and death, and appearance, so far as relates to the body, two hundred and fifty years after his death, in the second of the instructive and delightful volumes of Dr. Palfrey's History.

professed teacher has been declining, perhaps continually, until the beginning of this century.

In other respects, also, the boys were better fitted for college than they recently have been.

There were no cities. The greater part of the people lived in the country, nearly all on farms. In Boston there was little room for farms, and not much for gardens; but many of the inhabitants had gardens and farms on the islands of the Bay and at Muddy River, now Brookline, where their herds were kept. The boys spent most of their time in the fields and forests and along the rivers and the sea, hunting bears and deer, trapping foxes, shooting wild turkeys, wild geese, and wild ducks; or fishing, riding, driving, swimming, rowing, and sailing; or at work with those who were laying out roads through the woods, digging wells and ditches, making walls, and fences against the wolves, building houses, barns, fortifications, churches, ships, mills, boats, and ships, laying out and cultivating gardens, planting orchards, and engaged in all the labors of husbandry. They thus became hardened to the climate, and gained good constitutions and health, and moreover became acquainted with natural objects,—rocks and soils; animals, wild and tame, savage and civilized; the trees and shrubs of the woods, and the flowers and herbs of the gardens and fields; and saw the powers of water and of wind, and felt the effects of sunshine and cold and all the forces of the atmosphere. The elder boys belonged to the train-bands, which, under able officers, were drilled — not over twice or thrice a week, the law provides — to the use of the musket, the sword and the spear. Such were their summer occupations.

In winter, they helped to clear the woods and cut down the forest-trees, sledded the logs to the wood-pile and the timber to the mills, and assisted at first in hewing it, afterward, in sawing it into beams, posts, joists, planks, boards, clapboards, and shingles, or squaring it and building it directly into houses. The winter evenings, on those solitary farms, were probably spent in reading,— an easy and pleasant thing, before the existence of theatres, balls, concerts, and dram-shops. And they doubtless had their huskings and other merry-makings.

Has any system been devised to take the place of this, and give the young man, in a higher degree, full possession of all his powers and faculties of body and mind, or to give him, in the same degree, the masculine qualities of hardy self-reliance with cautiousness, manly courage with coolness, resolution with patience, and power of endurance with habits of strenuous and cheerful labor? What better discipline have we devised or are we devising for the drawing out and training these manly qualities?

A few men, whom we have known, have been obliged by force of circumstances, to approach this heroic early education. And it may be a fair question, Would Mark Hopkins, Francis Wayland, Daniel Webster, Jared Sparks, Cornelius Felton, Thomas Hill, have been finer specimens of humanity, or even better scholars and teachers, if they had been put, at seven, into schools, and kept there ten months of every year, till they entered college at sixteen, instead of giving their early years to the labors of the farm, the forest, and the workshop?

Milton calls "a complete and generous education that which fits a man to perform justly, skilfully, and magnanimously, all the offices, both private and public, of peace and of war." This primitive, heroic boyhood was not only a true preparation for the offices of a peaceful, private life, for the duties of town officer, magistrate, and representative to the General Court, and for those of privates and officers, in the wars always threatening from the Indians around, and often from the French at the North and the Dutch on the South; but it was the best preparation for the studies of the college, as it gave the student, for the object of his thoughts while engaged in those studies, instead of mere words, the facts of nature, real things and their properties and relations.

Everybody is now ready to admit the important place which natural and physical science should have in a liberal education; but all are not aware that such science, to be real, must be founded on personal observation. These boys were laying such a foundation. A boy engaged in stoning a well, in raising stones for a wall, or in drawing water from the well by an old fashioned well-pole, was studying the properties of the lever. In splitting logs, he become acquainted with the wedge; in making roads, with the inclined plane. In helping to lay out a farm, with a surveyor's chain and compass, so as to fix, justly and accurately, the bounds between neighbor and neighbor, he got the first elementary ideas which lie at the very foundation of geometry, and a feeling of the importance of doing justice, at the same time. In selecting, hewing, and shaping the different trees for all the purposes of the primitive essential arts, he became acquainted with the strength, elasticity, hardness, tenacity, and other properties, of all kinds of wood. Even in his play, he was still at his studies. In rowing, he was studying the lever; in sculling, the resolution of forces,—feeling as well as seeing. When he hoisted his sail by pulling at a rope passing round a truck at the head of his mast, he was studying the element of the pulley; when, to raise the sail to the utmost, he pulled out the middle of that rope fastened at the foot, to haul taut and belay, he was learning the properties of the rope-machine. When, sitting in the stern of his boat, he trimmed his sail to the varying wind, on a narrow, winding creek, or on Neponset River, or Charles, obliged often to come as near as possible to the wind, he was studying the resolution of forces, in the most favorable position in which they can be studied. When for the well-pole he substituted the windlass, and with it drew water from the well, he was learning the nature, by observing the uses, of the wheel and axle. When he dug a ditch or assisted in building a dam and arranging a flume and a gate for the water-power, he was studying hydrostatics and hydraulics. Arranging the stones for grinding corn, he was studying the combination of wheels; and, setting the stones to grind, the centrifugal force. The saw-mill and the wind-mill, when they were introduced, showed him machinery in more complicated action.[1]

Then again, in those early days, there were no spelling-books nor English grammars for children to waste their time upon. The deluge of children's books had not begun. Children learned their letters from verses in the Bible, — from those sublimest of all sentences: "In the beginning, God created the heaven and the earth;" "and God said, Let there be light, and there was light."

[1] I perfectly well remember standing, when a child, in a still morning, on the bank of a river, and watching a man engaged in chopping wood, at a distance, on the other side. I heard every stroke of his axe, but I heard it some little time after it was struck. It was my first lesson in acoustics and optics. I saw the slowness of the motion of sound compared with the velocity of that of light.

Boys and girls were obliged to read the few books they had, which were often the most excellent that we have, again and again, till they knew them thoroughly, almost by heart. They became, of necessity, familiar with the Gospels, with the beautiful histories of the Old Testament, the glorious poetry of the prophets, of Job, and the Psalms, the profound wisdom of Solomon and the divine wisdom of the apostles.[1] The little time given to the Latin language was spent in learning and using the words essential to conversation; and in studying the language of Cicero and Virgil, instead of the unintelligible generalizations of grammar, what John Milton calls "the most intellective abstractions of logic and metaphysics," so commonly begun with at the present day.

What a pleasant way of learning a language must that have been! — Walking about with the teacher over the farm, in the barn-yard, and in the woods; and learning from him how to speak, in Latin, of all they saw. How easy for persons so taught to continue the use of the language, in college! and how deeply fixed in the memory must all the usual forms of the language thus become! Whoever has had the good fortune to learn any modern language by hearing and speaking it alone for a few years, must know how imperfect and superficial, in comparison, is the knowledge obtained from books only.

Such was the necessary but real and noble preparation for college which was given to nearly all the boys in Massachusetts purposing to receive the highest education of the time. Has any thing better been yet introduced to take the place of such a preparation? Does the vast time given to arithmetic, destined to be never used; or the innumerable lessons in geography, destined to be speedily forgotten; or the volumes of choice and exquisite selections from the best and finest poetry and prose, most of it wholly beyond the capacity of those who are to read them, — give a better preparation? Are these an adequate substitute for readings from the book of Nature, from the works and word of God?

[1] The English language is spoken by the common people of New England far better than it is anywhere else. This is owing, I doubt not, to the fact, that they have always been familiar with the Old and New Testaments, in our beautiful translation.

In the year 1847, the President of this Society, — I heard it from his own lips, and know that he will pardon my telling the story, — himself a lineal descendant of John Winthrop, under whose administration the grant I have read, and the laws I am going to read, were passed, was sitting in the diplomatic gallery of the House of Commons, with Sir Robert Peel, to whom a letter from Edward Everett had introduced him, engaged in conversation; when Sir Robert suddenly interrupted himself, and said, "I must now leave you, as I see that Macaulay is going to speak, and I always want to hear what he says." He left him; and our friend presently heard, among other good things from Macaulay, —

"I say, therefore, that the education of the people ought to be the first concern of a State. . . . This is my deliberate conviction; and in this opinion I am fortified by thinking, that it is also the opinion of all the great legislators, of all the great statesmen, of all the great political philosophers, of all ages and of all nations. . . . Sir, it is the opinion of all the greatest champions of civil and religious liberty in the Old World and in the New; and of none — I hesitate not to say it — more emphatically than of those whose names are held in the highest estimation by the Protestant Nonconformists of England. Assuredly, if there be any class of men whom the Protestant Nonconformists of England respect more highly than another, — if any whose memory they hold in deeper veneration, — it is that class of men, of high spirit and unconquerable principles, who, in the days of Archbishop Laud, preferred leaving their native country, and living in the savage solitudes of a wilderness, rather than to live in a land of prosperity and plenty, where they could not enjoy the privilege of worshipping their Maker freely, according to the dictates of their conscience. Those men, illustrious for ever in history, were the founders of the Commonwealth of Massachusetts; but, though their love of freedom of conscience was illimitable and indestructible, they could see nothing servile or degrading in the principle, that the State should take upon itself the charge of the education of the people. In the year 1642," [should he not have said, 1647 ?] "they passed their first legislative enactment on this subject; in the preamble of which they distinctly pledged themselves to this principle, that education was a matter of the deepest possible importance and the greatest possible interest to all nations and to all communities; and that, as such, it was, in an eminent degree, deserving of the peculiar attention of the State."[1]

[1] Macaulay's Speeches, vol. ii. pp. 334 and 335, ed. of Redfield, New York, 1853.

That preamble is in these words: —

"It being one chief project of the old deluder, Satan, to keep men from the knowledge of the Scriptures, as, in former times, by keeping them in an unknown tongue, so, in these latter times, by persuading from the use of tongues, that so at least the true sense and meaning of the original might be clouded by false gloss of saint-seeming deceivers; — now, that learning may not be buried in the grave of our fathers, in the Church and Commonwealth, the Lord assisting our endeavors," — and here follows the law: —

"It is therefore ordered, that every township in this jurisdiction, after the Lord hath increased them to the number of fifty householders, shall then forthwith appoint one within their town to teach all such children as shall resort to him, to write and read, whose wages shall be paid, either by the parents or masters of such children, or by the inhabitants in general, by way of supply, as the major part of those that order the prudentials of the town shall appoint, provided, those that send their children be not oppressed by paying much more than they can have them taught for in other towns; and it is further ordered, that, where any town shall increase to the number of one hundred families or householders, they shall set up a grammar school, the master thereof being able to instruct youth so far as they may be fitted for the university, provided that, if any town neglect the performance hereof above one year, that every such town shall pay £5 to the next school, till they shall perform this order."[1]

A grammar school was then understood to be a school in which the Latin and Greek languages were taught.

In 1683, Oct. 10, we read, "The Court doth order that whenever a town has five hundred families, it shall support two grammar schools and two writing schools."

On June 14, 1642, the following law was passed:[2] —

"This Court, taking into consideration the great neglect of many parents and masters, in training up their children in learning and labor, and other employments which may be profitable to the Commonwealth, do hereby order and decree, that in every town the chosen men appointed for managing the prudential affairs of the same shall henceforth stand charged with the care of the redress of this evil; . . . and, for this end,

[1] Mass. Records, Nov. 11, 1647, vol. ii. p. 203.

[2] I had considerable doubt, and still have, whether this law or the one of 1647 were the one referred to by Macaulay; but, as this law really has no preamble, but only a short introduction in no degree remarkable, and, as it is almost wholly upon the matter of apprenticeship, I have concluded that it must have been to the other that he had reference.

they, or the greater number of them, shall have power to take account, from time to time, of all parents and masters, and of their children, concerning the calling and employment of their children, especially of their ability to read and understand the principles of religion, and the capital laws of this country, and to impose fines upon such as shall refuse to render such accounts to them when they shall be required; and they shall have power, with consent of any court or the magistrate, to put forth apprentices the children of such as they shall find not to be able and fit to employ and bring them up; . . . and for their better performance of this trust committed to them, they may divide the town amongst them, appointing to every one of the said townsmen a certain number of families to have special oversight of. They are also to provide that a sufficient quantity of materials, as hemp, flax, &c., may be raised in the several towns, and tools and implements provided for working out the same."[1]

Next to the law providing free public schools for all, this law providing for the accustoming of all children to labor, and their proper and sufficient training in some useful employment, shows most strikingly the wisdom and forethought of these men of Massachusetts. The observance and the perfecting of the former law, and the copying of it by other States, have been an immeasurable blessing to the world. The neglect of this latter law has been an equally vast misfortune.[2]

A very large part of the poverty found now among the natives of New England may be traced to this neglect. A great deal of the crime has this same cause. To this neglect, more probably than to any other cause, is due the great number of persons setting up in business, without any skill or knowledge or experience or any other qualifications, and soon failing; — ninety-seven per cent in the principal street in Boston, as was found a few years ago to have been the case for many years. To this neglect is owing that great army of middle-men, who, even now, are preying like vam-

[1] I have not quoted the whole of this law. It contains, at some length, farther provisions for the certain and safe employment of children of both sexes, in things useful to the Commonwealth.

[2] My own opinion is, that the education of no girl or boy ought to be considered finished, even so far as common schools are concerned, who has only had his mental, moral, and spiritual faculties developed, and knowledge given, principles fixed, and reverential habits formed. His bodily powers ought also to be exercised upon something useful, at every step in his course. This might be done without any loss to his intellectual nature, and with immeasurable benefit to his physical. Such an education would make every work and duty of after life more easy and pleasant.

pires upon the poor in this town and this country. The present very intelligent warden of the State Prison, Gideon Haynes, informs me, that "of the convicts committed to this prison in the last forty years, over eighty per cent had no trades." "I cannot with any certainty," he adds, "say how many of that number might have been saved by learning a trade; but from the fact that all received, who were capable of learning, have during the above period been taught one, and that only *nine per cent* of the number have been recommitted, I am satisfied that at least fifty per cent might have been saved by a good trade."

Those legislators sought, not only to prevent ignorance of law and of duty by universal education, but to prevent poverty and crime by universal intelligent industry.

A considerable portion of the inhabitants of all the large cities of the Atlantic coast are paupers. Here we have one cause. Is it too late to take measures to prevent much of the poverty and crime of Massachusetts, by laws requiring every child not provided for by the wealth of his parents with a thorough and learned education, to be brought up to some trade or other useful occupation?

A negro had been left, by one James Smith, at Portsmouth, and been retained in bondage. In the records of the General Court, for Nov. 4, 1646, we read, —

"The General Court, conceiving themselves bound by the first opportunity to bear witness against the heinous and crying sin of man-stealing, as also to prescribe such timely redress for what is past, and such a law for the future as may sufficiently deter all others belonging to us to have to do in such vile and most odious courses, justly abhorred of all good and just men, do order, that the negro interpreter, with others unlawfully taken, be, by the first opportunity (at the charge of the country, for the present), sent to his native country of Guinea, and a letter with him of the indignation of the Court thereabouts; and, in justice hereof, desiring our honored Governor would please to put this order in execution."[1]

Such was the sublime consistency of these men. Was there any earlier or more decided utterance against slavery and the slave-trade than this?

If this is not a serious challenge, what is? It should be remembered that, at the time when this indignant protest was

[1] Mass. Records, vol. ii. p. 168.

made, every other government on earth was, apparently, altogether indifferent to the existence and evil of slavery. It must be admitted that this lofty Christian tone of feeling did not last always. With the decay of education, this spirit of universal liberty decayed. Mingling with the rest of the world, the people of Massachusetts gradually lowered their standard, and felt and acted like the rest. Some of them held slaves. The oldest members of some of our oldest families must still remember them. Of cruelty towards them, I know not that there is even a tradition.[1]

The spirit of the laws I have read is purely republican. They protect the children and apprentices in their right to be instructed, against the indifference or cupidity of masters and parents, but leave it to the majority of the inhabitants of each town to provide the means in their own way. Further, — what was quite as essential to the accomplishment of the design of the law, they provide a standard below which the qualifications of a teacher in the grammar schools shall not fall. He shall "be able to instruct youth so far as they shall be fitted for the university," thus bringing within the reach of all the children of every town of one hundred families the means of preparing themselves for the highest course of instruction then or now existing in the country. Had this law continued in operation, youth from nearly every town in the Commonwealth would now be enjoying this privilege.[2]

The whole policy of the Puritan colonists in this matter ought to fill us with admiration. In their simplicity they conceived, and in their poverty executed, a scheme which had proved too high for the intellect and too vast for the power of every previous potentate or people, — the hitherto unimagined idea of universal education. Fugitives from the persecution of the Old World, and hemmed in between the waves of a stormy

[1] Those amongst us who have openly or silently sympathized with the spirit of this law, have for many years been accustomed to hear reproaches heaped upon us, because we allowed such disturbers of the peace as Garrison, Phillips, and May to go unhanged. The reproach now is, that such men did not arise two centuries ago, that this law was ever allowed to fall into oblivion, that such men as Garrison did not live amongst us always.

[2] Much of this, and several subsequent paragraphs, is taken from an article in the "North American Review," published many years since.

sea and the savages of a boundless wilderness, so little were they subdued by the hardness of their lot, that they regarded ignorance, irreligion, and sin as the only evils, and religious instruction, intellectual discipline, and proper employment, as the effectual remedies. Where shall their descendants look for a higher example?

How it came to pass that the early colonists of New England should form laws, for the advancement of education and the rights of men, of such wisdom, liberality, and forecast, it is not difficult to conjecture. The civil, and especially the spiritual, leaders of the first emigrations to Massachusetts were the most highly educated men that ever led colonies. They were independent, liberty-loving Anglo-Saxons. Their leader and many of his associates were brought up "among books and learned men."[1] They possessed, and they long continued to exert, an influence of the highest and noblest, because of the most disinterested, kind. They intended to form a Christian Commonwealth, all the members of which should understand and obey the laws of God and of the State. We may differ from some of their theological opinions; we may regret that, within half a century after the time of which we are speaking, the spirit of persecution, which had such frightful power in Britain and in most countries on the continent of Europe, reached and affected even them. We may regret, while we do not wonder, that they should have been misled by a belief that institutions and laws made for the Jews alone, in one stage of their progress, were intended for all mankind in every stage. But we may search the world in vain for more conspicuous, unselfish devotion to the cause of what they believed to be truth and the rights of humanity. Of the ministers of the fifteen or sixteen towns in Massachusetts,[2] the greater part had been educated at Oxford or Cambridge. And they were not educated men of an ordinary type. Archbishop

[1] Robert Ryce, writing to John Winthrop, on the 12th of August, 1629, says, "How hard will it be, for one brought up among books and learned men, to live in a barbarous place, where is no learning, and less civility." — See Historical Collections, 4th Series, vol. vi. p. 393.

[2] Palfrey's N. E., pp. 371–2. Newberry, Ipswich, Saugus, Salem, Charlestown, Weymouth, Newtown, Watertown, Boston, Roxbury, Dorchester, Hingham, Medford, Concord, Dedham; and Wessagussett, now Savin Hill and South Boston, or Mount Wollaston, now Quincy. Winnesimit, now Chelsea, belonged to Boston.

Laud did not meddle with ordinary, dull preachers. He silenced the famous preachers, — those that were distinguished for their learning and eloquence, their character and influence. Many of the men thus silenced came to Massachusetts. And they came not alone: their parishioners and friends, who loved them best, and most highly valued liberty of conscience, and least feared the terrors of the ocean and hardships of a savage wilderness, came with them.

Under date of Sept. 4, 1632, Governor Winthrop writes: —

"The 'Griffin,' a ship of three hundred tons, arrived. . . . She brought about two hundred passengers. . . . In this ship came Mr. Cotton, Mr. Hooker, and Mr. Stone, ministers; and Mr. Peirce, Mr. Haynes (a gentleman of great estate), Mr. Hoffe, and many other men of good estates. They got out of England with much difficulty, all places being belaid to have taken Mr. Cotton and Mr. Hooker."

Dr. Palfrey says of these men, and he knew of whom he was speaking, —

"In one ship came John Haynes, an opulent landholder of the county of Essex, and three famous divines, — Thomas Hooker, Samuel Stone, and John Cotton. They were men of eminent capacity and sterling character, fit to be concerned in the founding of a State. In all its generations of worth and refinement, Boston has never seen an assembly more illustrious for generous qualities and for manly culture, than when the magistrates of the young colony welcomed Cotton and his fellow-voyagers at Winthrop's table." [1]

Many of these men brought their libraries with them. Of one, John Harvard's, of two hundred and sixty volumes, we have the catalogue. There is not probably now a private library in America, of the same number of volumes, so well selected and so valuable. Many of the authors, such as Beza, Chrysostom, Calvin, Luther, Bacon, and Camden, and all the classical authors, — Homer, Plutarch, and Isocrates, Lucan, Pliny, Sallust, Terence, Juvenal, and Horace, — are hardly less valuable now than they were then.

Among them were the writings of Luther, who was not only the great leader of the Reformation, and the translator of the whole Bible into exquisite classical German, — which holds the

[1] Palfrey's Hist., vol. i. p. 367.

same place for its beautiful language amongst the Germans as King James's translation among the English, — but the most able, eloquent, and strenuous advocate of the highest education in the classical languages, in Hebrew, in History, Philosophy, Botany, Logic, Rhetoric, Music, and the Mathematics, for those who could afford such an education, and of schools for universal, elementary education, which all boys should be compelled to attend.[1] And in these writings they must have read such sentences as these: —

"It is brutish recklessness to act merely for the present time, and to say, as for us, we will rule now; but we care not how it shall be with those who come after us."[2]

"For the Prince of Darkness is shrewd enough to know, that, where the languages flourish, there his power will soon be so rent and torn that he cannot readily repair it."

"Let us bethink ourselves, that haply we may not be able to retain the gospel without the knowledge of the languages in which it was written. For they are the scabbard in which the sword of the Spirit is sheathed; they are the casket in which this jewel is enshrined."

"Hence we may conclude that, where the languages do not abide, there, in the end, the gospel must perish."

"The Sophists averred, that the Scriptures were obscure. . . . But they did not see that all that was wanted, was a knowledge of the languages in which it was recorded; for nothing is more plain-spoken than God's word, when we have become thorough masters of its language."[3]

"Had I passed my days in obscurity, and had I received no aid from the languages towards a sure and exact understanding of the Scriptures, I might have led a holy life, and, in my retirement, have preached sound doctrine; but then I should have left the Pope and the Sophists, together with the whole body of Antichrist, just where I found them."[4]

1 See Dr. Martin Luther's Address to the Councilmen of all the towns of Germany, *passim*. Barnard's American Journal of Education, vol. iv. p. 421.

2 American Journal of Education, vol. iv. pp. 432, 433.

3 Id., pp. 434, 435.

4 See how Luther valued the work of teaching: "As for myself, if I had children, and were able, I would teach them not only the languages and history, but singing likewise; and with music I would combine a full course of mathematics." — *Id.*, p. 437.

"Cheerfully let thy son study; and should he, the while, even be compelled to earn his bread, yet remember that you are offering to our Lord God a fair block of marble, out of which he can hew for you a perfect work." — *Sermon on Keeping Children at School*, p. 440.

"For my part, if I were, or were compelled, to leave off preaching, and to enter

We must remember that all this was written and published throughout Germany in 1524.

There is another thing to be taken into consideration, to account for the wisdom of this legislation. None were chosen to the Legislature but religious men, — men of spotless character, the best, wisest, and most trustworthy to be found, — men who would naturally make the best laws they could. From which of these United States are the best, wisest, and most trustworthy men now sent, and those only? To which Congress, within the memory of any person living, have only men of spotless character, the best, wisest, and most trustworthy to be found, been sent, from Massachusetts? To which branch of which legislature of the State, to which common council of the city, since the first, have such men and such men only been sent? The very thing which should always be considered a disqualification for a place in either of these assemblies is often the only qualification a candidate possesses, — the having some private interest to advance therein.

This law of 1647 was the establishment and the beginning of that great and wise system of common schools for the education of the whole people, which has been and is the honor of this Commonwealth, and which has been spreading, and is destined to spread, until it controls and guides the education of the whole people, not only in every State in this country, but of all States in every country.

From the beginning, the practice seems to have prevailed of transacting the business of the several towns at meetings of all the freemen. Every freeman was here naturally led to inform himself as to all the interests of the community, and was free to utter and urge his opinions. These town-meetings thus became societies for the discussion of real questions of public interest; schools, therefore, of training in argument, logic, and eloquence. These have continued, in all the *towns*, up to the present day, and must have had vast influence

some other vocation, I know not an office that would please me better than that of schoolmaster or teacher of boys. For I am convinced, that, next to preaching, this is the most useful and greatly the best labor in all the world; and, in fact, I am sometimes in doubt which of the positions is the more honorable." — *Id.*, p. 441.

in forming men to habits of thought and enlightened discussion.[1]

In 1632, the inhabitants of Dorchester designated twelve of their number to meet weekly for the consideration of public affairs. About the same time, Watertown chose three for the same purpose. In 1634, the people of Boston chose "three to make up the ten to manage the affairs of the town."[2] In 1635, Mr. Frothingham tells us of an "order made by the inhabitants of Charlestown, at a full meeting, for the government of the town by selectmen."[3] This is the element of representation; and "at the fifth General Court held in Massachusetts, twenty-four persons appeared, delegated by eight towns; 'namely, three each from Newtown, Watertown, Charlestown, Boston, Roxbury, Dorchester, Saugus, and Salem,'—to meet and consider of such matters as they (the freemen) were to take order in at the same General Court;"[4] and thus the government of Massachusetts first became truly a representative government.

The leaders and first legislators of Massachusetts were unconsciously laying the foundations and shaping the laws for a government and state of society wholly new. Every act of their legislation is therefore of the highest interest to the student of human progress. But as I found it impossible, in the space allowed me, to give more than a few glimpses of the spirit and action of their Legislature, I have selected the law founding the university, for the highest education; that establishing common schools, for universal education, and opening for all the path to the highest; that which required every individual to be fitted for some employment useful to the Commonwealth; and that which denounced and forbade slavery.

[1] Municipal government—the city—is an anomaly in a commonwealth. In all ages it has been the natural expression of despotism. Not the people of Italy, but the city of Rome, governed the world, as Paris has governed France. In a city the people annually meet, not together, but in wards, and surrender their liberties to men not always fit to govern justly; often to ambitious demagogues who have been devoting their time to intriguing for their own advancement. Faneuil Hall was the creation of a free town. It is almost out of place in a city. The natural tendency of things, in a city, is shown by the present condition of New York, governed by persons seeking, not the best interests of the people, but their own interest,—to make themselves rich.

[2] Palfrey's Hist., vol. i. p. 381.

[3] History of Charlestown, p. 50.

[4] Palfrey's Hist., vol. i. p. 372.

The schoolmaster was an important person, in those early days. Many of them were distinguished. There is room to speak of only a few. Dr. Bentley gives us a pretty full account of those of Salem for the first century and beyond. John Fiske arrived in 1637. He was educated at Cambridge, in England, and was possessed of a large property. He prepared for college Sir George Downing, a graduate of 1642. Mr. Fiske was frequently in the pulpit in Salem, and in 1644 became pastor of Wenham. Edward Norris succeeded Fiske, whose pupil he had been, in 1640, and continued forty-two years. He was succeeded by Daniel Epes, a Cambridge graduate, who continued till 1698. He was a magistrate and a counsellor. He was succeeded by Samuel Whitman, who was afterwards settled in the ministry; and he by John Emerson, who had been in the ministry, and continued in the school till 1711.[1]

To secure proper respect to the schoolmaster, his wife was to be accommodated with a pew next the wives of the magistrates.[2]

When, in 1643, forty-eight of the inhabitants of Weymouth determined to plant a colony in Seaconk, which they named Rehoboth, the fifth on the list was the schoolmaster. In the partition, by lot, of the woodland; and again, on the registry of lands, his name had the fifth place. Yet Rehoboth was then, as it is now, one of the small towns. It thus had one person, professionally a teacher, throughout the year. It now has schools three months in summer and three months in winter, each of them usually taught by a new teacher every quarter.

Ezekiel Cheever, born in 1614, came to New England in 1637; and, the next year, went with those who founded New Haven, began his services as schoolmaster in 1638, and continued there with great success till 1650; when he moved to Ipswich, and there taught with distinguished success and celebrity, making that town rank, according to Dr. Bentley, in literature and population, above the other towns in the county of Essex.[3] In 1661, Mr. Felt tells us, his agricultural operations required a barn, and that he planted an orchard on his homestead, thereby improving the soil of Ipswich, as well as the souls of her children, by

[1] Mass. Historical Collections, vol. vi. p. 240. [2] Id., p. 241.

[3] Barnard, American Journal, vol. i. p. 304.

healthy manual labor. It is to be regretted, as Mr. Barnard says, that the early practice of attaching a house, for the occupancy of the master, with a few acres of land for a garden, orchard, and the feeding of a cow, adopted from the Old World,[1] had not been continued in all the small towns. It would have been the means of securing, in each town, a permanent schoolmaster, educated for the office. If this practice had been retained, the lamentable decay of the schools throughout nearly all the smaller towns might have been prevented.

In November, 1666, Mr. Cheever removed to Charlestown; and thence, in 1670, to Boston, where his labors were continued for thirty-eight years. He was a good scholar, and made an excellent Accidence for beginners in Latin, which continued in use for very many years; but, if the account that Barnard gives of his discipline is to be relied on, he was in his feelings more of a savage than a Christian.[2]

There were other famous and able public schoolmasters; but there were not enough to supply the wants of the people, and thence the necessity of what were afterwards called "academies." Of one or two of these only have I time to speak.

By the will of Governor William Dummer, who died in 1761, his dwelling-house and farm at Byfield, in Newbury, were set apart for the establishment of a grammar school, to stand for ever on the farm. The property was given in trust, the rents and profits to be employed in erecting a school-house, and in support of a master; the appointment of whom was intrusted to a committee of five Byfield freeholders, acting in conjunction with the minister of the parish. The little school-house was built in 1762, and Samuel Moody — the famous Master Moody — was chosen to take charge of it. He continued its master for seventeen years, with an energy, success, and reputation which have rarely been surpassed. Very many of those destined to be the most distinguished men of Massachusetts in the various walks of life, were his pupils. They learned little else but Latin; yet the habits of promptness, independence of thought, exactness and thoroughness, which he formed in them, made all future ac-

[1] Barnard, American Journal, vol. i. p. 303.

[2] See Life of Rev. John Barnard, as quoted by H. Barnard, American Journal, vol. i. p. 308.

quisitions easy, and success, in most cases, certain. The endowment was not quite sufficient to maintain the master, and fees for tuition were found necessary. This, for some years, was the only conspicuous school in Massachusetts; candidates for the college being very generally prepared by the parish ministers.[1]

The example of Governor Dummer was followed by the Phillipses of Andover and Exeter, in the foundation and endowment, in those towns, of excellent academies, which soon reached the high reputation they have enjoyed up to the present day.

Samuel Phillips, of Andover, a pupil of Master Moody, a graduate of Harvard in 1771, an earnest patriot, a successful man of business, made town clerk and treasurer at the age of twenty-one, member of the Provincial Congress for four years, from 1775; a senator from the first election under the Constitution, and onwards, except one year, when he was lieutenant-governor, till his death; president of the Senate; and, before he was thirty, a judge of the Common Pleas, — this honored and honorable Judge Phillips founded Phillips Academy in Andover, in 1777, which, the next year, went into operation under Eliphalet Pearson.

His own share in the endowment was not large, but his influence secured $6,000 each from his father, Samuel, of North Andover, and his uncle William, of Boston; $31,000 from his uncle John, of Exeter, and $28,000 from his cousin William, of Boston.

This was the first incorporated academy; the act bearing the date of Oct. 4, 1780. One day less than six months from that day, that uncle John announced to his nephew the incorporation of Phillips Academy at Exeter.

The common schools and the town grammar schools continued to decline. In the busy world of Massachusetts, men of ability found more profitable employment; and the great truth was not yet discovered, that women, as teachers and managers and governors of boys even up to manhood, are often gifted, at least as highly as men. Most of the boys were fitted for college

[1] See Nehemiah Cleveland's admirable history of this school.

by the ministers of the gospel, among whom I have the best possible means of knowing, that the practice of teaching the elements of the Latin language, as a spoken language, very generally prevailed as late as one hundred years ago.

Academies and private schools grew more and more numerous; sometimes endowed by public-spirited individuals, sometimes by grants of land from the State, often by both, and usually supported, in part, by fees from the students. In 1834, there were more than nine hundred and fifty of these schools. Those under the supervision of resolute, judicious men, who knew the value of good teaching, and how to secure it; and sometimes others, by a fortunate accident, or a gracious Providence, — had good teachers, and flourished. But the greater number were *very* poor schools; so also were most of the town schools; and the belief and intimate conviction that most of the common schools were wretchedly poor, became, except amongst the most ignorant of the teachers themselves, and the most benighted of the people, almost universal.

The Act of 1789, up to which time the laws of which I have been speaking continued in operation, was a wide departure from the principle of the original law. It substitutes six months for the constant instruction provided for towns of fifty families; and requires a grammar teacher of determinate qualifications for towns of two hundred families, instead of the similar requisition from all towns of half that number of inhabitants. Still, however, far as it falls short of that noble democratic idea of the Puritans, of providing the best possible instruction for all, it would, if in force at the present day, render instruction of the highest kind accessible to the children of more than two-thirds of the towns of the Commonwealth.

By an Act of February, 1824, facetiously called, in the index to the Massachusetts Laws, "an act *providing for* the public schools," the law of 1789 was repealed; and, for all towns of less than five thousand inhabitants, instead of a master of "good morals, well instructed in the Latin, Greek, and English languages," a teacher, or teachers, must be provided, "well qualified to instruct youth in orthography, reading, writing, arithmetic, English grammar, and geography, and in good behavior."

This act was the severest blow the common-school system

ever received; not only because it shut from the poor children, of all but a few towns, the path which had always lain open to the highest order of education, but because it took away a fixed standard for the qualifications of teachers, and substituted no other in its stead. The common schools had hitherto been as nursing mothers to the gifted children of the indigent, who were often raised, through them, to better opportunities, and thence to the highest stations in society. This high duty they utterly abandoned. The poor boy of talent who, under the former system, would have received the elements of the best education, gratuitously, but of right, in his native town, was thenceforward obliged to find or beg his way to a private school or academy, or to remain, for ever, without a learned education. The candidate for the office of teacher, being released from the necessity of an acquaintance with the learned languages, which in most cases implied a certain degree of cultivation and refinement, and amenable to no rule measuring the amount of the mere elements, which only were required, was too often found to be lamentably deficient even in them.

The effects of lowering the standard of instruction in the public schools became, to attentive observers, every year more apparent. For a time, the better qualified teachers continued in the service; but they were gradually supplanted, in many places, by persons who, from their inferior qualifications, were willing to do the work for a lower compensation.

In 1830, a meeting of teachers took place in Boston, which led to the formation of the American Institute of Instruction, intended for the mutual benefit of actual teachers. It had its first annual meeting this year, and began its work with an Introductory Address by President Wayland, of Brown University, its first President. It was incorporated in 1831, and has continued till the present time, to hold annual meetings in various parts of this and other States, with addresses, lectures, and discussions, which have brought together many actual teachers and other friends of education from all parts of the country. Its good effects upon the teachers have been strikingly shown in the improved character and practical nature of their lectures and discussions.

One of the subjects year after year discussed was the condition of the common schools and what ought to be and might be done for their elevation. These discussions led, in 1836, to a Memorial to the General Court, from a committee of the Directors of the Institute, urging the importance of legislative action for the improvement of the common schools, particularly by raising the qualifications of the teachers, and asking for the appointment of a Superintendent of the common schools, and showing the ways in which he might exercise the most beneficial influence. This was referred to a committee, but led to no immediate action. In January, 1837, another memorial from the Institute was presented to the Legislature, praying that better provision might be made for the training of the teachers of the schools, and particularly "the instituting, for the special instruction of teachers, of one or more seminaries."

The cause of the common schools had been very ably pleaded by J. G. Carter,[1] at that time a member of the House, and earnestly and long and well advocated by our associate, Rev. Charles Brooks, of Hingham, in lectures in many places, two of them before the Legislature during this same session. This gentleman, indeed, for his long, disinterested, and unpaid labors in the cause of education, especially for his efforts to secure the establishment of Normal schools and a Board of Education, is entitled to be considered, more than any other individual, what he has been called, the Father of Normal schools.[2]

Elisha Ticknor, father of our distinguished friend and associate, George Ticknor, was the first in Massachusetts, — so far as I know, — to suggest the importance of an institution for the education of teachers, which he did in 1787, in the "Massachusetts Magazine." The next was Denison Olmsted, in 1817. In 1823, William Russell proposed seminaries for teachers; in 1825, Thomas A. Gallaudet did the same in Connecticut; and in 1826, Governor DeWitt Clinton in New York. Governor

[1] In Letters to the Hon. William Prescott, LL.D., on the Schools of New England, with remarks upon the Principles of Instruction, p. 123. Boston, 1824. And Essays upon Popular Education, containing an Outline of an Institution for the Education of Teachers, of sixty pages. Boston, 1826.

[2] Mr. Brooks lectured in nearly one hundred different towns and cities, — in every place where he was invited. By invitation of the Legislatures of Massachusetts, New Hampshire, Vermont, Rhode Island, Connecticut, New Jersey, and Pennsylvania, he delivered, to crowded assemblies in each, two or three lectures, besides speaking in most of the capitals between Boston and Washington.

Levi Lincoln, in his speech to the Legislature, June 6, 1827, earnestly recommends "measures for the preparation and better qualification of teachers," laments their present "incompetency," and suggests a public "institution for their appropriate education and discipline." In 1827, James G. Carter asked aid of the Legislature to establish a seminary, in vain.

In 1830, a branch of Phillips Academy in Andover was opened for the express purpose of educating teachers, but was soon closed.

On the 14th of January, 1837, in the Massachusetts House of Representatives, on motion of Mr. King, of Danvers, it was ordered that the Committee on Education be requested to consider the expediency of providing by law for the better education of teachers of the public schools. On April 14, of the same year, on motion of Mr. Carter, of Lancaster, a bill relating to common schools was taken up, and the House resolved itself into a committee of the whole for the consideration thereof; and, after some time spent therein, Mr. Speaker resumed the chair, and Mr. Winthrop, of Boston, from the committee, reported that the committee had had the subject referred to them under consideration, and that the said bill, with sundry amendments recommended by the committee, ought to pass; and the bill was ordered to a third reading.

Mr. Carter's report was as follows: —

"The Committee on Education to whom was referred so much of His Excellency the Governor's Address as relates to education, and to whom was also referred 'The Memorial of the Directors of the American Institute of Instruction,' and the petition of a convention of delegates from each of the towns in Plymouth County, and who were directed by order of the House, Jan. 14, 1837, to consider the expediency of providing by law for the better education of teachers of the public schools of the Commonwealth, have carefully considered those subjects, and report thereon the accompanying bill: Be it enacted, &c.: —

"Sec. 1. His Excellency the Governor, with the advice and consent of the Council, is hereby authorized to appoint eight persons, who, together with the Governor and Lieutenant-Governor, shall constitute and be denominated the Board of Education."[1]

[1] The first members of the Board were Edward Everett, George Hall, J. G. Carter, Emerson Davis, Edmund Dwight, Horace Mann, Edward A. Newton, Robert Rantoul, Jr., Thomas Robbins, Jared Sparks.

The remainder of the act designates its duties. The common schools were probably, at this time, at their lowest point of degradation. From what we can learn, they had, in most parts of the Commonwealth, been gradually declining, until, by this act, the Legislature showed its disposition to interpose and arrest their downward progress.

The Board of Education, at its first meeting, held June 29, 1837, appointed as their secretary, Horace Mann,[1] at that time President of the Senate of Massachusetts. Mr. Mann had been known to the individuals of the Board as a member of one or other branch of the General Court for the ten previous years, and especially as the principal mover and agent in the erection of the State Lunatic Hospital at Worcester.

He had, moreover, been recently engaged in the revision of the laws of the Commonwealth, and had been charged, together with another, with the supervision of the Revised Code; and was therefore as familiar, probably, as any other individual, with the laws, institutions, and interests of the State. Immediately on his appointment, he gave up a lucrative practice in his profession, and, abandoning all other pursuits, devoted all his energies, time, and thoughts to the work he had entered upon.

The most important and one of the first acts of the Board was the establishment of schools for the special education of teachers. Two Normal schools went into operation in the course of 1839: one at Lexington, for females; the other for pupils of both sexes, at Barre: the former, in July, under the superintendence of Cyrus Peirce, a man long and favorably known as a teacher, at Nantucket; the latter, in September, under the charge of Samuel Phillips Newman, a gentleman who had been for many years a professor, of high reputation, in Bowdoin College. The first of these schools was soon moved to West Newton; and thence, after some years, to Framingham, where it was finally settled, at a point within a few rods of the exact geographical centre of the State. The second was removed

[1] The almost universal expectation of teachers and others interested in the subject was, that J. G. Carter would be appointed. He was far better acquainted with the condition of education in Massachusetts, and had done, by his eloquent writings, more than any one else in making that known to the people. Advantage has been taken of his investigations and of his statements, but almost always without acknowledgment.

from Barre to Westfield, where it now stands. A third Normal school, for both sexes, went into operation at Bridgewater, Sept. 9, 1840, under the charge of Colonel Nicholas Tillinghast, a professor of high reputation at the Military School at West Point;[1] a fourth, for females only, June 2, 1853, at Salem, under the care of a man who had received his education as a teacher at the Normal School in Bridgewater.

In the establishment of each school, the inhabitants of the town, or their friends, provided a school-house, or made large donations for that object. The State sustains the schools, paying the salaries of the teachers and the necessary expenses of the school, granting aid to pupils of limited means residing at a distance, and making appropriations for apparatus and other helps in instruction.

All these schools are now in successful operation, and are accomplishing vastly more than their most sanguine friends ever dared to hope. They have greatly improved the old methods of teaching and introduced new. They have improved in modes of study, in thoroughness, and particularly in the study of subjects by topics, with personal inquiry, thought, and research, instead of servilely following the text-book. They have improved in the surprisingly ready use of the blackboard, upon almost all subjects, and of real objects and other sources of illustration; in method; and in the organization of schools and the theory of discipline after a lofty standard. They have substituted real *teaching* for the old way of *hearing lessons*.[2]

[1] Mr. Tillinghast introduced into the Normal schools excellent modes of teaching arithmetic and other branches of science, which have been greatly improved by his pupils, and by them, directly and indirectly, introduced into the other schools. He was extremely well qualified for his position in all respects, except one, — he was ignorant of the Latin and Greek languages; and he felt and often said, that a person cannot teach *language* without something of this attainment. He always lamented his want in this respect; and, I believe, shortened his life by his attempt to make up for it, when the labor necessary to carry on the school was constantly as much as he could bear. His ignorance of Latin shortened his sleep and his life. He felt that if he could have devoted to the study only a year or two, before he was old enough for science, he would have far better understood every thing which he had to learn.

[2] In a recent conversation with the faithful and able teacher of the school at Bridgewater, he gave an account of his way of teaching mineralogy. A single instance may suffice to give an idea of his method. For learning a lesson on granite, each pupil was furnished (instead of a text-book) with a piece of the rock, and the names of the three constituent minerals, whose properties he was to study.

And, in accomplishing this, the very object of their institution, and as a means of accomplishing this, they have been and are teaching, in an admirable manner, all those branches of knowledge which are deemed most important for the rising generation to be acquainted with. The Normal schools are thus colleges of purest character and noblest aim, perfectly suited to prepare females for their special vocation in life, that of teaching children from birth up, — a vocation which is really, taking all things into consideration, the highest vocation on earth.[1]

No teacher, though he may have given his life to the work, can spend an hour at one of these schools, without feeling how much time he might have saved, and how much better and pleasanter and more useful his whole life's work would have been, if he could have had two years of such preparation at the beginning of his career.[2]

By the exact knowledge, habits of investigation and thought, and clear understanding given to the great numbers who have in them been prepared to take charge of the common schools of the State, nearly all these schools are now very much better than they ever were before. Let any one who has any doubt upon this subject, visit any of the schools, Primary or Grammar, of this city, or of any town in the neighborhood.[3]

1 The best education for a teacher is really the best education that a woman can receive, since it requires a thorough knowledge and understanding of whatever it is most important for everybody to know. If better colleges are wanted for females, they may best be had by carrying out the plan which the Board of Education have now under consideration, — that of lengthening the course at the Normal schools.

2 Many years ago, an officer, P. A. Sileström, was sent by the Court of Sweden to look at our schools. After witnessing, for two hours, the instruction given by young ladies in the Normal school then at West Newton, he told me, "This is worth coming across the Atlantic to see. This is a great discovery. There are maiden ladies in Norway who could easily be prepared to teach all the little scattered mountain schools in that country, — schools in regard to which the government have long been almost in despair."

3 In 1856, I went into Prussia for the express purpose of examining the gymnasia and, more particularly, the seminaries for teachers, after the model of which our Normal schools had been formed, in consequence of the knowledge given in the Report on them by Cousin, which had been introduced here by his correspondent, our friend and associate, Charles Brooks. I found no difficulty in gaining admission to them, through our minister Governor Vroom; and devoted a week to the examination of one of them in Berlin, which had been pointed out by the Minister of Public Instruction and Religion as a fair representative of the Normal schools of Prussia.

There is another thing which should not go without mention in the briefest sketch of the history of Education in Massachusetts; that is, the signal ability, intelligence, and thorough acquaintance with every thing relating to the instruction, moral elevation, and discipline of the schools, shown in the extracts from the Reports of the School Committees of every part of the State, which accompany the Annual Reports of the Board of Education.

The signal success of our Normal schools, and the supervision exercised over the common schools, have been possible only through the existence and wise management of the School Fund, of whose legislative history it is therefore necessary to speak.

In January, 1828, the Committee on Education, in the House of Representatives, in a report made by the Hon. W. B. Calhoun, declared that means should be devised for the establishment of a fund having in view not the support, but the encouragement, of the common schools, and the instruction of school-teachers.

In January, 1833, Mr. Marsh, of Dalton, suggested the expediency of investing a portion of the proceeds of the lands of the Commonwealth in a permanent fund, the interest of which should be annually applied for the encouragement of common schools. The committee say, —

"It is not intended, in establishing a school fund, to relieve towns and parents from the principal expense of education, but to manifest our

I patiently heard every teacher and every class, in every study they were pursuing, and saw the instruction given by some of the pupils to classes in the Model school.

I had kept myself acquainted with all the operations of the Normal schools in Massachusetts, from the time when Father Peirce began with his class of three girls, at Lexington, to the end of the school-year in 1855; and I was obliged, to my infinite surprise and gratification, to come to the conclusion, that there was not a single point in which the Massachusetts schools were not immeasurably superior to the Berlin. Our course of studies was better, our methods of instruction and discipline, the intelligence and vivacity of our teachers; but the greatest difference was in the character of the materials out of which the future teachers were to be made. Instead of the bright, earnest, wide-awake, intelligent Yankee girls, who formed eighty per cent of the pupils in our Normal schools, I saw only ungainly, awkward, dull young men, of whom it was impossible to help feeling, that most of them were there because they were too lazy to work, and too stupid to hope to succeed in any calling which required intelligent, thoughtful activity.

In the gymnasia, I speedily came to a different conclusion; for, while I nowhere saw — in mathematics, in natural philosophy, astronomy, and kindred branches — instruction given better than I had often seen at Cambridge, and in the High School in this city, in instruction in the elements of language, and the subsequent course in Latin, in English, in French, and especially in their own German, I was obliged to admit that they were far beyond what I had, then, anywhere seen here.

interest in, and to give direction, energy, and stability to, institutions essential to individual happiness and the public welfare. . . . Therefore we recommend that a fund be constituted, and the distribution of the income so ordered as to open a direct intercourse with the schools; that their wants may be better understood and supplied, the advantages of education be more highly appreciated, and the blessings of wisdom, virtue, and knowledge, carried home to the fireside of every family, to the bosom of every child."

In February, 1834, a committee, after a very able Report, full of most valuable suggestions, reported, by their chairman, A. D. Foster, an Act to establish the Massachusetts School Fund:—

"That all unappropriated moneys now in the Treasury, derived from the sale of lands in the State of Maine, and from the claim of the State on the United States for military services, be appropriated to constitute a permanent fund for the aid and encouragement of common schools."

This, the "Massachusetts School Fund," went into operation Jan. 1, 1835.

By an Act passed in 1854, the fund was enlarged to a million and a half of dollars, by the transfer to the Fund of 2,944 shares of the stock of the Western Railroad Corporation held by the State. By a law of 1859, the School Fund is to be further increased, from the proceeds of the sale of lands in the Back Bay;[1] and it has been thus increased by the addition, from that source, of the sum of $456,930.06; making it, since the 1st of January, 1866, $2,000,000; to which sum, for the present, it is limited.

"The establishment of the School Fund," says Governor Boutwell, "was the most important educational measure ever adopted by the government of the Commonwealth; and, in connection with the organization of the Board of Education, it has wrought a salutary change and reformation in the character and influence of our public schools."—"With the fund, it is possible to obtain accurate and complete returns from nearly every town in the State. Without it, all legislation must prove ineffectual. By the aid of the fund, all material facts are annually made known to the State; without it, each town is kept ignorant of what its neighbors are doing. With the fund, we have a system; without it, all is disjointed and disconnected."[2]

One-half the income of this fund is annually "distributed among the cities and towns of the State, in proportion to the

[1] Twenty-fourth Report of the Board of Education: Secretary G. S. Boutwell's Report, p. 74.
[2] Id., p. 76.

number of children in each, between the ages of five and fifteen years;" on condition, however, that no apportionment shall be made to a town or city which has not sent in a report, and which has not raised by taxation, for the support of schools, during the previous school-year, a sum not less than one dollar and fifty cents for each person between the ages of five and fifteen. This sum is now increased to three dollars for each child.

From the other half of the income of the School Fund must be paid "all money appropriated for other educational purposes," such as the support of the Normal schools, schools for the blind, for the deaf and dumb, for feeble-minded persons, &c.

By the wise and careful distribution of the former half of the fund, with its conditions, the inhabitants of the towns and cities in the Commonwealth have been induced to raise, by voluntary taxation of themselves, sums for the support of the schools, which have been constantly increasing from 1837 to the present time. The mere increase for 1867 "amounting," according to the able secretary of the Board, "to $362,328.87; a sum added in a single year nearly, or quite, equal to the entire amount raised by tax in 1837."[1]

The small bonus of twenty cents, or at most twenty-five cents, for each child between five and fifteen, has been used as a lever to induce the people to raise by voluntary taxation, every year, from twenty-nine to forty times that sum, in all the towns of the Commonwealth.

We were recently told, in an admirable school report, by one of our associates,[2] who is as careful in his statements as he is eloquent in the enforcement of truth, that, in France, two and a half millions of children are taught at a cost of over six millions of dollars, that is, at $2.06 each child; and that, in 1856, the total expense of primary instruction, for 3,850,000 children, was over eight millions of dollars, or $2.07 for each child; by primary instruction being meant all instruction below that of the colleges.

In Massachusetts, in 1867, the money raised by voluntary taxation, for 261,408 children, between five and fifteen, including only expenses for wages, board, fuel, care of fires and school-rooms, was $2,355,505,[3] that is, $9.10 for each child; and "the

[1] Thirty-first Annual Report, p. 39. [2] Rev. R. C. Waterston.

[3] This money undoubtedly comes mostly from the rich, and the greatest gainers are the poor. Yet it is voted readily, and paid most willingly. "Government can-

amount from taxes, tuition, and funds, and expended on public schools, private schools, and academies, exclusive of the expenses of buildings and school-books, is $3,160,665.94; which is equal to the sum of over $12 for every person in the State between five and fifteen years of age."[1]

Besides these, we know what large sums are annually spent in buildings and in school-books.

There is another work, another change, which has been silently and constantly going on, under the guidance of the Board of Education and the secretaries, and through their great organs the Normal schools and the enlightened experience of the people, not less important than any other that has been spoken of. The common schools have, every year since the establishment of the Board, been taught and managed by a larger number of females than in any year before. To take only the last eleven years that have been reported. The whole number of different persons employed as teachers in the public schools, during the year 1856, was 7,153, of whom 1,768 were males and 5,385 females.

The whole number employed in 1867 was 7,759, of whom 1,020 were males and 6,739 females; showing an addition, in eleven years, to the number of female teachers, of 1,354, or 123, on an average, each year; and a diminution in the number of male teachers of 748, or 68 a year, the number of schools having increased in those eleven years from 4,300 to 4,838.

In the matter of compensation to female teachers, there always has been, and still is, a deplorable disregard of propriety, right feeling, and justice. The average wages of female teachers in 1837 were $11.38 per month; less than $3 a week. They are now, or were in 1867, $26.44 per month, that is, $6.61 a week; an increase of 50 cents a month each year for thirty years. But still what a wretched pittance for such services! Absolutely unintelligent labor, mere digging, is better paid than the intelligent, refining devotion and care of highly educated teachers.

not," as Mr. Webster said, "subject the property of those who have estates to a burden for a purpose more favorable to the poor, and more useful to the whole community. This is the living fountain which supplies the ever-flowing, ever-refreshing, ever-fertilizing stream of public instruction and general intelligence." — *D. Webster's Speech in Massachusetts Convention of* 1820.

[1] Thirty-first Annual Report of the Board of Education and of the Secretary, Hon. Joseph White.

One can hardly help feeling that the mere cleaning of streets, digging of ditches, and raising crops of potatoes and cabbages, — all to be forgotten in a year, — are more important, in the eyes of the fathers of the people, than the refinement, elevation, and delicate training of their children, on which their own happiness, after middle life, will depend, more than on all other causes together.

Now, are not the legislation of Massachusetts, in regard to the School Fund and the Normal schools, and the action of the agents of the State in carrying this legislation into effect, in perfect keeping with that legislation of our Fathers, which, as we have seen, is the object of praise and admiration throughout the world? In this one particular, we have not fallen below their high standard. We have, through our Governor and Council, selected, year after year, from all the inhabitants of the State, such persons, to form the Board of Education, as seemed best fitted, by their wisdom, experience, and knowledge of the wants and actual working of the schools, to take charge, without pecuniary remuneration, of the interests of education; and we have required the Board "to lay before the Legislature an annual report of school returns, and of all the doings of the Board, with such observations upon the condition and efficiency of the system of popular education, and such suggestions as to the most practical means of improving and extending it, as the experience and reflection of the Board dictate."[1]

The Board have chosen to the office of secretary, who is the organ of communication between the State, its officers and representatives, and all the schools of the State, men — Horace Mann, Barnas Sears, George S. Boutwell, Joseph White — as signally well qualified for the office as could be found in the State, perhaps in the world.

1 Twenty-fourth Report, sec. 3, p. 64.

Cambridge: Stereotyped and Printed by John Wilson & Son.

www.ingramcontent.com/pod-product-compliance
Lightning Source LLC
LaVergne TN
LVHW021320110826
845150LV00003B/631

9781425556884